Britain and Europe

Series Editor: Keith Robbins

Britain and Europe

In preparation, volumes covering the periods:

1300–1500   Anne Curry
1500–1780   Ralph Houlbrooke
1789–2005   Keith Robbins

Already published

Britain in the First Millennium   Edward James
Britain and the Continent 1000–1300   Donald Matthew

Britain and the Continent
1000–1300

DONALD MATTHEW

Emeritus Professor of History at the University of Reading

HODDER
EDUCATION
PART OF HACHETTE LIVRE UK

First published in Great Britain in 2005 by
Hodder Education, part of Hachette Livre UK,
338 Euston Road, London NW1 3BH

www.hoddereducation.com

British Library Cataloguing in Publication Data
A catalogue record for this book is available from the British Library

Library of Congress Cataloging-in-Publication Data
A catalog record for this book is available from the Library of Congress

ISBN: 978 0 340 74061 3

Typeset in 10/12 Sabon by Phoenix Photosetting, Chatham, Kent

What do you think about this book? Or any other Hodder Education
title? Please send your comments to educationenquiries@hodder.co.uk

Contents

Alienorae Pauloque
egregiis vetustatis liberis

General editor's preface

Years, decades, centuries, millennia come and go but Britain's relationship with its European neighbours remains consistently complicated and, on occasion, acutely divisive. It forms the stuff of contemporary political arguments both in 'Britain' and 'Europe', debate which is sometimes strident and ill-informed.

The heat may perhaps be excused on the grounds that there are issues of personal, national and continental identity at stake about which people have strong feelings. The ignorance, however, is not excusable. Whatever views may be taken about contemporary issues and options, here is a relationship which can only properly be understood if it is examined in the *longue durée*. That is what this series aims to do.

It becomes evident, however, that in regard to both 'Britain' and 'Europe' we are not dealing with fixed entities standing over against each other through two millennia. What may be held to constitute 'Britain' and what 'Europe' changes through time. The present is no exception. In a context of political devolution how Britain and Britishness is defined becomes increasingly problematic as new patterns of relationship across 'the Isles' emerge. And what are perceived to be new patterns turn out on examination to be reassertions and redefinitions of old identities or structures. So is it also with 'Europe'. The issue of 'enlargement' of the current European Union brings up old problems in a new form. Where does 'Europe' begin and end? At long last, to take but one example, the Turkish Republic has been accepted as a candidate for membership but in earlier centuries, for some, Europe stopped where the Ottoman Empire began, an outlook which can still linger, with violent consequences, in the Balkans.

In effect, therefore, the series will probe and chart the shifting of boundaries – and boundaries in the mind as boundaries on a map. Where Britain 'belongs', in any era, depends upon a multiplicity of factors, themselves varying in importance from century to century: upon ethnicity, language, law, government, religion, trade, warfare, to name only some. Whether, in particular periods, the islanders were indeed 'isolated' depends in turn not only on what they themselves thought or wanted to believe but also upon the patterns prevailing in 'Europe' and what might be thought to constitute the 'mainstream' of its development. The historians in this series are well aware that they are not dealing with a simple one-to-one relationship. They are not committed to a common didactic agenda or rigid formula. Different periods require different assessments of the appropriate balance to be struck in tackling the ingredients of insularity on the one hand and continental commonality on the other. Propinquity has itself necessarily brought the communities of Britain into closer contact, in peace and war, with some continental countries than with others and to have established (fluctuating) affinities and enmities, but the connection is not confined to immediate neighbours. Beneath the inter-state level, different sections of society have had different sorts of relationship across the Continent. There is, therefore, in reality no single 'British' relationship with something called 'Europe' but rather multilateral relationships, sometimes in conflict and sometimes in cooperation, across Europe both at the state and non-state levels, which have varied in content and intensity over time. And what has been happening in the 'wider world' has in turn affected and sometimes determined how both 'Britain' and the countries of 'Europe' have perceived and conducted themselves.

The study of a relationship (just like the living of one) is one of the most difficult but also the most rewarding of tasks. There is, however, no single title for this series which really does justice to what is being attempted. To speak of 'Britain and Europe' does indeed risk carrying the imputation that Britain is not 'part of' Europe. To speak of 'Europe in British Perspective' would mislead as to the extent of the concentration upon Britain which remains. To speak of 'Britain in Europe' or even of 'Europe in Britain' both have their difficulties and advantages. In short, in the event, there is something for everybody!

The difficulty, though perhaps also the urgency of the task, is compounded for historians by the circumstances of history teaching and learning in schools and universities in the United Kingdom where, very largely, 'British History' and 'European History' have been studied and written about by different people who have disclaimed significant knowledge of the other or have only studied a particular period of the one which has been different from the period in the other. The extent to which 'British history' is really a singular history and the extent to which it is a particular manifestation of 'European history' is rarely tackled head-on at any level. This series attempts to provide just that bridge over troubled waters which present European circumstances require. It is, however, for readers to decide for themselves what bridge into the future the past does indeed provide.

Keith Robbins
University of Wales, Lampeter

Preface

How people from these islands interacted with the Continent in the period
treated here has not previously been considered at any length. Reading the
evidence, I can understand why: nothing in the sources suggests that the
nature of relations between the British Isles and the Continent then seemed
to need discussion. What was once taken for granted has become controversial. This book does not seek to explain how the change came about. It
concentrates on trying to show how straightforward interaction with the
Continent once was.

English medieval history begins with the arrival of Germanic immigrants
in Roman Britain. The story of settlement culminates in the tenth century
with the unification of the various English kingdoms by the rulers of
Wessex, now regarded as providing for the foundation of the English state.
Academic study of medieval history has traditionally concentrated on showing how institutions of government developed thereafter, the records of the
various departments of state offering unrivalled opportunities for historical
investigation. Historians have long since broadened their field of study, but,
thanks to its influence on our subsequent history, no achievement of the
English Middle Ages has won more historical respect than the precocity of
medieval government. A disadvantage of this admiration has been a tendency to exaggerate its dominance in medieval affairs and overlook the
importance to society of matters not directly subject to royal supervision.

The modern western world has radically different values from those of
the Middle Ages. Medieval historians who admire bureaucratic administrations lack sympathy for the royal ambitions responsible for them. As
democrats, if not republicans, historians may, just, appreciate the continuity provided by hereditary kingship, but they have no time for hierarchical
social order and the hereditary aristocracies that kept society and state
going. Modern ideas about religion make it equally hard to do justice to
medieval churchmen. Their defence of clerical privilege and encouragement
of superstition offend modern principles. Historians who bravely take up

the challenge of writing about the great majority of the population, labour under the disadvantage of being brought up in industrialised society with no experience of what is required to wrest a living from the soil. Even as townsmen, modern historians are not spontaneously drawn into the kind of collective activity once characteristic of urban life: disputes with rival towns, neighbourhood solidarity, fellowship in craft guilds. How strange it seems to us that, at a time when most men were capable of defending themselves without policemen, this did not result in chaos. Medieval modes of social constraint elude our understanding. To get round the difficulty, historians attempt, like anthropologists, to apply modern social theories and read off whole patterns of behaviour from the merest scraps of evidence available. How important a part writing actually played in medieval societies is unfathomable: for all essential purposes they functioned without it. Even today, the oral transmission of culture remains more important than is commonly recognised or officially approved.

In writing this book I have worked on three assumptions. First, in the period discussed the peoples of the British Isles did not think of themselves as basically different or detached from their continental neighbours. Second, interaction was not a matter controlled by government: individuals and communities managed their own 'foreign' interests as they thought fit. Third, historical evidence about their attitudes and activities is pitifully inadequate for writing any comprehensive account. Like fireworks, what is known for certain only fitfully lightens the darkness of our understanding.

Donald Matthew
Reading
December 2004

1

Introduction

Few contemporary issues have become more contentious than how Britain relates to its continental neighbours. Arguments often turn, at least in part, on how things worked in the past and history has always been invoked in any discussion about national identity. Over time, however, the themes deemed of most significance for this purpose have changed. For centuries, it seemed obvious that the Protestant Reformation had been fundamental for creating national autonomy; for lovers of liberty and freedom of conscience the key event was the Glorious Revolution of 1689. When interest shifted to the character of the general population, historians examined the social legacy of the Industrial Revolution and the moral ambiguities of Victorian imperialism. Now we are preoccupied about where we belong in the world and how we relate to our neighbours, near and far. Attempting to understand how we have got where we are has become a major topic of historical interest.

Whereas the memory of recent events obviously colours any approach to the way these issues are viewed, it is not self-evident that events of many centuries ago can still have any impact on public consciousness. The Middle Ages are not, however, without relevance in this regard. The European Community itself began by looking back to Charlemagne, who had ruled over most of France, Germany and Italy. In England, the Norman Conquest and the Hundred Years War are both sometimes invoked as factors to be taken into account when explaining English attitudes to the French. However remote, these events from the past have been woven into concepts of what living in Britain is all about. While recognising the fact, it is not easy to explain how such historical events can still help to shape the national outlook.

It is certainly not a matter of official propaganda inculcating national legends. Popular conceptions of the past now owe more to television and the cinema than to the little history taught in schools. Those who dominate the media appear to have picked up their ideas about the past in a very haphaz-

ard manner. National myths, long since discounted by professional historians, survive in the popular imagination. They have become part of what
people want to believe about the kind of society they belong to. New
national myths can soon take root if they are deemed essential for modern
purposes. In both Scotland and Wales, the past has been reinvented to provide historical 'justification' for the devolution of separate political authorities. In Scotland, those responsible for the new national institution installed
at Edinburgh have devised a parliament quite unlike the Estates of the
Scottish kingdom before 1707.[1] In Wales, Edward I's suppression of the
principality of Llewelyn of Snowdonia in 1282 has been falsely represented
as an English takeover of the whole of modern Wales. The so-called
'Principality' for which an assembly was devised has no historical precedent
in pre-Edwardian Wales. Comparable rewriting of the Irish past from the
late nineteenth century fed the rancour of nationalists insisting that the
English had been trying to dispossess the Irish of their original nation for
seven centuries. The past has been cheerfully rewritten to suit modern
requirements.

Myth-makers do not care whether their history is sound or not, but historians do. The general public can hardly be unaware of the harm regularly
done by the kind of history that seeks to unite the 'nation' by identifying
which neighbours constitute the national enemies. This historical tradition
naturally leaves the present unequal to confronting the problem of how
Britain relates to its continental neighbours. This is where turning to the
Middle Ages becomes an advantage since national interests did not then set
the peoples of Europe against one another. Because British relations with
the Continent cannot be presented in terms of competition or alliance, the
factors actually involved have to be analysed afresh. During the three centuries discussed in this book, 'Britain' no more presented a united front to
Europe than Europe itself to Britain. Some basic assumptions of much modern discussion have therefore to be discarded.

Attempts to understand how Britain relates to the Continent commonly
proceed from three basic ideas. The first is that Britain is small compared to
continental states. With an area of nearly 89,000 square miles, England,
Scotland and Wales together may amount to less than Italy (about 118,000
square miles); even so, the island of Great Britain is hardly inconsiderable.
When taken along with the other islands of the archipelago, including
Ireland (32,500 square miles), the area of the whole territory amounts to
nearly 122,000 square miles. Though still smaller than France or Spain, the
United Kingdom, as a purely European power (even without counting the
'empire'), was never insignificant.

Second, many British patriots like to think of their history as one about
islanders living in splendid isolation, separated and protected from the
untrustworthy people of the mainland by water. The idea that islanders
remain cut off from their nearest continent does not withstand examination.
The original islanders had arrived by sea and could as easily travel back

again. Their ability to prevent others entering or attacking 'their' island, let alone settling there, has always been limited. Not until the union of the crowns of England and Scotland (1603) and then of Great Britain and Ireland (1801) was it practicable to throw a protective cordon round the whole archipelago. This lasted for little more than a hundred years. Since the secession of the Irish Free State from the Union (1922), the complexity of the problem in earlier times has re-emerged. The implications for British security were fully exposed in the Second World War. Any confidence that Britain can somehow remain detached from the Continent draws historically on a selective memory of what was effective only for a very short period. Even then the United Kingdom did not stand aside from the problems presented by Napoleon, the 'Eastern Question' or the violation of Belgian neutrality after 1914. British intervention in continental affairs itself played a part in creating the kind of European political order all its peoples have had to live with. It is disingenuous to disclaim a major responsibility for this. The mythical character of the Channel as a barrier is exposed by the curious fact that the Atlantic Ocean is never comparably treated as though it impeded contact with North America.

Third, the view that islands as such form natural social and political units overlooks the existence of several politically divided islands: Hispaniola, New Guinea, Borneo, Timor, not to mention the familiar problems presented by the cultural divisions of Ireland, Cyprus or Ceylon. For Britain, division has lasted longer than union. The 'south' began to develop in a different way from the 'north' as a result of its experience in the Roman Empire. Wales became what was left to the Celtic people of the west after the Germanic settlements in England. In the period dealt with here, Britain comprised many cultures. The interaction of all the British Isles with the Continent cannot be presented as though there were a single story to be told.

Diversity of the British Isles

If the island of Britain itself already comprises a number of different cultures, the concept becomes even more misleading when the whole archipelago is taken into account. In the twelfth century this was not conceived as a unit, let alone a 'British' one. The British Isles have long since been so called because Britain is the largest island of the group. Understandably, this is resented in Ireland, but this hardly amounts to an adequate reason for speakers of English to seek alternative names for it. Ireland is far from being a negligible quantity in the whole, but it is geographically smaller and, when seen from the Continent, screened from it by its larger neighbour. This was not without its advantages. In the Roman period, Ireland, being more remote, was spared conquest. If the acquisition of Britain seemed necessary for the completion of the imperial project, Ireland did not register in Rome in the same way.

Despite their size, neither Britain nor Ireland successfully dominated the minor islands of the archipelago. In earlier times these were more significant than now appears. Henry of Huntingdon, medieval author of a popular history of the English, did not suppose that there were only two islands worth mentioning. He named three others: 'Orkney', Man and Wight. In Huntingdon's time the Orkneys were subject to a local earl who, when not autonomous, acknowledged the king of Norway as his lord. Man itself was then still a separate kingdom, more closely connected with Ireland and the Norse of the Hebrides than with England. Only in the thirteenth century, after the fates of Ireland and England had been locked together, did Man lose its capacity to act independently. Yet, after seven centuries, the status of Man is still anomalous. Like the Channel Islands, it provides a persistent reminder that the only valid explanation of the constitutional oddities of these islands is historical. Wight is not otherwise noticed by Huntingdon and why he singled it out is obscure, but he was not the only historian to regard it as worth separate notice; the *Gesta Stephani*, another twelfth-century text, gives a precise description of it. In the mid-thirteenth century disaffected sailors used it as a base to harry merchantmen.[2]

England was unquestionably the most powerful of all the political societies in these islands and for this reason proved capable of exercising a decisive impact on affairs beyond its bounds. Although the lands of England comprise only two-fifths of the archipelago's total area, as the most favoured for agricultural exploitation they have been the most densely populated. Reliable statistics about the relative sizes of the various peoples of Britain become available only in the nineteeenth century when England supported a population nearly five times the size of Scotland's, not quite twice that of Ireland and sixteen times greater than that of Wales. Such figures at least give an impression of the relative weighting of the different parts of Britain by that period. In the absence of more exact information, it is not unreasonable to assume that they were comparable in earlier centuries. Estimates of the size of the Scottish population at the end of the thirteenth century put it as a sixth of the English, only a slightly less favourable ratio than the nineteenth-century one.[3] In Ireland, the population after the Act of Union had probably grown as a result of the more recent development of agriculture; in the Middle Ages, when the Irish economy was still mainly pastoral, the population is more likely to have been proportionately smaller. Given these figures, it is misleading to think of England, Wales, Scotland and Ireland as though they were, like sporting sides, all of comparable weight. They were significantly different in wealth and standing. By any standard, England, even on its own, was the heavyweight in British affairs, its role in Britain determined not by any peculiar aggressiveness of its population but by its overwhelming economic and cultural strength.

English dominance of the British Isles explains why many people both at home and abroad frequently fail to distinguish between Britain and England. The very complexity of these islands may have encouraged the search for at least one common factor. England, as the original homeland of the language now spoken throughout these islands, is used as a synecdoche for Britain. The worldwide diffusion of English does not, however, create modern illusions about English political power. Political dominance never overlaps completely with language. Even in the twelfth century, when a united England was ruled by powerful kings, they did not command the allegiance of all native speakers of English, for English-speaking Lothian, once part of the old Northumbrian kingdom, had been taken by the king of Scots into his Gaelic-speaking kingdom.[4] English medieval kings also ruled peoples in Cornwall and Wales who were not native English speakers. Even before the Norman Conquest, the kingdom was not monoglot.

England's closer proximity to the Continent gave it a rarely acknowledged advantage over its neighbours in these islands. Since cultural innovations from the Continent normally reached the archipelago from across the shortest sea route, England itself was always the earliest to feel the effects. This had political consequences. Significantly, it was not where the indigenous peoples could manage their affairs with the minimum of contact with outsiders, but in England, the part of Britain most open to pressures from the near Continent, that the most resilient political society developed. After the withdrawal of Roman armies, the arrival in considerable numbers of settlers from Germanic-speaking lands laid the foundations for the later dominance in these islands of the English. Before their arrival, all the inhabitants of Britain were Celtic speakers. Those natives who were left in the west by the settlements of the English invaders laid the foundations for later Welsh culture. Had it not been for the way these Germans settled, they would have been absorbed on their arrival into the existing Romano-British society, as happened elsewhere in the Roman Empire when the barbarians settled there. Since those earliest years, the English and the Welsh have interacted differently with the Continent. The Welsh kept up communications with continental Celts, as in Brittany. Gerald of Wales recognised that the languages of the two peoples were mutually intelligible.[5] Nor did the English, who had come from non-Romanised Germany and had been mainly responsible for the collapse of Roman-type government in Britannia in the fifth century, show any disposition thereafter to turn their backs on the near Continent. They proved much more eager to establish contact with the barbarian successor states of the empire, as soon as this was practically possible, than to complete the subjugation of the rest of Britain.

Early English preference for cultivating relations with near continental neighbours allowed Celtic societies to survive as such in the remoter parts of the archipelago. This deeply affected the later history of all these peoples. Differences of language were particularly important. In every continental province of the Roman Empire, Latin had been sufficiently widely spoken to have become the basis for various vernacular speech forms, which survived the collapse of formal Roman government. By contrast, in Britannia, Latin never became the basis of any vernacular language. After the collapse of the

Roman administration, it continued to be used for religious purposes and, for the Welsh, learning to write it had to be done the hard way in school because they spoke a quite different language. Isolated, however, from the rest of the Latin world, the Welsh most unusually also took to writing in their own vernacular. Although it is uncertain at what point they began to do so, their oldest poetry relates to events of the sixth century. The Irish, who had had only informal contacts with the Roman Empire, did not begin to accept Christianity until the fifth century, effectively, that is, after the collapse of imperial power in the west. Without coercion from any government, the Irish clergy learned Latin for religious purposes but made no difficulties about using the Irish vernacular language, even in writing. They too had to maintain schools and encourage learning about a Latin culture of which they had no direct experience.[6] Nowhere on the Continent was the vernacular ever used in writing, except briefly in Visigothic Spain, where, after the triumph of Catholic Christianity, Latin was reimposed as the language not only of religion but of culture.

These insular peculiarities powerfully influenced even the English settlers in Britain. Before migrating, the English peoples had known no Latin. Only after the arrival of Christian missionaries was Latin apparently written in England. Even so, the law code of the first Christian English king, Ethelbert of Kent, was redacted not in Latin but in English.[7] Had the missionaries themselves been responsible for introducing writing into England they would, surely, as everywhere else in the lands of the Roman Empire, have used Latin. This makes it look as though the English had already found a use for writing somewhat earlier. In England, anyway, Roman Christianity never attempted to suppress writing in the vernacular as it did elsewhere. The English use of their own vernacular in writing had far-reaching implications for the future, not only in Britain but abroad. These peculiarities about the formal status of the vernaculars in Britain helped to keep the peoples of the islands distinctive, not only from the Continent but from one another.

As far as English itself is concerned, it may seem more insular than it was. To what extent all speakers of Germanic languages on the North Sea littoral were mutually intelligible in the Middle Ages cannot be established. As late as the mid-thirteenth century, Matthew Paris regarded the English and German languages as similar enough to justify the election of Richard of Cornwall as king of the Romans in 1257.[8] In the absence of any standard form of the language or of formal instruction in vernacular speech, communication between different groups may not have been notably more difficult than it was between the different forms of English. Another reason for linking English as a spoken language to others of its linguistic family on the Continent is that the most famous piece of surviving Old English literature, *Beowulf*, does not relate to any English adventure but to a Danish one. The interaction between the English and the Danes who raided, settled and governed in England in the ninth and tenth centuries indicates another way in which the English continued to interact with the Continent. Such contacts mattered more to the development of the English kingdom than its relations with its Celtic neighbours.

Even if the Germanic peoples of the Migration Period are presumed to have spoken mutually intelligible languages, they did not all arrive in Britain together. Politically their settlements developed into several different kingdoms. They even recognised more basic differences than those of mere kingdoms, since some were called Angles, others Saxons. For the peoples in the rest of Britain, they were all called Saxons, as still in modern Scots, Sassenachs. The same term was used for them in Ireland. Only in England itself did the term English prevail. Why was this? The most plausible explanation is cultural. After the various Germanic peoples had accepted Christianity, they were perceived by the Northumbrian historian, Bede, as sharing an essential unity within the Western Church. Since Northumbria had been settled by Angles rather than Saxons, Bede called his *Ecclesiastical History* that of the English, not of the Saxons, no doubt consciously playing on the similarity of the words *Angli, angeli,* a conceit he attributed to Pope Gregory I.[9]

Bede's ecclesiastical inspiration obliged him to contrast the English peoples who had received their Christian beliefs from the Roman mission with the Welsh Christians. Not only had the Welsh failed to undertake missionary work among the invaders, they proved reluctant in other respects to conform to the usages of the Roman Church. For Bede, Britain remained divided, even by religious practice, with the English as loyal participants in the faith of the whole Western Church and clearly committed to the Continent whence they had come. Bede did not falsify the facts. The different parts of Britain had received Christianity from various sources. The Christian religion had originally reached Britain under Roman aegis. In the fifth century, it must have been very weakly grounded if the English invaders were put under no pressure to convert when they settled. They even proved strong enough to have suppressed most traces of Christian organisation in the territories they occupied. Britons who remained under English domination were either happy to revert to paganism under their new Germanic conquerors, or had little option but to do so. Beyond the settlers' reach, Christians in Cornwall and Wales preserved their Latin religious culture while losing contact with the Roman world. This outcome was in marked contrast to what happened on the Continent. There Catholic Christianity was so deeply entrenched that all the barbarian peoples who settled in the Roman Empire, even those already converted to Arian Christianity, were in the end obliged to accept the religious practices of the lands they came to rule.

The strength of continental Catholicism was such that the English themselves were drawn into its orbit, converted not by the efforts of Christians already in Britain but by missionary efforts from Gaul and then Rome. The importance of these continental links for English Christianity is fully borne out by the experience of Northumbria. The first Christian missionaries there had been brought in by King Edwin, originally from Deira, the southern part of the kingdom, who had become acquainted with the new religion while in exile at the court of the king of East Anglia. In his brief reign, conversion made little progress. After his death, kings from Bernicia, the northern part of the kingdom, took over. Oswald, likewise in exile but to the north, had first learned of Christianity from the Irish monks established at Iona; when he returned to Northumbria as king, Oswald accordingly invited missionaries from there. This strain of Christianity took root during the next thirty years. By the middle of the seventh century Northumbria had also become the most powerful of the several English kingdoms. Yet instead of using this authority to bring the other English churches into line with Iona, King Oswy, at the Synod of Whitby, decided to favour Rome in matters of church discipline. His decision in favour of the continental rather than the insular tradition shows how attracted the most northerly of the English were to keeping up their links overseas, even at the cost of breaking with ties closer to home. The direction of the English Church thereafter became subject to the ideals of continental Catholicism, responding sensitively to papal decisions and varying fashions in monastic observance as these changed over the centuries. By contrast, after the sixth century the Celtic-speaking peoples in the other parts of Britain who maintained links with one another seem to have remained relatively detached from the practices of other western Christians. The consequences of these differences were long-lasting.

The impact of continental affairs continued to affect developments in England after the conversion period. Under the Vikings, notably, most of the native English kingdoms collapsed altogether. The survival of Wessex stimulated a military counter-attack, which in the end brought most of the former separate English kingdoms into a single united kingdom. Though the Vikings did not spare other parts of these islands, they did not there provoke comparable countermeasures. In Ireland the Vikings never succeeded in taking over any existing kingdom. Nor were they ever completely absorbed into any of the Irish kingdoms. Their coastal enclaves did not threaten the power of Irish kings of the interior and were consequently left to their own devices. In the twelfth century, Irish annalists still insisted on regarding them as foreigners. The unification of the English as a result of their confrontation with the Danes proved decisive, not only for the history of England but for the rest of Britain. In time, the new monarchy was able to assert greater pressure elsewhere in the archipelago than any of the other still small authorities. Yet without the stimulus given them by the Danish settlement, the English might have remained as divided as the Irish.

England and the Continent

By the unification of the various English kingdoms in the tenth century, England had become one of the strongest kingdoms of the west well before

English kings acquired properties of their own on the Continent. Most of its continental neighbours were all much less powerful. Just across the North Sea, what are still thought of as the small states of the Low Countries were themselves not united, with each province ruled separately by different princely families. Marriage alliances between the families of English rulers and the princes of this region were renewed in almost every generation from the time of Alfred of Wessex. Both sides valued friendly relations. Regional princes also then dominated the affairs of France, the major state of modern Europe. When compared with his continental neighbours, the king of England was a very imposing figure. The only ruler of greater standing on the Continent was the German king who ruled also in northern Italy. After Otto I was crowned in Rome in 962, he and his descendants were called Roman emperors. No ruler in the west was treated with greater respect. With Germany, English relations going back to the age of settlement and reinforced over the centuries had been cemented politically by the marriage of Otto I to one of King Athelstan's sisters. The friendship of the English and Germans was still appreciated on both sides in the mid-eleventh century. This brought the two most powerful political forces of the Germanic world together.

The renewal of Danish raiding in the late tenth century against the south of England made it imperative to secure additional protection from across the Channel by an alliance with the duchy of Normandy, 'founded' in 911 and still in contact with its Viking kinsmen. At first, this alliance did not seriously alter the course of English relations with the Continent and the successful Danish conquest of England inevitably emphasised the predominantly Germanic character of the kingdom. But the Norman Conquest itself, which intensified English involvement with the Continent, eventually gave it an entirely new thrust. Whereas the natural direction of English interests overseas had been across the North Sea and Straits of Dover to other Germanic lands, after 1066 attention was focused across the English Channel. By the marriage of Henry II to Eleanor, duchess of Aquitaine, in the mid-twelfth century, English kings acquired other interests further south, which regularly took English mariners to the Bay of Biscay.

England's kings expected to move freely across the sea as and when they wanted, often at very short notice. No other western European kings of this period, not even in Scandinavia, went to sea more often. Just as the Vikings had taken to their ships more easily than any other group of barbarian marauders in search of booty and conquests, so too the Normans. In southern Italy the Normans, unlike the Lombards, their barbarian predecessors, quickly followed up their successes on the mainland by further adventures against the North African coast and across the Adriatic Sea. In the north, the Norman monarchy in England had a maritime awareness which suited English requirements perfectly. Government and subjects alike adjusted promptly to the new situation. This had implications for the way England was perceived on the other side of the Channel. For French rulers and 'government', the lands of the English king abroad were not a matter of foreign affairs at all. To all intents and purposes, from the eleventh century England became a factor in French politics.

Long before English kings became closely involved in continental affairs, clergy from these islands had taken such contact for granted. From the time of Augustine's mission, which inaugurated regular communication between the church of Canterbury and the papacy, English clergy cultivated their connections with continental churches and rulers as well as benefiting culturally from the legacy of the Christian Roman Empire. The early English Christians were aware that the ancestors they identified with had come from Germany and were remarkably prompt in assuming responsibility for taking the benefits of Christianity back to the ancestral lands in order to bring the pagan Germans into their Christian world. They did this with the active encouragement of the Carolingian rulers, themselves rulers of Germanic speech. In this great effort of conversion, Irish monks too made an important contribution, thanks to a hallowed tradition of leaving their own land to travel in exile as *peregrini*. They established monastic communities in German lands that continued to recruit monks from Ireland for centuries. In both England and Ireland commitment to missionary efforts became an enduring feature of their churches. When the pagan Vikings began to settle in England they were required to convert and, as Scandinavia itself was drawn into the Christian world, the kings of Denmark, Norway and Sweden turned confidently to English clergy for help with the conversion of their own peoples and the organisation of churches in their kingdoms.

Over the centuries, the contacts made by English clergy abroad were not subject to royal control or supervision and became extremely diverse. They could be institutional, like associations of prayer between English and continental monasteries. Later, when university education developed in the twelfth century, English students abroad established personal relationships with their teachers or fellow students. Something similar, though much less profound, has occurred since the Second World War through international research projects and university exchanges. In the Middle Ages the easy intercourse of educated people across western Christendom was not something supplementary to national education, but basic to the concept of education itself. Those who derived their learning from the Continent acquired a moral point of reference outside the kingdom. This should not be understood to mean that Englishmen educated abroad became any less 'patriotic' on that account. Stephen Langton, who had studied for many years in Paris and been called to Rome as cardinal, wrote convincingly about the strength of his feeling for his native country since childhood.[10] Clergy who dutifully accepted the call to serve the Church far away from their home country did not find it easy. As a Carthusian, Hugh of Avalon could not refuse the invitation to help establish a new house of his order in a land with which he had no previous connection, but he still had problems about adjusting to foreign ways, unfamiliar food and the standards of strangers.[11] But however devoted their local churches and saints, their patrons, even their kings, clergy were cognisant of their place in the international order. They were patriotic but not nationalist, counting in their struggles as much on the foreign friends they had made as on the sympathies of fellow countrymen. As the best educated men of their kingdoms, the clergy did not leave the care of their interests abroad to royal agents; they naturally assumed the responsibility themselves. There was no one formal ecclesiastical organisation anywhere in Britain able to negotiate on behalf of all, even with the papacy; everywhere, local prelates managed their own affairs.

The authority of the Roman Church did not originally inspire equal respect in all parts of Britain. In the remoter parts of the archipelago, where the introduction of Christianity owed nothing to the papacy, it was only as they were brought into more intimate contact with England that the Scottish, Welsh and Irish clergy began to perceive the potential advantages of cultivating their own papal connections. Information about how these contacts were first developed is somewhat fitful. Does the notice that when the Welsh bishop Joseph of Llandaff died *c*.1045 he was at Rome signify something unusual?[12] Or were earlier Welsh contacts with Rome for some reason simply not noted? Visiting the shrines of the holy apostles may actually have been more frequent than the evidence suggests, but only in England were Roman contacts deliberately cultivated from the beginning to institutional effect.

Quite apart from the Canterbury tradition, political considerations counted here. The English king, unlike other kings of these islands, consistently kept a close eye on the activities of his bishops. Not only was royal influence on the English Church a factor in its well-being; later, the king's political force on the Continent made it impossible for the pope to ignore his interests. After the Protestant Reformation, the matter of British relations with the papacy assumed a controversial character and this prejudiced understanding of how the links with the papacy arose in the medieval period. The acceptance of Christianity in England had owed much to the initiative and support of local kings; the enduring importance of royal support for the Church was never forgotten. Kings, who had at first been understandably wary of foreign missionaries, might have become uneasy about the likely effects for their own influence of becoming members of the international Church. In fact, the new commitments were not perceived as incompatible with more local political loyalties. Disputes which inevitably arose between kings and their clergy were regarded as deeply distasteful, to be resolved as quickly as possible. Neither side insisted on the differences between the universal and the local commitment; neither required one to be sacrificed for the sake of the other. But since the papacy itself was sufficiently autonomous to challenge even kings of England on occasion, it was not until Henry VIII had finally broken with Rome that he could escape from the moral constraint of the universal Church and become for the first time undisputed sovereign of his own kingdom.

The close relation of the clergy with a 'foreign' power like the papacy has no secular parallel. Nevertheless, after the Norman Conquest the intimate relation between England and France did create a situation with some similar features. The greatest English magnates and many of their vassals had estates of their own on the Continent which many intended to keep alongside their English lands as a family concern. Like their kings, they went to and fro across the Channel. For their Norman lands they owed service to the king of France and in this sense they too might be considered servants of two masters. The king of France, however, was in no position to take advantage in England of the fact that these 'vassals' possessed extensive lands in his own kingdom. Aggrieved Norman barons only rarely attempted to inveigle their king's French overlord into their own quarrels and such moves had no success. The king of France, unlike the pope, had no means of commanding moral submission to his diktat: English secular politics were autonomous. Unlike bishops, barons expected to resolve their differences with the king without foreign aid. Although they were no more isle-bound than the clergy, there is much less precise information about their visits abroad. Those with Norman estates regularly travelled further than others, either on their own account or with their king. The mustering of forces for military campaigns and the transmission of intelligence information were matters of course. Chronicles allude to baronial participation in tourneys, the great sporting contests of the period, but there is nothing in writing to show how these were organised. Formal invitations could have been delivered orally by messengers.

The exposure of other Englishmen to the Continent followed from the determination of English kings to take the place they thought they deserved on the European stage. All the king's subjects were positively encouraged to look outwards, but as we move down the social scale our sources of information dry up. Although nothing can be confidently asserted about the great majority of the population, this does not mean that the meanest persons in the kingdom must have remained unaware of foreigners and foreign places. Since the medieval English educated elite had identified its interests with the international order of the Church, this too had great significance for the intellectual and moral outlook of Christian people. The clergy did not keep their ideas about abroad to themselves. By their education and later by the offices they occupied in Church and State, they encouraged laymen to look abroad with the same confidence so that it was not only dedicated missionaries who went across the sea for religious reasons.

The Church encouraged pilgrimages to distant holy places, either out of sheer devotion or as a form of penance. Laymen duly left these islands to make arduous journeys overseas as far as Jerusalem, Rome and Santiago de Compostela. These could take months, walking across many strange lands. Some went more than once in their lives. Tenth-century English coins found along the routes of northern Spain prove that English pilgrims must have already become devotees of St James. The English had a hospice of their own at Compostela in the twelfth century, the only nation known to have such an amenity, further evidence for the popularity of the pilgrimage.[13] Pilgrims could be of very humble social condition but only by a miracle would their journeys be thought worth mentioning. The pilgrimage of the Essex countryman Thurkill of Stistead was only recalled because his devotion to St James was rewarded in 1206 with an extraordinary vision of the afterlife written up by the neighbouring abbot of Coggeshall.[14] At Bury St Edmunds, the pilgrimage to Rome of one of the abbey's villeins attracted notice because of his miraculous rescue at sea by St Edmund himself.[15] Only because Godric, the hermit of Finchale, inspired sufficient devotion for a monk of Durham to write about his life do we learn incidentally about his colourful youth as a merchant and pirate in the North Sea and the three visits he made to the Holy Land.[16] The numerous pilgrims who did not acquire saintly reputations were of no concern to contemporary chroniclers. Pilgrimage was not a pleasure cruise. Foreign travellers were not proportionately as numerous as modern holidaymakers, but their journeys certainly made a deeper impression, for conditions of travel were far more testing.

Whether pilgrimage was imposed or chosen, it was expected to be temporary; exile might be permanent. In the early period, disputes with kindred or personal enemies might oblige men to flee abroad. After the unification of England, political dissidents, forced to take refuge, often chose Flanders or Ireland. In 1051, Earl Godwin and some sons went to Bruges, Harold to Leinster. Political exiles may have constituted 'expatriate' communities, awaiting a favourable opportunity to launch attacks on England for their own reinstatement, and obviously maintaining contact with friends to keep informed about the situation. Some exiles had foreign kinsmen. Aethelred II escaped temporarily to Normandy, his wife's homeland; the children of Edmund Ironside prudently fled as far as Hungary to elude notice. After the Norman Conquest, some exiles were established in the Byzantine Empire; others took refuge in Denmark. Clergy who temporarily fell out with kings after the Norman Conquest were welcomed by friends or in religious houses sympathetic to their causes. While Archbishop Langton and four English bishops were in exile at Amiens, they were called in to settle a dispute between the local bishop and his chapter.[17] The Cistercian house at Pontigny, which had provided a refuge for Becket, likewise offered sanctuary to one of his successors at Canterbury, Edmund of Abingdon. When he died there, the French monks promoted his cult and attracted more English pilgrims.[18] Similarly, Lawrence O'Toole, archbishop of Dublin, who died unexpectedly at Eu in 1180, was venerated there as a saint.[19]

Saintly exiles were revered and their sufferings recorded. The fate of criminal exiles did not have comparable interest. Yet there were probably many of them. The operations of royal justice in England from the late twelfth century drove many of those accused of serious crimes out of the kingdom. Apart from the rules stipulating how they should be escorted to the ports, nothing more is known of where they went or how they fared. Suspected criminals able to evade appearance in court were outlawed and some of these may have skulked in bands, taking refuge in out-of-the-way places. Others presumably went overseas, and perhaps made a living there. Exiles and outlaws once out of England probably followed well-beaten paths, known about even in England and leading them into the most remote parts of Europe. In the Middle Ages the English appreciated the possibility of a kind reception abroad. The extent to which this has been true in more recent times is systematically overlooked in England, but the Scots and the Irish have never underestimated the importance of being received sympathetically on the Continent. Willingness to receive foreigners in need also attracted continental exiles to England itself. French nobles were said to have dissuaded Louis IX from attacking England in 1242 because they needed an independent England as a bolt-hole for when they they fell out with their own kings.[20]

Englishmen who needed no urging from kings or clergy to take themselves overseas were those who saw their way to making a profit by doing so. Well before the Conquest, merchants who were wealthy enough to have taken their merchandise across the seas three times at their own expense were ranked as thegns.[21] Climbing the social ladder was probably not the principal spur for their activities. Aelfric's *Colloquies* fill out the picture of the eleventh-century English merchant by explaining how his imports of valuable commodities contributed to the general well-being. The precious objects he brought into the kingdom were specified as purple cloth, silks, rich clothing and dyes, precious gems and gold; wine, oil, spices; ivory, metal goods and glass.[22] Whether the merchant took goods overseas to pay for these costly imports or relied on payment in cash is not stated, but other evidence from about the year 1000 corroborates Aelfric's view that foreign trade had much to offer the kingdom. A record from Pavia refers to an agreement between the kings of the English and the Lombards, undated but probably from the mid-tenth century, which aimed to prevent further ructions between English merchants and the Lombard customs officials. In return for exemption from payment of the 'tenth' the English king was to pay 50 pounds of refined silver every three years, two large greyhounds with gilded collars, two embossed shields, two lances and two fine swords, with a further douceur to the master of the treasury, namely two coats of miniver and two pounds of refined silver.[23] The English evidently regarded the Lombard trade as worth protecting and the agreement shows what goods were traded. There is no later information about this traffic apart from the fact that King Cnut on his Rome journey of 1027 negotiated with the king of Burgundy for concessions allowing English merchants and those who travelled for devotional reasons to move freely through that kingdom.[24] An early eleventh-century record of the tolls exacted in London sheds light on the situation in reverse by listing various foreign merchants who traded in England: men from Rouen bringing wine, whale or large fish, Flemings, men of Ponthieu, Normans and Frenchmen, traders from Huy, Liège and Nivelles and men from the German Empire. The main English import was of wine but, unless their trade was in permanent deficit, they must have exported goods of even greater value.[25]

The strongest proof of English wealth from the tenth century is shown by the high quality of the royal coinage. This was maintained by attracting silver from abroad (mainly Germany). Not much evidence about the affairs of medieval merchants has survived for early periods, mainly because until urban literacy became more common from the thirteenth century commerce may have dispensed altogether with written records. Making allowance for the scale of international trading may be difficult, but does not justify the common assumption that the medieval economy was one of basic self-subsistence. Movement between the islands and the Continent was managed from both sides for commercial purposes, providing and selling goods of basic supply, as well as those of specialised craftsmanship and luxuries. Travelling merchants had moreover to be men of steel, ready to defend their own persons and property if attacked. Only exceptionally were kings able to offer them assistance with their business operations.

Instead of thinking that relations between Britain and the Continent concern only governments, as modern views are inclined to suppose, we need to recognise that they are conducted on a very broad front. Governments may now be empowered to act on behalf of all, but they are still not the only players in the game. Nor are interests of government necessarily the same as those of all the people in whose names they purport to act. Governments sometimes find reasons of their own to inhibit the interests of manufacture, commerce, sport or finance. Whatever governments may profess about acting in the general interest, in practice they pay greatest attention to those believed to have the most political clout.

The mobility of islanders

Island peoples are natural seafarers and every bay and harbour will have been busy with boats great and small. The mobility of medieval populations may be seen at its most extreme in the crusades, but even these indicate not merely a propensity to take off for distant lands but confidence in overcoming the difficulties of travel. Those intrepid enough to entrust themselves to the sea are, however, the people least likely to leave records of their journeys or get their deeds narrated by historians. Nobody doubts the importance of the Germanic migration into fifth-century Britain for the subsequent history of England, but because all the immigrants were illiterate its course is one of the most obscure episodes medieval historians have to deal with. Centuries later, much-travelled merchants, even those who kept records of their merchandise and business accounts, still left no reports on their journeys or their impressions of the world. Our understanding of medieval seagoing often depends on the most oblique evidence, like the many miracles at sea worked by various saints for frightened devotees caught in storms or terrorised by godless pirates. The greater frequency of sea-traffic from the mid-eleventh century may be gauged not only from the increasing popularity of Nicholas as the saint most commonly appealed to at sea by distressed travellers but by the evident anxiety of other cult centres to promote the efficacy of their own saints in this respect. At Bury, the powers of St Edmund at sea were recorded even before 1100; in the twelfth century, at Durham, those of Cuthbert, at Canterbury, those of Becket.[26] Trouble at sea was a familiar hazard and these stories prove that sea journeys were assumed to be everyday experiences. The sea offered the best way of leaving home, finding adventure and exploiting opportunities for trade and settlement. The inhabitants of these many islands were familiar with seagoing and not necessarily content to navigate home waters or confine their attentions to one another. The sea lanes they explored were just as naturally followed by their continental neighbours, from the North Cape to Cadiz.

The geography of the British Isles itself positively invites taking off in several different directions so that the contact made with the Continent varied according to region. After the Norman Conquest, much of southern England probably cultivated close ties with the Norman ports across the Channel. But Kent had for centuries maintained closer relations than other southern regions with the near Continent across what in the twelfth century was as often called the Flemish Sea as the British Ocean.[27] In the early stages of the Germanic migrations into England, it would have been natural to keep in touch with communities in Germany in order to encourage fresh settlers and help shore up the new settlements. Habits originally developed for practical reasons were maintained over time for economic and religious motives. England's largest city, London, owed its prosperity to its continental commerce, down the Thames and across the North Sea to Germany. It was its commercial prominence that eventually made it the focal point of English national government. Further up the east coast, Danish settlement reinforced long-standing contacts with Scandinavia.

The rivers of eastern England provided easy access to the interior as far as they were navigable. At the time, water transport was indispensable for bulk purchases and rivers are prominently indicated on the earliest maps of England.[28] Produce destined for distant markets went down the rivers and across the seas. Major towns were those accessible by water. By contrast, communication overland was laborious and consequently restricted. When market towns developed in the twelfth and thirteenth centuries, their commercial range was expected to be within manageable walking distance for prospective vendors. Accepting the common assumption that a man could walk twenty miles a day, the thirteenth-century legal treatise known as Bracton expected market towns to be no more than seven miles off, if there was to be time for transacting business and getting home again in daylight.[29] Such limited horizons did not prevail in coastal regions.

Although it is easy to see that Germanic immigrants who settled in the coastal regions to the south and east are less likely to have lost contact with their original homelands than those who moved further away, it would be mistaken to suppose that the most remote parts of these islands were insulated from events overseas. Northern waters brought the coastal districts of Scotland, Ireland and Wales experience of their Scandinavian neighbours.[30] Many of the inhabitants of these districts were of Scandinavian origin and accustomed both to receiving visitors from the north and visiting the Norwegian royal court themselves. The Anglian colonisation of Northumbria and the Irish links with the early Church there had set up communications at a much earlier stage. Irishmen from the south-east of the island took advantage of easy access to Wales to travel through 'Celtic' waters from Wales to Cornwall and Brittany. Contacts between Brittany, Wales and Ireland were after all ancient before the end of Roman rule in Britain. Gerald of Wales refers to the direct route between Ireland and Spain: the sea journey took three days, whereas to cross Ireland from east to west took four. Legends about the origins of the Irish people take direct communication with Spain for granted.[31] Even further away, Irish hermits had found their way to Iceland before the Norwegian settlers arrived in the ninth century and made such ocean journeys regular occurrences.[32]

The openness of the whole British Isles to maritime traffic does not alter the fact that those who could cross to the Continent at best within a few hours enjoyed a different sort of contact from those in the west and north, for whom shores to be reached entirely by water were that much further off. For them, the near Continent was more safely reached by using a land route across parts of Britain. In the twelfth century, St Malachi reached the Continent by crossing from northern Ireland into Galloway and then through southern Scotland before following the eastern coast of England to the Low Countries.[33] The Irish of the north may have generally preferred the route through Gaelic Scotland to the one across England. There is little to show what routes were normally followed, though the movement of Irish monks to their establishments on the Continent is certain.

In the absence of any conception of 'territorial waters' (until the great powers agreed in the nineteenth century to accord them recognition in international law), the comings and goings of the coastal peoples of northern Europe were not normally subject to governmental controls.[34] At certain crossing points, opportunities to exploit travellers might be taken to collect tolls or intercept messengers, but whole coastlines could not be watched, still less could the open seas be regularly supervised. There is nothing to show what concern political authorities showed about shipping until the Viking attacks stimulated the kings of Wessex to think of how to organise effective naval forces and intercept invaders before they landed. An edict of Aethelred II issued in 1008 shows what naval service was then expected from the kingdom. As late as 1049 Edward the Confessor deployed many ships in the Channel when asked for help by the emperor Henry III against

Baldwin of Flanders.[35] Yet royal naval forces did not prove sufficient to prevent either the Danish or the Norman conquests. Both these peoples, after settling down in the kingdom, then kept in touch with their old homelands. Their confidence at sea can only have enhanced the naval capabilities of the kingdom, without making England any more of an island fortress in this period than it had been earlier. In the rest of the British Isles there were no central authorities at all to supervise local activities or keep out foreign intruders. Local naval forces coped with their own defences and took advantage of their opportunities to plunder at will.

The availability of shipping remained, essentially, a matter of private enterprise. Most seamen had full-time activities of their own, either as merchants, shipping both their own goods and those of others, or as fishermen or even as pirates, taking their chances with others like themselves, an abuse of power which kings were in no position to suppress. In times of war, the king relied on what naval forces were already available to keep the seas clear of his enemies. Henry II was sufficiently concerned about finding ships when needed to forbid the sale of them abroad, but assumed that it was common practice.[36] By the thirteenth century, commercial shipping was available in almost any of the English kingdom's ports and there was nothing to stop ships venturing to foreign shores on their own account. Information about the shipping available in other parts of the British Isles is much less specific, but twelfth-century Irish annalists frequently refer to the deployment of large numbers of ships, not only in the Irish Sea but on the Shannon and in the north.[37] Norse expansion in northern waters was made possible and sustained by superior naval strength, and the establishment of Norse trading towns in Ireland followed from commercial as much as military calculations. Those with interests at sea had their own agenda and did not act as disinterested defenders of any national security. Seamen traded overseas and could be as familiar with foreign places as were the king, clergy and nobility with places abroad of interest to them.

England had many sources of information to draw upon for understanding the nature of the continental world; rather less, it would seem, about the other peoples of these islands. From their experiences, merchants acquired knowledge of ports and weather conditions at sea. Clergy visited and studied in schools and monasteries on the Continent, making friendships and contacts that proved valuable to their communities at home. Travellers who returned home to report on what they had seen and done were reliable sources of information, able if required to voice, for example, what they thought of the papal Curia, the king of France, the demand for English wool or the relative safety of travel in Muslim lands.

Laymen who might travel as far as the Holy Land were no less aware of the size of their world than the educated clergy. Many people would have had some general understanding of the shape of Christendom, and were able to place their own concerns in the larger whole that they knew of. Their conversation helped to inform others who did not travel in person. Some information might have been unreliable, for stories retold up-country might have taken on the wonderful colours of legend. Lucian, monk of Chester, had heard stories about India from travellers which he dismissed as shameless lies, but the shipmen from Aquitaine, Spain and Germany he saw in the port of Chester would have been trustworthy informants about their own lands.[38] In coastal regions, where the greatest densities of population were anyway situated, the comings and goings of travellers provided generally sound intelligence about the nature of places on the other side of the water. In this way all the clergy of the great churches could learn about the affairs of the papacy, the Holy Land or places of pilgrimage. Their views of abroad were not necessarily identical with those of their informants: their concerns were affected by different considerations. Matthew Paris, the thirteenth-century chronicler, knew a great deal about the activities of the papacy in his own times but, never having been to Rome himself, put his own slant on what he heard.

The many reasons the English in particular found for going overseas may even have stimulated exceptional curiosity about foreign shores. William of Malmesbury added a long account of the crusading campaigns to his history of English kings and was the first English writer to have heard of sugar cane and appreciate that it could assuage hunger when sucked.[39] At the end of the twelfth century, Roger of Hoveden thought readers of his chronicle would appreciate his detailed description of the lands along the sea route to the Holy Land and back, providing information of both political and economic interest.[40] Half a century later, it was an English Franciscan, Bartholomew, who provided all Christendom with its most consulted single-volume encyclopaedia, where he described in alphabetical order all the known places of the world. Much of his material was lifted from earlier authorities like Pliny and Isidore of Seville, but for parts of northern Europe Bartholomew relied on personal information or report. In any case, the book shows how information became available to those who looked for it, even if they did not themselves travel.[41] The public display of maps of the world in thirteenth-century England proves that geographical curiosity had prompted efforts to devise visual representation of what was known.[42] Whether the information found on such maps was taken from literary sources, previous maps or from fresh information, it is evidence that there were people curious to know something about the world beyond Britain. This may help us to understand why English writers of chronicles more often recorded information about their continental neighbours than their French or German contemporaries bothered to do. In their outlook, the English were far from being 'insular'.

National sentiment

In modern times, schooling, political institutions, sport, language and common assumptions about a shared past all seem to be important factors for the development of any sense of national solidarity. In the Middle Ages it is difficult to suggest how any of these could have helped to foster nascent national sentiment. Quite the reverse. Conscious effort was devoted rather to inculcating respect for local residence, kinsmen, or lords who offered protection and patronage. Not even speaking a common language could have been sufficient to promote a sense of belonging to one nation. A great number of different languages were spoken locally throughout twelfth-century Europe, but Europe was not compartmentalised politically into opposed linguistic regions, as it is now, because the spoken vernaculars were not taught in schools or used as media for cultivating cultural values. Differences in the manner of speech defined distinct and geographically limited regions. Those who moved outside these limited districts had perforce to acquire speech patterns, even foreign ones, with wider diffusion. After the Conquest, French speech was widely heard in England and, since French in some form was spoken in many parts of Christendom, it became a kind of lingua franca. This offered the English a linguistic advantage they seem to have appreciated. England was the sole medieval country where a Germanic language was radically changed in syntax and vocabulary by the influence of French. Only widespread bilingualism can have been responsible for transforming the character of the language spoken by the totally uneducated. The general population became so familiar with hearing French spoken that it simplified its own speech accordingly. The dominant French culture of English 'society' in this period effectively precluded the early appearance of any deep sense of rupture between the English and the French. In his Latin commentary on difficult words in the Bible, Alexander Neckham provided vernacular equivalents, not in English but in French.[43]

The kind of evidence we have does not allow us to assess whether the English and the French felt antagonism for one another in the twelfth century. The nearest we come to sensing such feelings relies on the interpretation of some Latin poetry. Sophisticated audiences evidently enjoyed comparing the respective merits of priests and soldiers as lovers or the rights of pope and antipope, so disputes between kings gave rise to comparable literary exercises. In a conflict poem, written by Pierre Rigor, a canon of Reims, about the political differences between Louis VII and Henry II, resolved by the marriage of Henry's heir to Louis's daughter Margaret in 1160, the two parts of the poem may be seen as presenting two distinct 'national' points of view, with Louis's party naturally emerging in the better light. Such a literary production can hardly be interpreted as an expression of French national feeling. Poets were not interested in voicing popular opinions or in the differences between peoples.[44] It is doubtful whether there were any generic sentiments about other nations, apart from wonder at their different customs. Since there were no opportunities for meeting rival fans of national teams, there was no occasion to foster national hatreds. By the mid-thirteenth century, when French writers in the north had become more confident about using the vernacular to voice shared opinions, they cheerfully mocked the inconclusive efforts of Henry III to acquire a military reputation in France.[45] At that time there were only occasional bursts of open combat, so French writers more commonly ridiculed the English for what were considered their idiosyncracies. At Fontainbleau in 1200, when Philip II of France entertained King John of England and his men, the French had a good laugh because the English preferred to drink the inferior wines and would not touch the best.[46] The French also mocked English ways of speaking French, which may or may not be a sign of nationalist sentiment. Only later did Englishmen become shamefaced about their French and it took even longer for them to insist on speaking and writing only in English. Language was not a shibboleth before 1300. Although making fun of foreigners is now frowned on, it hardly amounts to proof of national antipathies.

Not even memories of past experience were used to promote national self-consciousness. It might be supposed that the Vikings would have inspired Englishmen with some dislike and distrust of Danes as such, but there is no sign that Denmark had come to be viewed as a national enemy. The English kingdom successfully absorbed its Danish elements and friendly association across the North Sea continued after the cessation of Viking raids. In the twelfth century, Englishmen continued to obtain ecclesiastical posts in Norway and English saints were venerated there. The impressive number of English churches dedicated to Olaf testifies to the mutual attractions of the two peoples.[47] The traditional privileges enjoyed in the city of London by Danes and Norwegians most likely date from the time of Cnut and passed unchallenged for centuries. In 1069 Danes were welcomed, at least in parts of Yorkshire, as almost fellow countrymen against the Normans. The English built up no national prejudice against Scandinavians on account of much earlier history.

The Norman Conquest is now held to have provoked strong antipathy among the English to their Norman conquerors and to have encouraged Normans in turn to despise the English for their military defeat. Such ideas appear to depend more on modern beliefs about what proud people ought to feel about national humiliation than upon any hard evidence. The rhetoric of William of Malmesbury has been cited, but his own birth of mixed parentage was certainly not exceptional and proves that there was no social separation of the 'races'. Whereas Normans usually distinguished themselves from the French, the Bretons or the Angevins, the English did not discriminate and treated all alike as speakers of French. Anyway, within a century, no difference between those of English or French ancestry was detectable.[48] If anything, as the Normans themselves settled down as English residents the English grew closer to the French, abandoning their old Germanic names in favour of Tom, Dick and Harry, all French. Popular English prejudice about the French developed later as a result of their military experiences abroad during the Hundred Years War.

Travellers apparently undeterred by difficulties of communication in a foreign language and meeting foreigners on a regular basis did not throw up artificial barriers by asserting their own nationality. As to the idea of 'foreign-ness', it was not necessary to be born abroad. In medieval towns residents without civic or burgess rights to office or status were 'foreigners', meaning 'not insiders'. The 'foreigners' most in the public eye were other Englishmen from neighbouring towns or communities whose commercial or artisan activities appeared to encroach on local privilege. In London, even the merchants of Dunstable were resented as foreigners. At Yarmouth in the thirteenth century, the townsmen were more favourably disposed to visiting Flemings than to Englishmen from the Cinque Ports with whom they regularly had disputes, scuffles and worse.[49] There was no disposition to perceive outsiders from far afield as somehow different. Their reception depended on their intentions. Those who came with force to seize property would be resisted and attacked; others travelling in small numbers for trade or as pilgrims did so in expectation of a quiet reception. Englishmen themselves similarly ventured overseas on their own business, confident of finding suitable conditions for their activities and reliant on their own ability to cope abroad, without the protection offered by government passports or consular offices to smooth their way and remind them perpetually of their nationality.

Whenever the placing of foreigners became an issue, their status was indicated not so much by their nation or their native speech as by their particular place of origin, not as Germans, but from Cologne or Lübeck; not as Flemings, but from Malines, Douai; not as Italians, but from Florence, Pistoia, Siena, Piacenza. Insistence on their local affiliation does not resemble our appeal to national citizenship. The purpose of such identifications was simply to know to which authorities it was appropriate to make representations about redress of grievances caused by citizens of that place in England. These identifications carried no implications about the supposed characteristics of the place in question. It was, no doubt, also relevant to appreciate that whether the authority was that of a prince, bishop or a town council over errant merchants, it was invariably of lesser dignity than that of the king of England himself. English kings had no reason to encourage their subjects to develop any emotional hostility to the subjects of other rulers.

Without any formal education about English 'values', it is unlikely that the English as such could have already acquired any distaste for foreign nationals. When objections were raised in the thirteenth century, it was not to foreigners as such but to specific foreign-born subjects of the king (*alienigenae*), and for very pertinent reasons, namely that they not only appeared to enjoy greater favours from the king than Englishmen but had abused their position to turn the king against his native-born subjects. These protests have since been hastily interpreted as evidence for innate English xenophobia. This seems plain wrong. English medieval society was confident of its own strength, welcomed strangers and considered the offer of hospitality as one of the greatest virtues; the English should not be considered as atavistically hostile to strangers.

It is sometimes alleged that because post-Conquest English kings themselves had lands on the continent they dragged their subjects unwillingly into royal affairs of no national importance. Defining the national interest may not itself be so straightforward as it sounds and deciding what it might be is anyway normally considered a prerogative of governments. Modern governments, even allegedly democratic ones, often have reasons of state for policies which many, even most, of their subjects do not understand or approve. Medieval kings did not, of course, seek popular approval for their policies, and whether these were appreciated by their subjects was not important for their success. But it is actually not difficult to offer a plausible rationale for them. The various peoples of the English kingdom, especially those in the south, had a basic interest in keeping open their lines to the Continent, preferably by maintaining as many separate links to their near neighbours as possible. Politically, this encouraged English kings to prevent the emergence of any one ruler powerful enough to hinder English activities on the Continent. Under Charlemagne there had been no scope for English political intervention there and at the time no English king was powerful enough to think of doing so. The collapse of the Carolingian empire changed this. From the late tenth century, the dukes of Normandy had raised a barrier between England and the French kings. After 1066, Normandy itself provided an easy entry into France and thus offered England an exceptional opportunity to cut a great figure there. For several generations the kings of France remained too feeble to challenge the English presence. English interests may therefore be described as keeping France weak, and seeking to weaken it as it grew stronger. Their efforts in this direction were not completely futile. Only the unification of the Low Countries under French princes and the successful reassertion of French royal strength from the late fifteenth century effectively blocked English continental initiatives. The result of English withdrawal was to seal French dominance there. While Germany remained divided, only Spain challenged French pretensions and the Anglo-Spanish alliance became the bedrock of English foreign policy. All this took time. In the twelfth century, England had become a major factor in continental affairs, courted by many and fully abreast of what it could do. Although England was not a vassal state of the French kingdom, the English shared fully in the cultural life of French lands in this period and could be accepted as honorary Frenchmen.

The domestic advantages of having kings who were often absent should not be minimised. As long as they were not present to rule as they chose, they were obliged to set up forms of administration that worked according to routine. Absent kings chose to insist that their English subjects properly discharged their duty to help keep the king's peace. It is no accident that the enduring peculiarities of the English judicial system first took shape in this period. In addition, royal military campaigning in France on the whole kept

England itself at peace for most of the twelfth and thirteenth centuries. Royal warfare abroad did not even have the effect of turning English soldiers into English patriots, for kings could afford to make extensive use of hired mercenaries and did not rely on recruiting Englishmen to fight for them. Even in the fourteenth century, kings used such sundry warriors as could be assembled, some serving as military duty, many simply for wages. It was getting money out of parliaments that forced kings to make Englishmen think of France as a national enemy.

English concentration on the Continent had far-reaching implications for the rest of Britain and the slow emergence of a national dimension in the disputes between the kings of France and England has its parallel in Britain itself. There, however, a sense of national identity did begin to develop from the late thirteenth century, originally in connection with the reactions of the Welsh and Scots to the attempted takeover of native societies by Edward I. In Scotland, Edward's blithe assumptions that he could direct the government of the northern kingdom and quell disobedience by military occupation were shown to be unjustified. His experience of Welsh opposition to his lordship did not open his eyes to the strength of national sentiment. It clearly never occurred to him that Scots too might resent his projects for their kingdom. In the case of both the Scots and the Welsh, reliance on native soldiers to defend their lands against Edward I has an obvious bearing on how they became aware of their 'national' solidarity by warfare. But fighting together was not necessarily sufficient to achieve any 'national' ambition. In both Wales and Ireland, resentment at English domination did not bring about independent political authorities; it only exacerbated the sense of being distinctive from the English.

The nationalist question has recently been taken up as part of a systematic campaign to rescue the non-English inhabitants of these islands from alleged disparagement by historians. Understandably, the chief exponents of such views have been Scottish, Welsh and Irish historians. In some ways, such redress has made it easier to grasp the complex nature of the medieval situation in these islands. However, the further claims that under the Norman kings the English began to despise the 'backward' parts of the British Isles in a manner now labelled 'racist' and that the English aimed to impose an 'imperialist' agenda have seriously prejudiced understanding.[50] William of Malmesbury, who has been accused of a contemptuous attitude to the 'Celtic fringe', did not derive his ideas about the differences between the civilised and the barbarous from any sense of national superiority but from his reading of classical writers. Malmesbury certainly saw England as part of the civilised world of his day and correctly perceived that the other peoples of Britain were still living in a mainly pastoral economy without sophisticated monarchies and disciplined noble hierarchies.[51] This is far from representing evidence of English arrogance and it is inappropriate to read his words in the light of recent (and contentious) theories of 'political correctness'. Correct it is certainly not. The English approach might be more usefully compared with that of those who now think it justifiable to introduce 'humanitarian' or 'multicultural' values to 'backward' undemocratic societies without them. Both then and now, it seems reprehensible to let 'traditional' values stand in the way of 'modernising', that is adjusting to the perceived values of the 'real' world. Because champions of the new claim an exclusive right to ideological rectitude, they are always infuriated by those who refuse to accept that any change must necessarily be for the best. But claiming to be more 'enlightened' than others is only another form of 'imperialism'. Fortunately, a number of more recent studies have shown how open medieval English society could be to influences from remoter regions and allow for much closer interaction than some earlier writers had claimed.[52]

In this period, only some clergy were intellectually arrogant enough to think of imposing their values on others and their ability to do so remained limited. It was not only Muslims or Jews within their reach who resisted clerical pretensions, for Christian laymen, who were more vulnerable to religious pressure, did not abandon all their own values in the hope of escaping eternal torment. However confident they might be about their own way of doing things, the English were in no position to impose colonial status on their nearest neighbours. Such outside influences as penetrated the rest of the British Isles did so initially at the hands of native rulers, bishops or monks. Not all the support they needed came from England for they had their own lines of contact to the Continent. England, as that part of Britain closest geographically to the Continent and most open to influences from that direction, was, however, the natural conduit of the same influences round the rest of Britain. It is difficult to see how things could have turned out otherwise. After its unification in the tenth century, England had acquired a dominating position with regard to the other more traditional societies of the archipelago, so it could only be a matter of time before they experienced English pressure on them, in one form or another. At that stage, even notionally, they were not national entities. Over the period studied in this book, the emergence of national consciousness and the sense of belonging to English, Scottish, Welsh and Irish nationalities was one of its most important features. Likewise, however, contacts with abroad also failed to persuade the peoples of these islands that they had more in common than they did with people from the continental mainland. Britishness was not a product of the Middle Ages. On the contrary, some of them preferred their continental friends and allies to their fellow islanders.

|2|

The Norman Conquest and its implications

1066 and All That, the title of the popular parody of the English history textbook, takes it for granted that the year of the Norman Conquest is the most memorable date in English history. The prominence accorded to the Conquest is not of recent origin. As far back as 1577, Holinshed began his account of continuous English history at 1066. If the reign of the first Norman king, William I, makes an acceptable starting point for the study of English history, then in this emblematic fashion English history begins with a foreigner. Nevertheless, the new king chose to insist on his rights, as the heir nominated by his kinsman, Edward the Confessor, to remove Harold Godwinson as a usurper. Twenty years after his conquest, far from thinking that his alien regime had successfully obliterated all memory of earlier legitimacy, William I ordered the survey of England recorded in Domesday Book to set down the state and obligations of landholdings on the eve of the Conquest as well as in 1086. King William's deeds were recorded by the English vernacular chronicle in the traditional manner, even if it noted some novelties in his style of government. The king's Norman nominees as bishops and abbots built new churches, but to honour old English saints.

Norman willingness to recognise the value of the English past has been systematically underplayed, though even those determined to think of the Normans as destructive, domineering bullies, credit them with the saving grace of establishing a form of government strong enough to protect England from further foreign encroachments. In this way, the last successful foreign violation of English shores has been approved for endowing England with one of its most cherished characteristics – immunity from foreign pressures. Curiously, from that time to the present, the ruling dynasties of England have all been of foreign extraction: Norman, Angevin (Plantagenet), Welsh (Tudor), Scottish (Stewart), Dutch (King Billy) and Hanoverian. The various forms of royal government introduced by different dynasties for their own purposes might well be included on the list of advantages brought to Britain by immigrants. Relations with England's continental neighbours over subsequent centuries owed much to royal familiarity with the prevailing political order abroad.

The Conquest itself would not have occurred had the fates of England and Normandy not already been closely connected for many years. At the end of the tenth century, after papal mediation, the Confessor's father Aethelred II had been married to Emma, daughter of the Norman duke Richard I. The pope hoped to promote friendship across the Channel in order to contain and deter raiding from Scandinavia, then still pagan. Normandy and England were in different ways already prominent players in the confused affairs of the northern seas in the Viking period. The Norman Conquest of England in 1066 was no isolated adventure. It was but one decisive event in a series going back generations. By throwing a political bridge across the Channel, the Norman kings demonstrated the strength of the western end of the Viking world over its old homelands and made the political might of the English monarchy a powerful force in western European affairs.

This pre-eminence of the English kingdom in northern Europe would not have occurred had the several distinct regional English kingdoms not been brought under the sway of Wessex in the tenth century. Before the earliest Danish invasions, the strongest English kingdoms had been Northumbria or Mercia. Had either of those two ultimately become responsible for uniting all the other English kingdoms, the later history not only of England but of Scotland, Wales and probably Ireland too would have developed differently. The domination of Wessex established southern English hegemony in united England. However, Danish settlement in eastern coastal zones still tilted English interests towards the North Sea and Scandinavia. At the end of the tenth century, the Danes were able to take advantage of the fact that united England was, nominally and unprecedently, ruled by a minor to renew their assault. The kingdom was for a time rich enough to buy off the attacks, but the Danes, alerted to the kingdom's wealth and vulnerability, were not to be diverted. In 1013, King Sweyn of Denmark drove the English king from his throne and took his place. Sweyn's own rule was short-lived but his son Cnut reigned in England for eighteen years and ruled with comparable vigour in Denmark as well. Significantly, Cnut saw the potential dangers from the south and covered his flank by his marriage to his English predecessor's Norman widow, Emma. Their son Hardecanute later ruled in England and Denmark, albeit briefly. Cnut's international standing was recognised when he went to Rome in 1027 for the imperial coronation of the German king, Conrad II. Relations between Cnut and Conrad were reinforced by the marriage of Cnut's daughter Gunnhilda to Conrad's heir Henry at Nijmegen in 1036.[1] Norman success in 1066 is often allowed to obscure the impact of the earlier Danish kings in bringing the young, wealthy kingdom to prominence.

In this story, the key problem about the Norman Conquest is not why the English allowed themselves to be conquered by the Normans, but why the

Normans proved more successful than their Danish or Norwegian rivals in taking over the kingdom and keeping it. The answer is usually held to lie with the superior military skills of the Normans, though historians may differ about which military skills were most important. After the Conquest, the nature of the Norman military settlement provided for effective local defence against renewed Danish attacks and this deflected most subsequent raiding from the north into less well-defended parts of these islands.

Norman effectiveness in defending their conquest and pushing hard on its northern and western borders cannot obscure the fact that earlier eleventh-century English military resources had been far from negligible. Stout, if intermittent and divided, resistance was put up against Sweyn and his son, Cnut. In 1066, Harold II did defeat the Norwegian host near York, very far from his home bases, and his army fought courageously against the Normans at Hastings in a day-long battle. England was not easily conquered, but after the unification of England once a crucial battle was lost the whole kingdom became the prize of the victor, Sweyn or William. Unification under Wessex had diminished Englishmen's enthusiasm for fighting one another. Within a generation or two, they saw sense in preserving a united kingship, even under a foreigner. The alternative was to suffer the rigours of bitter resistance against a foreign oppressor which would keep the kingdom in a woeful state of war. The attitude of the English in the eleventh century was realistic. The foreign origins of England's kings did not prejudice the success of their rule and could have been an advantage: they were not perceived as partial to one part of their kingdom rather than another, as Harold Godwinson, former earl of Wessex, for example, probably was. This has given the English monarchy a lasting characteristic in standing above merely local affiliations.

The avantage for a southern-based monarchy of political union with a major military power south of the Channel is obvious: it reinforced the position of the economically and culturally richer south. But the abilities of the Norman ruler himself were also considerable. Before his coronation in England William, who had succeeded to the duchy of Normandy as a child in 1035, had since 1049 shown his gifts in both government and warfare. As king, he is said to have tried to learn English, without success; in middle age, he would have also found it difficult to change in other ways.[2] After the unification of England, English kings had moved in a more confined space and their functions had become more ceremonial as their military responsibilities had diminished. Under Edward the Confessor, military activities had usually been assumed by his earls; he himself acquired a reputation for saintly inactivity. After 1066 no English king could afford such peaceableness without losing respect. At heart the Norman kings remained military commanders, but this was not because they were unable to adapt to a new role. On the contrary, from the Conqueror's time English kings who ruled over more than England had to find a style of authority able to impress peoples of different origin: initially, Normans as well as English; later, others

too. They moved rapidly and without warning across their extensive dominions and, if they were to retain credibility as rulers, had to know how to
command respect in diverse circumstances, consider different options on a
broad front and achieve some success in their schemes. The effects of the
new active kingship for the development of government in England were
profound. No other kingdom in the west was more innovative and energetic, or needed to be.

The cohesion of the Norman kingdom depended not merely on the kings,
but on the style of their relationship with their followers. William had
attracted to his campaign soldiers from many parts of western Europe and,
after Harold had been defeated, Normans were not the only men of importance for William's kingship. Even the decision to take the English crown
was allegedly made at the instigation of a Poitevin, the viscount of Thouars,
when the Norman barons appeared more hesitant.[3] Quite apart from his
hopes of getting English loyalty for his government, William continued to
count on the services of the many Bretons and Flemings who had joined his
force. The Bretons had long been subjected to Norman bids for overlordship
and some of them welcomed the opportunities William's campaign offered
for their own advancement. In Flanders, William had relied initially on the
benevolence of Count Baldwin V, his father-in-law. Flanders was particularly important to the success of any invasion, as the place from which exiles
had normally forced their way back into the kingdom. Many Flemings had
joined the conquering army and some were initially rewarded with lands in
England. The exploits of the nobly-born Arnulf, lord of Ardres, for example, show him serving the Conqueror in England under the auspices of
Count Eustace of Boulogne. He received English estates and lived there long
enough to father three sons, from three different women, and pay for their
education and settlement in life.[4] Arnulf's domestic life in England provides
a glimpse of what campaigning might actually mean for soldiers. Most of
them were not of noble rank or rewarded in England with estates. When
paid off they returned home, like a serf of the monastery of St Trond who
had come to England, also probably as a soldier, and lived there for some
years before returning with the freeborn woman he had taken to wife.[5] The
importance William attached to retaining Flemish support was tested
shortly after the Conquest when a dispute about the succession to the
county arose between the sons of Baldwin V. The Conqueror's right-hand
man, William FitzOsbern, his deputy in Normandy, joined the king of
France on behalf of Count Baldwin VI and was killed in battle along with
Baldwin. English kings gave high priority to keeping Flanders friendly and
later counts became regular pensioners of the king. English kings vied for
generations with the kings of France as to which of them could rely on
Flemish support. Brittany was not quite so significant in this respect because
of its isolation in the west and its greater distance across the sea from
England. Nevertheless, English kings remained committed to making
friends in Brittany and, by the fourteenth century, it became a major theatre

of war between England and France. The Conquest was responsible for opening a new chapter in England's relations with the people across the Channel. William's original coalition had brought together the major interests on the other side of the sea facing England and the influence of these other French lands on the Norman settlement can be overlooked. Culturally this was responsible for drawing England into a novel relationship with French speakers and weakening its traditional Germanic ties.

Whatever hopes the Conqueror had placed in leading English lords, after the rebellions of 1069 he was obliged to recognise that the Normans were the followers most committed to backing his kingship. By 1086, William had become so much more dependent on them that even the number of Breton and Flemish followers in England had shrunk. This created a new kind of relationship between the king and the most powerful men in the kingdom. In the past great lords had, for the most part, attained eminence by virtue of their families' long-standing wealth and reputation; the lords of Norman England owed their positions and their wealth entirely to the king, who rewarded them for their service and loyalty as he chose. Even in the Church he appointed mainly Normans as bishops and abbots. The king's Normans perceived that the defence of his kingship rested on their shoulders and that he was no more able to dispense with them than they with him. He needed not only their arms, but their advice: they had to act collectively in their common interest. The reciprocal character of the new order in politics was to have a lasting effect on English government. Without previous experience of ducal Normandy where the great men expected to act in concert with their leader (*dux*) rather than be ruled by a king, the Normans in England would not have known how to manage the new responsibilities they acquired after 1066.

By 1086, the king had established a new nobility entirely of his own choice. No previous ruler of England, and none since, enjoyed such an advantage. This new social order looked to the king for further favours and feared his displeasure. The kingship itself became the principal source of patronage, directly assigning the major offices and estates, suspiciously overseeing grants at a lower level which might conflict with its interests or diminish its resources. The kings of Germany and France never disposed of comparable powers and their kingdoms were accordingly organised differently from the English. The Normans rewarded by the Conqueror were not necessarily always docile, but they recognised that if they failed individually to retain his confidence they had no other 'family' right and could count on no local solidarity from their English tenants to save them from ruin. Not all the families enriched in 1066 stayed the course, but those who retained royal confidence and respect did acquire within a generation or so both a sense of what their birth entitled them to and what their friends might do to help them. By that time the king himself realised that if he enjoyed formal superiority as 'feudal' lord he had to take the interests of his barons into account and rule in accordance with customary law.

The substantial evidence of Domesday about the installation of new Norman landowners can overshadow the lasting effects of the Conquest on English towns. The Norman ecclesiastical organisation, unlike the situation in pre-Conquest England, was firmly based on the episcopal cities and one of the major reforms introduced by the new archbishop of Canterbury, Lanfranc, was to get rural sees transferred to major urban centres. Although it is estimated that by 1066 one-tenth of the English population was already urban, even busy towns like Lincoln and Norwich did not become the sees of bishoprics until after 1066. By the time Norwich had become the permanent seat of the East Anglian bishop, a French commercial district had already been set up in this flourishing town. Similar French settlements were established elsewhere, notably at Southampton and probably at Northampton and Nottingham, but quite small local centres, like Ilbert de Lacy's base at Pontefract and Earl Alan's castle at Richmond, also attracted French urban settlers. Some towns of the western region were authorised to adopt the 'Law of Breteuil' (a Norman town belonging to William FitzOsbern), probably to encourage further urban settlement since these customs offered particularly favourable terms for struggling newcomers.[6] It was in connection with urban commerce that Jews too arrived in London from Rouen, though they did not spread to other towns until a generation or so later. All these factors, in their way, must represent intensified trading between England and the Continent.

The principal act of government that subsequently influenced English relations with the Continent most was royal insistence on retaining family lands in France. Although this came as a direct consequence of the Norman Conquest, it was not an inevitable one. In 1087, on the Conqueror's death, he arranged for the dominions he had united to be divided, recommending his second son William as king in England, while the old king's continental possessions passed to the oldest, Robert. Neither son was satisfied with this partition and it took twenty years to reunite the Conqueror's legacy. It proved, however, impossible to accomplish this from Normandy. The strength of the English kingdom, as restored by William I, had left the ability to do so with the kings, not the duke, despite the fact that Robert as the oldest son had the strongest claim on the loyalty of the Normans. His younger brothers, William and Henry, successive kings in England, made it a matter of policy to acquire control of the Norman duchy. Though this was a personal decision of kings, the royal initiative was supported by Norman lords in England and not forced on them from Normandy itself. Barons well provided for in England could, like the Conqueror, have planned a division of their lands between insular and continental sons. Unlike the Conqueror, they did not think this was necessary or desirable. They had no impression that their trans-Channel dominions were not viable; nor did they think of the Anglo-Norman realm as a short-term anomaly. The Conqueror's sons regarded the partition of 1087 as no more than a gesture of respect for an ancient legal distinction drawn between a man's inherited properties, his first-born's birthright, and his personal conquests, to be disposed of as he chose. It could not be allowed to stand in the way of political good sense which required the union of England and Normandy. The link between England and the continental holdings of its kings could not, moreover, have been maintained for centuries had kings and others taken the (modern) view that the continental dominions should have been disposed of as an inconvenient, costly and unnatural burden.

The outcome was not an aberration born of carelessness, but brought about deliberately and renewed in the face of considerable difficulties. Far from being blinded by sentiment, English kings were realistic about the problems presented by Normandy under Duke Robert. The immediate danger was that Robert as the oldest son did attempt to deprive his younger brother William of his English kingdom and that many barons in England found reasons to back Robert's rights. William, perhaps surprisingly, proved able to hold on to his kingship from his English resources alone but, after the danger had receded, William Rufus as naturally tried to forestall any renewed threats from that quarter by carrying the war into Normandy. Robert's inability to prevent this active intervention in the duchy's affairs demonstrated his powerlessness to control his own barons there and the potential of the English kings to carry the war into the land of the conquerors. William II and Henry I both had a legitimate interest in covering their hold of England by carrying the war into the duchy.

The benefits of the new arrangement were practical. England had no longer to be defended at the Channel, but on the frontiers between Normandy and the lands of the kings of France and of the counts of Anjou. This strategy provided England itself with an exceptional period of internal peace. Warfare, whether constant or intermittent, was confined to the remote borderlands of Normandy or of other parts of the British Isles – a situation almost without parallel in western Europe at the time. This had profound consequences for medieval English institutions of government which were insulated from the pressures of domestic warfare. Whereas pre-Conquest English kings had hardly ever ventured outside their kingdoms, all post-Conquest English kings took continental journeys and military campaigns for granted. Inevitably, all those who had business to do with kings accompanied them, or chased after them in efforts to expedite the settlement of their own affairs. On their travels, kings made acquaintance with men whom they took into their service and might reward with property or office back in England. In this way, for example, William I met William, abbot of St Carileph in Maine, and brought him back to England to be bishop of Durham on the dangerous northern border. Absentee kings, far from provoking English discontent and the search for a home-grown ruler, seem to have stimulated an unprecedented enthusiasm in England for getting involved abroad.

The consolidation of the 'west'

Closer involvement in continental affairs was not, however, merely the result of Norman kingship; it was a further consequence of fundamental changes on the Continent itself. Viking activity had disturbed the tranquillity of lands adjacent to northern waters for two centuries; the incursions of the nomadic Magyars had likewise disrupted the peace of central Europe since the early tenth century. When the Saxon kings defeated the Magyars and obliged them to settle down in Hungary and accept Christianity at the beginning of the eleventh century a new era opened. The new order in central Europe induced in lands further west a sense of security unknown since the Roman frontier had been breached by the barbarians in the fifth century. Easier communication between the west and the Eastern Empire at Constantinople also alerted western Europeans to the troubled fortunes of the Christian east. The culmination of this process of re-establishing direct contact across the whole Christian continent was reached at the end of the century with the launch of the first crusading expedition to the Holy Land.

Hitherto, the Roman Empire at Constantinople had borne the main burden for the defence of Christendom against its Islamic enemies and sought no assistance from western Christians. However, when the Turks defeated the emperor at Manzikert in 1071, they threatened to put an end to Christian control of Anatolia and a new policy was called for. The first emperor of a new dynasty, Alexius Comnenus, judged that suitable military assistance might be obtained from the Christian west and asked the pope to appeal for auxiliaries to be sent east. The pope stimulated what proved to be an unquenchable enthusiasm in western Europe for taking an active interest in Levantine affairs. By their very nature, the crusades indicate that, however far away, Latin Christians regarded the eastern Mediterranean as a proper concern of their own. Their insistence on pursuing their own agenda in the emperor's own 'backyard' indicated how confident they became in rejecting the role assigned to them at Constantinople as the emperor's biddable allies. This willingness to support enterprises so far away and without direct impact on their immediate interests indicates that something had shifted in the west. The eastern emperor, who saw western soldiers simply as desirable auxiliaries, had not realised what lay behind their resolution. His summons brought the 'west' into being as a historical force.

The west had for centuries lived culturally in the shadow of the Roman Empire. Not only had successive Germanic leaders since Charlemagne attempted to claim some legitimacy for the powers they exercised over defeated neighbours by claiming to rule as 'Roman emperors', but even in Britain, the tenth-century kings of Wessex, who succeeded in making at least an enlarged kingdom of England out of what had once been the Roman province of Britannia, also adopted the language of empire, using the prestigious title *basileus*, rather than *rex*, 'king', a term appropriate only for a local barbarian ruler. In Germany, comparably, the Saxon dynasty had brought under their own sway large parts of the former Western Roman Empire, based on the axis of the Rhine and Po valleys, but also extending east beyond the old Roman frontiers to include all the Germanic peoples as far as the territories of the Poles and Magyars, Christians of non-Germanic origin. On the strength of his achievements, Otto I had been able to revive the Western Roman Empire for himself in 962 and yoke Germany to Italy, creating a new frame for European political order.

His empire comprised so many disparate peoples that religious belief was their most important common bond. To give this Christian element greater prominence, the emperors needed the assistance and cooperation of their own bishops and of the Roman Church these bishops honoured. Nearly a century after Otto I, in 1046, the emperor Henry III, mindful of traditional imperial responsibilities, was drawn into a dispute about rival popes. When he settled the confusion by appointing one of his German bishops to the papacy, his intervention initiated a radical reform of the Church at Rome itself. Within a few years, a succession of German popes had reinvigorated this venerable institution, rescuing it from its preoccupation with local Roman politics and inspiring it to give more attention to its universal responsibilities, in line with the broader concerns of the emperors themselves. By the time of the Norman Conquest, the papacy was already encouraging clergy all over the Western Church to work for the ascendancy of spiritual over secular interests. To strengthen their authority at Rome itself, popes recruited distinguished clergy north of the Alps, first from Germany and Lorraine, then from Burgundy and other parts of France. Popes summoned clergy to synods in Rome; popes themselves travelled in the north to champion their programmes or simply to escape enemies in Italy. The papacy had begun to transform its Roman base into a supranational institution. Between them emperors and popes worked for the revival of the Christian empire sabotaged six centuries before by the barbarian invasions.

The emperors' efforts to bring the papacy into closer harmony with their political objectives nevertheless provoked some clerical dissent. Within ten years of the Norman Conquest, a new pope, Gregory VII, was prepared to denounce the German emperor himself for his rejection of papal claims to superior 'authority'. Condemning the new young emperor's indifference, even opposition to papal objectives in church reform, Gregory went so far as to encourage civil war in Germany. This stirred up disorder which lasted for over forty years. The call for spiritual renewal had become openly divisive. Contemporaries were understandably troubled by the implications. Correctly, they perceived that a new concept of public order was proposed which could not easily be contained. At stake proved to be the future of the western world: the superior claims of what was right, because spiritual, over the practical calculations of political power. In this construction, the duty to pronounce on righteousness belonged not to the empire (the 'State') but to the Church as established by God for his own divine purpose. Since the impact of this shift in western perceptions has reverberated to the present day, it is understandable that in the eleventh century many people, without being able to foresee the long-term effects, were already aghast at the temerity of churchmen in challenging traditionally respected authority. Hitherto, the empire had claimed priority as divinely ordained to provide for the world order into which Jesus Christ had himself been born. Hereafter, the 'State' was constantly obliged to engage in argument with its moral critics about what course of action to follow.

That churchmen felt confident enough to turn against secular protectors who defied their spiritual counsel shows that they no longer lived in fear of brutal pagan enemies. They thought the right moment had come to set about reshaping Christendom according to its properly religious purposes and that, since kings were spiritually subject to bishops, the clergy should take the lead in this task. Cut free from dependence on secular power, however, spiritual leaders appeared in a variety of forms. New ideas about how to lead the religious life suddenly proliferated. Nor could new religious foundations dispense altogether with secular patrons able to get them started; there proved to be no easy way in practice of excluding laymen from ecclesiastical affairs. There was room for manoeuvre.

Medieval reformist clergy should no more be taken at face value than contemporary idealists. Whatever their propaganda implied, they also had vested interests of their own to consider. The situation was more confusing than polemic allowed, but the 'reform' movement gave a new and exciting charge to life in the western world. It made greater demands on the invention and fervour of the most idealistic members of the Christian community. It rapidly became clear that it would not be easy to restrain all the energy released or channel it into useful courses. For a time, the Church of Rome itself appeared as a leader, or at least a figurehead, for all the diverse proposals to bring about 'reform'. The papacy was the only institution in a position to do so because it was able to count on widespread respect for Roman ideals. At stake was acceptance of the Church as uniquely privileged in the social structure of the west.

Under papal direction, the idea of the 'Roman' legacy was given a new meaning, one which severed its old umbilicus to the empire. As a result, other aspects of Roman life, law, literature and architecture, all came to be reappraised and adapted for new purposes. Encouragement from the political empire, as had been the case under Charlemagne, was not essential. To justify its leadership of the reform movement, the papacy provided itself with a specious history of its own universal authority. The old Roman Empire had at least recognised that there were geographical limits to its dominion, if only where it met its match in Persia. The medieval empire acknowledged that it had a frontier at least on the east where it met the authority of Constantinople. By contrast, the Roman bishop recognised no limitations to his rights as God's representative on earth. Without this confidence, Pope Urban II and his successors could not, before the end of the eleventh century, have called for Christian reinforcements for the Holy Land and attempted to direct their operations. The crusades had been launched to help the eastern emperor; they became an instrument of papal policy.

The greater prominence of papal leadership from this point was due not only to the appeal for help from Constantinople, but also to the disarray in the Western Empire, prompted by Gregory VII's recent willingness to countenance defiance of the German king's authority. In this conflict the Western Roman Empire lost any immediate expectations of extending its geographical range to include such parts of the former Roman Empire as still eluded its grasp. In 1037, the emperor Conrad II had taken over the kingdom of Burgundy. A few years later in 1046, as the Norman mercenaries of south Italian princes had conquered provinces hitherto ruled by the Greek emperor in Apulia, the emperor Henry III had taken the homage of the Norman leader and clearly expected that these provinces too would be incorporated into his Western Empire. This did not happen. Instead, as early as 1059, the new Norman leaders escaped the imperial embrace and obtained papal approval for their conquests.

In the late eleventh century the difficulties of the empire may have seemed only temporary and no more serious than those faced by the kings of France. French historians have never allowed themselves to become particularly apprehensive about the possible fate of the kingdom at that time, but the auguries were not good. The ruler of the strongest northern province, Normandy, was a king across the water; in the Loire valley, the counts of Anjou were engaged in building up a coherent dominion of their own. The French kings themselves were committed to constant warfare with the castellans of their own domain lands and their practical powers in the provinces of their kingdom were negligible, even where they were accorded formal deference. For most of the twelfth century, French kings laboured ineffectually to acquire an apparatus of state comparable to that of Ottonian Germany. Had that German Empire not been challenged by the disloyalty of so many of its clergy in the eleventh century, the emperor might have been more successful in asserting his theoretical authority in France itself, as he had so recently done in Burgundy. The French kingdom was saved by its clergy. Whereas the more intransigent clergy in Germany set out with papal encouragement to undermine the notion of respect for the Roman emperor, clerical interests in France remained compatible with those of the much weaker kings. The French clergy accordingly did much to promote the French royal revival in the twelfth century. In return kings benevolently conceded ecclesiastical privileges to all persons of clerical status. The development of a new European order rested on the ability of kings to secure cooperation from their bishops. This provided a pattern for rulers across the Channel.

England and the reform movement

The Norman Conquest occurred at a time when neither France nor Germany had been in a position to influence events and the Norman monarchy was soon perceived to be a new force in the international order. Not all chroniclers approved. In Germany, Frutolf's chronicle recorded 'the miserable subjugation of England by William the Norman, who made himself king, exiling almost all the prelates, killing the nobility, reducing the lesser folk to the servitude of his knights and forcing the wives of all the native people to marry the newcomers'.[7] Adam of Bremen took a more favourable view of the 'Bastard's' victory. He treated Harold Godwinson as a usurper and thought God had punished the English for their sins. The appointment of the scholarly Lanfranc as archbishop and the expulsion of thousands of English clergy who lived irregular lives offered the kingdom a fresh start.[8] One way or another, William's achievement was undeniable.

We may speculate to what extent putative heirs of Harold Godwinson would have played a similar role to the Norman kings in this new European order. Despite his own Norman upbringing, Edward the Confessor had done comparatively little to prepare for any Norman succession. Some of the Normans he introduced into the kingdom had provoked hostility, for Edward ruled in a culture which was predominantly Germanic. The continuing influence of Danes at court and in the country had recently reinforced the Germanic elements. Edward himself added to Germanic influence by making Hermann bishop of Ramsbury in 1045 and Giso bishop of Wells in 1060. Through them the ideas of the German bishops' reform programme had already reached the English Church. Giso, who came from the region around Huy, established a community of canons for his cathedral *ad modum patriae meae*.[9] Hermann accompanied Archbishop Aldred to Rome in 1050 and met the emperor, Henry III, at Cologne in 1053. Influence from the Rhineland also probably explains why Harold, who had himself visited Germany before he became king, founded a house of secular canons at Waltham. England's reputation for disciplined clergy was sufficiently high to attract the attention of two of the three original founders of the Arrouaisian order, Heldemar of Tournai and the German, Cono. The historian of the order reported that while they were developing their ideas about how to lead the clerical life they had served as chaplains to William the Conqueror and Queen Matilda.[10] This English background for the Arrouaisian canons casts an unexpectedly favourable light on the character of the English secular Church in the mid-eleventh century.

Since the Conquest had been undertaken with the blessing of Pope Alexander II, it might anyway have been expected to turn the Conqueror into a firm ally of the papacy in its dispute with the empire and so weaken England's earlier friendship for its Germanic kinsmen. English ties with Rome were long-standing. Peter's pence was paid to the papacy in token of English respect. Archbishops of Canterbury dutifully obtained from Rome the pallium which confirmed their metropolitan authority. After 1066, formal deference to Rome remained significant but, if anything, the Norman clergy were less submissive than the English had been. In particular, Lanfranc, an Italian from Pavia, who had been both prior of Bec and abbot of Caen before his promotion to Canterbury, kept papal pretensions at arm's length. King William I and his archbishop disapproved, probably in equal measure, of Gregory VII's attitude to political authority and to metropolitan bishops who barred papal access to their own bishops.[11] The Norman kings were accordingly able to secure in England a form of royal control over the churches which later made it possible for England, alone of European kingdoms, to preserve the traditional model of relations between Church and State. Had the Conquest occurred after, rather than before, Gregory VII's pontificate, the result would have been different. Instead of inaugurating a 'reform' on behalf of ecclesiastical interests, William exercised an authority over the Church which prevented the papacy from ever acquiring sufficient influence to weaken the commitment of the bishops to the king, as happened in Germany.

When Archbishop Anselm, in dispute with William Rufus only thirty years later, insisted on consulting the pope about his position, his stance in England was greeted with bewilderment. Anselm's own personal acceptance of the claims of papal authority had been made as abbot of Bec in Normandy. His refusal to submit to royal direction when he became archbishop offended the (Norman) bishops in England, showing that they were then still far from accepting his unqualified reliance on the papacy.[12] It was Anselm's exile on the Continent which opened the eyes of his English followers to what Gregory VII had wrought in the Western Church.

As the Anglo-Norman monarchy got into its stride Normandy, rather than Rome or Germany, became the principal point of contact between English churchmen and the Continent. This brought about change, inspired not so much by ecclesiastical idealism as following inevitably from the appointment of so many men of Norman origin as bishops and abbots in England. At the very least, the new prelates provided personal links between their Norman religious houses of origin and their new posts. This could lead to arrangements for mutual prayer fellowships, acquisition or exchange of books or borrowing of clergy. When Herbert Losinga established a new bishopric for East Anglia in Norwich, he not only sent some of his cathedral monks to Fécamp, where he had himself started the religious life, to learn monastic discipline; he also borrowed books he could not find in England and sent a member of his own household to learn how to cook in the abbey's kitchen.[13] At Norwich, however, Losinga had to start an entirely new cathedral in East Anglia's principal town.

Because the Roman cities of Britain, unlike those of the Continent, had not retained their influence as centres of Christianity after the Germanic settlements, England had been converted like other parts of Christendom beyond the old frontiers of the Roman Empire mainly by the efforts of monks and the establishment of monasteries. The English Church remained heavily indebted to this original monastic influence and in this strongly resembled the Irish Church. But the Roman mission of Augustine, himself a monk, had also reintroduced episcopal structure into the English Church, but not for the most part into old Roman cities. In the tenth century, monks had reaffirmed their dominance in the English Church by setting up monastic communities in several English sees; bishops themselves were commonly recruited from monasteries. Bishop Leofric had already moved his see from Crediton to Exeter in 1050, but it was only after 1066 that Lanfranc required a more systematic approach, establishing church government in major centres, as it had originally worked in the Roman Empire. The Normans were enthusiastic promoters of the religious styles they were familiar with, providing for better diocesan management by appointing archdeacons to give bishops more control over their own affairs. Whatever new zeal was in evidence, there was no wholesale attack on traditional vested interests. English families in London, for example, retained their cathedral prebends in the new period. Some Norman bishops intended to set up a body of secular clergy in their cathedral chapters, as found in Normandy, but the English monastic traditions were in some places too strong for them. At Winchester, the bishop relented and accepted the monastic community of St Swithin as his chapter. At Durham, as at Norwich, a monastic chapter was newly installed where there had been none before. At Bury St Edmunds and Glastonbury the monks resisted proposals by their local bishop to appropriate their monastery as the site of a new cathedral. Because Lanfranc was himself a monk, the ecclesiastical reforms he fostered in England tended to reinforce the traditional monastic outlook of the English Church rather than impose the pattern of secular cathedral chapters familiar in France.

The Norman blueprint for change was not forced through regardless of the cost but few English churches were immune to the effects of injecting senior Norman clergy into their highest offices. No doubt all this shocked conservative institutions but the extent of disruption varied considerably from one religious house to another. Not all of it gave dissatisfaction to the communities concerned. At Canterbury, notably, the regime of Archbishop Lanfranc pleased the monastic community better than that of his English predecessor, Stigand, a secular priest. Because their communal life gave monks a greater sense of solidarity, resistance to any innovations was strongest in some monasteries: mere innovations in the chant and liturgy could be sufficient to provoke protest. In other communities, the new superiors were more conciliatory, winning approval for their prompt defence of their house, seeking privileges from the king and promoting veneration of its saints by building in their honour.

The introduction into England of Norman building practices provided the kingdom with grandiose ecclesiastical and military monuments, still regarded as the most obvious signs of the Conquest. To satisfy the high standards expected of these buildings, fine white stone was imported from Caen, which was ideal for moulds and carving. Lanfranc, former abbot of St Etienne, was responsible for building his new cathedral at Canterbury entirely of Caen stone, and it was accordingly used for the rebuilding at Canterbury in 1175. In the next century it was imported for Westminster Abbey and the Tower of London, notwithstanding the fact that by then England was politically separated from Normandy. The quality of Caen stone ensured that it was more widely used in England than any local stone.[14] The impetus the Normans gave to splendid ecclesiastical building in England lasted nearly five hundred years. From the first it provided for local needs by drawing on what was known of contemporary techniques abroad. At Hereford, Bishop Robert from Lorraine drew his inspiration from Charlemagne's church at Aachen. Moreover, English buildings were not slavish imitations of foreign models.[15] English masons rapidly began to innovate on their own account. But from the first the Norman prelates insisted on setting a new standard in magnificence, not only for cathedrals, but for monastic churches.

What may be true of the material cadre of the religious life did not so quickly disrupt its inner character. Before the Conquest, England had many long-established Benedictine houses, most founded by saintly religious and often maintaining close links with distinguished monasteries across the Channel. There the most easily appreciated of the skills cultivated in English monasteries was the decoration of religious manuscripts.[16] English stylistic devices were taken up by foreign monks and English artists branched out to pioneer a new style of narrative illustration. There was no pretence that they were not masters of their chosen fields.[17] Innovations in monastic organisation, as found in Burgundian religious houses like Cluny and Cîteaux, at first attracted little attention in England. Though the Normans had adopted some of the features of Cluniac reform earlier in the century, no Cluniac priory had been founded in Normandy. Likewise, after the Conquest, the only stake Cluny acquired in England was the priory of Lewes founded by William de Warenne. As to Cîteaux, although an Englishman, Stephen Harding from Sherborne, had played the leading part in the reform movement, no house of this religious order was established in England until the bishop of Winchester founded Waverley in 1128. Rather than work with these famous monastic centres, the Normans preferred to maintain their own close ties with their family houses in Normandy and assigned them land, churches and tithes in England. Such endowments were provided in every part of England and for the most part retained for centuries.[18]

Normandy did not engross all the attentions of English monks. In traditional Benedictine practice, each monastery was independent and maintained its own connections, so that after the Conquest monasteries like Peterborough and Ramsey did not think of severing their particular links with Denmark. William I took advantage of this, using Abbot Aethelsige of Ramsey as his envoy to King Sweyn. William Rufus encouraged English influence in Denmark by authorising Evesham to supply monks for a monastic chapter at Odense in 1095 to please the English bishop there.[19] The Normans appreciated the need to cultivate goodwill across the North Sea if they were to be spared constant assaults on their conquest and church-men willingly lent themselves as negotiators for this purpose. William I induced even Archbishop Adalbert of Bremen to speak on his behalf to King Sweyn of Denmark.[20] Canterbury itself was not of much help in dealings with the north. When Archbishop Anselm wrote to the archbishop of Lund, it was not because of any direct contact between himself and Denmark, but at the instigation of a Roman cardinal, a former pupil of his at Bec. Anselm took a somewhat perfunctory interest in the north, tactfully congratulating the earl of Orkney for acquiring a bishop but merely expressing a hope that religious progress would follow.[21]

In place of the pre-Conquest English involvement with the Germanic world, the Normans provided a self-confident entry into zones where Norman mercenaries had already made the Norman name feared and respected. After they had established their princely powers in the south, the Normans remained close to their kin and neighbours in Normandy. The bishop of Coutances, Geoffrey of Montbray, who played an active part in England, had raised money for rebuilding his cathedral by touring south Italy.[22] Many opportunities for ecclesiastical advancement existed in the Norman dominions of southern Italy and some Englishmen, as well as Normans, found a welcome there. These Norman conquests had effectively stretched the frontiers of Catholic Europe well beyond their familiar bounds. Pope Urban II summoned a council to Bari in 1098, the first pope to have travelled so far south for centuries. Eadmer, an English monk of Canterbury, who subsequently wrote a life of Anselm, was in attendance on his archbishop at this council. There he saw the bishop of Benevento wear-ing an embroidered cope, finer than the pope's own vestment, which Eadmer recognised as of English workmanship. He recalled having heard as a young man from older monks at Canterbury about a bishop of Benevento who had come to England collecting alms for an impending famine in south Italy. The bishop had sold his church's relic of the arm of St Bartholomew to Cnut's queen, Emma, and received the cope at Canterbury when the relic was deposited there.[23]

Some Englishmen went even further than south Italy. The eastern emperor at Constantinople who maintained a body of troops traditionally recruited from Scandinavia welcomed English exiles as members of his Varangian guard. According to the (late) Confessor's saga, when the English realised that they could not expect any more help from Denmark in their resistance to the Conqueror, Earl Sigurd left England with three earls, eight barons and 350 ships, sailing to Constantinople via the straits of Gibraltar. The emperor Alexius received them and granted them lands in his empire which they called 'England'.[24] The story cannot be corroborated from else-where, but correctly emphasised the Scandinavian affinities for the English in the eleventh century and implied that their defeat at Hastings had in no way compromised their military reputation. English soldiers certainly fought for the emperor in the Balkans, as it happens, against the Normans, so that the contests between the two peoples were in a sense resumed on a second, distant front.[25] There is further evidence of the contact between England and Constantinople in the eleventh century. A lead seal belonging to John Raphael, a prominent Byzantine official of the 1060s and 1070s, was discovered at Winchester in 1962, indicating that an imperial embassy (not otherwise documented) had been sent to England within a few years of the Conquest.[26] But diplomatic ties with the east were older than this. According to William of Malmesbury, Edward the Confessor had a dream about the Seven Sleepers of Ephesus and sent to Constantinople for information about this miraculous event. Malmesbury writes as though nothing could be simpler than an enquiry to a ruler 3000 miles away.[27]

In the eleventh century Constantinople was still the greatest city of Christendom and it was the source of religious cults which gained western adherents in the eleventh century. Both the feasts of the Immaculate Conception and of St Nicholas, bishop of Myra, had reached England before 1066, that is earlier than in most parts of the west, and England was to play an influential role in obtaining wider support for these cults.[28] English devotions have plausibly been explained in terms of the established links with Normandy and through Normandy with the Normans in south Italy and their experience of Orthodox monasticism there, but direct communication with Constantinople cannot be excluded. Either way, before the end of the century we hear of Coleman, an English nobleman who had built a church in Constantinople jointly dedicated to Nicholas of Myra and Augustine of Canterbury. Joseph, a monk of Canterbury, found fellow countrymen in the city influential enough to secure him access to the imperial chapel and relic collection.[29] Well-educated Englishmen had a 'patriotic' interest in the imperial city because Constantine, its founder and the emperor responsible for making the empire Christian, had been first proclaimed emperor in Britain and his mother Helena was born there.[30]

Contact between north-western Europe and the Near East was most obviously fostered by enthusiasm for pilgrimages. The eleventh century, after the conversion of the Magyars and before the Crusades, was the heyday of the purely pilgrim routes to the east (albeit with armed escorts for the larger parties). How frequently did people from the British Isles make the journey to Jerusalem itself before the Conquest? The Londoner, Ingulf, later abbot of Crowland, is reported to have gone to the Holy Land while still a young man, accompanying the bishop of Mainz in the great pilgrimage from Germany in 1064–65. Though the reliability of Ingulf's chronicle as a whole has been doubted, the story of how well the pilgrims were received by the venerable Sophronius II, patriarch of Jerusalem, with music and bright lights, received corroboration when this patriarch's leaden seal was also discovered at Winchester in the excavations of 1963.[31] That foreigners are found visiting England should not cause surprise. England had not only powerful rulers to be placated, but its own famous religious shrines. Malmesbury may not have been among the best known of these, but one of the miracles performed there by St Aldhelm, founder of the monastery, was for a fratricide from Cologne who had been sent on penitential pilgrimage as far as Jerusalem, only to be denied spiritual comfort until he reached this corner of England.[32]

These incidents point to channels of communication across Europe not otherwise documented. The exile of the sons of Edmund Ironside in Hungary is a reminder of English awareness of the very fringes of Latin Christendom. Edmund's son Edward returned to England in 1057 at a time when the king of Hungary, Andrew I, was married to a Byzantine princess, Anastasia. Contemporaries knew more about one another by word of mouth than our present information allows us to demonstrate. The Norwegian king, Harold Haardrada, who invaded England in a bid for the crown in 1066, had spent many years at Constantinople in the imperial Varangian guard and married a Byzantine wife. After his death, she married King Sweyn of Denmark. Similarly, Anna of Kiev, Russian wife of Henry I, king of France, as a widow married the French count, Radulf of Vermandois. At the highest social level at least, some knowledge of eastern lands could be acquired in the west simply through family contacts. The east was also a source of costly merchandise. Early in the twelfth century, Maurice, an Irish monk based in Germany, wandered with only one companion as far as Kiev where the prince made him a gift of precious furs. These he sold on his return to merchants in Regensburg for 100 marks to raise money for his monastic building.[33] Politics, ceremonial and commerce already hung together.

The Viking legacy

Since the late eighth century, the single most important influence upon the well-being of these islands had been the Scandinavian diaspora as it had gathered strength and character. The most important long-term consequence of this was to create a situation in which one united English kingdom emerged. Elsewhere in Britain Scandinavian settlement did not provoke comparable reactions. Welsh vulnerability at sea left the coasts exposed to Norse fleets, like that which attacked in 1052. St David's was regularly raided from as far away as Orkney. In their internecine quarrels, the Welsh princes themselves did not hesitate to employ Norse contingents as Gruffydd ap Rhydderch did against Gwent in 1049. When the Welsh sacked Hereford in 1055 they had Norse allies, probably from Dublin.[34] Gruffydd ap Cynan, prince of Gwynedd, was born of mixed Welsh-Irish parentage in Dublin in 1055 and was proud of his Norse ancestors. In his several campaigns to obtain and hold on to his father's rights in Gwynedd, he was able to recruit forces from Ireland, the Hebrides and Norway. His

Norwegian and Irish forces were not reliable, but they had no ambitions of their own in Wales. They joined in for booty, not conquests.[35]

In Ireland, the Vikings established coastal enclaves with fortified ports to protect commercial activities in the Irish Sea and beyond.[36] Dublin's effective independence was secured by being established on the fault line between the kingdoms of Leinster and Meath. After Cnut's visit to Rome in 1027, the Norse king of Dublin, Sihtric, himself also went to Rome and on his return established a bishopric in his city. The pressure to convert probably came from the English Danelaw.[37] Had the Irish been responsible, they would surely not have allowed the 'Ostmen' to acquire autonomous ecclesiastical organisations of their own.

To the north, the Norse settlements of Orkney and the Western Isles left an enduring legacy. In the Shetlands, it was even stronger and clergy of Bergen had property there until the sixteenth century, much as the Norman monasteries held lands in England.[38] There is no hard evidence that the Norwegians took much interest in mainland Scotland, though Viking inroads in the ninth century have been proposed as a factor which precipitated the otherwise mysterious takeover of the Pictish kingdom by the Scots.[39] More obvious is the fact that Viking destruction of the Northumbrian kingdom gave the kings of Scots north of the Forth the opportunity to settle their own affairs without fear of English intrusion. Even so, to the north and west the authority of the Scottish king remained circumscribed by Norse rulers. When the earl of Orkney decided to accept Christianity, he turned not to the Christians of Britain but to the archbishop of Bremen, then the only major prelate in the north. At the end of the eleventh century, the Scottish king Edgar acknowledged that the Western Isles lay within the orbit of the king of Norway.[40]

The remoter parts of Britain may not have been subjected to the same pressures from the Continent as England, but they did not live in blissful isolation from the rest of the world. Nor, once converted, did Scandinavians lose interest in exploiting their opportunities for maritime adventures in the waters round Britain. All the natives of the northern region moved by water, on plundering expeditions or in search of allies and patrons in their local conflicts, keeping in touch with one another and held together by communications across the open seas. People who took naturally to the waters had little interest in creating larger, more stable political structures, but in the period of Danish kingship in England they had already begun to feel some pressure from the greater weight of England. After their easy entry to England itself was barred by the Norman Conquest, the peoples of Scandinavia were obliged to deflect their attentions to the north and west. The Norwegians, in particular, became determined to assert some authority over the scattered settlements of Norwegian origin. King Magnus's descent on Anglesey in 1097 reaffirmed Norwegian maritime supremacy at a point at the very heart of the system in the Irish Sea. Magnus even became involved in Ireland, where he was killed in 1103, but his campaigns had been sufficient to renew respect for Norwegians in the region and they remained a power to be reckoned with in the north for another century and a half.[41]

Magnus's determination to assert himself in the Irish Sea is a sign that control of it had become a matter of concern by the late eleventh century. Adam of Bremen provided a description of the northern waters, revealing how familiar north Germans had become with the idea of sea journeys as far as Greenland and 'Vinland'.[42] Within the system, contacts between the western shores of England and the eastern coast of Ireland began to have great importance. Domesday Book gives evidence for the flourishing condition of Chester which had a reputation for the marketing of marten skins, certainly acquired somewhere to the west or north.[43] The development of Bristol in this period was unobtrusive, but sensational. In 1086, although Bristol had burgesses, it was still only part of a royal manor. Fifty years later, its castle sustained a long-drawn contest with the king of England, a kind of commercial republic in the west, firmly integrated into the feudal domain of a great Welsh marcher lord. The Margam annalist noted apprehensively that a Norwegian fleet which arrived in the autumn of 1124 spent the winter at Bristol with the obvious intention of resuming its normal marauding activities as early as possible in the new year. William of Malmesbury describes it as a port with ships from Ireland, Norway and other lands overseas.[44] Of the nature of Bristol's commerce, the traffic in English slaves to Ireland is ominously singled out by the monastic sources and not only because it inspired a sustained campaign by Wulfstan, bishop of Worcester, to bring about its suppression.[45] A century later there were still English slaves in Ireland.[46]

On the Irish side of the sea, Norse Dublin, as a coastal town, had notable naval strength: in 1094, its king put a fleet of ninety ships to sea. The native kings began to appreciate Dublin's growing importance and competed to get recognition of their overlordship in order to secure military and naval forces from Dublin for their own campaigns against one another. The rulers of Dublin could count on the support of the kings of Man so that the dominance of Leinster over Dublin was challenged by Godred, king of Man, who had possession of the town for a few years (1091–94). King Murtagh of Munster then reasserted Irish power.[47] But none of these kings was able to integrate Dublin into their own kingdoms and for the annalists of traditional Ireland the inhabitants remained strangers, 'Ostmen'.

Conflict in the region made possession of the Isle of Man itself a matter of importance. For a time, the Norse kings of Dublin had prevailed, but by the late eleventh century Godred Crovan, son of the Icelander Harald the Black who fled to Man after the battle of Fulford Bridge, had imposed himself as ruler. Five of his descendants ruled in turn until the middle of the thirteenth century. It was the importance of Man that brought King Magnus of Norway back into play, but his death in 1103 left the local kings free to maintain their practical independence. They carefully nursed their relations with the kings of both England and Norway, but it was Alexander III of Scotland who received the submission of the last Manx king, Magnus, in 1264.

The Normans and the British Isles

Because the lands and islands of the archipelago were already linked together in various ways, it was hardly possible that a major shift in political force, like that achieved by the Norman Conquest of England, would not have serious implications for the rest of the region. The union of Normandy with England effectively closed the Channel to the Danes and the Normans' own confidence at sea helped them to hold off any challenges which the Danes and Norwegians were still, for a time, prepared to mount. Initially, however, the remoter parts of the archipelago were not much affected by the changes wrought in England. Their rulers had themselves no immediate reasons for engagement with the near Continent and maintained no regular contact with their counterparts abroad, except those of Norway. These regions were brought indirectly into relations with the near Continent through the effects of Norman rule in England.

For generations, the English had been engaged in pushing back the indigenous inhabitants to the west and north, but after the unification of England the momentum had fallen off. Already in the eighth century a limit to further western expansion had been set by the construction of Offa's Dyke. Nothing comparable was achieved in the north. Rather, English authority was forced into retreat. As a result of the Danish invasions the old Northumbrian kingdom, which had stretched into what is now southern Scotland, collapsed and the king of Scots took advantage of the Danish settlement in England to occupy Lothian uncontested. Cnut had forced his way into Scotland where he was received by three native kings in 1030, but accepted the loss of Lothian as permanent. English intervention in the north occurred spasmodically. Earl Siward's invasion of 1054, which ousted Macbeth's son Lachlan, restored the exiled Malcolm III to his father's throne.[48] Twelve years later, Harold II defended his kingship in the north by defeating the Norwegian invaders. The troubled condition of Northumbria as a more autonomous region encouraged the earls, where possible, to seek accommodation rather than confrontation with their Scottish neighbours. There was no linguistic frontier to be drawn between the northern English and those of Lothian: culturally they were one people. Understandably, until the late eleventh century English kings were more concerned about the defence of their own vulnerable positions in the richer parts of the kingdom to the east and south than with asserting any pressure on their neighbours in the island of Britain. At the time of the Domesday inquest in 1086, the royal administrative arm did not stretch into what became County Durham, though William appointed the bishops there and before the end of the century King William II had planted a castle on the Tyne. England was beginning to assert itself again in Britain.

The ability of the Norman kings to intrude into the affairs of neighbouring lands in the British Isles depended on the fact that for the first time in generations rulers did not have to concentrate their energies on protecting themselves from maritime assaults along the eastern and southern coasts of England. Surprisingly, engagements across the Channel did not deter the Normans from becoming more effective in advancing the English dominion in the British Isles than their stay-at-home English predecessors.

Aggression was originally provoked when the peripheries proved willing to allow refugees from Norman England to make use of their facilities for threatening William's conquest. William I was already alerted by the Danish invasion of 1069 to the dangers for his rule if his most northerly earldom was not firmly subjected to his authority. His ability to prevent the secession of Yorkshire from his kingdom was an augury of what was to come. Institutionally, he delegated the responsibility by creating several different military commands in the north to replace the single authority exercised by the pre-Conquest English earls of Northumbria. Thus over the years new Norman 'earls' by name or function were established for Northumberland, Durham, Richmondshire, Holderness and York itself. To the north, Malcolm III of Scotland, who had taken an interest in English affairs since his youth, gave the Norwegians some support in their campaign against Harold Godwinson in 1066. His willingness after the Norman Conquest to receive the English prince Edgar Aetheling and his sisters, one of whom, Margaret, he took as wife, gave comfort and support for an English resistance movement in the north. William I could hardly overlook this. In 1072, attacking by land and sea, William advanced into 'Scotland' proper, that is, beyond the Forth, and obliged Malcolm III to come to terms, become William's vassal and give hostages for his good behaviour.[49] The implications of Malcolm's subservience were not spelt out and in no way inhibited his rule of Scotland, but his practical dependence on William's forebearance had become clear and William's potential beyond the normal limits of the 'frontier' was exposed.

None of this deterred Malcolm from maintaining what seemed to him his proper interests as king, continuing to give succour to Edgar, his brother-in-law, in 1074, or raiding as far south as the Tyne in 1079, when he was checked by the Conqueror's oldest son, Robert. After William I's death, Malcolm invaded England again while William II was in Normandy. This provoked another royal expedition, which concluded, as in 1072, with Malcolm's submission to the king and his promise on oath to obey William II in all respects (1091). Two years later, when Malcolm asked for a revision of the terms of their agreement, Rufus summoned him to Gloucester but then refused to receive him. Malcolm returned to Scotland and sought to recover credit by an invasion of England. He was surprised and slain, along with Edward, his oldest son by Margaret. This precipitated a crisis in the Scottish succession.

In line with older tradition, Malcolm's brother Donald claimed the throne and was opposed by Duncan, Malcolm's son by his first marriage. With assistance from Rufus, Duncan invaded Scotland and was allowed to oust his uncle on the significant condition that he kept Englishmen and Frenchmen out of the kingdom, a clear sign of the resentments Malcolm III's reign had aroused.[50] When Duncan was treacherously slain and Donald restored, a second invasion was launched from England. This time, Edgar, the oldest of Margaret's surviving sons, was installed as king. Despite the dissatisfaction of some Scots with the nature of changes identified with Margaret, their inability to withstand determined pressure from England had been exposed. As Margaret's sons learned how to reconcile dissaffected Scots to their rule, better relations with England covered their flank. Their English royal ancestry was no longer feared by the Norman kings as a danger to their own power; rather, it became a means of bringing the Scottish kingdom into closer relations with England. Rufus reinforced the military hold on the north he had established at Newcastle by seizing Carlisle in 1092, where he built another castle and arranged for the settlement of English peasantry round about and Flemings, probably in the town itself.[51] English power in the north by 1100 no longer depended on the abilities of the earls of Northumbria, but upon a number of strategically placed Norman lords, with impressive military followings and castles at their disposal. If necessary, kings left Normandy to deal personally with particularly critical situations, a sign of the importance they attached to this new frontier. Even so, the immediate purpose of protecting their own domains accomplished, English kings left Scottish kings to refashion their kingdom as they chose, on condition that they caused no trouble in England itself and proved personally reliable.

The importance of these interactions with England for introducing change into Scotland is certain. The demonstration of English might in State and Church obliged Scottish kings to realise that they would have to assert comparable authority of their own if they were not to degenerate into mere cat's-paws of English kings. Scotland may have become aware of new religious influences before the reign of Malcolm III, for his predecessor Macbeth had made a visit to Rome in 1050, memorable for a lavish display of almsgiving: no more is known about this visit than the brief notice in Marianus's chronicle.[52] About the same time, Earl Thorfin of Orkney also visited Rome.[53] These visits do not appear to have had the effect of opening Scotland to reforming clergy, but Scotland was obviously not totally out of touch with Rome in mid-century. When Malcolm III's wife Margaret took up the cause of church reform, however, she looked not to Rome but to Archbishop Lanfranc in England.[54] Due to his influence, the Benedictines were introduced into the Scottish Church which had hitherto kept faith with traditional monasticism. Margaret's reputation as a Scottish saint was assiduously cultivated at her foundation of Dunfermline and by her royal descendants. A book describing her pious life was written by Turgot, a former prior of Durham who was promoted by King Alexander I to the see of St Andrews.[55] Margaret may herself have encouraged veneration of St Andrew as Scottish patron, given the respect for Andrew in her native Hungary. Margaret's English connections did not, however, reconcile Malcolm III to the archbishop of York's attempts to assert metropolitan rights in his kingdom.[56] Despite their apparent vulnerability to pressures from England, the Scots were already able to pick and choose what they considered innovations of benefit to themselves.

On the borderlands between the English and the Welsh there was some superficial similarity with the situation in the north, since Welsh attacks from time to time caused damage to Englishmen and English property. Until this time, responsibility for dealing with the Welsh had fallen principally upon the earls of Mercia and the structural organisation of pre-Conquest England had precluded more extensive campaigning. The success of Gruffydd of Gwynedd in imposing himself over other Welsh princes and raiding in England had brought Earl Harold Godwinson to the west. Harold's defeat of Gruffydd in 1063 had removed the immediate danger.[57] Awareness of what was needed in the way of local defences had caused the Confessor before 1066 to entrust some Norman kinsmen with responsibility for building castles in the March region. Typically, the Normans after the Conquest sought to resolve the problems of the frontier lands by identifying several different critical crossing points and entrusting each to a different commander, particularly to the three earls at Hereford, Shrewsbury and Chester, with lesser barons in the interstices. Fragmentation of the Norman defences was a consequence of the perception that by 1066 there was no longer a leading Welsh 'king' to be confronted. Wales was not as attractive as Scotland as a place of refuge or support for English malcontents, perhaps because differences of speech and culture made it more difficult to establish amiable relations between the two peoples. The Conqueror himself was not committed to further conquests in the west and the Norman marcher lords, perhaps reacting instinctively as their fellow countrymen had done on the borders of Normandy itself, perhaps only alert to their occasional opportunities, pressed forward to enlarge their domains where they could.[58] Before the end of the eleventh century the Normans had accordingly penetrated into Wales all along the line. In Powys, Robert of Bellême, earl of Shrewsbury, left an enduring legacy by importing Spanish horses with a view to improving the bloodstock, but not all the Norman advances could be sustained.[59] Magnus of Norway's campaigns stiffened local powers of resistance and, as a result, Chester remained a border fortress into the thirteenth century. The greater thrust into south Wales was chiefly provoked by the need to curb the aspirations of the Welsh ruler of Morgannwg and Gwent. Not all the spectacular success achieved before 1100 in south Wales can be explained in terms of greater Norman energy. Norman determination may have contributed to the disarray of the Welsh themselves in coordinating resistance but local geographical conditions enabled several different Norman families to establish separate lordships in south Wales which subsequently made it more difficult for the Welsh to reverse the situation in any one great campaign.

The impact of these Norman incursions into south Wales on the Welsh themselves is nowhere better illustrated than by ecclesiastical affairs. No more than the Scots had the Welsh already developed territorial dioceses on the conventional pattern. Nor had Welsh bishops hitherto had to learn from experience how to deal with masterful local rulers. There the general arrangements in the 'Celtic' Church assumed that the local family would provide patronage and fill the offices of the Church without interference from outside. There was no metropolitan bishop in Wales. The few Welsh clergy who maintained relations with the papacy had no reason to think that such contacts would protect them, as the Normans began to infiltrate Welsh regions, disrupt the ecclesiastical order and set up monastic cells for their own favoured foundations in England or Normandy. Welsh bishops in dispute with secular lords or ecclesiastical rivals accordingly turned to Canterbury. Archbishop Anselm wrote on behalf of Bishop Wilfred of St David's to leading Norman lords in west Wales, urging them to respect the rights of the bishop and pay the correct ecclesiastical dues. Llandaff, in the south, the Welsh see geographically closest to England, was even more exposed to English pressure. Before 1100 Llandaff was the only Welsh see in recognisable order by contemporary continental standards.[60] Bishop Herewald, an Englishman, had been the first to appreciate that acceptance of Canterbury's jurisdiction might help him to gain firmer control over his own affairs against rival clergy. The new situation owed more to the willingness of Welsh bishops to seek Canterbury's support for their own causes than to any ability of Canterbury, even with secular support, to make metropolitan jurisdiction effective. Nevertheless, Canterbury disposed of greater resources than York had commanded for exercising metropolitan jurisdiction in Scotland. Canterbury succeeded in keeping the initiative and its interference proved fatal to the cause of any effective Welsh resistance on the ecclesiastical front. By the time the bishops of St David's, the see most remote geographically from England, attempted in the twelfth century to secure papal support for their own metropolitan status, it was too late. As the Norman lords extended their hold in south Wales, the future pattern of English infiltration into Wales had already become clear. The Welsh were gradually drawn into the Norman network as the English had been, much more abruptly, a generation earlier.

The eleventh-century Normans had no intention of invading Ireland, but their presence in England and Wales had predictable repercussions across the Irish Sea. After the Norman Conquest, sons of Harold Godwinson took refuge in Leinster and used it as a base for their attacks on England. By making a present of their father's banner to its king they may have hoped to tempt him into active military assistance.[61] Ireland was traditionally both a place of refuge and a source of auxiliary soldiers for Welsh princes, and once the Normans themselves had arrived in west Wales they were irresistibly drawn into contact with their Irish neighbours. At first relations were amicable. Murtagh, king of Munster, a powerful figure in Ireland, accepted Arnulf of Montgomery, lord of Pembroke, as a son-in-law who nursed hopes of becoming Murtagh's successor.[62]

According to the *Book of the Taking of Ireland* written *c*.1050, the Irish people had arrived in Ireland from Spain, having wandered from their original homeland in the Middle East, but by the eleventh century there is little evidence for regular contact between Ireland and the Continent. Such information as we have is spasmodic. The cryptic notice that the high-king Turlough of Munster received five Jews in 1079 and sent them back to their own land, probably to Rouen or London, typically comes without explanation and had no consequences: Jews did not settle in medieval Ireland.[63] What had they been seeking? Had they been rebuffed, or concluded that Ireland offered them neither business opportunities nor security? Irish kings were not altogether cut off from the rest of the world. Alerted perhaps by Cnut's own Rome journey, several Irish kings visited Rome in mid-century, some to die, some as exiles.[64] No more than in the case of Macbeth did these royal visits have tangible consequences for the reform of the Irish Church. It seems strange that only Irish kings and not clergy are reported in the Irish annals to have made contact with Rome, though there was a community of Irish clergy in Rome at the end of the eleventh century.[65] Piety took some Irishmen further still. In 1080 one minor king of Munster went to Jerusalem on pilgrimage.[66] He too may have passed through Rome, though he could equally have crossed through Germany, where Irish monasteries still flourished. These monasteries provide the main evidence for Irish relations with the Continent.[67]

The outlook of the Irish Church in the eleventh century was still shaped, as it had been for centuries, by monks committed to respect for the older traditions of 'Irish' asceticism. The Viking raids of the ninth century had helped to drive other Irishmen overseas as refugees. In the late tenth century an Irish community had been established at Cologne, where Marianus Scotus, the famous computationist and chronicler, arrived as an exile in 1056. Over the next twenty years he moved about in Germany, meeting other Irish monks at their bases in Fulda, Paderborn and Mainz, where Marianus died sometime *c*.1082. His chronicle pays little attention to the turbulent events of German church history in his own time. This cannot have been because as an *inclusus* he was shut off from the world, for he noted the Roman visits of Scottish and Irish kings as well as other events in the distant British Isles, such as the deaths of kings and even the Conqueror's devastation of Yorkshire. Such information as passed between Ireland and Germany was presumably the source of those brief entries in the Irish annals which concern events in the eleventh-century empire but cease abruptly after 1052.[68] Contact between Ireland and Germany may have suffered, however, from the open breach between the emperor Henry IV and the pope after 1080.

The religious orthodoxy of the Irish Church was never in doubt, but ecclesiastical reformers from the Continent were troubled by many irregularities they perceived in its organisation.[69] The reform programme required bishops to assume more effective control of their dioceses and work together for greater uniformity in matters of religious discipline. After the Conquest, the Norman bishops in England had taken a firm line on asserting episcopal rights and were able to build on the prestige accorded to bishops from the earliest days of the missionary movement. In Ireland there was no such sentiment to build on. Irish bishops did not even have cities from which to exercise their authority and lacked bodies of cathedral clergy pressing for observance of episcopal rights; they were not concerned about authority and precedence. The claims of the bishop of Armagh to respect depended on his status as the 'coarb' (successor) to St Patrick; the office was even transmitted by family connections. The coarb sought no confirmation of office from the pope.

In Ireland, there was no body of opinion which reckoned to benefit from church reform. There was no single king, as in Scotland, to patronise and control reform programmes; nor at this stage were the Irish obliged to make haste with reforms of their own by the infiltration of Norman border barons, as happened in Wales. Ireland might not seem particularly oppressed by secular lordship, for lay patronage of the Church had not taken there the forms of proprietary control which reformers so strongly denounced on the Continent. Nevertheless, the affairs of Irish churches and leading families were deeply entwined and from a reformers' point of view merited attention. Apart from what reformers judged to be irregularities in Irish rules for consecrating bishops, it was Irish laymen's disregard for the rules forbidding marriage within prohibited degrees of kinship which most distressed outside observers. Irish monks may have retained their own austere traditions, but these had little impact on the moral conduct of Christian laymen. The Irish clergy were not in fact well placed to direct the lives of laymen in the ways continental clergy took for granted. Old Irish law was interpreted and maintained by a special group of lawmen and Irish bards preserved the memory of laymen's great deeds.[70] In most parts of Christendom, sole responsibility for the transmission of culture was shouldered by the clergy; in Ireland, they had secular counterparts who had no intention of giving way to monks.

The earliest evidence of Irish churchmen taking any interest in closer contact with the Church outside Ireland comes naturally enough from Dublin. Patrick, an Irishman, was sent to Archbishop Lanfranc in 1074 for consecration as bishop. Patrick had formerly been a monk at Worcester, so his English contacts pre-date the Norman Conquest.[71] Canterbury's part in smoothing the way towards incorporation into the Anglo-Norman realm for Welsh clergy points to the potential importance of comparable involvement in the consecration of a new bishop of Dublin. The willingness of Dublin and Patrick himself to involve Canterbury in Irish ecclesiastical affairs must indicate not only dissatisfaction with the conditions prevailing in Ireland itself, but some readiness to embrace a new order of discipline from overseas. No doubt encouraged by this initial invitation, Lanfranc wrote to the king of Dublin, urging him to accept Patrick's advice about needful reforms. Rather more ambitiously, Lanfranc also wrote to the king of Munster, then high-king of Ireland, recommending him to assemble all the Irish clergy and legislate to abolish evil customs.[72] In this, Lanfranc may have responded to a papal initiative, since the high-king received a similar letter from Gregory VII.[73]

Both the pope and the archbishop regarded it as natural and urgent for the high-king to take the lead in bringing about the outcome they desired. There is no reason to think that many Irish churchmen were already eager to welcome any such moves. Nevertheless, the reform movement had got its foot in the door at Dublin. Archbishops of Canterbury consecrated two more bishops for Dublin before the end of the century and another Irishman, a former monk at Winchester, was consecrated as bishop of Waterford, another Ostman town. Canterbury's involvement in Irish affairs must have aroused further English interest in Ireland. The close relations between Canterbury and the Irish Church clearly owed much to the promotion to Irish bishoprics of Irish monks professed in English monasteries, but the choice of bishops was made in Ireland, not in England, and the willingness of Irishmen to live as monks in England indicates that they welcomed such opportunities to make contacts across the sea.[74] In Ireland, Lanfranc of Canterbury inspired sufficient respect for the Irish bishop of Munster, Domnall, to consult him about the validity of certain Irish beliefs about the salvation of infants and to throw in a question about literary matters. Lanfranc replied at length about the religious issue but declined to enter into discussion of profane learning on the grounds that as a bishop he had renounced any earlier interest in it, with the implication that Domnall should do likewise. In the milieu Lanfranc was familiar with, the Irish no longer enjoyed a reputation for learning and he was not interested in Domnall's opinions.[75] When Anselm succeeded Lanfranc at Canterbury in 1094, he appears more conciliatory, seeking to explain his appointment to his fellow bishops in Ireland as men deserving respect, not only those who had been in England but also to the same Domnall. Admittedly, he too encouraged them to press ahead with the enforcement of stricter discipline and offered to give them any help he could, but he did not assume any superior right of Canterbury to direct their efforts.[76]

The Norman Conquest of England carried unforeseen implications for the rest of the British Isles for generations to come. For better or worse, from this time forward, the English came to mediate between the rest of the archipelago and the Continent. Historians of the Conquest have traditionally concentrated on the domestic consequences, but set in its contemporary context it is clear that the arrival of the Normans in England soon began to have effects elsewhere in these islands. The consequences for the Continent were no less profound. For centuries, English kings were no longer content to remain observers; they became active players in continental politics, not merely because of the estates they owned in France, but because they were too rich and powerful as kings of England to opt out of the great issues of the day.

|3|

Pushing against the frontiers

The crusade and the British Isles

The capture of Jerusalem by Christian forces from the Latin west on 15 July 1099 has left a profound impression on both Christians and Muslims. For the first time, western Christians signalled their concern for the region where their religion had taken its origin and their determination to deploy their forces to protect it. Northern Europe played a prominent part in the First Crusade, providing three of its main commanders, all of them having some connection with England. Robert of Flanders was first cousin to the Conqueror's sons. Eustace of Boulogne, older brother of Godfrey de Bouillon, chosen Defender of the Holy Sepulchre after the fall of Jerusalem, already possessed extensive lands in England before his marriage to the English queen's sister on his return to the west. Robert, duke of Normandy, on whose behalf many Normans had been prepared to fight in England after Rufus's accession in 1087, certainly had Englishmen in his contingent alongside Normans and Bretons. Some English and Scottish crusaders may have formed a separate company under Edgar Aetheling. One of the Aetheling's *miles*, Robert, son of Godwine, played a heroic role in the Holy Land, saving King Baldwin from capture near Ramla, but himself suffering martyrdom in Cairo for refusing to become a Muslim.[1] The English were at least as deeply implicated in the affairs of the crusades as others, though because neither of Robert of Normandy's younger brothers, William Rufus and Henry I, kings of England, apparently paid much attention to the needs of the Holy Land, English historians once tended to underrate English interest in the crusading venture.[2] Even Henry I himself cannot have been indifferent. On the death of his crusading brother-in-law, Stephen of Blois, Henry I acted *in loco parentis* to his sons.

English involvement can also be shown in other ways. An eyewitness chronicler of the First Crusade, Ralph of Aguilers from Le Puy, gives a circumstantial account of English crusaders who had arrived by water round the coast of Spain in thirty ships, a naval contribution only surpassed by the contingents from Pisa, Venice or Genoa.³ Nothing more is known about how these ships were mustered or led, but in themselves they prove that the call had reached a lower social level than the nobility, either in London or in other great ports with appropriate shipping. Such crusaders needed no great lords to inspire or coerce them. Even monks desired to depart. The abbot of Cerne prepared a ship for this purpose and cannot have been the only one. Anselm urged his bishops to prevent monks sailing because it was incompatible with the monastic profession.⁴ English interest in distant maritime traffic was no flash in the pan. The part taken by English sailors in the Second Crusade of 1147 is fully recounted in the chronicle written to celebrate their part in the Portuguese capture of Lisbon from the Muslims.⁵ It is highly unlikely that English sailors would have contemplated such expeditions had they not already been familiar with the maritime route to the Holy Land and aware of the problems of provisioning entailed by such long voyages. Sigurd, king of Norway, travelled out to the Holy Land by water, c.1105, spending the winter in England on the way as a natural port of call on a familiar route. His exploits in the east were recounted admiringly in England.⁶ The trips made by Godric of Finchale in his early years as a pirate may also be evidence of the same traffic. After the calling of the First Crusade in 1095, greater familiarity with these routes would have developed, whatever the case before.

The principal English chroniclers of the age, Henry of Huntingdon, William of Malmesbury and Orderic Vitalis, the English-born monk of St Evroul in Normandy, all gave the crusade generous coverage in their works. Malmesbury made extensive use of written sources but felt confident enough of his own historical acumen to interpret the campaigns afresh. Like other monastic chroniclers, writing for edification and making use of other written sources, he garnished his narrative with details taken from returning crusaders or from inspired travellers' tales.⁷ In his own monastery Saewulf, a merchant who had become monk, wrote a memoir of his journey to the Holy Land in 1102 and the chronicler had probably heard him talk abut his experiences.⁸ Some crusaders returned with less edifying experiences to relate. One of Arnulf of Ardres's English sons, Anselm, had been taken prisoner and only returned home after many years. His family were so scandalised to hear that he had not only become a Muslim but intended to remain one that they rejected him and he returned to the east.⁹ A crusader less impressed by Levantines was Bohemond of Antioch, who made a tour of France in 1106 to raise men and money for another campaign to the east. Henry I prevented him from crossing into England for the same purpose, fearful that Bohemond would win over men the king himself needed for his own campaign against Robert in Normandy. Even so, Bohemond's progress through France was followed closely in England. A letter he wrote in September 1106 trying to persuade Pope Paschal II to accompany his new expedition to the east is known only from a copy in a Lincoln manuscript.¹⁰

Early manuscripts of the *Gesta Francorum*, which celebrated Bohemond's crusading prowess, and of other accounts of the crusade known to have been in England helped generate interest in the crusading venture.[11]

William of Malmesbury believed that so many persons had been caught up in the excitement that even the Welsh, Scots, Danes and Norwegians on the very fringes of Christendom had taken the cross, but gave no details about these Welsh and Scots crusaders. The later journey of one Welsh prince to Jerusalem in 1125 was only undertaken as a penance for murdering his brother. Eighteen years later, the *Brut* chronicler thought it worth noting the death by drowning in the Aegean of a band of other Welsh pilgrims from Dyfed and Ceredigion on their way to Jerusalem.[12] Such notices are too casual to convey any real idea of what the Holy Land meant in Wales. For Scotland, the evidence is scarcely better. The French chronicler, Guibert of Nogent, remarked that the eagerness of the Scots troops to lend their aid to the great cause inspired some ridicule when they arrived from across the sea, barelegged and wearing shaggy cloaks with their purses hanging from their shoulders. In desperation at not being able to make themselves understood by speaking, they gestured with their fingers to try to explain the purpose of their journey.[13] King Alexander received gifts from the Holy Land of Turkish armour and an Arab horse, no doubt trophies taken by returning Scots warriors. Alexander also presented Murtagh, king of Munster, in 1105 with a camel, described as being of wonderful size.[14] Irish annals, most unusually for contemporary historical records, barely allude to the crusade at all. The campaign of 1147 was there described as being launched to extirpate the power of the Jews.[15] Even if this were the result of mere confusion about the actual situation in the twelfth-century Holy Land, such a mistake could not have been made in England.

Once the crusaders became established in the Holy Land, their difficulties continued to impinge on the peoples of the west through the urgent need of men and money to sustain their campaigns. Provision for the military establishment was one of the objectives of the Order of Templars, founded by Hugh Pain, a knight from Champagne where King Stephen's older brother, Theobald, was count. Hugh visited both England and Scotland. In the first half of the century, the Templars were assigned over twenty properties in England; for these, they obtained as many as sixty charters from Stephen's reign alone.[16] Stephen's wife Matilda seconded his generosity: she was the heiress of the crusader, Eustace of Boulogne. Stephen's enemy in Normandy, Geoffrey count of Anjou, was the son of Fulk, who became king of Jerusalem by his second marriage to Melisende, the heiress. The difficulties of Stephen's reign were not so great as to blot out all sense of responsibility for kinsmen and friends in the east. When Louis VII of France departed on crusade in 1147, Earl Warenne and the bishop of Chester joined his company. The text of a song composed in French to prompt others to join the king's crusade has only survived in an Anglo-Norman version, but provides a rare glimpse either of how the campaign was managed or how it inspired enthusiasm.[17] England belonged to that part of the world where crusading idealism was most cultivated.

The crusading movement is the most striking manifestation of the laity's sensitivity to the call of religion. Hitherto, laymen had been admonished by clergy that their only hope of redemption was to abandon their blood-stained lives in the secular world and enter a monastery. Hereafter, clergy conceded that laymen, without formally renouncing the world, might obtain spiritual rewards by devoting their belligerent energies to the recovery of Christ's homeland from the infidels. On crusade they were encouraged to display their talents and prove their courage for a righteous cause, rather than exhorted to renounce aggression altogether. This confidence that it is just to fight for a good cause has helped shape the European consciousness ever since. In modern times, though Christian authorities themselves now judge the crusade to be incompatible with religious teaching, the zeal to fight for causes deemed praiseworthy has not been eradicated.

England's involvement in Mediterranean campaigning may have been encouraged by its connection with the Norman states established in the south. When Duke Robert returned from the east, he travelled back through south Italy where he acquired a bride, Sybil of Conversano; she came with an appropriately lavish dowry, offered by her enriched family eager to secure such a prestigious marriage. Forty years later, when the archbishop of York, William FitzHerbert, went into exile, he found a refuge in Sicily with King Roger II to whom he was distantly related twice over.[18] Roger was known for attracting men of talent to his service. Two of his most prominent ministers were Englishmen. Thomas Brown who worked in Roger's chancery had previously been in the service of King Henry I of England, leaving his homeland after Henry's death because he was not sufficiently appreciated by the new king, Stephen. After twenty years, he was summoned back to England by Henry II who created a new post for him in the Exchequer as a special auditor; he worked there for another twenty years.[19] There must have been good reasons to remember his abilities. His departure from Sicily coincided, however, not only with Henry II's accession but with the death of Roger II, whose successor, William I, did not take comparable care to retain him. Brown's career proves that information about attractive postings moved easily over more than 1000 miles. Roger II's other English minister, Robert of Selby, shouldered even greater responsibilities: as chancellor, he served as the king's deputy on the mainland of south Italy. John of Salisbury on a visit to the kingdom was impressed by his prominence and appreciated his lavish hospitality.[20] Sicily had become a land of opportunity, not merely for Normans but for Englishmen.

The impact of the crusading movement on western Europe was immediate, profound and long-lasting. It is impossible to summarise in a few words the effect on all those who went east and returned to tell of their experiences. The English chroniclers' accounts of the great events reveal their excitement, satisfaction and exasperation when their expectations were disappointed. How their emotions influenced their ideals and actions can only be guessed at, but there could be practical consequences. When, after his return from Jerusalem in 1120, Earl Haakon built a round church in Orkney, there can be no dispute that he was impressed by the church of the Holy Sepulchre.[21] Experiences out east probably had some impact in other ways, though it is much more difficult to pin down the connections. Western crusaders will have suffered from the unusual conditions they encountered, the climate, the food and the diseases. The religious order of the Hospitallers developed to provide hospices for the needs of pilgrims rather than to minister to the sick, but the provision made for the endowment of the order in the west shows that a new concern for the welfare of the needy had taken root. The social pressure stemming from the growth of towns and the religious revival would have both acted anyway as spurs for the establishment of houses providing care. In England, occasional foundations of hospitals had been made before 1100, but the number grew rapidly in the twelfth century and most towns had at least one. What impact did greater familiarity with the lands of the Mediterranean have on this? The efforts made by scholars in the twelfth century to make available Greek and Arabic medical knowledge proves that they had become aware of what advantage they might derive from such learning. Ordinary western visitors may well have been impressed by the medical expertise available in the Levant and encouraged their own doctors to take an interest in learning more. Simply as travellers they appreciated the places of refuge provided in difficult areas along pilgrim routes, and the English were notable for their financial contributions to these institutions. They often stopped off at a house at St Gilles in Provence and the cult of St Giles spread into England where it was identified with care for the crippled and for lepers. Though it is no longer believed that leprosy reached the west only as a consequence of the crusades, setting up houses specifically for those with leprous conditions became commonplace from this period.[22] The influence of the Mediterranean is plain from the saints most often chosen as patrons of hospitals. London alone had hospitals named after saints Bartholomew, Giles, Antonin, John of Jerusalem, Mary of Bethlehem and Thomas of Acre.[23]

Another aspect of hygiene could have been influenced by the crusading venture. The bathing establishments of the eastern Mediterranean were inevitably patronised by visitors from the west. It cannot be shown, however, that this did anything to stimulate the provision of comparable establishments back home. How many English visitors to Naples sampled the baths at Pozzuoli, as the ailing emperor Frederick II is known to have done? The English had their own hot springs. At Bath these were much frequented by the sick in the twelfth century and monastic writers gleefully reported what incidents they could to prove that saintly miracles were even more efficacious than bathing. This did not deter everyone. The waters at Leamington Spa were sufficiently appreciated to attract even early-morning bathers in the mid-thirteenth century. Irish and Norse fighting men were on occasion surprised and killed in their baths. As might be expected, little is known about such basic matters as washing practices in the Middle Ages.[24]

The English pursuit of learning on the Continent

About some of the other consequences of the crusading movement, it is possible to speak with more confidence. The crusades encouraged western Christians to push against the frontiers of the world they knew and discover what lay beyond the immediate horizon. The regular routes they opened to the east enabled a number of Englishmen to take the opportunity to cultivate intellectual interests not adequately catered for in northern Europe. This has implications for our understanding of the state of English learning at this time. The English did not leave as novices, but already well schooled to pursue more advanced study. In the eleventh century England still enjoyed the high reputation for mathematical scholarship it originally owed to Bede. At that time a number of distinguished scholars of mathematical and astronomical learning appeared in Lorraine whose work was promptly followed up in England. One of the earliest visitors from this region was Gerland of Besançon, a famous teacher and author of a *Computus* who was himself later attracted to Sicily where he became the (sainted) bishop of Agrigento. Gerland's own visit to England had no obvious repercussions on English learning, but two other Lorrainers, Walcher, who became prior of Malvern and Robert, later bishop of Hereford, had considerable impact. In 1092, Walcher made the earliest recorded observation in Christian Europe of an eclipse of the Moon with the astrolabe and appears to have initiated English interest in such studies.[25]

The leading figure for the encouragement of natural science in the next generation was Adelard of Bath, whose family had probably come from the Continent. As son of Fastred, he witnessed documents from the bishopric of Bath, where two bishops in succession, Giso and John, were of continental origin. John, renowned as a doctor and patron of learning, encouraged Adelard to pursue studies in Tours, his own birthplace. At some point thereafter Adelard became aware that to improve his scientific understanding he would need to travel further. In the early twelfth century he visited Salerno and Sicily. His earliest dated work is dedicated to William, bishop of Syracuse, whom he respected for his mathematical learning. Somewhere he learnt enough Arabic to make translations after his return to England in the 1120s. His versions of Euclid and Arabic works on mathematics and astronomy became influential for the promotion of scientific learning both in England and abroad.[26] Manuscripts of this period show that by this time even Arabic (that is Hindu) numerals were becoming known in England. One of Adelard's pupils, N. Ocreatus, wrote a work, *In Helceph*, notable for its early use in the west of mathematical symbols for zero.[27] Otherwise unknown, could this scholar have been an Irishman (O'Grady)? If so, he could have been a link between Adelard and the Irish computationists of the Rhineland.

Adelard was not alone in perceiving what might be gained intellectually for Latin learning from new contacts in southern lands. Peter Alfonsi, a Spanish Jew who became personal physician to Henry I, also used his knowledge of Arabic to advance astronomical knowledge in England.[28] By such means, England began to benefit intellectually from contacts with the Islamic world. Robert of Ketton (in Rutland), after study in France, possibly at Chartres, went to Spain to learn Arabic. At Barcelona he studied geometry and astronomy with Peter of Tivoli and became a friend of Hermann of Carinthia (or Dalmatia). In 1142 Peter, abbot of Cluny, then on a visit to Spain, commissioned Ketton to make translations of Arabic religious works, including the Koran. Peter had realised that there was more to the religion of Islam than had previously been suspected and that the learned refutation of Muslim teaching he thought desirable would have to be based on a clearer understanding of what Muslims actually believed. Ketton obliged but, once his version of the Koran was completed in the summer of 1143, immediately resumed his scientific studies, translating a work on alchemy, Al Kindi's *Astronomy*, and the *Algebra* of Al Khwarizmi, which became the basic Latin textbook on the subject. Although he was appointed archdeacon of Pamplona, Ketton had returned to England by *c*.1150 when he compiled a set of astronomical tables for the longitude of London.[29]

The Christian reconquests in Spain had made it easier to take advantage of the many learned men to be found in the old Muslim lands. To help with the work of translation, Jews often acted as intermediaries. Arabic was the native language of Abraham ben Ezra, a distinguished Jewish scholar from Tudela who had left Spain about 1140 and spent many years in Italy and France before reaching London early in the reign of Henry II. Before his death there in 1164, he continued with his writing, mainly to make the Ashkenazi community there aware of the Sephardic traditions of Talmudic scholarship.[30] He was remembered by the Jewish community in England and his influence on Gentile learning is not demonstrable. His presence, nevertheless, offers additional proof that England was on the circuit of learned men of many kinds in the mid-twelfth century.

From this time, travel on the Continent in pursuit of learning became regular. Most students went no further than France. Although some laymen attended the northern cathedral schools, the great majority of these students were clergy. The explanation for this educational exodus is two-fold. Part of the attraction was the new learning of some innovative thinkers; for the rest, the nature of education in England itself where clergy may have suffered from one institutional disadvantage. The most intellectual cathedral sees in post-Conquest England were monastic, particularly Canterbury. Such monastic centres could not offer teaching appropriate for secular clergy to rival those of the province of Reims across the water. Well before the Norman Conquest, men from that region had become bishops in England

and begun to promote the development of secular cathedrals. Their connections abroad would already have encouraged English students to pursue further education in those schools. The most ambitious English students took study abroad for granted. Before Paris itself became the great magnet for students mid-century, the most famous teachers were concentrated in Laon and Reims, whose schools were attended by students from all over the western world. If the English were to benefit from the best available modern learning, that is where they could find it. The fact that so many prominent clergy attended the school at Laon should not be interpreted as proof that England was inadequately provided with establishments for education. Rather the reverse. We are informed that there were schools with excellent teachers to be found, not only in English towns but even in villages. The French teacher Thibaud of Etampes found it worth his while to open a school in Oxford.[31] It was because Englishmen were so well prepared that they appreciated the possibility of getting the most advanced learning of the day in foreign schools like that of St Victor in Paris or at Laon. Even after English schools had been notably improved at the hands of the new Norman bishops, students continued to go abroad. They were keen to do even better.

The connection between Laon and England can be illustrated from a work written *c.*1146 recording miracles obtained through the efficacy of relics of Our Lady of Laon.[32] To raise money for the cathedral building the canons decided to advertise the relics by taking them on tour. The first tour was so successful that one of the canons, himself an Englishman, suggested bringing them to England. Miracles duly occurred at each of their ports of call: Dover, Canterbury, Winchester, Christchurch, Exeter, Salisbury, Wilton, Bodmin, Barnstaple, Totnes, Bristol and Bath. On their travels in these southern towns, the canons were well received particularly by Englishmen who had attended the lectures of Master Anselm of Laon, one of the most respected early twelfth-century teachers of theology. Some of these pupils subsequently became prominent: William of Corbeil, archbishop of Canterbury, Archdeacon Robert of Exeter and Agard, bishop of Coutances (but then still prior of Bodmin) as well as Alexander of Lincoln and Nigel of Ely, the two episcopal nephews of Bishop Roger of Salisbury. The canons also received a warm welcome at Barnstaple from the wife of Joel of Totnes, described as their *comprovincialis*, sister of Guernendus de Pinkney from Amiens. Only one incident of discord marred their happy experiences in England. Down in Cornwall, then no popular tourist destination, one of the canons' servants flatly refused to believe a local man's curious assertion (at the site of King Arthur's tomb in Bodmin) that Arthur was still living. This provoked a brawl. Generally, the canons of Laon counted on a friendly reception, not merely from those with previous connections with their city but wherever they went.

Some Englishmen themselves achieved early prominence as teachers on the Continent. Adam of Petit-Pont, a famous logician in Paris, was so highly regarded that a twelfth-century manuscript (now at Munich) provided with a full-page illustration of Lady Dialectic shows her leading devotees in the four corners of the picture, Adam appearing alongside Socrates, Plato and Aristotle, no mean tribute to a learned Englishman.[33] After his successful career as a teacher, Adam returned to England where he wrote a work designed to enlarge a beginner's Latin vocabulary by giving a detailed description of his house and family.[34] Adam had been a canon of Paris and probably died in France, though he has been confused with another later Adam, a Welshman, who was also a canon of Paris and may have taught there before becoming bishop of St Asaph in 1175. It is difficult to assess how other parts of the British Isles responded to the new opportunities for schooling abroad. When Bernard, the queen's chaplain, a Norman, was appointed as bishop of St David's in 1115, the Welsh annalist then considered this a snub to the learning of the Welsh masters and did not welcome the new learning.[35] But some later Welshmen, like Bishop Adam and Gerald of Wales, obviously came to appreciate what foreign study could do for them.

The monastic network

The ideals of English religious life in the earlier Middle Ages had been set by monks. Since the Conquest, many monasteries had reinforced their links with particular houses overseas by formal agreements for mutual prayers. Such an arrangement was reached between Canterbury Cathedral and the church of St Michael at Sigeberg, Cologne, about 1125, probably in connection with the death that year of Henry I's son-in-law, the emperor Henry V.[36] Monasteries valued these connections, sending partners news about the deaths of monks and asking for prayers on their behalf. In the early twelfth century the deaths of several great religious figures on the Continent were reported in England by messengers carrying rolls on which each monastery they visited was invited to write messages of condolence.[37] The deaths of Bruno, founder of the Carthusian order, of Mathilda, abbess of Caen, daughter of the Conqueror, and of Vitalis, founder of the order of Savigny, were accordingly notified to a very great number of different houses, some of which appear on all the rolls, others only once. Vitalis had undertaken preaching tours in England which probably accounts for the fact that he was well enough known for nearly seventy English religious houses to put their names to his roll.[38] These rolls provide picturesque evidence for the religious network, as well as showing how news travelled through the Christian community. The English may have been known for their benevolence towards foreign visitors: Alexander Neckham praised the English for their generous disposition.[39] Probably on that account, Andrew, an Italian ascetic originally from Vallombrosa, who had founded a monastery at Chezal-Benoît near Bourges, came to England begging help and returned highly content, with many ornaments for his church and money to relieve the poverty of his monks.[40] Another continental monk, Gelduin, who resigned as abbot of Anchin in order to resume his former life as a recluse, came to England for quite other reasons – in search of the necessary isolation. Even so, the date of his death in 1123 was known at St Omer.[41] St Omer had close ties with England and even attracted Englishmen to take their monastic vows there. The monk Helias, who was professed at St Bertin's, produced some beautiful manuscript illuminations for his monastery, showing familiarity with native English workmanship.[42] England might not seem a very likely place for would-be hermits to choose. Nevertheless, we hear of another foreigner, a Danish layman called Henry, who settled on Coquet Island and resisted all the efforts of fellow countrymen to persuade him to return home. Taking into account the number of English hermits and recluses, it may be that in western Europe only Italy had more than England.[43]

Monastic contacts were much more diverse than those of the secular clergy. Some reflected changes brought about by the Norman Conquest when a large number of foreign churches, mainly in Normandy, received donations of property in England. Small priories were sometimes established. At the very least, a few monks were sent from the mother house to superintend its acquisitions and secure the transmission of some of the produce, like grain or cheese, back to France. Little of the comings and goings of these monks is known in detail, but at the time they were not of minor consequence. The abbey of Fécamp, for instance, enjoyed possession of the major ports of Rye and Winchelsea. Eight similar religious establishments were founded in south Wales where they were comparably responsible for establishing the closest Welsh links with the Continent. Five of the mother houses were in Normandy; the others were in Paris, Maine and Anjou, so that Welsh contacts were quite spread out.[44]

The old Benedictine tradition was not the only monastic influence on the British Isles in this period. In late eleventh-century France reformers had become dissatisfied with the autonomous style of the old houses and begun to experiment with ways of providing for greater supervision of discipline by inspection from abbeys of great reputation. They also advocated more uniformity in liturgical uses for their orders than bishops then expected in their dioceses. Because of its reputation for strict monastic observance, the Burgundian monastery of Cluny (founded in 911) had been entrusted with the reform of many French religious houses in the eleventh century. Cluny did not acquire any English priories until after the Conquest, but even then its greatest impact on English religious practice was realised through prestigious houses like Reading, founded by Henry I, or Faversham, founded by Stephen. From the first these were abbeys, not priories, and, as royal foundations, totally independent of Cluny itself. The Cluniac style of monastic observance was by then already somewhat unfashionable but still respected in noble families. Henry I himself became a notable benefactor of Cluny and made his nephew, Henry of Blois, after a noviciate at Cluny, abbot of

Glastonbury and bishop of Winchester, two of the best endowed religious houses in England.[45] Henry of Blois kept up his friendship with Abbot Peter of Cluny and his stature in the kingdom was recognised by Pope Innocent II, who made him resident papal legate in England. Henry was a great traveller on the Continent, a discriminating patron of building, libraries and illuminated manuscripts, as well as a collector of Roman antiquities. He made the pilgrimage to Compostela, but not to Jerusalem.[46] He was, by any standard, an imposing figure and well able to survive the persistent hostility of Bernard, abbot of Clairvaux, the most tireless censor of what he regarded as monastic worldliness.

By the late eleventh century the Cluny network had become so unwieldy that its whole reforming programme had been called in question, notably at Cîteaux. Although Stephen Harding, an Englishman, had become the leading spirit in this reformed house, it was the strident advocacy of the Cistercian order by Bernard of Clairvaux which made it a great power in the Western Church. After the first Cistercian house was established in England (1128) new foundations came thick and fast. Bernard himself played no part in this expansion and only interfered in English affairs when Cistercian abbots in Yorkshire concerned about the choice of a new archbishop of York invoked Bernard's help and that of the Cistercian pope, Eugenius III. The Cistercian order promoted such solidarity. All the abbots of the order were required to attend annual chapters at Cîteaux itself. Formally, therefore, all the Cistercian houses of Britain were kept informed about the order's affairs. The movement gained early adherents in the north of England and from there spread quickly, not only into Scotland but even further. A Norwegian bishop on a visit to England persuaded the abbot of Fountains to plant a Cistercian colony under Abbot Ralph at Lysa in 1146. In his old age, Ralph returned to die at the mother house, Fountains.[47] From Kirkstall, another Cistercian house was founded near Oslo. The Cistercian affiliations rekindled the earlier religious links across the North Sea in a new form.

Cluny and Cîteaux are the best known of these congregations of monks, but there were many others which multiplied the strands binding the new houses to the international order. Bernard of Tiron (diocese of Chartres) was a monastic reformer patronised by Count Theobald and Countess Adela of Blois and through them by Henry I of England. A house of the order was founded early on in Wales by Robert FitzMartin, but it was in Scotland that the order was most favoured. David of Scotland, while still earl of Huntingdon, impressed by what he had heard of the saintliness of Bernard of Tiron, invited the abbot to send monks for a monastery established on the Tweed at Kelso in David's fiefdom of Lothian. Bernard's biographer recalled how David himself later made the long journey from the 'Arctic' zones in order to meet Bernard in person, only to find on his arrival that Bernard had died. Kelso's international connections were reinforced when it became one of the earliest Scottish monasteries to seek a privilege from Pope Innocent II and its building plan was actually modelled on the churches of the Rhineland.[48] David also drew on other religious orders for the rejuvenation of the Scottish Church. Houses for canons from Arrouaise and Prémontré were established from which suitable candidates for Scottish bishoprics were taken. A comparable case occurred in England, where Stephen, as count of Mortain and lord of Lancaster, was so impressed by the itinerant preaching of Vitalis of Savigny that he provided for the foundation of an abbey at Furness in 1128. In 1134, the king of Man entrusted Furness with responsibility for choosing a bishop for Man and this house was also drawn into founding daughter establishments in Ireland.[49]

Confidence in their native traditions may have protected Irish monks from succumbing to the novelties of the monastic practices developing in Burgundy, but they were not without continental friends and contacts of long standing. In this the Irish were in quite a different position from the Scots. Detailed information is scanty. An Irish monk who was studying abroad in various cities of *dulcis Galliae* is known only because he reported a miracle he had witnessed at Liège. He gives no information about what he studied there.[50] In 1100, Irish clergy were certainly in touch with Irish communities both in Bavaria and in Cologne, as well as in Rome itself. A new Benedictine house for Irish monks was founded at St James, Regensburg as late as 1119 and soon flourished enough to spawn several dependent houses. It was recruiting monks in Munster *c.*1130 and again in mid-century.[51] Evidence for economic links between Ireland and Germany at this time is provided by the coins of German type minted at Clonmacnoise, Dublin and Ferns *c.*1135. [52] The style of the Cormac chapel at Cashel, built *c.*1134, the earliest piece of 'Romanesque' architecture in Ireland, has been explained in various ways, but even if English or French influence counted for more than German, the fact remains that the then abbot at Regensburg was a member of the same MacCarthy family which founded the chapel. Some Irish high crosses of the same period also show awareness of contemporary monumental sculpture, as practised on the Continent, but not in England.[53]

This phase of Irish religious history is best known for the introduction of Cistercian monks at Mellifont in 1142 by Malachi, bishop of Down (1136–48), but Malachi's interest in the Cistercians came rather late, only after nearly twenty years as a reforming bishop. When still bishop of Connor, he visited Savigny's Lancashire house *c.*1126 before it was moved to Furness, and duly patronised the establishment of a Savigniac colony at Erenagh in his diocese. Its success was encouraging enough for Furness itself to found a second house at Dublin about 1139. As bishop, Malachi may have always been more interested in setting new standards for diocesan clergy by promoting the religious life of secular canons, dedicated to austerity of life and liturgical celebration. Malachi visited the Austin house at Guisborough (founded 1119) and the even stricter house at Arrouaise. Here he was credited with introducing canons of that order into all the bishoprics of Ireland.[54] This is an exaggeration, but it is true that from the 1130s regular canons were established alongside the churches of many Irish bishops. Edanus, bishop of Clogher (1138–78), himself attracted canons from Arrouaise in 1142. Malachi's own influence on Irish practice may have been more limited than his continental friends believed. The French monks originally sent to start the Mellifont community returned to Clairvaux with very jaundiced impressions of their Irish fellows. Malachi's reputation for sanctity rested essentially on the advocacy of Bernard of Clairvaux, who wrote a *Life of Malachi* shortly after his death. Bernard was gratified by Malachi's open sympathy for the Cistercian order, but had little understanding of the situation he faced in Ireland.[55]

All the religious reformers of the period inspired the foundation of new houses in England, Scotland and Ireland before 1150, but it was not only the great monastic innovators who found backers in these islands. Robert FitzWalter and his wife Sybil, returning to England from a pilgrimage to Rome by way of St Gilles, were intercepted by bandits and only rescued by the miraculous intervention of Ste Foy. Out of gratitude, they hastened to pay their respects at the shrine of the saint at Conques and were so impressed by the monastic community there that they persuaded two monks to return with them to England. There, Robert and Sybil endowed a monastery at Horsham St Faith, giving it property in East Anglia and London.[56]

The pilgrimage to Santiago de Compostela itself remained very popular with the English. In the mid-twelfth century, the Bay of Biscay was known to the Arab geographer Edrisi as the English Sea, suggesting that communication by water was well established.[57] Visiting the shrine of St James could also inspire the foundation of new monastic houses. On his return from the pilgrimage, the original founder of the priory which eventually came to rest at Wigmore visited the learned canons of St Victor in Paris, where there were already a number of English canons.[58] As a result, the Victorines became responsible for the new priory dedicated to St James and in due course their reputation for discipline and scholarship inspired the foundation of five more dependent priories in England. In the course of the century, the number of English religious houses grew prodigiously and the clerical proportion of the population must have more than doubled. The effects of this for the encouragement of literacy as well as piety have to be imagined, for no contemporary was in a position to assess the enormous changes they brought. Not all of this expansion should be attributed to influences from overseas, but the English more than held their own with France in their commitment to the religious life.

Monks were no longer generally recruited as children and were not therefore estranged from the world beyond their immediate cloister. They collected information from whatever source. The stable monastic community also provided a favourable environment for keeping records of what was happening of note in the world and historians still rely on monastic sources for knowledge of this period.[59] Monastic prejudices may diminish the value of their testimony about the world beyond their own experiences and their weakness for marvellous tales, miraculous cures and *Schadenfreude* about their enemies once blackened their reputation as historians. Nevertheless, thanks to them we are well informed about travellers abroad and their visits to holy shrines as far away as Jerusalem, but including churches with reputed saints in places not otherwise well-known attractions. Some of the stories reached the chroniclers in garbled form, but behind all of them there was once some traveller. English monastic chroniclers seem to have been more interested in noting information about the rest of the Latin world than Welsh and Irish annalists. Occasionally, they were so fully aware of distant happenings that the only information now available about them comes from these reports.

The exceptional development of historical writing in twelfth-century England owed much to the Norman Conquest itself. Even the Normans who settled wanted to know about the English past of their new land. To satisfy the requirements of lay readers in Lincolnshire, Gaimar's *L'estoire des Engleis* was written in French.[60] The vernacular was also used in the *Anglo-Saxon Chronicle*, which was still being added to in the early twelfth century, but most historical authors of the Anglo-Norman world wrote in Latin for a more sophisticated and international readership. The stimulus for their intellectual efforts was the world chronicle of Marianus Scotus, which had been introduced into England from the Rhineland by Robert, bishop of Hereford.[61] On the Continent it was so popular that it was continued by a whole succession of historians. In England it served rather to prompt monks of Worcester to write a more complete narrative of English history, and it was from Worcester that William of Malmesbury took his inspiration. William of Malmesbury, the most learned of English historians, was half-English, half-Norman. Taking Bede as his model, he set out to tell the story of the English from Bede's day down to his own. His first patron was Henry I's queen Matilda, herself a descendant of the Old English royal house.[62] Although in the hands of these writers history became far more than a set of brief annals for each year, what the native English historical tradition owed to its continental connections should not be overlooked.

The interest in storytelling, so obvious in the histories, was channelled for religious purposes into collecting records of the marvellous events attributed to the intervention of the saints. In England, a precocious devotion to the Virgin Mary had been responsible for the celebration of the feast of the Immaculate Conception at Canterbury even before 1066, and the earliest collection of Marian miracle stories was made at Bury St Edmunds in the time of Abbot Anselm, nephew of Archbishop Anselm. Abbot Anselm enriched the collection of English stories with additional miracles from Italy which added to its interest for continental scholars. Abbot Anselm had originally been sent to England as legate by Pope Paschal II and been denied entry by Henry I. Subsequently, the king had taken a shine to Anselm and appointed him at Bury, one of the most flourishing English monasteries.[63] He was not the only Italian Henry appointed abbot in England. Henry's physician, Faritius, went to Abingdon in 1100. English monasteries were not culturally confined to the Anglo-Norman world.

In the first half of the twelfth century, Peter Alfonsi's *Disciplina Clericalis* and the Marian miracles demonstrate the importance of England for the development of a new literary genre, which only later had a wider diffusion on the Continent: the short-story collection. Wales also became a storehouse of marvellous tales. Henry I's Welsh interpreter Bleherius, a fluent French speaker, related the story of Perceval to the troubadour count William IX of Poitou.[64] Soon after Henry I's death, Wales became much better known outside England through the rapid diffusion of Geoffrey of Monmouth's *History of the Kings of Britain*, the original source of stories about King Arthur.[65] That Wales had an ancient tradition of storytelling is confirmed by the work now generally known as the *Mabinogion*, redacted in Welsh prose no later than the early twelfth century, though not widely disseminated.[66] Telling tales from the mythical past also appealed to twelfth-century Irish taste, for a similar collection of stories, the *Book of Leinster*, was compiled there.[67]

Organising the Western Church

Among the holy places most frequented by the pious and curious from the British Isles, Rome was certainly pre-eminent. The journey was made to the shrines of Peter and Paul; only Rome had the resting places of two apostles. But Rome was beginning to have additional drawing power as Gregory VII and his successors summoned regular councils of bishops from all over Latin Christendom and asserted the papal right and duty to supervise the conduct of the episcopate. In England, the pull of the papacy on the episcopate was not particularly strong until the early years of the twelfth century. In his last years, even Archbishop Anselm was not best pleased to find Pope Paschal II so unhelpful on the issue of Canterbury's authority over the archbishop of York. But his belief that he needed papal approval for his efforts to secure the rights of Canterbury opened the way for archbishops of York themselves to seek papal protection from Canterbury's arrogance.[68] Canterbury's insistence on getting papal endorsment of its claims made it difficult for it to oppose other clergy who sought papal intervention in their affairs, whether they were the archbishops of York, suffragan bishops of the province of Canterbury or abbots in their province hoping to exclude Canterbury's own meddling. Within a few years, many abbots of wealthy monasteries obtained papal privileges protecting them from the interference of local bishops. In return they were prepared to offer the papacy modest annual payments. The costs of the transactions were borne by the petitioners. Other clergy who found themselves aggrieved for whatever reason also took their cases for reconsideration to the Holy Father and cultivated friends at the Curia who promised to advance their interests. The contacts between the English and Roman churches developed rapidly in the generation after 1120. All clergy in pursuit of privilege accepted that they needed a supreme judge on earth of their rights and willingly acknowledged the universal jurisdiction of the pope as the only possible source of decisive judgements.

The Roman Church was not felt to be alien. English clergy might themselves enter directly into its service and build up connections of some value to their countrymen at Rome. Robert Pullen became papal chancellor in 1143. Nicholas Breakspear became Pope Hadrian IV in 1154. The acceptance of papal discipline in twelfth-century England was not the result of the missionary endeavours of Roman agents, working subversively like Counter-Reformation Jesuits in Elizabethan England. Acceptance of papal direction, or supervision, rested entirely on the willingness of native clergy to take their problems to Rome and uphold what already seemed to them its incontestable right to defend ecclesiastical jurisdiction and privilege. Legates and letters sent from Rome could not enter the kingdom without royal consent and special pleading from English sympathisers. Rome was expected to serve English needs, not vice versa.

What was true of England did not count for so much in other parts of Britain, though even there some clergy discovered the advantages of seeking papal friendship. This was particularly true of those who were unwilling to submit to the supervision of Canterbury in their affairs. Like Anselm, they too began to take their grievances and ambitions for independence to Rome for adjudication. In Wales, Bishop Urban of Llandaff appealed directly to Pope Calixtus II in 1119 for help with his efforts to recover the rights and properties of his see, which he alleged to be the *magistra ecclesia* of Wales.[69] Oddly, Urban, who had been consecrated in 1107, had not taken such action earlier; possibly the example of Thurstan of York alerted him to what the pope might do to help. Until his death in 1134, Urban made a nuisance of himself with three successive popes and badgered at least two cardinals on behalf of his church, attending papal and legatine councils in England, France and Italy. From the first days of Innocent II's troubled pontificate, Urban and his agents dogged the pope's steps from Rome into exile in France and back. He obtained many papal bulls confirming the properties he claimed for his diocese and papal letters to the king, to the archbishops of Canterbury, to the clergy of his diocese, to its barons who had appropriated his property and to the bishops of Hereford and St David's who had, according to Urban, encroached on Llandaff's rights. Though Urban's diocese did not recover the properties his predecessor had ruled over in the heyday of King Caradog ap Gruffydd of Morgannwg, his efforts were successful in giving Llandaff a territorial integrity unprecedented in Wales. Urban's original appeal to the pope stated that the revenues of his see were worth no more than £2. When he began to build a new cathedral in 1120, he needed the archbishop of Canterbury to offer indulgences to those who helped with the costs, a device endorsed by the papal legate in 1125. How such an impoverished see paid for Urban's Roman embassies is a mystery, but Welsh clergy became convinced of the advantages of this tack. In mid-century, the *Book of Llandaff* showed its appreciation by opening with a lengthy description of Rome, its walls, its gates and churches.

Llandaff was not the only Welsh bishop to appreciate what Rome might do for its local interests: Urban's complaints about Bishop Bernard of St David's obliged Bernard to cultivate his own Roman connections. Bernard welcomed the opportunity Stephen's reign gave him to break away from dependence on Canterbury. For this reason, Bernard gave consistent support to Matilda of Anjou, the only bishop to do so, safe in the depths of west Wales. Bernard concentrated on trying to get papal recognition of the metropolitan status of his see. This involved visits to the papacy. Surviving letters to him from cardinals show how he intrigued at the Curia to find support.[70] His failure to adduce proof of the effective independence of Wales from English overlordship discredited his case in Rome, but Bernard and his successors were not deterred and their claims to metropolitan status were vigorously prosecuted for the rest of the century. Either way, with or without an archbishop of their own, the Welsh expected that Rome would provide their main hopes of getting some modification of unwelcome developments.

Though Bernard introduced the Cistercians into Wales, his own foreign connections did not apparently bring much change, or encourage others to follow his example. His purpose was to protect Welsh independence by presenting old truths in new clothes. Thus in his time the Welsh life of St David written by Rhigyfarch in the late eleventh century was translated into Latin. About the same time, the lives of several other Welsh saints were likewise given Latin form by other Anglo-Norman clergy. Significantly, such modernising was the work not of the native Welsh but of the newcomers, like Bernard himself.[71] They were not bent on stamping out Welsh heritage, only in adapting it to new conditions for their own purposes.

Such initiative as there was for change and reform at St David's was the direct result of Henry I imposing a clerk from overseas. In Wales the king took the initiative in promoting clerks of the new type as bishops. Since complaints were promptly voiced that they knew nothing of the Welsh language or customs, they can have had little impact on the parochial clergy and people. At Bangor, where the Welsh under the prince of Gwynedd proved strong enough to reverse the Norman advance into north Wales, Hervey, a Breton made bishop by the Normans in 1092, was simply expelled. Instead of trying to reinstate Hervey, Henry I compensated him handsomely by making him bishop at Ely when a new bishopric was established in that venerable monastery. Henry I's ecclesiastical policy was not conceived as part of any systematic plan to open the way for greater Roman interference in the Welsh Church. On the whole, his pragmatic approach was justified. The Welsh bishops were not able to wriggle out of Canterbury's jurisdiction.

In the estimation of reformist contemporaries, Scottish bishops without an archbishop of their own should have been subject to the metropolitan archbishop of York and popes proved reluctant to set aside this form of organisation, originally proposed by Gregory I for the Church in Britain half a millennium earlier. In Rome, popes underestimated the potential of the small Scottish kingdom to preserve its independence. Michael, the first bishop of Glasgow, was sent by King Alexander to York for consecration but the king had no intention of allowing the archbishops of York to exercise jurisdiction in his kingdom. Michael's successor, John, obtained his consecration at Rome. York's pressure on Scotland was felt most directly by the bishops of Glasgow, who were necessarily alert as to how they might best defend their interests. English occupation of lands south of the Solway in Cumbria had actually deprived Glasgow of property it claimed for the Church. To stave off any further encroachments, Bishop John obtained a declaration of Glasgow's property rights, which was put into writing, the first such statement in Scotland. Although any hopes of recovering lost estates were reluctantly abandoned after a new see of Carlisle was set up in 1133, bishops of Glasgow had learnt how to defend themselves.

The Scottish Church had not previously been loyal to Rome in the way of English Canterbury. Before King David's time bishoprics in Scotland, as in Wales and Ireland, had lacked territorial definition and institutional structures. On David's accession there were only four recognisable bishoprics in the kingdom; at his death, thirty years later, there were nine.[72] The process of replacing traditional arrangements with those required by reformers was slow. At St Andrews, proposals to move out the traditional Scottish order of Culdees in order to establish a conventional cathedral chapter were first aired in 1124. Twenty years later the Austin chapter of Carlisle (by then under David's authority) was adopted as a suitable model for St Andrews and papal approval for a gradual absorption of the Culdees obtained. This was so ineffective that the Culdees still had their own abbot in the 1180s and attempts to enforce the rights to the succession of Culdee prebends were still being made in the mid-thirteenth century. Such shortcomings were not allowed to become an excuse for encouraging York's pretensions to introduce reform. Scottish bishops counted on the king to add his own robust defence of Scottish peculiarities to their supplications at Rome. The acquiescence of the papacy to this state of affairs is unexpected. The authorities of the kingdom itself were left with the task of creating a Church structure along Latin lines. There was no insistence upon the papacy's own scheme of ecclesiastical government, once this proved to be incompatible with the realities of the situation.

Reforming movements in the Church remained much more dependent on royal patronage in Scotland than in England because there was less spontaneous enthusiasm for change. The drive came from David I's determination to keep control of any innovations. He learnt to manoeuvre in a tricky situation and take the papacy into account without abandoning his own purposes. David's decision to try to interfere in English affairs after Henry I's death created a new state of tension between his kingdom and England but, even so, this did not impede David's close relations with the Continent. He received Malachi of Down on his way to and from the Continent, as well as the papal legate Paparo, who reached Ireland in 1152 across Scotland when he was denied admission to England by King Stephen. The independence of the Scottish Church from York's domination was not achieved by a refusal to enter into relations abroad, but by adroit use of multiple contacts that left the Scottish king master of the situation.

Since there was no uniformity about the nature of papal relations with the churches in the various parts of Britain, its experiences elsewhere offered the papacy little guidance about how to deal with the Irish. In the early twelfth century Murtagh, king of Munster, appeared to be powerful enough to take the lead in pushing through the changes favoured by convinced church reformers. Murtagh secured the appointment of his bishop of Killaloe as papal legate in 1101 and followed this up by offering the bishop of Munster the royal seat on the Rock of Cashel and moving his own capital to Limerick. There his new bishop, Gilbert, also become resident papal legate in 1107, an office he only resigned in extreme old age in 1140. Gilbert wrote a book on church discipline, *De statu ecclesiae*, which recommended the introduction of uniform Roman practices in the liturgy to replace the many debased forms then prevalent in Ireland.[73] How he reckoned to implement this programme is not clear and the only known manuscripts of his work come from England. Admittedly in 1111 Murtagh brought many, though not all, of the Irish clergy together in council. Plans were drawn up for the territorial definition of the Irish bishoprics, with two archbishops, at Armagh and Cashel, for Ireland's traditional halves, north and south. Each of the thirty-odd Irish kings was to have his own bishop. The decisions of this council are known only from a text copied by a seventeenth-century antiquary from the annals, now lost, written by Gillachrist, abbot of Clonmacnoise.[74] A curious feature of the proposals given here is that they totally ignored the existence of a bishopric at Dublin. Did the council simply accept that Dublin was subject to Canterbury's jurisdiction? Dublin was, however, for that reason one of the Irish bishoprics most open to reforming ideas.[75] The council's programme was anyway not realised. Within a few years, the eclipse of Murtagh's political influence in Ireland doomed his projects for change. In his place Turlough O'Connor from Connaught, a region untouched by reforming zeal, became the most powerful king in Ireland, spending most of his long reign in combat and giving church reformers little encouragement.[76] Armagh does not seem to have been eager to make the most of the place assigned to it within the Roman scheme, and Celsius, the coarb of St Patrick, strove to reinforce his own authority all over Ireland. When he died in 1129, the Irish annals approvingly described him as the chief bishop of western Europe, obeyed by both the Irish and by foreigners, by this meaning the inhabitants of the (Norse) coastal cities.[77]

Gilbert of Limerick's role in Celsius's time is obscure. He remained in close touch with the Church in England, which may have prejudiced success in Ireland and encouraged false expectations in England. A successor to him at Limerick was actually consecrated at Canterbury in 1140, without ever being able to take his see. The reformer most encouraged by Celsius was Malachi, bishop of Connor (1124–36) and briefly Celsius's successor at Armagh (1132–36). Significantly, Malachi decided that he could not remain at Armagh in the face of objections raised by the family which had occupied the see for generations. One of its members, Gelasius, abbot of Bangor, became archbishop (1137–73) and Malachi resumed his pastoral activities as bishop at Down (1137–48). The episode is instructive because it shows that however much the Irish respected the see of St Patrick, the church of Armagh itself showed little enthusiasm for the reforming programme of Malachi. As champion of papal authority, this would have diminished, not augmented, Irish respect for Armagh's own position. After the death of Gilbert of Limerick, Malachi himself took up the matter of Irish Church organisation and tried to get the approval of Pope Innocent II for the proposals of 1111. Far from seizing this chance to bring about reform, the pope temporised, insisting that until all the Irish bishops could agree about reorganisation, he would do nothing. The stumbling blocks were two: how should Dublin be incorporated into the Irish Church and how could the agreement of Turlough O'Connor be secured? Agreement on these points was attained by a meeting in 1148 and Malachi set out for Rome to obtain papal approval, but died on the journey. Four years later, Pope Eugenius III sent his legate with four pallia for four archbishops. Dublin was separated from Canterbury by becoming an archbishopric and Turlough's consent was obtained by giving Connaught its own archbishop at Tuam.[78]

This scheme was designed to fit the realities of the Irish situation at the time, but having four archbishops, even reserving a formal primacy for Armagh, deprived the Irish Church of any hopes of achieving effective direction. This left the several kings of Ireland as the real masters of what happened next. Later in the century minor modifications were still being made to suit their interests. Satisfied in their own kingships, none of them showed any concern for the affairs of the whole Irish Church. The new province of Dublin which was intended to dispose of Canterbury's claims to jurisdiction in Ireland instead provoked Archbishop Theobald into taking countermeasures. In 1155, he secured from the English pope Hadrian IV a bull, 'Laudabiliter', granting the island of Ireland to the new king of England. Hadrian claimed that the Donation of Constantine gave him the right to do this.[79] Nothing more was done at the time about Hadrian's grant, but down the centuries it has not been forgotten.

The impression Ireland gave of being steeped in ancient religious traditions may have enhanced its credentials as a plausible location for imaginative depictions of the afterlife. In the late 1170s an English Cistercian monk at last wrote down a story that had probably been around for the past thirty years. According to this another monk, Gilbert, had been sent from England to found a monastery at Baltinglass, an event dated 1148. Owen, one of the king of Leinster's knights assigned to act as Gilbert's interpreter and assistant, told Gilbert about a visit he had made to a cave on an island in Lough Derg (Co. Donegal). There he had been conducted through the various divisions of the Other World at a place known as St Patrick's Purgatory. Owen's frightening experiences had changed his life and he had immediately made the pilgrimage to Jerusalem. Once in writing, Gilbert's story of St Patrick's Purgatory became well known, particularly through translations into the vernacular.[80] By the end of the twelfth century, the reputation of Lough Derg drew impressive numbers of pilgrims.

About the same time as Owen's visit to Lough Derg, another well-connected Irishman, this time from the kingdom of Desmond, had his own different vision of the Other World. For three days after suffering a seizure, Tundal appeared to his friends to be dead. When he recovered, the young man also completely changed his style of life and took a crusading vow. He related what he had seen in his vision to an Irish monk, Marcus, who shortly after this, in the year 1149, called at Clairvaux where Abbot Bernard was engaged in writing his life of Malachi (d. November 1148). From Clairvaux Marcus moved on to the Irish Benedictine house of St James at Regensburg, where he wrote up his account of Tundal's vision for the abbess of a neighbouring convent. For her benefit, Marcus provided a brief description of Ireland, naming the two Irish ecclesiastical provinces (Armagh and Cashel) and claiming that there were thirty-four *precipuas civitates*, which can only be intended as a reference to bishops since their 'sees' can hardly have been described as cities. The main interest of the work lay in its detailed depiction of the various torments and joys to be expected after death. This was so much appreciated that the account was soon turned into German verse in which form it became extremely popular in Germany.[81] Because of his contact with Bernard, Marcus has been suspected of writing to advance the cause of church reformers in Ireland, but his book had no success in Ireland itself. That both these texts about the Other World had an Irish origin is intriguing but it was really thanks to non-Irish interest that Ireland acquired a reputation for other-worldly experiences. The effect of the stories was to feed a religious imagination subsequently better served by Dante Alighieri.

The papacy and the kings of England

Spontaneous enthusiasm for finding new ways to live the Christian life in the early twelfth century took shape in a variety of proposals for religious reform. Sometimes to its embarrassment, the papacy came to be considered the natural patron of all these diverse reform movements and judge of their merits. All this helped to change its role in the Western Church in the first half of the twelfth century. From being the ghostly heir of the apostles, presiding over the churches of their city, popes had become dispensers of privileges and judgements on all matters touching the clerical estate. The popes had become so detached from the holy city itself that even when excluded from it by disaffected citizenry (as often happened) they were still able to exercise their authority from their temporary places of refuge.

Had the new papal programme been asserted against rulers of the Old English royal house it would surely have been admitted without any hesitation at all. In fact, the change of ruling family had an important bearing on the outcome in England, for Henry I, like his predecessor William II, resented anything he deemed likely to diminish his royal dignity. At the beginning of his reign, Henry I was most displeased by Archbishop Anselm's claim that the pope had forbidden royal investiture of bishops. Though Anselm typically preferred to go into exile rather than consecrate bishops invested by the king, it did not take too long for a way out of the difficulty to be devised. Neither the king, nor the English bishops, still less the pope, desired to make an issue out of questions about royal rights. A botched settlement was conveniently arranged as early as 1107. The king retained his right to nominate bishops and the individual churches secured appointments of men active on their behalf and friendly enough with the king to receive royal favours in the form of privileges.

Henry I did not consider himself defeated by the pope and remained confident enough of his own independence to negotiate for his daughter's marriage to the German emperor, Henry V, at a time when Henry V was himself still engaged in controversy with the pope over investitures. The significance of this quarrel was fully appreciated in Henry I's dominions. One of the strongest defences of the traditional rights of kingship in the Church, attacked by reformers, was written at Rouen.[82] Henry I's clergy never contemplated persistent defiance of royal authority out of loyalty to the Roman Church and Henry I probably felt some sneaking sympathy for his new son-in-law. The fortunes of the emperor were watched closely in England. Henry V's bullying tactics with Paschal II were enthusiastically written up by a clerk from these islands, David the 'Scot', probably an Irishman, who had taught at Würzburg before entering imperial service. William of Malmesbury criticised David's narrative as more of a panegyric than a history, but Henry I appreciated him and made him bishop of Bangor in 1120. The survival of all the relevant documents about Henry V's negotiations with Paschal II in an English manuscript provides irrefutable proof of how promptly intelligence was transmitted to England.[83] Many of those involved in negotiating the marriage of Henry I's daughter to Henry V were clearly sympathetic to the emperor's position.

A marked improvement in relations between the king and the papacy became possible after the death of Paschal II, helped by the fact that the new pope, Calixtus II, was a distant cousin of the king. If Henry I had at first expected a completely free hand in settling any difficulties with his bishops, he took a broader view once popes showed how much they respected his power, valued his friendship and appreciated his support, as after the schism of 1130. Henry I discovered that he had little to fear from recognising papal authority over the English Church: the pope did not automatically back bishops in their quarrels with the king. And whereas in England Henry I could get away with petty behaviour, like detaining papal legates or intercepting papal letters, as ruler in Normandy he was obliged to humour the papacy. English kings were in no position to carry their objections to the point of rejecting papal authority altogether.

Henry's attitude was continued by his successor Stephen, who promptly sought and obtained papal recognition of his kingship in 1136. The pope's benevolence was confirmed when he appointed Stephen's brother, Henry, bishop of Winchester as resident papal legate in England. Relations with the papacy under Stephen did not always remain so cordial, but Stephen had little difficulty about asserting royal rights, even against papal opposition. Archbishop Theobald several times took refuge from the king in exile, but always came back to make his peace. The papacy consistently supported Stephen against Matilda over the succession and showed no interest in weakening the crown in the ecclesiastical interest. In England the episcopate hardly wavered in its support for Stephen and showed no eagerness to drag the papacy into the domestic quarrel. Their moderation at this critical juncture had long-term consequences. Subjected to no violent innovations, the forms of church governance in England allowed some ancient practices to survive. Royal protection was not rebuffed because it did not frustrate the essentials of the new churchmanship.

An unexpected consequence of the conflicts between a self-assertive monarchy and the papacy was that it stimulated intellectual interest in public affairs. Well-educated clergy were retained in royal service, where their learning was deployed, particularly to help promote the development of royal justice and devise exact procedures for the audit of the king's finances. The pressure to raise more money was connected with Henry I's military difficulties in Normandy, another sign of how the king's continental dominions had implications for the elaboration of royal administrative offices. Henry I improved his financial position, first by exacting heavy money penalties for offences against royal pleas and second by stricter accounting at a new body, the Exchequer. This last clearly owed much to the computational skills for which Englishmen became famous. Knowledge of the abacus had been introduced from Lorraine into England by Robert, later bishop of Hereford (d.1095), and the sound workings of the royal Exchequer depended on the mathematical competence of its clerks. One of these, Thurkil, himself wrote a treatise on mathematical problems, including fractions, in the second decade of the twelfth century.[84] Only slightly later, Philippe de Thaon, making use of this treatise, wrote a little book on computation in Anglo-Norman, evidently for use by laymen and with the expectation that making such knowledge available would be appreciated. Up-to-date scientific knowledge put at the disposal of the king's officials helped to make England one of the best organised of medieval states. In addition, the views of some reformers that the clergy should play no part in secular governments were rejected by clergy regularly engaged on royal business. In some ways, the kingdom retained its 'old-fashioned' patina, but it was neither an Old English survivor, nor a new-fangled 'French' colony, but *sui generis*, a genuine creation of the post-Conquest kings within the old English kingdom.

Relations between secular rulers

Post-Conquest English kings dealt far more often with foreign rulers than their Anglo-Saxon predecessors had done. As dukes of Normandy, they brought their concerns with close neighbours in France to their activities as kings in England. Henry I was second cousin to King Louis VI of France and first cousin to Count Robert of Flanders and to the count's sisters, one of whom married first the king of Denmark and then the Norman duke of Apulia. Henry himself married a sister of three successive kings of Scots; his only legitimate daughter was married first to the German king and Roman emperor, Henry V, and then to the count of Anjou; his son and expected heir, William, also married a daughter of Count Fulk of Anjou. In Henry's lifetime the widowed Fulk was persuaded to go out east and marry the heiress of the kingdom of Jerusalem and so himself become a king; Henry's sister was married to Count Stephen of Blois-Champagne. With connections like these, no English ruler could escape playing a part in the relationships of these early twelfth-century foreign kinsmen. Though Henry I himself rarely ventured outside the boundaries of his own dominions, his messengers kept him informed and his neighbours took notice of his attitude to their affairs. No other king of the period enjoyed such diverse contacts with his peers and his preoccupations had consequences for his subjects.

The king did not meddle abroad with matters of no moment to himself and his right to settle any issues of 'foreign' policy was not challenged; his activities did not put his kingdom at risk. At the very least, England's French-speaking kings had French lands which they had no intention of neglecting. As kings of great authority, wealth and prestige, they rated only the respect of other major rulers as important. The heirs of the duke of Normandy aimed to shine as rulers of European standing; the acquisition of the English kingdom had given them the means to do so. Their dignity was acknowledged by other prominent rulers of the west – the pope, the emperor, even the king of France. Recurrent struggles with the king of France were unavoidable. The king of England might formally be his vassal, but in every other respect was his equal, if not superior, in real power and consequence. Suger, abbot of St Denis, one of the French kings' chief advisors, expressed awe and admiration for Henry I as a ruler.[85]

The Conquest had been responsible for stimulating new contacts with the French, not merely in Normandy itself but with Flanders, Brittany and the lands towards the Loire and beyond. This was partly because French political life had by then become so fragmented that the kings of France could not themselves throw up any barrier to the English presence. Several different French lords accordingly negotiated on their own account with English kings. Their combined weight thwarted the hostility of Louis VI of France when he launched ineffectual efforts to challenge Henry I's family interest in the duchy of Normandy. The advantages afforded to England by a united purposeful English monarchy and a divided France were obvious. The king of England could affect French political affairs, through one or other of the French provinces subject at different times to him, Normandy, Anjou, Poitou and Gascony.

Henry's assumption of the crown on the death of Rufus in a hunting accident in August 1100 pre-empted the rights of his older brother Robert, then on his way home from the crusade. Henry expected Robert to contest his hold on the English kingdom and in fact Robert did twice challenge Henry in England itself. Henry managed to hold his own and in turn defended his kingship by attacking Robert in Normandy. After Robert was captured at the battle of Tinchebrai in 1106, Henry kept him in prison until his death in 1134. Henry was consequently regarded by some Normans as no better than a usurper and the king of France never accorded him any formal recognition as duke. In 1119, admittedly, after winning a battle at Brémule, Henry obliged Louis VI to take the homage of his heir, William, for Normandy. William did not, however, then assume government of the duchy and when he was drowned the following year Henry went on ruling Normandy as before.

Robert's imprisonment obliged Henry to give constant attention to the restless condition of Normandy where several attempts were made to overthrow him; whatever it cost, he was determined to hold on to it. His ability to do so was not a matter of course. It took nineteen years from 1087 to 1106 for English kings to reunite the kingdom and the duchy as ruled together by the Conqueror. By pursuing this policy in Normandy itself, Henry I spared England from becoming the terrain of conflict, but it is not sufficient to think that he simply treated Normandy as an outer defence of his kingdom. His obstinate commitment to the duchy set up tensions with the French king and made him desperate for alliance with neighbouring French counts, Anjou, Blois and Flanders. He also appreciated approval from more distant friends in Germany and at Rome. That Henry played with foreign princes for his own benefit is blatant. Quite unscrupulously he courted the Angevins as the princes most likely to help him make trouble for the French king but, when the time came, declined to endorse the hopes of

Geoffrey of Anjou, husband of his only legitimate daughter Matilda, for the English succession.

After Henry's death in 1135, the link between England and Normandy continued as a basic preoccupation of the king. At first, Stephen appeared to have little to worry about, though his cousin Matilda, countess of Anjou, Henry I's sole surviving legitimate child, attempted to assert her own rights to the duchy. Within two years Stephen, more successful than Henry I, had induced the old king of France, Louis VI, to recognise Stephen's son Eustace as duke of Normandy. The relationship was strengthened in 1140 when Eustace married the sister of the new king of France, Louis VII. The French king allowed Stephen peaceful occupation of Normandy because Henry I's formidable alliance with Anjou had by then broken down. No longer in fear of an overwhelming coalition in the north, and encouraged by his own marriage to the heiress of Aquitaine to feel more confident in his kingdom at large, Louis VII had no reason to neglect the advantages of good relations with the king of England. Count Geoffrey of Anjou was not, however, discouraged and, taking advantage of Stephen's own weaknesses after his defeat at Lincoln in 1141, eventually succeeded in conquering Normandy for himself. Reluctantly, Louis VII agreed in 1144 to recognise Geoffrey as duke. While Louis was absent on crusade, Geoffrey unceremoniously entrusted his son Henry with the duchy of Normandy. When Louis returned in 1150, he naturally chose to reassert his own authority and oust Henry in order to restore his brother-in-law, Eustace. For whatever reasons, the kings of England persisted with their determination to rule in Normandy.

Henry I's mother had been a Flemish princess and previous English rulers had been making marriage alliances with princes from the Low Countries for two centuries. Flanders had long served both as a place of exile for political dissidents and as a launch pad for would-be invaders. The political challenge facing Henry I at the beginning of his reign easily explains why he negotiated an alliance with his cousin, Count Robert of Flanders, in March 1101. The text of this agreement provides the earliest surviving English example of a 'treaty' with a foreign power.[86] Its purpose was to settle the terms whereby the count would provide the king with up to 1000 Flemish knights when he needed them, in England or in Normandy. Ostensibly it is not concerned with Henry's disputes with his brother Robert of Normandy, but with his fear of an invasion of England by the king of France, Philip I. Although Philip's son, Louis, had a few months earlier quarrelled with his father and taken refuge at the English court, there is no reason to think that on this account Philip contemplated any invasion of England. Henry's real concern was the expected invasion of his brother Robert (though this did not occur until the summer) and Philip's possible support in his bid for the throne. The purpose of the treaty was to define Count Robert's own obligations as a French royal vassal in any such emergency. Henry was prepared to allow the count to do the minimum necessary to retain his French fiefs and also to perform services due within the German Empire. To secure an ally, Henry I had to take cognisance of the very complicated set of obligations incumbent on the count of Flanders. Henry's alliance with Count Robert added a new formality to the situation, but was not otherwise an innovation. What is new is the king's expectation that he could manipulate the count of Flanders in the interests of his own concerns in Normandy and France. The count himself was willing to play along with Henry for his own purposes rather than to fall in with the requirements of his direct overlords, the kings of Germany and France. Despite his obligations to these rulers, the count chose to ingratiate himself with the king of England, at a price which Henry I was prepared to pay because Flanders was central to his calculations. The sheer complexity of political arrangements on the near Continent enabled king and count to get away with their pact, which underlines the enviable standing the king of England had acquired since the Norman Conquest. English kings regularly renewed their 'treaty' with the counts of Flanders until Philip II of France brought the county firmly under his own supervision.

The importance to England of the Low Countries had been clear well before the Norman Conquest. Quite apart from Flanders, the major county of the region, the count of Boulogne had already proved his worth. Eustace II, husband of the Confessor's sister, gave the Conqueror his support and consequently obtained great influence and estates in England. Early in Henry's reign, his oldest son, Eustace III, was married to Mary of Scotland, the younger sister of Henry's own queen Matilda, another sign of Count Eustace's importance in Henry's scheme of things.[87] The link with Boulogne across the Channel became stronger still in the reign of Stephen, who himself became count of Boulogne by his marriage to the heiress Matilda. It mattered even more after Stephen began to lose control of Normandy. Stephen's major military forces were led by William of Ypres, he owed his financial credit to William Cade of St Omer, and the chronicle most favourable to his cause was written by someone from that region. The consistent support offered to Stephen by London can be explained by reference to the commercial value of relations across the narrow seas. Flemish merchants in London knew about the murder of Charles the Good, count of Flanders, in Bruges in 1127 within two days. London kept in close touch with important foreign news.[88]

English political links with Germany had been initiated in the early tenth century by the marriage of King Athelstan's sister Edith to the German king Otto I and renewed by that of Cnut's daughter to Conrad II's son Henry. A similar pact was brought about by negotiations for the marriage of Henry I's daughter Matilda to the emperor Henry V from 1110. Imperial recognition of Henry I's royal standing was strongly appreciated in England and English relations with the empire enhanced the political weight of those territories through which communications were maintained in the Low Countries. Henry also received an envoy sent by the Emperor Alexius Comnenus from Constantinople. The emperor's representative was an

Englishman from Lincoln who made a gift of relics to the abbey of
Abingdon. Unfortunately, the monastic chronicler was more interested in
the benefactor's piety than explaining the nature of his mission to the king.
The fact that a man from Lincoln should act as the emperor's messenger in
England at this time may seem surprising; another is said to have acted on
behalf of King Magnus of Norway. Townsmen cultivated their own foreign
contacts without being bidden by Henry I.[89]

Henry himself is not known to have sought friends in Scandinavia.
Across the North Sea, Denmark no longer posed a threat to English security.
The continuing strength of relations with the peoples of the north may,
however, be illustrated from ecclesiastical sources as Englishmen helped the
Scandinavian churches to take root in the early twelfth century. The Danes'
need of a worthy life of the sainted king Cnut IV, assassinated on the eve of
his descent into England in 1086, was satisfied about 1120 by an English
cleric in exile who was familiar with the Anglo-Saxon hagiographical tradition.[90] A rich Norwegian family retained the services of an English chaplain
who was falsely accused of violating a lady of the house, but owed his life to
the miraculous intervention of St Olaf.[91] In the same period, those responsible for building the church, later cathedral, at Stavanger, had learnt their
craft in Norfolk and the first known bishop there was an Englishman,
Reinald, who fell foul of King Harald Gilli and was executed in 1135.[92] The
English connection was responsible for introducing the Cistercians into
Norway in 1146 and when the Cistercian pope, Eugenius III, was invited to
set up separate metropolitan jurisdictions for the kings of Norway and
Sweden, he tactfully sent an English cardinal, Nicholas Breakspear, presumably as one most likely to prove congenial in Scandinavia.[93] The jurisdiction
of the archbishop of Nidaros included the bishopric of Man and the northern islands; the new arrangement therefore had a direct bearing on ecclesiastical organisation in Britain. Breakspear introduced another Englishman,
Henry, into Scandinavia. Henry was consecrated bishop of Uppsala but
King Eric of Sweden was so impressed by his qualities that, after successfully
conquering the Finns, Eric made Henry bishop of Åbo (Turku), for 'Finland'
where he soon incurred martyrdom.[94] In the diocese of Uppsala, the feast
days of many English saints, most from before the Conquest, came to be
observed: the martyred kings Oswald, Edmund and Edward; the queen-
abbess Etheldreda; the hermit Guthlac, and the abbot Botulf, along with
several bishops, Cuthbert, Wilfrid, John of Beverley, Swithin, Dunstan,
Willibrord; Becket was the only late addition to this list.[95]

There is no evidence of Henry I having had any direct dealings with
Spain, but he cannot have been entirely ill-informed about it because his
personal physician, Peter Alfonsi, came from there. Moreover, after the
death of Alfonso VI of Castile (1065–1109), who had been a generous benefactor of the monks of Cluny, Henry took over his role as patron of the new
monastic buildings there. Alfonso had been respected outside Spain as a
great Christian warrior against the Muslims and many Normans had will-

ingly gone to Spain to help efforts for the recovery of former Christian lands. This probably explains why Bishop Diego of Compostela asked Archbishop Anselm if he could arrange for some more Norman soldiers (*milites*) to be sent out to Spain to fight the Saracens. Anselm had to reply that no troops could be spared because of troubles at home, but the invitation implies respect for the Norman military reputation from far away.[96] A few years later, *c*.1111, Diego was also reponsible for rescuing some Englishmen from enslavement as pirates when their ship was captured by the people of Galicia.[97] What they were actually doing in Galician waters is unknown, but Englishmen were certainly familiar figures there, if only as pilgrims to Compostela.

Henry's diplomatic connections with other rulers had one picturesque consequence: fellow monarchs had heard about his passion for collecting unusual wild animals and sent him presents for the royal menagerie.[98] This private zoo, kept at Woodstock, of lions, leopards, lynxes, camels and a porcupine sent from Montpellier, excited wonder and curiosity. Its origins were older than Henry himself. Rufus had already presented the count of Guines with a bear from Woodstock. The count put it to 'work' and its exploits were described in the count's family history. Unfortunately, no account of how the royal beasts were handled has been preserved, but the necessary framework must have functioned regularly because the royal animals were occasionally paraded in public. On a visit to Caen, probably in 1115, a monk from Fleury, Radulf Tortuaire, saw a young lion of six months and the king's leopard, lynx, camel and ostrich as they processed through the streets.[99] Henry I may have maintained a separate zoo in Normandy itself, but there was no reason in principle why the king's beasts should not have travelled with him and his household, as his falcons certainly did.

The ramifications of Henry's alliances may be contrasted with those of the other kings of the archipelago in his day. His brothers-in-law of Scotland, for example, had nothing comparable and most rulers of Wales and Ireland were not even linked to the Continent through their personal ties to Henry I. Only by taking service with Henry I did the Welsh prince, Owen, go to Normandy in 1115.[100] The heir to the Manx throne was raised at the court of Henry I. The foreign rulers of most importance to the peoples in the west of these islands were the Norwegian kings. On occasion, rulers from Man, the Hebrides and the Orkneys visited the Norwegian royal court in connection with the affairs of the islands of the archipelago.[101] They did not need to engage in political negotiation with many different interests as Henry I did in France. The Irish annals rarely extended their interest in events outside Ireland further than Wales, Scotland and England. Even these were usually limited to a record of the deaths of rulers; only on rare occasions did they note those of popes. Quite exceptionally, Irish annals reported the occurrence of an earthquake in the Alps in 1118, almost certainly an indication of an otherwise unrecorded Irish visit to Italy.[102]

The kings of England were far from planning to make themselves masters of all Britain, but Henry I, building on the recent successes of Rufus in the north, aimed to consolidate his hold on the northern part of his own kingdom. To do so, he found ways of keeping his brothers-in-law, the Scottish kings of his time, sweet. King Alexander was married to one of Henry's own illegitimate daughters and was sufficiently well disposed to join Henry I on campaign in Wales in 1114.[103] The youngest of Queen Matilda's sons, David, was married to the heiress of the earldom of Huntingdon in 1114 and remained respectful of Henry after he became king of Scots, ten years later. Through these personal relationships, the Scots were exposed to the same continental influences as the English, even if there was no formal 'Norman' conquest of Scotland. William of Malmesbury commented on the way David of Scotland as an English earl had become a speaker of French. Already as earl and later as king, David attracted Anglo-Norman lords into Scotland to help with the refashioning of the kingdom.[104] In this way, Scotland held a place of its own in the French feudal world. By providing the means for the regeneration of Scotland under David I's own direct rule, the Norman impact had the unexpected consequence of leaving the Scots to make their own independent contacts abroad.

The twelfth-century kingdom, much smaller than England, was a conglomerate comprising Scotland proper (between Forth and Moray) and Galloway, both then still Gaelic-speaking areas, along with Lothian. Moray even had its own line of kings until 1130. David's brother Edgar had accepted the claims of Magnus of Norway to the Shetlands, Orkneys and Hebrides and David himself was actually more interested in extending his royal authority into northern parts of England than further north into a purely 'Scottish' kingdom. After taking possession of Carlisle, he treated it, for a time, as his royal seat and his coins, the earliest to be struck in Scotland, were minted there.[105] The irresistible spread of the English language across the kingdom from its base in Lothian points to its cultural importance for the development of a united kingdom. The kingdom of Scotland was not created by a patriotic defence of Gaeldom from the 'Celtic' highlands, but achieved politically under rulers able to subordinate the culture and language of Picts and Scots to Anglo-Norman influences. The kings began to build up a new kind of regal authority, drawing on English experience.

The rivalry between the English and Scottish kings for control of northern England in the end led to a definition of the geographical border beyond which the rule of English kings would not operate. Disputes about the line of the frontier understandably troubled the loyalty of lords with lands in the contested zones. Locally, such disputes may have provoked bitterness, but it is a mistake to interpret this as evidence of racial prejudice. The peoples concerned were too similar; the confusions of lordship too great. English expressed hatred of the Scots only when the kings of Scotland unleashed soldiers from the remoter parts of their kingdom, like Galloway, as in accounts of the Battle of the Standard in 1138.[106] In warfare these men, unlike David's own contingent, seemed uncouth to the English. The king and his Lowland subjects were not seen as aliens, or indeed as anything but temporary enemies.

The shifting frontiers of Welshry and Englishry may also have created some local antipathies, but the shifts themselves demonstrate that there was still no hardened frontier spirit to intensify hostilities. Even the more persistent Norman conquests, mainly in south Wales, failed to crystallise national feeling, since the newcomers soon became part of the mixed settlement pattern. Welsh sources name the invaders as either French or English, calling attention to the fact that they did not speak Welsh; what 'nation' they might belong to did not matter. Likewise they precisely identified by language the groups of Flemings sent by Henry I to colonise parts of west Wales, where they appear to have retained their distinctive characteristics for centuries.[107]

The confusion of tongues and traditions in their lands may have made it more important for the several rival princely families to deal with local situations as best they could. The major princes of Powys, Deheubarth and Gwynedd vied with one another to achieve short-lived predominance. Within princely families competition between rivals brought endemic conflict. Fathers fought sons and brothers one another, more often at one another's throats than concerned about outsiders. The Welsh annalists who followed these disputes with such close attention were indifferent to more distant events. In these family disputes, the English/French might even be enlisted as allies, whereas real hatred was vented on family rivals, savagely mutilated in revenge and with the express intention of forestalling trouble in the next generation. This kind of behaviour in warfare has no parallel in England, either in the twelfth century or earlier.

Welsh experience of English manners of combat will also have served to alert them to military innovations: the earliest record of the Welsh building a castle comes under Gruffydd ap Cynan in 1116.[108] Warfare against the English obviously did not serve to instil a new spirit of Welsh nationalism. No confidence can be placed in the apparent evidence for it in poetry. Courtly Welsh poets, mainly in the north, wrote persuasively of the need for the Welsh to rally to their own prince in his stand against the invader, but the poetry was designed to exalt the prince not inspire the people. By praising particular princes, the poets even undermined any basis for promoting Welsh national unity.[109] Promoting respect for princes was the principal object of the *Life* of Gruffydd ap Cynan (who died in 1137) written about 1170, the only Welsh work of its kind. The author made a deliberate effort to present Gruffydd as a ruler aiming to 'modernise' Gwynedd by promoting settled agriculture and building fine churches, but emphasising Gruffydd's wish to draw inspiration from Irish rather than English models. Gruffydd himself was half-Irish Norse and lived in Ireland as an exile from a rival Welsh prince until he was able to return with an Irish force to recover his principality (1115).[110]

Ireland, like Wales, was ruled in the early twelfth century by a number of princes, called there 'kings'. Competition between rulers for recognition as high-king or overlord was keen, but no institutional continuity of office had been realised and the personal eminence of one high-king was rarely transmitted to his natural heir; it normally passed to a rival capable of challenging his power. Irish princes in the twelfth century were prepared to make use of any 'foreigners' willing to help them with their own brand of warfare, harrying other Irish rulers and rounding up great numbers of cattle as the principal spoils of war. Ireland was quite familiar with raiding expeditions from Man, Hebrides and Galloway and the Irish knew how to defend themselves. In matters they thought important, they kept abreast of such novelties as castle building. As early as 1124, Turlough of Connaught, the part of Ireland least touched by outside influences, already knew about building castles. Irish kings were not in awe or fear of foreign fighting men.[111] Such raiders created only temporary problems. When King Magnus of Norway set about reasserting Norse strength in the Irish Sea at the end of the eleventh century, he had achieved some success in Anglesey before venturing into Ireland where he made an alliance with the king of Munster in 1103. But in Ireland he was soon out of his depth and presented no serious threat to Irish interests. Yet the Norse presence had been reintroduced into the island which remained closely interested in Norse pretensions. Magnus had arranged for the marriage of his heir, Sigurd, to an Irish princess, but Sigurd abandoned his wife and returned to Norway before going east on crusade. This was not the end of Magnus's influence in Ireland, for he apparently procreated another son during his brief stay, who, as Harald Gilli, later succeeded in charming his way into making himself king of Norway for a short time.[112]

Political exiles had not found it difficult to interest Irishmen in supporting them. Even a Norman settler in south Wales, like Arnulf of Montgomery, had taken refuge in Ireland when his family fell out with Henry I. Murtagh may have taken up the cudgels on Arnulf's behalf. William of Malmesbury claimed that relations between Murtagh and Henry, normally excellent, had soured on one, unspecified, occasion. According to Malmesbury, Henry's threat to impose a ban on commerce had been sufficient to persuade Murtagh to climb down. Malmesbury believed Irish trade to be entirely in the hands of English and French inhabitants of the towns and that the native Irish were penniless and ignorant of agriculture. He clearly exaggerated, but had grasped an important difference between the two islands.[113] Previous contact between England and Ireland, like the links between Dublin and Canterbury from the late eleventh century and allusions to trade through Chester and Bristol, provides only glimpses of arrangements of obvious importance on both sides. Ireland could even be a source of luxury goods. High-quality vellum was acquired there by Master Hugo of Bury St Edmunds for painting miniatures in manuscripts.[114] Gilbert of Limerick modestly offered Anselm a gift of little pearls, which does not mean that they were not appreciated.[115] Trade must have been conducted in more basic goods than these. A version of the story of St Brendan was written for one of Henry I's queens, a small indication of the interest taken in Irish culture across the Irish Sea.[116] From the ecclesiastical point of view, Ireland may have seemed rather out of step with other parts of western Europe in the first half of the twelfth century, but in secular terms it was not conspicuously different and certainly not perceived as a likely victim of foreign conquerors.

The success of the crusaders in establishing themselves in the Holy Land is only the most conspicuous example of the way western Europeans began to assert themselves in the first half of the twelfth century. There was a conscious and deliberate break with tradition and a willingness to experiment with new ways of living the Christian life and a readiness to explore unfamiliar territory. The English entered willingly into the spirit of the new age. The Scots needed more coaxing under their kings, who were persuaded that they could best serve their own interests by taking charge themselves of political and cultural innovations. Elsewhere in these islands there was more reluctance to come to terms with the unfamiliar, but even the attempts to refurbish traditional positions are signs of recognition that adjustments to a new order of life in the Western Church could not be resisted. Because the impulses were moral and intellectual they had as powerful an effect on secular as on ecclesiastical affairs. What this meant for the British Isles became crystal clear in the second half of the twelfth century.

|4|

The Angevin Empire:
English influence on the
Continent at its zenith

From his earliest youth, Henry of Anjou became committed to gaining recognition of his claims to what he considered his mother's rights in Normandy and England. By the time Henry succeeded Stephen as king of England in October 1154, he was already duke of Normandy, and had succeeded his father as count of Anjou. By his marriage to Duchess Eleanor, mere weeks after her divorce from Louis VII, king of France, Henry had also become duke of Aquitaine. Within three years of his accession in England, he had recovered lands in the north seized some years before by the king of Scots. In 1159 he tried, this time unsuccessfully, to secure recognition of his lordship from the count of Toulouse, but in 1161 at least regained the Norman Vexin (which Louis VII had obtained in 1144 from Henry's father) as the dowry of Louis's daughter for her marriage to Henry's own infant son. With the marriage of Henry's third surviving son, Geoffrey, to the infant heiress of Brittany in 1166, that territory too became, in effect, another piece in the Angevin conglomerate. In the course of his reign, Henry secured recognition in Ireland of his lordship (1172) and took the homage of the king of Scots and numerous Scots lords (1174). This assembly of lands is commonly referred to by historians as the Angevin empire.[1] Between 1154 and 1204 the Plantagenet kings were lords of more lands and peoples abroad than in England. Understandably, they spent more time out of their kingdom than in it. The significance of all this for the histories of both England and the Continent has not been disregarded, but in England a narrow concern for domestic issues under Henry II and his sons has tended to hamper assessment of the Angevin empire. For many writers, the shackling of England to the duchy of Normandy by the Norman kings seemed bad enough; to extend royal responsibilities to the Bay of Biscay represented sheer folly.

Henry did not rule abroad as English king; his was no English empire. Without England, Henry as master of Anjou already dominated western France, from the Channel to the Pyrenees. Angevin predominance in the

French kingdom goaded kings of France into doing all they could to thwart Henry's activities. After 1170, Louis VII was able to fan the resentment of Henry's sons at the insignificant role they enjoyed in their father's scheme of government. Louis's son, Philip II, proved an even more resourceful opponent. Yet John's total loss of Normandy and Anjou in 1204 was more obviously a consequence of his own mistakes than of Philip's cleverness or the inevitability of French victory.

The ability of the Angevin 'Empire' to survive for so long at least proves that it was no political monstrosity. As a truly French empire centred on the Loire, it offered a means of linking together the provinces of west France without compromising their autonomy. Although it was not legitimised there in terms of a royal title, Henry, as king of England, enjoyed the respect accorded royalty. There was no more idea of 'Anglicising' Henry's French lands than of considering England itself as a French colony, though England was culturally as 'French' as Aquitaine. On neither side of the Channel was 'foreignness' an issue. This alone has been sufficient to discourage English interest in the empire's problems and compromise understanding of its achievements.

The Angevin Empire, now seen as an anomaly of many diverse dominions, was not a unique aberration in the twelfth century. In the Europe of Henry II's day, supreme political authority was wielded by a handful of great princes who all presided over comparable conglomerations. In their company Henry II himself enjoyed a pre-eminent reputation. The great princes strove to maintain peaceful relations between themselves and resolve disagreements by occasional meetings, frequent exchanges of messengers, regular negotiations and proposals for promoting mutual amity by marriage alliances. Henry's oldest daughter, Matilda, was married to Henry, duke of Saxony, the most powerful figure in Germany after the emperor Frederick I (1168); only the early death of one of Frederick's own sons forestalled his marriage to the next daughter Eleanor.[2] Instead, she married Alfonso VIII, king of Castile (1170). The youngest, Joanna, married William II, king of Sicily (1177), reinforcing a link with the Normans in the south forged in the mid-eleventh century. Henry also negotiated marriages for his princely friends, obtaining a bride from Portugal for his pensioner Count Philip of Flanders (1183) and for King William of Scotland from his own kin (1184).[3] Even the Greek emperor claimed kinship, for his wife was a cousin of Eleanor of Aquitaine. Henry's contacts stretched from one end of Europe to another. His subjects were caught up in his schemes whether they realised it or not. They could endure the consequences or take advantage of the opportunities opened up to them.

The European family of kings was united in recognising the moral authority of the Roman Church. Though the most remembered problem of Henry II's reign is his dispute with Archbishop Becket, there was never any danger that it would provoke rejection of papal jurisdiction in his kingdom. At the beginning of the reign an Englishman, Nicholas Breakspear, was elected to rule the Latin Church as Pope Hadrian IV. After his death in 1159 a disputed election created uncertainty about who should be recognised as lawful pope. Significantly, Henry II and Louis VII of France threw their joint weight behind Alexander III against the pope championed by the emperor Frederick I. For eighteen years Frederick persisted in his intransigence, but at last he accepted that he had failed to convince his fellow rulers of his right to set up antipopes of his own. At Venice, Frederick acknowledged Alexander (1177), as other kings had long since done. With the emperor back in the fold, the pope was able to assert his own spiritual sovereignty over all earthly authorities by summoning a Church council to the Lateran palace in 1179, attended by an impressive number of bishops. The British Isles were well represented: Canterbury, Bath, Hereford, Norwich and Durham from England; St David's and St Asaph from Wales; the Scottish bishop of Ross; the Irish archbishops of Dublin and Tuam with four bishops from the province of Cashel.

Such an international meeting of clergy had no secular parallel, but lay princes did not begrudge the Church its assembly. They acknowledged the limits of their own powers to dictate in ecclesiastical matters. Their own conflicting interests forced them to appreciate what the papacy could do to reconcile their differences. Because they relied on the regular intermarriage of their families to effect lasting alliances, they became ever more dependent on popes granting the necessary licence to marry within the prohibited degrees. Secular princes also found willing agents of their domestic administrations among the clergy, whose services they rewarded by grants of bishoprics. None of this compromised the ability of secular princes to enlarge the scope of their activities in other ways. They aimed to provide for the stability of their far-flung dominions by traditional means, that is by warfare and the provision of landed estates or revenues for favoured vassals.

As king of England, Henry II excited much wonder, if not admiration, in his own time. From the first, he was active, determined and quick to exploit his opportunities, but his rule was shaped by an (unwise) reliance on the strength of family feeling, most pathetically revealed by his concern for his youngest son, John. According to the chronicler of Laon, the eastern emperor offered to set John up in his empire by marriage to a Comneni princess. Henry rejected this handsome proposal on the grounds that John, so far away, would be unable to offer his brothers any assistance in their difficulties.[4] The idea that the empire could be held together by family sentiment exposes the simplicity of Henry's political ideas. Having rejected an alliance with the Comneni, Henry willingly considered a marriage for John with a princess of Savoy. This provoked suspicions that he hoped to make Savoy a base for dominating the affairs of both Lombardy and Burgundy. Any such ambitions would have tested even Henry's stamina. It made good sense all the same to find friends in the Alpine region. Savoy was not a remote Alpine land of no importance to England. Very early in Henry II's reign, probably in connection with an embassy to Frederick Barbarossa, the king's men had become familiar with the valuable services provided by the hospice of St Bernard. To show his appreciation, Henry II endowed it with two estates in England which supported a priory at Hornchurch, east of London, a valuable listening post on movements in and out of Italy. Further proof of movement between England and Savoy at this time is provided by the small collection of English and Savoyard coins discovered some years ago on the St Bernard pass, lost presumably by some unlucky traveller.[5]

Given his resources and ability, Henry might have become even more domineering, but he retained some sense of what was possible. He persevered in treating his overlord in France, the king, with formal respect. As count of Anjou, he was proud of his right to the title of royal dapifer. At Philip II's coronation in 1179, his sons vied with one another as to which of them should discharge the dapifer's ceremonial functions.[6] Henry himself gave the young Philip advice on how to govern, though Philip learned most from watching Henry's disputes with his own headstrong sons.[7] Henry's commitment to his royal duties impressed contemporary writers and his affairs were closely followed on the Continent, and not only in his own lands. In the province of Reims, the chronicler at Laon, apparently an Englishman, kept himself well informed about English events. Reims itself was not out of touch with England: Ralph de Serra, an English pupil of Becket's, became dean of the cathedral there. Often engaged by the papacy as judge-delegate, he acquired legal experiences which made him useful to the monks of Canterbury and their professional relationship was sealed by a gift of his books to the monastery and commemoration in the monastic necrology.[8]

The entanglements that resulted from extended foreign interests and the king's frequent absences provoked no domestic discontent, but could threaten trouble for the kingdom. One aborted invasion was planned by Matthew, count of Boulogne, brother of Philip of Flanders, who amassed a fleet of 600 ships in 1167 for this purpose.[9] Henry II's most serious setback came in 1173–4 when his sons, instigated by Louis VII of France, broke into open revolt. In England the rebellion received no popular support. Such difficulties as arose were fuelled from outside the kingdom. Earl Bigod brought a force from Brabant and Flanders to attack his local enemies in East Anglia, assaulting Cambridge and the abbey at Bury St Edmunds. A more serious danger was presented by William, king of Scots, who invaded Northumberland. After his defeat and capture at Alnwick, the main disturbances in England subsided. William was Henry II's cousin and family connections played their part in bringing him into the rebellion of 1173–74. He was also personally concerned to recover the earldom of Northumberland which he had briefly enjoyed before his older brother, Malcolm IV, had ceded it back to Henry.[10] That the Scots had been drawn into political contact with the Continent is a notable feature of this episode. For this development, Henry II was himself principally responsible.

Relations between the English and Scottish kings had hitherto been of mainly domestic interest. Since the time of David I, the kings of Scots had held lands in England and on that account did homage for them anyway. Acknowledging Henry II as his overlord, the young king, Malcolm IV, had joined Henry on his campaign against Toulouse in 1159 and received knighthood in a ceremony at Poitiers from Henry himself. Malcolm's brother, William, had also participated in this campaign and shortly after he became king in 1165 went again to France to take part in a tournament.[11] A quarrel with Henry II there prompted him to offer his friendship to Louis VII of France, showing that even before the rebellion of 1173 he saw the potential value of his own alliance to Henry's enemies. The policy of later Scottish kings in seeking alliance with the kings of France against the kings of England can be discerned in embryo.

The king of Scots was a minor, if not negligible, figure in the continental affairs of his day. Both Malcolm IV and William, sons of Ada of Warenne, were French speakers from infancy and moved naturally in the same cultural environment as Henry II himself. Malcolm arranged for the marriages abroad of both his sisters, Margaret in 1160 to Conan, duke of Brittany and Ada in 1162 to Florent, count of Holland. Counts of Holland had not previously married outside the empire and Florent courteously sent the abbot of Egmond to fetch his bride.[12] Commercial contacts are not known to have been significant and the most likely explanation for the meeting was Barbarossa's hopes of drawing Malcolm onto his side in the matter of the papal schism. King William himself, after a rakish youth and middle age, married only in 1184. At first he too looked to the empire for a bride. When the pope forbade a match with a Welf kinswoman, Henry II arranged for William to marry another of his relations, Ermengarde of Beaumont. The prospect of an alliance with the Welfs was revived when William's daughter Margaret, then his heir presumptive, was sought as a bride for Otto of Brunswick, Richard I's favourite nephew. This proposal so alarmed Philip II of France that as soon as William's son and heir, Alexander, was born in 1201 Philip offered him one of his own daughters as a wife.[13] The Scottish royal family had been accepted into the fold. Thanks to their contacts with Henry II, both Malcolm IV and William made their own connections with the Continent and helped foster Scottish assimilation of French culture. Jordan Fantosme believed King William favoured foreign-born men above native Scottish lords.[14] An early thirteenth-century English chronicler writing of disturbances in the Scottish kingdom went further still, asserting that the kings were effectively French in speech, habit and customs, and aimed to reduce the restless Scots population to obedience.[15] There was some justification for this extravagant claim. In Galloway and in the far north, Scottish kings were confronted by local chieftains who were effectively independent and uninterested in adapting to the new 'French' fashions of the Scottish kingship.[16] After William had failed to recover lands in Northumbria, he had little alternative but to deploy his military resources in the outlying parts of 'Scotland'. His victory over forces from Caithness and Orkney was celebrated in a Latin poem, written in the style of Matthew of Vendôme, and so provides further evidence of Scottish cultural links with France. Scottish military campaigns were now as worthy of cultivated poetic attention as those of other western princes.[17]

In Wales, Henry II's attempts to recover the ground lost to native Welsh princes in the disturbances of Stephen's reign were thwarted. The princes made enough show of force to deflect Henry from this purpose and in return for acknowledging Henry's formal position as overlord were accordingly left to manage their own territories by themselves.[18] Whatever satisfaction this gave at home, it sent the wrong signals abroad: the Welsh were treated there as subjects of the king of England. To the pope, Gerald of Wales acknowledged that since Wales was not a kingdom, it was a 'portion' of England.[19] Wales already operated in an environment dominated by those who regarded Henry II and his sons as the real masters of their destiny.

Although no Welsh princes became as familiar with continental Europe as the kings of Scotland, Wales itself was sensitive to the fortunes of the Angevin Empire. Henry II's domestic affairs could not fail to interest the Welsh. When Becket was driven into exile, Owen, prince of Gwynedd, entered into a correspondence with him about how his new bishop of Bangor might be consecrated without disparagement of Canterbury's rights. Owen may have found a useful go-between in a Welsh clerk, Llewelyn, known in England as Alexander, a cheerful member of Becket's household who became archdeacon of Bangor.[20] Owen also wrote to Becket's patron, Louis VII, in 1165, seeking an alliance, reckoning that his military confrontations with the English would be appreciated by Henry's enemies abroad. The French royal chancellor, Hugh de Champfleury, duly reassured Owen about this, but when Owen tried to get Louis VII to put military pressure on Henry II in order to get some relief for himself in Wales, Louis proved not much of an asset as a military ally.[21] Gerald stated flatly that the lack of foreign friends was a serious weakness of the Welsh in their confrontations with the English. In the rebellion of Henry II's sons in 1173, Rhys, prince of Deheubarth, prudently sent his son Hoel with a body of troops overseas, as a token of his duty to the king.[22] Unlike William of Scotland, Rhys nursed no illusions about turning the rebellion to his own advantage.

The French altogether failed to appreciate Welsh military potential: William Marshal, earl of Pembroke, recalled that the French found it ridiculous for Henry II to employ Welsh soldiers.[23] Henry II, who also employed mercenaries from the Low Countries, took a different view. Like other mountain peoples, the Welsh acquired a fearsome reputation as light-footed soldiers, particularly as archers. According to Gerald of Wales, Henry II boasted about Welsh prowess to the eastern emperor at Constantinople.[24] English rulers could not do without them. In the 1190s, both John as count of Mortain and his enemy, the royal chancellor William Longchamps, bishop of Ely, mustered sizeable numbers of Welshmen to confront one another, 'spear to spear'. (Gerald says that lances were the favourite weapon of men from Merioneth.[25]) Very early in the next century, John arranged for a body of Welsh infantry and equestrian archers to take service with Sverre, king of Norway. Welsh soldiers saw more of the world than their own princes did.[26]

Henry also became personally responsible for drawing Ireland into closer contact with the Continent. The English pope, Hadrian IV, had granted Henry II lordship of Ireland in 1155 but Henry did nothing to make good this claim. Ten years later, when the high-king, Rory of Connaught, drove Dermot MacMurrough, king of Leinster, out of his kingdom, Dermot went to Poitou and appealed to Henry II for help. Henry authorised Dermot to recruit forces in England but took no immediate steps to interfere in Ireland himself. Although Dermot tried to secure Welsh support, no Welsh princes were persuaded to invade Ireland on his behalf, though as a gesture Rhys of Deheubarth released one of his prisoners, Robert FitzStephen, so that he could participate in the campaign.[27] The English earl Richard Strongbow of Clare was only drawn into Dermot's schemes on the understanding that by marrying Dermot's daughter, Eva, he would be entitled to succeed Dermot as king in Leinster, a proposition acceptable in English feudal law but contrary to Irish practice. Strongbow did, however, have the troops and brought both Welsh and Flemings from Pembrokeshire into Ireland.

In the past the Irish had frequently joined in Welsh disputes; now it was the turn of lords from Wales to cross the Irish Sea. The whole venture rapidly turned into a serious movement for the conquest, not just of Leinster, but of other parts of Ireland too. The situation became very disturbed and the high-king, Rory O'Connor, showed no ability to master events. When he tried to buy off Strongbow's claims on Leinster in return for the surrender of the port towns Dublin, Wexford and Waterford, he showed he did not appreciate what advantage they offered as points of entry for potential enemies.[28] They were simply not 'Irish' enough to bother about. By 1171 both Dermot's auxiliaries and his enemies were desperate for a settlement and called on Henry II to intervene. Because of Becket's recent murder, Henry was glad of the chance to get out of England until tempers cooled. Without needing to take any military action himself, Henry secured recognition of his lordship from his own invading vassals and from several minor Irish 'kings' themselves. The willingness of enough Irish lords to accept Henry's power, if only for their own purposes, brought Ireland willy-nilly into the orbit of the Angevin Empire.[29]

The attitude of most Irish prelates was even more submissive. At the time of Strongbow's arrival in Ireland, Christian, bishop of Lismore and former abbot of Mellifont, was acting as resident papal legate. He had earlier enjoyed some support from the kings of Leinster and Munster, but the new high-king, Rory O'Connor, was indifferent to the papal reform programme. Undeterred by papal censure of Henry for his part in Becket's murder, Christian assembled Irish bishops at Cashel who promptly recognised

Henry's lordship without being coerced.[30] Within months of Henry's return, Alexander III approved of the submission Irish bishops had already made. Henry II's Irish lordship at last drew Ireland into full contact with the rest of the Western Church. The auguries could not have been more propitious. Gerald of Wales actually refers to the single monarchy that Henry II had established by his strength over the whole island of Britain within the sea.[31] Henry II did not really unite the British Isles, but the Scots, Welsh and Irish had all accepted that his power and his contacts made it impossible for them to disregard his intentions. England's own links with the continent brought its neighbours into direct contact with affairs overseas.

The clergy and the development of institutional learning

Modern narratives which put secular affairs at the heart of their accounts misrepresent one aspect of twelfth-century reality. The best-known name of any twelfth-century Englishman throughout Europe was Thomas Becket. He owed his own far-flung reputation for sanctity to the fact that Henry II had made what happened in England of general concern. Becket himself campaigned against Henry on the grounds that the king, by aiming to enforce outdated and local custom, scorned the universally recognised laws of the Church. The quarrel, which engaged the energies not only of Englishmen but of the papal Curia and the king of France, had an international dimension from the first. Three further strands may be discerned in any account of Becket's continental relations. In the first place, his own travels, both while chancellor, as Henry's representative, and later as archbishop in exile, alongside the influential people he met or corresponded with, gave him personally a high profile in the continental society he frequented. Herbert of Bosham listed among the distinguished men he attracted to his circle a number of Italians, or Lombards, some of whom later became eminent, like Lombard of Piacenza, archbishop of Benevento, and Humbert of Milan, later Pope Urban III.[32] Such Italians gave Becket a better idea of the local conditions influencing papal policy. Though Becket would not go to Rome and prefered to remain nearer England among French friends, he had met the pope and several cardinals while Alexander III had been in French exile. Becket knew some cardinals well enough to write to them in a personal way. He sought to keep well informed about all contemporary affairs with any likely bearing on his quarrel with the king. He was aware of the relevance to his quarrel not only of the pope and the king of France, but also of the activities of the German emperor, Frederick Barbarossa, and of the strange customs found in the churches of Hungary and Sicily which might be regarded as precedents for tolerating the equally idiosyncratic practices of the English Church.

Second, after his murder in December 1170 the shocking details of his death at the hands of Henry II's henchmen were widely reported all over Europe. They were commemorated in histories, verse and saga. The notion that he had died for the Church as a whole in defiance of royal tyranny appealed particularly to the clergy, who did their best to promote the cult.[33] Within months, stories of the miracles worked by the sainted martyr drew pilgrims to his shrine at Canterbury, sometimes from considerable distances.[34] Before 1173 William of Canterbury had noted the arrival of a merchant from Brindisi and a young man from Genoa. The explanation for Becket's posthumous reputation may seem difficult to credit in modern terms, but there are recent examples of how hysterically the general public can react to violent death. Within a few years he was believed to have worked miracles not only in England and Scotland, but in Denmark, the Low Countries, Normandy, Auvergne, Périgord and, via Aosta, as far as southern Italy. The bishop of Evreux told a story about a rich Saracen of Palermo who was converted to Christianity when vouchsafed a vision of Becket. Becket's miracles incidentally cast some light on the foreign travels of Englishmen. Unfortunately hagiographers did not explain what had induced Wimarga of Luton to go on a pilgrimage to St Gilles in Provence, why William of Monkton in Thanet was on his way to Rome, or what Robert and William were doing at sea off the Brittany coast. When a young man, George, left Sandwich for foreign parts, his reasons for doing so are not given. Robert of Cricklade called on Becket while walking from Catania to Syracuse; but why was he in Sicily at all? Ivo of Lynn was on his way to Norway; it is only supposition that he was a merchant. In the north Becket's cause had considerable resonance at a time when Archbishop Eystein had quarrelled with the king of Norway. In Iceland too Becket became a popular saint. Several independent versions of his saga were composed in the vernacular.[35]

Arising out of this respect for Becket's sanctity, a third strand of importance for the present purpose may be distinguished: representations of the martyr were soon found all over Europe, the earliest in mosaic at Monreale, foundation of Henry II's son-in-law, King William II of Sicily. Henry's daughter Eleanor, who became queen of Castile, introduced the cult into Spain, but cannot have been responsible directly for promoting his reputation in Catalonia, where dramatic scenes of Becket's murder were painted on the walls of the church at Tarrassa *c.*1180. In the thirteenth century, the enamel workshops of Limoges produced more caskets for the custody of Becket relics than for any other saint.[36]

Quite apart from the flood of pilgrims who descended on Canterbury, Becket's reputation for sanctity had international repercussions for the church of Canterbury itself. Becket's own exile and his posthumous reputation set up unprecedentedly intense relations between Canterbury and northern France. The king of France, Louis VII, came in person to pray at Becket's tomb in 1179 and made a gift of French wine to be delivered annually to the monks; the gift was enhanced by his son Philip II in the next century. After Philip II's death, Canterbury's links with the French court were reaffirmed as late as 1232, when the monks assured the regent Queen Blanche (daughter of King John's sister Eleanor of Castile) that she was remembered in their prayers.[37] Becket's sojourn in exile at the Cistercian house of Pontigny forged another link with Canterbury. One of the lives of Becket was written by a monk of Pontigny and another was written by a wandering jongleur, Guernes of Pont Saint Maixent (near Senlis) who had once met Becket. Guernes actually came to England to do research for his verse life.[38] When Archbishop Edmund of Abingdon went into exile in 1238, he too took refuge at Pontigny where his reputation as a saint was also fostered after his death in 1240. These connections in northern France help to explain how it was that when it became necessary to rebuild the cathedral after the fire of 1174, the monks of Canterbury came to engage the master builder, William of Sens, to provide as modern and magnificent an edifice as the times would allow.[39] The chronicler Gervase described the building operation with exceptional care and pride. Canterbury had much to celebrate.

The monks at Canterbury felt sufficiently confident thereafter to browbeat the papal Curia into blocking the attempts of Archbishops Baldwin and Hubert Walter to set up a house of canons either at Hackingbridge or Lambeth, feared by the monks as potential rivals. The monks knew how to make the most of the saintly relics in their midst. Becket's standing helped them to see off his successors' plans for 'modernising' the Church's administration. They invoked the intercession of their friends and patrons, including the king and queen of France, numerous bishops and cardinals. They sent frequent envoys to the Curia where they maintained several monks at a time. (When five monks and the prior died of the pestilence in 1188, others were still there to carry on the mission.) The agents reported on the events at the Curia, the characters of the popes on whom their hopes rested, the exorbitant costs of diplomacy and the hardships of travel. One monk wrote doggedly in mid-February from the Alps to explain why local conditions had not made it possible for him to send a letter from the Great Saint Bernard pass. Nobody could doubt the monks' commitment and competence to defeat their own archbishop. They had European friends and experiences all their own.[40]

In many respects Becket's martyrdom did not alter the nature of relations between the English Church and the papacy: Becket's exile had already released a cascade of letters between the two. Its most important after-effect was to quicken the pace of English interest in the collection and assimilation of papal decretals. In this way English jurists came to share in the labour of preparing for the codification of canon law in the next century.[41] An English Master Richard wrote a treatise on procedure at canon law much esteemed by more famous canonists of the day.[42] Bologna had become the centre for such legal work; the university there already attracted students from all over the west. Jocelin, a scion of the Bohun family, later bishop of Salisbury, had been an early student at Bologna where his son, later Bishop Reginald of Bath, was probably born and certainly studied. His nickname in England was 'the Italian', or 'the Lombard'.[43] He became a figure of international reputation and his connections abroad probably explain how he came to be charged with responsibility for a campaign to refute the heretics of southern France; parts of Henry II's empire were themselves affected. Reginald was also sent on missions where tact was required, as when he successfully negotiated at the Grande Chartreuse for the appointment of Hugh of Avalon as prior of Henry II's foundation of Witham.[44] Reginald's cousin (and successor at Bath), Bishop Savary, was equally cosmopolitan. Savary was also cousin to the emperor Henry VI who made him his chancellor for imperial Burgundy.[45]

Numerous other Englishmen achieved distinction of various kinds abroad. John of Canterbury, who ended a remarkable career as archbishop of Lyon, enjoyed an enviable reputation as scholar, politician and holy man. When Henry II's daughter was taken to Spain for her marriage in 1170, John, as bishop of Poitiers, was the only Englishman among the grandees from Aquitaine to accompany her.[46] Richard, bishop of Syracuse, then archbishop of Messina, who had studied in France, became a leading member of the junta in the Sicily of Henry II's son-in-law William II.[47] John of Salisbury became bishop of Chartres, being denied promotion in England because Henry II found him personally unacceptable. King Waldemar of Denmark made his English chancellor, Ralph, bishop of Ribe.[48] King Sverre of Norway promoted Martin, his English chaplain, to be bishop of Bergen.[49] How Milo II, *patria anglus*, became bishop of Thérouanne is not known but when Becket went into exile Milo escorted him to the papal court and corresponded with John of Salisbury.[50] If traditional English connections in the north of France made it possible for Milo to obtain episcopal office there, it is more difficult to understand how the Cistercian Englishman, Isaac, became abbot at L'Etoile in Poitou. Nothing is known of his personal life apart from his friendly relations with Becket's circle, but his copious and learned writings were accorded great respect in the Cistercian order.[51] Gervase of Tilbury, who served several different patrons, most likely had his own anecdotal writing to thank for his final appointment as historiographer to the German emperor Otto IV, Henry II's grandson.[52]

Comparably productive, but less successful, was Ralph Niger who had studied theology and law in Paris, served both Henry II, until Becket's murder, and then his son, the young king, but obtained no ecclesiastical preferment.[53] This left him with the leisure to write a number of works, 'de re militari', a commentary on the Book of Kings and two chronicles. Perhaps with vain hopes of ecclesiastical advancement, he submitted all these works for the approval and attention of powerful men in the Church, Archbishop Conrad of Salzburg (whom he had known in connection with Becket), Bishop Maurice of Paris, Archbishop William of Reims, uncle of King Philip

II, Pope Clement III himself and various cardinals. His chronicles are exceptionally well informed about Danish affairs, probably on account of Niger's contacts with Danish students in Paris and with German clergy. After his belated return to England, he became a canon of Lincoln and acquired a house in London. Although he was entrusted with no special responsibilities in old age, his broad knowledge of contemporary men and their affairs could have made him well worth listening to.

In fact, it was not only the most prominent clergy who knew their way about abroad. A curious example of how even a mere scribe might travel is provided by the case of Mainer of Canterbury, who copied a handsome three-volume Bible in France about 1175, possibly for St Lupus, Troyes. Although the Bible was beautifully illustrated, Mainer may have been responsible only for the script. At the end, he gave his name and an account of his family, explaining in Latin the meanings of the English names of his father, Wimund, and his mother, Liveva, who lived for more than eighty years. He also knew the names of his (paternal?) grandparents. In his own generation, his brothers and sister had been given the more fashionable names: Ralph, Robert, Gerald, John and Dionisia. Even abroad this professional scribe did not forget his English family. Other French churches took advantage of English facilities for building up their libraries. The canons of the Norman house of Ste-Barbe-en-Auge had manuscripts copied in their English dependency and even the distinguished house of St Victor in Paris acquired manuscripts written in England, perhaps in its own English priories. The English had a reputation abroad for illuminated manuscripts even before the Norman Conquest, though it may have faded somewhat as the Normans began to assert their own influence on the writing of English books. After 1120, however, the illumination of manuscripts in England entered a new phase. Bibles and psalters were provided with highly elaborate initials and in many instances with full-page decorations. The use of psalters in devotion appears to have encouraged the practice of providing them with full-page illustrations not of the Psalms but of stories from the Bible, summarising in pictorial form the history of salvation from the Creation to the Last Judgement. This device will have helped the devout to relate the meaning of the Psalms to the Christian dispensation. This type of decorated psalter was not produced on the Continent until quite late in the twelfth century and certainly then only as a result of English example. At what point English psalters became known abroad and by whose agency is not demonstrable. Could the popularity of the Becket cult have been a factor? Becket's exile in France and that of Henry the Lion in England a little later both had the unlooked-for effect of reinforcing cultural ties across the sea. That the psalters were highly prized when first introduced is clear. One made for Archbishop Geoffrey Plantagenet (1189–1212) was used soon after his death by Blanche of Castile to teach her son, the young St Louis of France, how to read. A luxurious example intended for the French queen, Ingeborg of Denmark, and another said to have belonged to Blanche of

Castile herself both incorporated the names of many English saints in their liturgical calendars and owe much to the style of English art, even if they were not illuminated by English artists. There is no reason indeed why, like the scribe Mainer of Canterbury, English illuminators should not also have worked on the Continent.[54]

Information about English commoners who travelled or settled abroad is sparse, but experience of foreign lands was not confined to a few exceptional people. Quite humble clergy took petitions to Rome. A few English crusaders unable to get beyond Italy claimed to have obtained papal letters of excuse allowing them to return to England before completing their journey.[55] Only because he acquired a reputation for sanctity after his death c.1192 do we know of an English priest called William who ministered at Pontoise.[56] Even more perplexing is the story of a certain Mathildis. A brief notice about her appears in the Prémontré chronicle because she had become an object of local curiosity at Lapion in the diocese of Laon. She had embraced a life of voluntary poverty and spoke little to her neighbours who found her speech difficult to understand. For some reason she was fancifully supposed to be a 'Scot', even the daughter of the king of Scotland. The chronicler was sufficiently intrigued to meet her. She told him that she was actually from Romney in Kent, but not why or how she had taken up a holy life alone so far from home.[57] Possibly she had begun a pilgrimage and simply abandoned her original intention. The humble may be numerous and historically inconspicuous, but on occasion prove quite astonishing.

The interests of the English clergy abroad took them chiefly to Italy and France in this period. In Italy, their chief anxiety was often how to get the cash needed for their affairs. English clergy at the papal Curia had recourse to local merchants for paying immediate debts. Peter of Blois refers to the willingness of Flemish and Roman merchants in Rome itself to lend money to needy Englishmen.[58] By 1177, the monks of Malmesbury were so indebted to Italian merchants that the pope ordered an investigation.[59] The monks of Canterbury borrowed what they needed in Bologna. Witnesses to a debt of a mere £10 contracted there by the chancellor of Canterbury were spared the expense of testifying before the civic authorities in Bologna when Pope Lucius III mandated the archbishop to examine them himself.[60] The rapacity of the Bolognese moneylenders disgusted Gerald of Wales. Needy foreigners were cornered into borrowing from them at exorbitant rates because in Italy the cost of borrowing urgently needed money was much greater than in Troyes, at the heart of the Champagne fairs, where terms were more competitive.[61]

Gerald went to Rome three times in the hope of securing greater autonomy from Canterbury for the see of St David's.[62] He was a candidate for the see himself. Although he made out that he was denied the appointment for fear he would use his office as a platform for advancing the cause of Welsh nationalism, he admitted that his ambitions were thwarted more by infighting among the Welsh clergy than by the venality of the Curia or the malevolence of Canterbury. Gerald's writings allow many twists of this tale to be followed in some detail. His cheerful self-confidence may have amused more than it impressed his superiors. According to him, he enjoyed intimate conversations with Innocent III, to whom he offered copies of his own works. He claimed the pope kept the *Gemma Ecclesiastica* on his bedside table and lent other works to his cardinals. Gerald comments himself on his relations with different members of the Curia. He made a fourth visit to Rome when he was well over sixty and had no qualms about becoming a brother of the Hospital of the Holy Spirit, the English School, in order to augment his allowance of indulgences. Gerald obviously did not find any Welsh community in Rome but Welsh laymen certainly visited the city: Cadell, son of Gruffudd ap Rhys, is recorded to have gone to Rome on pilgrimage in 1153.[63]

Lists of the attractions of the city, its gates and churches occur in several twelfth-century manuscripts, two of them written in Wales. Practical problems about making ends meet in Rome no more diverted visitors from appreciating its marvels then than they do now. The dilatory procedures of the Roman Curia may have given those obliged to hang about in the city greater opportunities to spend their leisure more instructively visiting the vestiges of antiquity at their feet. Henry, bishop of Winchester, who brought ancient statues back to England in mid-century, is the earliest known English collector of antiquities in Italy, but it is unlikely that he was the only connoisseur. John of Salisbury, one of the best educated Englishmen of the day, admittedly mocked Henry's interest in pagan sculpture but twelfth-century popes themselves took great interest in the antiquities of the holy city and this alone would have encouraged others to do likewise.[64] They were also made aware of new building in Rome. In March 1197, Bishop Savary, then in Rome, attended Celestine III's consecration of the church of San Lorenzo in Lucina.[65] For the benefit of such travellers, an elaborate guidebook to the holy city was composed, probably by an Englishman, Magister Gregorius.[66] Gregory's work differs from others of its type by the interest he took in describing the pagan as well as the Christian monuments of the city, and the scorn he poured on the more credulous anecdotes touted by local guides. Gregory's preferred authorities were the cardinals themselves. Some of these features of his guide are characteristic of contemporary English historical writing and seem designed to meet the expectations of English readers and their interest in the past.

Rome was not the only place on the twelfth-century grand tour. Gervase of Tilbury relates stories about the monuments of Naples which had Virgilian associations of great significance to men of education.[67] The natural wonders of Italy were reported by the English chronicler Roger of Hoveden. As a government official, Hoveden was much intrigued by the peculiar form of the Sicilian king's seal and drew a picture of it in his work. Ralph Niger also remarked on this.[68] The attractions of the southern Norman kingdom for English visitors have been a matter of comment from the twelfth century to the present.[69]

Some of the difficulties of journeys to Italy were alleviated by the availability of hospices, like the one dedicated to St Brigid which was established for 'Scoti' at Vercelli, an important staging post for northern travellers. The hospice statutes promulgated by the local bishop in 1180 asserted that the original foundation had been made some forty years back by Bonifacio, treasurer of the cathedral, but provided no explanation for his interest in the Irish. Cardinal Guala Bicchieri who returned to his native Vercelli after his legatine mission in England issued fresh regulations for the hospice in 1224. Guala's interest in the British Isles had been reinforced by the gift of a church in Cambridgeshire to his own Austin foundation at Vercelli.[70] This set up regular communication between the Italian town and England. Evidence for contact with the 'Scoti' is sparse, but relations between Vercelli and Ireland were still maintained in the early fourteenth century, by which time wars in Italy had depleted the hospice's own resources. It sent a plea to Scotland and Ireland for financial help in providing for the multitude of pilgrims from those lands. The recent papal jubilee may have temporarily augmented the number of such travellers.

Because there is little direct evidence for Irishmen travelling regularly to Italy, this does not mean they did not do so. Gerald of Wales remembered a 'good' Irish bishop who, for two years, was constantly travelling to and from Rome and passing through St David's, often being obliged to wait for a favourable wind at the church's harbour.[71] Gerald had forgotten his name and took no interest in what business took him to Rome. Typically, his importance for Gerald was that he had approved Gerald's own claims to the see of St David's. Several Irish bishops attended Alexander III's Lateran Council in 1179. That 'Scots' were familiar figures in Italy and easily recognisable is the basic assumption of Jocelin of Brakelond's story of how his abbot, Samson, while still young, had been in Italy when the papal schism broke out in 1159. In order to elude imperial supporters on the lookout for adherents of Alexander III, Samson had taken to dressing like a 'Scot', that is slinging his boots about his neck (to save shoe leather, a familiar jibe about Scottish parsimony).[72]

Despite the importance of Italy for twelfth-century students, a far greater number went to northern France and felt more at home there than they ever could beyond the Alps. Students from all over Christendom flocked to the great schools. There was no problem about language. Instruction was given in Latin, familiar throughout the Western Church. Abbot Samson had studied in Paris before he became a monk in 1168.[73] Gerald of Wales himself went to Paris three times for extensive periods of study in the mid-1160s and 1170s, first mastering and teaching the basic course of Trivia and then returning to study both Law and Theology. Spells abroad must have been considered indispensable by those who were most ambitious for successful careers: there were not as yet the same opportunities for advanced study in England. Many Englishmen clearly benefited from contact with fellow students from other lands. There were several Danes studying in Paris, some of whom returned home to become bishops. More unexpected might seem the contacts made with Hungarians. Becket's English protégé Gerard de la Pucelle, a famous teacher in Paris, counted Archbishop Luke of Esztergom among his former pupils.[74] Walter Map, archdeacon of Oxford, had also known Hungarian students while he was in France and some English clergy found their way to Hungary. (A Master Robert *Anglicus* was one of three clergy at Esztergom accused of tampering with papal privileges.[75]) Before the end of the century Hungarian students could be found at Oxford, subsidised for several years by Richard I.

Shared experiences in the schools provided the basis for lasting friendships which could be made to serve political purposes. Peter of Blois, archdeacon of Bath, felt justified in asking Cardinal Conrad, archbishop of Mainz, for his help in getting Richard I released from German captivity by reminding him of their student days together.[76] When Abbot Samson went to see Richard in Germany, he probably anticipated meeting old student friends in Cologne.[77]

Student life already made a strong impression on young clergy. Some of the most appreciative descriptions of life in Paris were written in the Anglo-Norman environment. The Canterbury satirist, Nigel Wireker, poked fun at the English scholars in Paris who took advantage of the good food they had there and the quantity of wine they drank.[78] The '*de disciplina scholarium*', a work then assumed to be by Boethius, was very popular in thirteenth-century England where it may have been written.[79] In Paris, the writer had met students from Germany and Spain. John of Hauvilla, probably from Normandy, dedicated his literary work *Architrenius* to Walter of Coutances, at the moment of his translation from the see of Lincoln to the archbishopric of Rouen in 1184.[80]

One of the most prestigious Paris schools was the abbey of St Victor founded in 1113. Its scholastic reputation was established by the German, Master Hugh (who died in 1140). Richard 'Scot', one of Hugh's pupils, wrote many works much admired in the twelfth century.[81] Almost nothing is known about his life or how he came to leave Scotland but by 1162 he had become prior under Abbot Ervisius, an Englishman whose arbitrary and dishonest administration damaged the abbey's reputation.[82] Several influential Roman clergy who had studied at St Victor became so distraught that they secured papal intervention. Ervisius cannot have been as disreputable as his critics alleged since Louis VII thought well enough of him to make him godfather of his heir, Philip, in 1168. Although Ervisius was eventually deposed, in retirement he was not easily silenced. He too had connections in Norway.[83] His sister was married there and her sons studied in Paris. English and Norman interest in St Victor was substantial. There were already English canons there *c.*1140 when plans were being drawn up to establish the first Victorine house in England. This house, when it at last found a permanent home at Wigmore, received as abbot Master Andrew, a Biblical scholar of considerable repute in Paris for his knowledge of Hebrew and concern to establish the literal meaning of Old Testament texts. It is not certain that he was born in England, but anyway contributed to England's intellectual reputation.[84] The house in Paris had close contacts with England. A canon lent Henry II's treasurer money which was not repaid; a papal chaplain lent money to an English canon, Robert of Bristol. The best known of the English Victorine houses was established at Bristol by Robert FitzHarding in the 1140s, now Bristol Cathedral.

Other continental schools frequented by English students are less well known, but there were many. Gerard de la Pucelle was tempted to accept an invitation to teach in Cologne at a time when the Becket dispute made it awkward for him in Paris to avoid taking sides. In 1189, Hugh of Avalon met Gilbert de Lacy while he was studying in the schools at Saumur.[85] Gerald of Wales recruited compatriots studying at St Omer when he went to Rome in 1199.[86] A Scottish student at Angers only attracted notice because he got himself ordained subdeacon without being qualified.[87] Given the unexpectedly large number of *magistri* who turn up in twelfth-century Scottish documents, there must have been many Scottish students abroad, most probably at Paris.[88] King William's own interest in making friends in France could have encouraged Scots to follow his example. The king and his bishops needed men familiar with the Continent and able to negotiate on their behalf with the papacy.

About one Scot's experiences abroad we are comparatively well informed. Adam of Dryburgh, born to a small landowner of Berwickshire, became a canon in the Premonstratensian house at Dryburgh which Adam describes as being in the land of the English and the kingdom of Scotland, testimony to the still ambivalent character of Lothian.[89] His several works show him to be well versed in the style of Biblical criticism cultivated at St Victor in Paris, where he may have studied. He had certainly lived for a time at the mother house of his monastery at Prémontré and went on a tour of France with its abbot, during which he visited the Charterhouse at Val St Pierre. When Gerard, abbot of Dryburgh fell ill, Adam took over the running of the house *c.*1184, but withdrew to become himself a Carthusian in the only English house of the order at Witham in 1188. These brief glimpses of Adam's travels show that service on behalf of the monastic order took its members to some far-flung destinations.

Without patrons interested in recruiting educated men for their service, Irishmen lacked the incentive of the English and Scots to study abroad. Little is actually known about the formation of this generation of Irish clergy. A Gospel book written at Armagh in 1138 has a commentary derived from notes made by an Irish student of Peter Lombard; Lombard's *Sentences* were copied in 1158 by Michael the Irishman (*Hiberniensis*), possibly a monk from Clairvaux. Irish glosses written into a commentary on Plato's *Timaeus* prompted a suggestion that an Irish scholar had studied at Chartres.[90] An Irish hagiographer had studied in France and Liège before coming home in the 1160s. Flan O'Gorman's return to Armagh as chief lector in 1154, after twenty-one years of study in both France and Germany, looks like a move intended to follow up the changes in Irish ecclesiastical organisation of 1152, but how exactly he influenced the school at Armagh is not demonstrable.[91]

By the late twelfth century, the attractions of the continental schools in France and Italy were reaching their peak. Clergy with continental experience of the great centres of European learning, particularly Paris for theologians and Bologna for law, returned home to posts of great prominence. Robert of Melun, who had taught in Paris, became bishop of Hereford in 1163 and Gerard de la Pucelle, who had also taught there for nearly twenty years, returned to England as bishop of Coventry. When Bishop Hugh took charge of the diocese of Lincoln, William de Montibus, who in 1180 was teaching in Paris at Mont Ste Géneviève, became resident theologian (1189–1213) and revived the languishing reputation of its school.[92] He composed various works intended to help parish clergy discharge their pastoral responsibilities and in his own day won a considerable reputation. Alexander Neckham, who wrote his *De Laudibus divinae sapientiae* in Paris *c.*1180, returned shortly after to take charge of the school at St Albans, possibly glad of the opportunity to cultivate his independent interests in scientific learning.[93]

Neckham derived some of his chapters in *De natura rerum* from a commentary on the *Aphorismi* of Urso of Calabria, a famous Salernitan doctor.[94] The school of Salerno had attracted foreign students since the early twelfth century and some manuscripts of its standard works had reached England at an early stage. About 1175, a manuscript of a work by Marius, a contemporary Salernitan teacher, was written in England.[95] When Neckham himself became head of the school at St Albans, the monastic prior was Master Matthew, Abbot Warin's brother. Matthew had himself studied physic at Salerno and when he returned to become a monk brought with him two of his disciples and colleagues, Fabian and Robert of Salerno. Abbot Warin made use of medical knowledge to improve conditions in the monastic infirmary, appointing a doctor and providing suitable medicaments. He also made further provision for a house of 'leprous' nuns and the hospital of St Julian. Under his regime, his nephew, a master of *decreta* and laws ran the school after Neckham had withdrawn to Cirencester. Education at St Albans owed much to Italy. Warin funded the school's library generously, though the monastic historian criticised the abbot's patronage because it was done from the monks' revenues. At St Albans John de Cella, Warin's successor as abbot, was a polymath, respected as being as 'brilliant in grammar as Priscian, in literature as Ovid and in physic as Galen'.[96] The books English students acquired abroad might later enrich monastic libraries. Thomas de Marleberge studied in Paris, Rome and Bologna and built up a varied collection of books on medicine, law, philosophy, theology, poetry and grammar which he gave to the library at Evesham when he became prior.[97]

Since a number of Englishmen acquired international reputations as doctors, it would be instructive to know what had first stimulated their interest in medicine. No formal medical training was available in Britain. Natural curiosity must have been enough to drive a few determined students to look for superior scientific learning in faraway places. The example of St Albans indicates that the chance arrival of skilled practitioners, abbatial patronage and institutional continuity were mainly responsible for improvements, even if the monks, the immediate beneficiaries, did not appreciate their good fortune.

After study in Paris, his interest in medical science took Neckham's contemporary, Daniel Morley, to Toledo where he joined the circle of Gerard of Cremona, the prolific translator of Arabic works into Latin.[98] Daniel learnt the *rationes Arabum*, hearing for the first time about Galen, Aristotelian cosmology and the influence of the stars in medicine. He returned to England *c.*1187 and, at the end of the century, composed his *Philosophia*, the earliest treatise to make use of the *De elementis* of Isaac Judaeus. This work made the Latin west familiar with an Arabic treatise on astronomy by al-Farghani and two scientific works '*de ortu scientiarum*' and the '*liber celi et mundi*', then ascribed to Aristotle. A third member of this group, Alfred of Shareshull (near Lichfield), had also studied in Spain, where, with the assistance of a Jew, he translated from the Arabic two works thought to be by Aristotle. The '*de plantis*', of which a great number of manuscripts are known, was actually written by the Greek Nicholas Damascenus in the first century but it remained the chief source of botanical theory in the west until the sixteenth century. Alfred added to its usefulness by writing a commentary, about 1210/15. The *de mineralibus* was actually part of a work on chemistry and geology by Avicenna but Alfred inserted it into the fourth book of Aristotle's *Meteora*. Alfred also wrote a commentary on this text, of which only one manuscript is known, but other *Meteora* manuscripts have glosses attributed to Alfred. The importance of these works for Latin scientific learning is not in doubt. Apart from his translations, Alfred wrote a work '*de motu cordis*', dedicated to Neckham, which was a text still recommended by the Arts faculty syllabus in mid-thirteenth-century Paris. Alfred's views on the independent existence of the soul attracted the attention of later philosophers, but essentially he was himself not so much a teacher as a scholar of Arabic learning who made his findings known in Latin.[99] Roger of Hereford, who dedicated his *Compotus* to Bishop Gilbert Foliot, does not seem to have moved in Neckham's circle, but shared its scientific interests and had probably himself studied in Spain. His chief importance lies in his adaptation of the astronomical tables compiled for Toledo, as modified for Marseilles, to the longitude of Hereford, completed in 1178.[100]

These pioneers were not responsible for establishing any lasting schools but it is from this period that the earliest evidence comes for institutional learning at Oxford. In 1184 Gerald of Wales decided to make a public reading of his new book, the *Topography of Ireland*, at Oxford, 'where of all the places in England, the clergy were most strong and pre-eminent in learning' and there were already a number of doctors in diverse faculties.[101] Even so, ten years later when warfare prevented Gerald's return to Paris he did not consider resuming his studies in Oxford but went to learn more theology under Master William at Lincoln. Oxford may simply have enjoyed a better reputation for other courses of study. Apart from attracting Hungarian students from overseas,[102] two young Frisians, Emo and his brother Addo, came to Oxford after periods of study in Paris and Orleans with a particular interest in various legal books, including the *Decreta*, *Decretales* and the *Liber Pauperum* written by Vacarius for English students.[103] The Oxford schools still operated in the shadow of Paris, but held some attractions for continental students.

England was in fact full of men with foreign connections. The Becket controversy naturally received a lot of attention in France, as letters written within the circle of John of Salisbury testify. One of Salisbury's friends, Peter of Celle, abbot of St Rémi, Reims thought of visiting Becket's shrine. Though he never did come to England he corresponded with several Englishmen.[104] At the request of a monk of Norwich, he started a correspondence with another monk of that priory. He wrote to a priest of Hastings to whose son he had become spiritual father. Some of the letters concerned the affairs of his own monastery's priory at Lapley in Staffordshire. In one to the bishop of Coventry, he begged the bishop to restrain the archdeacon's court from fining the priory for its faults so that he could himself as abbot inflict corporal punishment on the monks. Even for practical purposes, a French abbot needed to know how the English Church dealt with miscreants. An old friend who became a canon of Merton Priory asked for a copy of Peter's pamphlet on claustral discipline. In reply, Peter recalled the conversations they had once enjoyed together. Peter received a letter praising another of his works, '*de panibus*', from a monk of Reading. The longest and most elaborate of all his letters was written to Nicholas, a monk of St Albans, whom he had known many years back (perhaps at Paris). They had subsequently lost contact after a disagreeable altercation. When contact was resumed they argued again, this time about the doctrine of the Immaculate Conception of the Virgin, which Nicholas stoutly defended against Peter's objections.[105] The matter was discussed at great length and proves not only how controversial it was, but how much it stimulated monastic intellects at the time. Since several defenders of this teaching came from England, Peter was puzzled enough to wonder why England should provide a congenial environment for views not received in France or approved by Rome. He did not ascribe this to the influence of a particular teacher and his school, nor to the liturgical practices of a church like Canterbury where the feast was observed. Instead Peter ventured to think that it was 'in the nature of their land . . . that unsubstantial fantasies slide easily into their minds; they think their dreams to be visions and their visions to be divine'. (Not all Peter's impressions of England were so visionary for he had heard that in England 'men were more often drunk than sober'.) The letters of this foreign monk show him to have had a quite lively impression of the state of England in his time and its differences from France.

One Cluniac poet, Richard of Poitou, expressed deep admiration for England, praising its *terra ferax, fertilis angulus orbis, dulce solum, plena iocis, gens libera, nata iocari*. In the poem celebrating his arrival in England, he already acknowledged its 'liberal' character, the *libera gens, libera mens, libera lingua* (free people, open minded, frank speaking). Richard must be counted among the earliest and most enthusiastic of French Anglophiles.[106] This happy state of affairs made England itself a congenial refuge for exiles. Richard's claim that the English were open-handed is confirmed by Neckham who wrote that the people of England did not know the meaning of meanness, a view also found elsewhere. Archbishop Eystein, in exile from Norway, spent three years (1180–83) sheltered in various English monasteries and returned with ideas about how to complete the building of his new cathedral at Nidaros inspired by the new work being done at Canterbury.[107] Fountains, which had a daughter house in Norway, preserved the fullest manuscript of Eystein's *Life of Saint Olaf*; the network of Anglo-Scandinavian relations set up generations earlier was obviously still viable. The Icelander, Thorlak, who was at first in Paris, continued his studies at Lincoln, either for reasons of economy or because he wished to study with some particular master there.[108] He had returned to Iceland by 1170 and subsequently became bishop of Skalholt. Some religious visitors to the British Isles ventured to more remote districts. The relics of St Petroc were stolen from Bodmin and taken to Brittany in 1177. This episode also has an unexpectedly exotic dimension, for when the relics were eventually recovered they were placed in an ivory casket of Muslim workmanship and Sicilian provenance which still survives.[109]

Formal links between monastic houses, particularly in orders like Cîteaux, were responsible for the most regular interchange of information between the British Isles and the Continent. In the absence of other evidence about Wales, for example, the occasional entries concerning continental events in the Annals kept at the Cistercian monastery of Strata Florida, founded in west Wales in 1164, can be explained by the annual visits to Cîteaux made by the abbot.[110] The murder of the abbot of Clairvaux by one of his own monks in 1176 was bound to secure a mention. At Margam, a Cistercian house in south Wales, the Annals were significantly more receptive of foreign information, probably reflecting the fact that it had been founded by an Anglo-Norman baron. Here, amid notices of the damage inflicted on the house from time to time by the native Welsh, the annalist gave an elaborate account of a fanatical movement of religious zealots in 1163 in the Périgord, a part of the Angevin Empire rarely mentioned in English chronicles.[111]

Similarly, in Ireland, some clergy had acquired new friends abroad in the

Cistercian order. Ominously, the first appearance of the Irish in the records of the Cistercian general chapters under the year 1184 indicates that the practices of the Irish houses already excited suspicion: all the abbots of the order were warned against recognising Irishmen as bishops without strong evidence. In Ireland, even the Cistercians did not always come up to contemporary continental expectations. Mael, abbot of Mellifont, who quarrelled with the general chapter and refused to receive the inspector sent from Cîteaux in 1191, was accordingly suspended from office in 1192. Nevertheless he was appointed bishop of Clogher in 1194 and after his death three years later buried in his old monastery at Mellifont.[112] The monastic reform in Ireland did not produce all the benefits expected of it by its advocates.

Learning and government

Devised for the needs of the reforming Church, the new learning had far wider implications for the rest of medieval society. English kings took the best educated men of the day into their service and the royal administration developed rapidly in the course of the twelfth century, thanks in no small measure to the trained clergy and the laymen influenced by the methodical thinking of the schools. The loose structures of the Angevin Empire itself obliged the king to devise government machinery capable of working in his absence. Royal powers were delegated to justiciars with defined and limited functions; because they were not given a free hand to rule as they pleased, their rule was more predictable than the king's. The king's continental responsibilities did not become a bone of contention between him and his English subjects. This may seem strange. Whereas in the first half of the century Henry I shared a concern for the duchy of Normandy with many of his barons, under Henry II the English barons had no personal stake in his continental lands, apart from Normandy. There was no settlement of Angevins or Gascons in England, nor of Englishmen abroad. Englishmen could, however, take up appointments in Henry's continental dominions. In Normandy itself a Cornishman, Walter of Coutances, became archbishop of Rouen and the Norman Exchequer was reorganised by Richard of Ilchester. The first mayor of the commune at Caen was English. William, abbot of Reading, became archbishop of Bordeaux; one of his successors at Reading ended his career as abbot of Cluny.[113]

Some Englishmen cheerfully pursued Henry II into his French domains on their own account, chiefly to expedite their legal disputes, rather than await his return or, indeed, rely on those who deputised for him in England. The most famous of these impatient litigants, Richard de Anesti, travelled all the way to Toulouse in 1159 and spent three weeks there until a favourable opportunity presented itself to achieve his end with the king. Even this was not enough to settle his case. Over the many years of his protracted lawsuit, he had occasion to send agents to Rome twice and to Normandy several times, all in connection with his efforts to get confirmation of his better right to succeed to his uncle's estate than his uncle's daughter by a marriage the Church deemed unlawful. Though his suit only concerned property in England, Anesti found it expedient to take himself abroad and had to keep informed about the situation overseas.[114]

From Henry II's surviving charters it can be seen that Anesti was not alone, even if we are better informed about the cost and frequency of his travels than about others. With Henry near Toulouse in 1159 was the bishop of Rochester, or his agent, along with Templars who there secured a royal charter confirming rights to a mill on the River Fleet in London. Cistercians from Rievaulx met the king in this period at Cahors and some from Byland Abbey at Poitiers. In 1183, at Poitiers, the archbishop of Canterbury and the abbot of St Augustine's resolved their differences before the king. Many documents concerning England were issued in Normandy throughout the reign and Henry could as easily make decisions about his English affairs from the depths of Gascony as in England itself.[115] Did the English regard the need to go abroad and get documents for their affairs from the king as vexatious? Or did they take advantage of business trips to travel, meet friends or visit shrines?

The French provinces were not uniform and in no way deferential to the legal practices of the French royal domain lands. The long association between England and Normandy involved reciprocal effects on the laws of both, but they remained distinct from one another. The England of Henry II is famous for its precocious development of a common law for all the king's free subjects, but parallels can be discerned in other provinces where, in due course, statements of customary laws were composed in Normandy, Anjou and Poitou, all equally precocious. English legal scholarship has traditionally treated the development of common law as a uniquely English phenomenon, but given that changes in legal procedures were not confined to England, English developments could be usefully studied as part of a general transformation of European justice in this period.[116]

The promotion of judicial institutions in Henry II's dominions owed something to the king's own reputation in judicial matters and astuteness in judging disputes. As an arbiter of quarrels, he arranged a satisfactory settlement of the disputes between the kings of Castile and Navarre.[117] Yet the king's character is insufficient to explain why English litigants became so eager to avail themselves of royal procedures. The judicial activities of Henry II's law courts owed much to novel procedures devised in response to new social pressures for resolving civil disputes about property and for containing criminal activity. But the king's offer of legal remedies would have been insufficient without a widespread willingness to work with the king's courts and accept their judgments. The treatment of criminal cases in royal courts rested on the obligations of neighbours to denounce suspects to the king's government and detain them until they could stand trial. The use of summary royal procedures to secure titles to land diminished the attractions of alternative courts which proceeded more slowly and had less power to implement their rulings. The machinery of official justice rested therefore on the traditional responsibility of the neighbourhood to settle disputes of general interest by legal means. In this way, the government acquired not only supporters but critics (when it functioned defectively) and in the longer term a public able to protest (as in Magna Carta) because it was dissatisfied with the king's performance of his duties.

Quite apart from any particular English preference for settling disputes in royal courts rather than by traditional means, like arbitration or violence, the changes in English legal procedure at this time could not have remained unaffected by the revival of the formal study of Roman law. Everywhere this had caused twelfth-century Europeans to think afresh about legal procedure, the nature of proof and the search for legal remedies.[118] Its most immediate impact came through the concern of churchmen to provide themselves with a body of canon law to define and defend their privileges. The English clergy had taken an interest in these matters, even before Becket insisted on the superior claims of canon law over local custom. From early in his reign, Henry II had shown that he had no intention of allowing hallowed royal rights to be overturned by claims to clerical privilege. These appeals to legal principles could not fail to have an impact on the practical enforcement of customary law. The courts needed to find men able to sit in judgment, as well as men prepared to come forward and give evidence or denounce crimes. Henry made extensive use of his bishops and abbots as judges in royal courts and they applied what legal principles they knew to the matters in hand.

Nor is it difficult to demonstrate the influence of new styles of learning on the common law. The earliest written account of procedures in the royal courts, which was composed about 1187 and passed for the work of Ranulf Glanvill, the king's justiciar, makes this plain.[119] Writing played a very small part in English legal procedures at the time, so the fact of describing the procedures in writing at all proves that men with experience of formal learning took an interest in these matters. Throughout the text, the author follows a simple method of exposition. At each stage in legal proceedings, there is a choice open to the litigant. If he chooses one path, the next stage is described; if another, the process will differ. The influence of twelfth-century scholastic teaching of logic is obvious. Whatever common law owes to its native traditions, to develop as a form of royal justice it drew on the contemporary learning of the continental schools. Gerald of Wales, who had studied law in Paris, quotes Justinian's *Codex* and *Digest* frequently. Ralph Niger has an encomium of Justinian. English interest in legal studies was sufficient to bring Master Vacarius, an experienced teacher of law and a legal advisor, to England where, like a few other Italians of the day, he received a benefice.[120] To pretend that learned law had no part to play in the development of the English legal system is disingenuous. The revival of learned study of the law had more immediate repercussions in England than anywhere else in Europe outside Italy.

The development of strict rules of procedure in English justice has a parallel in administrative matters. The royal office of Henry II's time best understood by historians is that of the Exchequer. Once again, a treatise, written this time by the king's treasurer, Richard Fitz Nigel, openly displays the dependence of Henry II's officials on twelfth-century schooling by being written in the form of a dialogue between the treasurer as master and a disciple. The treasurer describes the activities of the Exchequer, taking pride in the orderliness of its operations and commending the work of its educated officials for the well-being of the king's government. The advantages derived by the Exchequer from Henry's contacts on the Continent are further demonstrated by the example of Thomas Brown. After service with King Roger II of Sicily, Brown was coaxed back to England and assigned a special role at the Exchequer.[121] How Brown's experience in Sicily might have enhanced his value in the Exchequer is not made explicit, but appreciation of Brown's administrative expertise in two very different twelfth-century kingdoms is certain. The procedures of the Exchequer also took for granted familiarity with the contemporary practice of arithmetic by clerical officials and secular sheriffs. The new learning with numbers had been enthusiastically accepted in twelfth-century England and the eagerness of kings to take advantage of it in their accounting procedures was, no doubt, as important as the learning itself for Exchequer purposes.

Historical attention inevitably focuses on rulers, but the articulation of effective royal government under the Angevins undoubtedly rested on the shoulders of well-educated and conscientious officials. The great actors on the world stage would not have achieved public success without the dressers, directors and teachers behind the scenes, most of them leaving no impression of their own distinctive personalities. Henry II was one of the first European rulers to make extensive use for his own purposes of men educated at the fashionable schools of twelfth-century Europe, or influenced by them. For the most part, they were Englishmen and not favourites found abroad. As clerks they were rewarded with ecclesiastical benefices, including bishoprics bestowed at the king's discretion. Henry's quarrel with Becket tends to obscure the extent to which his regime depended on close cooperation with clergy, as Becket's earlier career as Henry's chancellor so flagrantly demonstrated.

Among the rulers of the British Isles, only the king of England could be regularly found on the Continent, but it was not only in England that princely engagement with educated clergy had implications for government. The way things worked out differed from one country to another. In Wales, for example, princes from the time of Madog ap Mareddud, ruler of Powys (d.1160) began to employ clerks and issue official Latin documents, but better educated Welsh clerics had more controversial problems on their minds than improving princely chanceries.[122] Those most impressed by the great reforming programmes abroad were keen to impose the new standards expected, for example, in Christian marriage. They felt obliged to criticise Welsh laws countenancing traditional practices. The clergy themselves had no power to change the law, but their arguments provoked the Welsh lawmen responsible to revise the Laws of Hywel Dda, in order to make them more acceptable in the new intellectual climate.[123] The oldest surviving manuscript of these laws is the one in Latin composed for Rhys, whom Henry II appointed as justiciar for Deheubarth. The Welsh were understandably proud of their past cultural achievements and did not see the need to embrace without reservations the new modes of thought they had to encounter. Their culture was sure enough of itself to try to resist foreign moral pressure.

In Scotland, where David I had appreciated the advantages his kingdom could derive from a reorganisation of the Church, educated clergy had more scope for action. Unlike Wales, Scotland had fewer ancient traditions to defend against innovation. It sought rather to build up new and effective working practices. The pressure for change in legal matters could be satisfied by straight borrowing from England. Glanvill's handbook was taken over and became the basic text for the later lawbook, the so-called *Regiam Maiestatem*. Likewise, royal writs devised in England for the needs of landholders promptly appeared in Scotland, which had established tenures similar to those of feudal England. The Scots were not slavish about their borrowing, but used the writ form to initiate new procedures for their own purposes. Although the oldest manuscripts of Scots laws belong to the fourteenth century, English influence can only have been felt at a very early stage. Before 1200 the Scots had already become fully conscious of their institutional differences from England and selective about what they were prepared to borrow.[124]

The very similarities between English and Scottish institutions made it more important for Scotsmen who wished to keep English government at a distance to find ways to protect their differences. This objective was rendered more difficult after the failure of William's intervention in the rebellion of 1173. Henry II aimed to cover himself against further trouble by requiring not only the king but the Scottish lords and bishops to do him homage. The bishops objected. When Henry II and Becket quarrelled in 1164, Scottish bishops had hoped that papal support for Becket would weaken the position of Becket's enemy, Roger of York, and so lead to the cancellation of York's claims to ecclesiastical jurisdiction in the Scottish kingdom. Ten years later, William's submission gave Roger another chance. Now he could argue that the Scottish kingdom was no longer independent but had become part of Henry II's dominions. This was sufficient to make Scottish bishops vigorous defenders of the kingdom's interest at a time when the king himself had lost the initiative. Infuriated by Henry II's demand for homage, they obtained a papal denunciation of Henry II's action. This sharpened William's resolve to assert as much independence as he could. Emboldened by episcopal support, William even risked papal irritation by rejecting a papal judgement in the matter of a new appointment to the see of St Andrews.

William's intransigence with the papacy was a remarkable demonstration of his determination to exercise full rights in his kingdom. By 1180, Alexander was so exasperated that he revived York's hopes of recovering jurisdiction in Scotland and sought Henry II's intervention as overlord to help find a solution. The dispute over ecclesiastical issues in fact exposed the limited character of Henry's lordship: he had no coercive powers in Scotland.[125] Alexander III's successor, Lucius III, recognising the need to make a fresh start, sent William a golden rose. Symbolically, he acknowledged the king as an independent ruler. His bull was the oldest document preserved in the royal archive when it was catalogued a hundred years later: it had been appreciated.[126] Even so, the matter was only finally resolved when Hugh of St Andrews died, at Rome, in 1188. Within months, Pope Clement III took all nine Scottish bishoprics under papal protection and thus put the Scottish Church well beyond York's reach. (Argyll had not become separated from Dunkeld at the time of Clement's bull.) The papacy realised that the political independence of Scotland made subordination of the Scottish Church to York, outside the kingdom, unworkable. This papal privilege, *Cum universi*, was renewed by the next pope in 1192 and came to be treated in Scotland as an endorsement of Scottish independence.[127] The use of papal authority in Scotland to keep the English king and hierarchy in a distance shows what could be accomplished by Scottish diplomacy in Rome. Friendship with the Roman Curia cost little. Unlike the English, the Scots never paid Peter's pence and resisted any form of papal taxation. Thanks to the support of churchmen, William's government had been given a new lease of life after the ignominious surrender at Falaise. Henry II had been responsible for thrusting Scotsmen into the continental maelstrom, but they learned how to navigate on their own account.

Scotland's bishops made many different friends abroad. The Cistercian network explains why Abbot Joscelin of Melrose, on becoming bishop of Glasgow, obtained his consecration at Clairvaux from Archbishop Ekstein of Lund. Some Scottish bishops were of course consecrated in Rome itself. Although only one Scottish bishop, Arnold of Ross, attended Alexander III's Third Lateran Council in 1179, two other bishops were consecrated there. In Galloway, then less a part of the kingdom than an autonomous region, the bishops of Whithorn had regularly received ordination at the hands of York. Bishop Christian even refused to attend Vivian's legatine council of 1177 on the grounds that the papal legate in Scotland had no authority over him. But bishops at Whithorn felt awkward about their position and two diplomatically secured consecration from foreign bishops: in 1154 from the archbishop of Rouen and in 1189 in England from the visiting archbishops of Dublin and Trier.[128]

In Ireland, clergy in touch with continental churchmen enjoyed fewer opportunities to influence the affairs of government. Irish kings shared an aspiration to achieve recognition as high-king, a courtesy title dependent on their individual military superiority. This type of kingship appreciated recognition of its standing from the coarb of St Patrick at Armagh, but actually found little use for educated clergy in its government. Irish bishops invariably owed their appointments to their family connections with the royal families of Ireland but this relationship was not expected to assist kings with their own rule, nor oblige them to change their own behaviour. Nor did the responsibilities of the many bishops within their small dioceses require them to maintain large staffs of clerks as was the case in England. There were only limited demands for the issue of documents and only eight royal charters are known from before 1169.[129] These were prepared by the beneficiaries seeking royal confirmations and not by royal chancery clerks. Phrases in them show that the Irish clergy were more influenced by what they knew of imperial diplomas issued for Irish monks in Germany than by the style of English royal documents. This is easily understood. The Irish monastery at Regensburg was in touch with Cork in 1155 and a cell for this house established at Ross Carbery near Cork. Following the example of Frederick Barbarossa, who persuaded his antipope to canonise Charlemagne in 1165, the O'Brien family took an interest in getting one of its own ancestors recognised as a saint. King Dermot of Leinster himself employed a 'notary' to compose his documents; he also began to use a seal for authorising them.[130]

These German connections may have been responsible for making Irish kings wary of Alexander III and his allies among reforming churchmen. Irish kings were satisfied with the Church settlement of 1152. They were in no hurry to introduce further changes and there is little sign that as a result of it papal contacts with Ireland had been stepped up. Only a single letter from Alexander III to an Irish king is known. The pope thanked the king for his kind reception of a papal envoy and expressed the hope that the king would send a representative to the council Alexander had summoned for Tours in 1163.[131] Since the main thrust of reforming efforts was directed to changing the habits of laymen, kings were understandably reluctant to make many concessions to reformers who denounced their indifference to the rules prevailing elsewhere about marriage within the prohibited degrees of kinship, worse still, their practice of polygamy and divorce. Irish family law recognised no distinction between legitimate and illegitimate children, which encouraged disputes about the succession to property. The Irish paid no tithes and resented being asked for them. Some idea of the values of traditional society Irish idealists were up against can be glimpsed in the Irish annals, which remained indifferent to matters of most common interest to western chroniclers, such as the crusades, Church councils and the succession of popes.

Lack of support from Irish secular princes meant that since the 1130s the Irish bishops had concentrated their main efforts to effect change on establishing houses of Austin canons, probably as a way of providing examples of stricter religious discipline for clergy and higher standards of liturgical practice. Even in the west there were nearly a score of Austin canon priories, seven in episcopal sees, most between Limerick and Sligo, with only one in the south, at Cork.[132] Nothing is known about the effect these Austin canons had, either immediately or later, on the religious life of these regions. The one liturgical manuscript to have survived from twelfth-century Ireland has been attributed to an Austin house, but since the scribe had a defective grasp of Latin, this text does not bolster the order's reputation for learning.[133] After Malachi, the most saintly Irish bishop of the twelfth century was Lawrence O'Toole, archbishop of Dublin, a former abbot of Glendalough, who had no experience of life outside Ireland until his last years. Like Malachi, he died abroad. There, not in Ireland, the hagiographies of both saints were written, their miracles recorded and their reputations for sanctity boosted.

The immediate effects of Henry's lordship on Irish relations with the Continent can be measured by the regular despatch of papal bulls for Ireland, which begins in earnest in 1172, and the introduction of the twelfth-century religious orders, the Hospitallers in 1172, the Templars after 1180, the Premonstratensians at Carrickfergus in 1183, all patronised by the Anglo-Norman newcomers.[134] From this time, Ireland was exposed to the same kind of pressures for reform as England. From the English point of view, Ireland lacked many institutions they took for granted. By their standards, Ireland seemed like a wasteland, sparsely populated and crying out for 'development'.[135]

Those who established themselves in Ireland felt no scruples about providing for the management of the country along lines they were familiar with and which were, almost by necessity, opposed to traditional Irish practice. Where the English began to consolidate their hold the pattern of events familiar in England rapidly took over. The Irish adapted readily enough to arrangements that served their own interests. Treated as a 'foreign' enclave of Germanic settlers by the other Irish, Dublin for example had only been fully accepted into the Irish polity when it was recognised as an archbishopric in 1152. However 'alien' in Ireland, Dublin rapidly became the best endowed of all the Irish bishoprics and the one most recognisably Latin. In 1171, those whose affairs were bound up with the city already appreciated what greater advantages they could derive from the establishment of a government anchored on the other side of the Irish Sea. Those parts of the island which faced Wales and England inevitably gained most from closer relations with other parts of Britain and the Continent.

Other parts of Ireland did not reckon to benefit so obviously, but it was difficult to take effective rearguard action. Ecclesiastically, Armagh, for example, was forced into a corner. Though it retained some of its old allure, there was no future for it as an Irish Canterbury. When Tomaltach, bishop of Elphin, a nephew of Rory O'Connor, was chosen as archbishop of Armagh in 1180, Henry II was uneasy enough to encourage Malachi, bishop of Clogher, to challenge the appointment. Malachi went to Rome in 1186 to get papal confirmation of himself as archbishop, but died before he could return. Tomaltach resumed his seat and the papacy took no further action; he survived until his death in 1201.[136] When relics of Patrick, Bridget and Columba were discovered in the 1180s, Tomaltach was happy to be associated with John de Courcy's bid to make Downpatrick the centre of the cult.[137] Armagh was not geographically well placed to contest Dublin's new prominence and accordingly benefited less from direct contacts with the near Continent.

Although it is clear enough that not all Irishmen were put under comparable pressure to adjust to the novelties introduced by the Angevin dominion, evidence for the parts of Ireland which kept their distance is poor. Least affected was the west where the effective motors of Irish native society, such as they were, remained its secular lords. A few were prepared to take the initiative in promoting some aspects of the reformers' programme. Cistercian houses established in the provinces of Cashel and Tuam, though fewer than those in Armagh and Dublin, nearly all owed their existence to the urging of secular patrons. Domnall Mor O'Brien set up no less than three houses, and two kinsmen, two more. The rest owed much to the MacCarthy, O'Ferral, O'Cananan and O'Connor families. Hardly unexpected, therefore, is the fact that some of these foundations faltered after a few years.

The political confusion of Ireland after the invasions of 1169–72, when compared with England and Scotland, is reflected in the language used by historians then and since. They could not decide whether the invading forces should be regarded as English, Welsh, French or even Flemings (meaning the settlers from Pembroke); later historians have also been baffled as to whether to call the same groups Normans or Anglo-Normans as though the English as such were not involved. Rather than treat these events as a struggle between nations, it is more obvious that they precipitated a clash of cultures only comparable to that created in England itself by the Norman Conquest. In England, however, there was only one kingdom to be conquered and the Normans so rapidly achieved total mastery that its unitary character was preserved. Moreover, the Normans were themselves quickly absorbed into English society. In Ireland, the island remained disunited and the newcomers were only to a partial extent assimilated in the next generations. The intrusion of Angevin interests into Ireland should be accepted as inevitable given the political weakness of the Irish, the sheer exuberance of Plantagenet power and the eagerness of so many parts of Irish society to take advantage of this to ease Ireland more fully into European affairs. But, as in Wales, the native culture did not willingly make way for contemporary French culture.

Understanding the native Irish position is rendered more difficult because most of the historical information comes from the side of the invading forces. The so-called *Song of Dermot and the Earl*, written in French at the end of the twelfth century, celebrates the early stages of the English entry into Ireland at Dermot's behest and is remarkable for its presentation of the encounters between the two forces as between compatible peoples. Maurice de Prendergast had no difficulty about taking service with the king of Ossory and subsequently, when the king was in trouble with Strongbow, acted not only as go-between but insisted against Strongbow himself that the oaths sworn to respect a safe conduct should be honoured.[138] Maurice and the poet treated the Irish as worthy combatants. Ireland might be in need of 'development', but it was not to be reduced to a state of colonial subjection.

After his visit there in 1185, Gerald of Wales wrote two books about Ireland, both works of advocacy.[139] As a Welshman, he might have been expected to show more sympathy for the Irish position than he does. One of his main purposes was to extol the exploits of his own family whose contribution to the conquest, he believed, had been cut short by the interventions of the king and royal officials envious of Geraldine prowess. From his point of view, the English entry into Ireland had begun as a Welsh one. By the time he wrote, moreover, he thought that the momentum for royal lordship had already slackened and that the native Irish had learnt enough about the invaders to know how to keep up an effective resistance. Fresh measures were needed.

Henry II thought the same. In 1185, he sent his son John as Lord of Ireland to establish a new form of government. John was quite inexperienced and attached no importance to securing any cooperation from the Irish. He made grants to English vassals or adventurers happy to help themselves to lands in the possession of Irishmen previously well disposed to Henry II. The failure of John's expedition to establish any understanding with the Irish leaders was patent enough to arouse misgivings.[140] On the Irish side, it must have seemed equally clear in 1185 that total foreign domination was by no means inescapable. When contemplating any reshaping of their governments, however, native Irish rulers did not perceive that educated clergy in their service might offer them any advantages as rulers.

They may not have been convinced of being able to bolster their threatened independence by making friends overseas, but to do so they would have needed to promote the development of western ports like Limerick and Galway. Limerick, like Dublin, had been founded by the Norse as a trading city and commanded excellent maritime communications down the Shannon. The Anglo-Norman invaders appreciated the potential of Limerick and seized it for the first time as early as 1176, but their position so far west proved vulnerable and they had to withdraw. The bishops of Limerick in this period were still of Norse origin, but the Irish kings of Thomond were fully aware of the advantages of the city. Perhaps in the hope of securing the loyalty of the 'foreign' city, Domnall M or O'Brien and his son Donnchad founded and endowed a new cathedral there in 1172. This at least proves that the aesthetic and technical fashions of the continent could reach as far west as this under native supervision.[141] However, the town fell again into English hands *c*.1200 and King John promptly built a castle there. The native Irish princes lost their last chance of using Limerick as a base for consolidating their own political power in the west.

The imposition of Henry's lordship had by then already become controversial even in educated English circles. Gerald thought it necessary to combat criticisms that Henry II had inadequate grounds for his intervention. His arguments probably carried no more conviction then than they do now. He acknowledged that however Earl Richard's claims on Leinster might be justified, this provided no excuse for seizing lands in Munster, though Gerald did reject the slur that Earl Richard and his men were mere brigands (*predones*). In desperation, propagandists liked to invoke the moral failings of the Irish to justify the English campaigns, but even the most devout were not convinced by this. At Canterbury, William, the indefatigable collector of Becket miracles in the early 1170s, disapproved of Henry II's Irish campaign; for him the Irish, however barbaric, were still Christian. He was impressed that many soldiers in Ireland who had incurred much suffering were only relieved by Becket's miraculous powers.[142] The English were far from united about the merits of the new relationship with Ireland.

The culture of chivalry

The influence of educated men on lay society was not confined to the practical work of government. Secular society in general did not expect to learn much from educated clergy about how to run its affairs, but laymen were happy to be diverted, if not instructed by them. Educated men in search of employment found that talents to please, flatter and entertain were appreciated and rewarded. In the last third of the century, a new style of poetry was being composed in northern France for great princes. Drawing on their own familiarity with stories from Latin authors, the poets recast them in vernacular verse, as 'romances'. One of the most popular subjects for these stories concerned Arthur and his knights, a theme inspired by Geoffrey of Monmouth's Latin history of Britain. The romance broke with the tradition of recounting adventures to inspire emulation of great heroes and devised a new kind of plot, the love story, which appealed to both sexes. The writers used the form to explore the effects of emotions, advocate forms of polite behaviour and promote the idea that men should prove themselves worthy of the love of ladies by performing personal deeds of valour. The romances pay little overt attention to religion and the values held up for approval were recognisably worldly. In place of the ideals of Christian living advocated by churchmen, the poets set out an alternative code of behaviour appropriate for the well-born, respectful of virtue and concerned with relations between men and women of good birth and noble expectations. Under its influence, something like a code of polite manners for persons of good birth had penetrated most parts of the Continent by the end of the century.[143]

The new ethos of chivalry had originally been devised in northern France, but no royal courts in western Europe were more sensitive to its impact than those of Henry II and his queen.[144] Henry himself was more of a man of action than of leisure, but he was well educated and a patron of historians. His wife, Eleanor of Aquitaine, granddaughter of the troubadour count, William IX, naturally encouraged the cultivation of poetry. From her it passed both to her daughters and to her sons. Henry's oldest surviving son, Henry (who predeceased him), was admired as a model knight; his second, Richard, himself achieved a reputation as a crusader and a poet. Through Eleanor's daughters courtly literature passed into Germany and Castile, so that at the princely level it became truly international within a generation.

Given the original Welsh inspiration for the development of Arthurian romances, it is hardly surprising that French romances began to influence the character of traditional Welsh poetry. Characteristically, however, the Welsh also responded by injecting new life into native traditions. In 1176, surely inspired by Henry II's court, Rhys of Deheubarth invited poets from all over Britain and Ireland to what is now accepted as the earliest recorded eisteddfod.[145] That Ireland was already concerned about changes in taste is shown by the *Book of Leinster*, a compendium of Irish lore made in the twelfth century and designed to preserve older traditions as they came under threat. A slightly later work shows how educated Irish clergy retold the legendary stories of ancient tradition for a Connaught audience with chivalrous expectations.[146]

The Scots were more directly implicated in the new French literary fashions. In the *Conte de Graal*, written for Philip of Flanders, Chrétien of Troyes drew on Scottish information for his picture of the wilderness where Perceval was brought up.[147] Slightly later, the Romance of Fergus, an Arthurian-type adventure with the action located in Scotland, was probably written for Alan of Galloway, the semi-independent ruler there in the early thirteenth century. The continental author scatters references to places between Navarre and Syria in his narrative and has a poor grasp of Scottish geography, but the incorporation of so many Lowland Scottish names must indicate that a Scottish audience for the poem was expected. A 'king' of Scotland features in several other French romances of this period, along with kings of Moray and Lothian, adding to the impression that Scotland was at least known to continental writers of the period, however vaguely.[148]

The English contribution to the new literature was both more substantial and more innovative.[149] The prominence of English writers in the development of this 'French' literature may seem rather improbable but was actually a consequence of the fact that many English laymen were speakers of French and had begun using the vernacular in writing rather earlier than the French themselves. By far the oldest manuscript of the *Chanson de Roland* was written in England and William of Malmesbury confidently averred that it had been sung before the battle of Hastings to stir up martial ardour.[150] The English tradition of writing in the vernacular was enthusiastically embraced by the Normans in England from early in the twelfth century when Philippe de Thaon had composed useful handbooks in Anglo-Norman, a computus before 1120 and a bestiary written for Henry I's second queen, Adeliza of Louvain, c.1125.[151] Gaimar's English history served a similar kind of readership. In the process the vocabulary of spoken and written French had to be enlarged, finding new words for Latin expressions. Eagerness to improve their vocabulary explains why the courtly words of the new literature were rapidly adopted into the French currently spoken in England. By the 1160s they already turn up in the life of Edward the Confessor composed in French by the anonymous nun of Barking. In this way the world of learning had begun to affect vernacular speech, providing it with new words and new ideas. [152]

In this respect it comes as no surprise that some of the most original themes of the new literature originated in England, like the earliest version of the Tristan story attributed to Thomas of Britain which was available for Chrétien to use before 1174.[153] The English acquired such a reputation for literary discernment that the literary manual most widely used in the thirteenth century, the *Ars Poetica/Ars Versificatoria*, was written by an Englishman, Gervase of Melkley.[154] A less popular literary work, the *Liber Derivationum*, also written by an Englishman, Osbern of Gloucester, nevertheless enjoyed wide circulation on the Continent, being quoted before the end of the twelfth century by the famous canonist, Huguccio of Pisa, and finding its way as far as Bavaria and Austria.[155]

English laymen, as French speakers, expected to be provided with useful books as well as with entertainment. Such works did not exist in France itself and so could not be imported ready-made. The willingness of English writers to satisfy the demand is a sign of how comfortable they felt with the French language they spoke. The advantages for them are clear. French speakers were found right across Christendom as far as the crusading states, providing laymen with an international language of communication comparable to Latin for the clergy. It even served in contacts with some Muslims. Thus speakers of French provided Edrisi, the Arabic geographer of Norman Sicily with his information about the English coast from the Channel to the Wash.[156] Speaking French did not turn Englishmen into Frenchmen in any modern sense. William Marshal's youthful sporting ambitions took him to France where he regularly encountered the various competing groups of Burgundians, Normans, Angevins, Poitevins, Flemings, all speakers of French and compatible rivals. None of these various groups considered themselves 'French' simply because they spoke French and were all equally proud of their own *patria*.[157]

The ability to speak French offered Englishmen too many advantages for it to have remained a preserve of the upper classes. Englishmen who had not mastered its rudiments recognised that this was a handicap, not a matter of patriotic pride.[158] Some knowledge of the language was indispensable for those Englishmen involved in the king's courts of justice or those who moved outside their own local communities. In towns it must have been heard frequently. There are signs that by the late twelfth century Englishmen might seek help with learning French by an early adoption of the au pair system. This is implied by the story of a youth, sent from Normandy by his father to teach the son of a knight how to speak French, for whom Becket worked a miracle. The usefulness of French could not be in doubt. Richard of Devizes for some unexplained reason picked out Norwich, Lincoln and Durham as places where little French was spoken.[159] This would be surprising, but the implication that French was commonly spoken everywhere else is unavoidable.

Popular stories told in French about the fox and the wolf, at the beginning of the later sequence of Reynard the Fox tales, have enough familiar elements to pass for reworked folk tales. Their setting in rural society is far removed from that of the courts. Yet these stories display an early determination to take note of contemporary affairs and use the personification of the animal subjects as a means of satire. They were not short of subjects. Both the legal chicanery identified with the new legalisms and the hypocrisy of the privileged clergy began to excite criticism. Some stories of this type were written in Normandy about 1190 for the constable, Richard du Hommet.[160] The elaboration of such animal stories quickly became popular in England too. There is sufficient evidence of an artistic kind to show that Reynard the Fox was at least as well appreciated as a character here as he was in France.

Storytelling was not monopolised by professional poets. Lambert of Ardres in his history of the counts of Guines describes how Count Arnold got the men of his household to tell stories. One old soldier, Robert of Coutances, was not limited to recounting his own martial exploits. He had an impressive repertoire, diverting the company with the great deeds of Roman emperors, Charlemagne and Arthur of Britain, as well as those of Gormond and Isembard, Tristan and Isolde, Merlin and Morolf. Whether he had read these stories or only heard them recited, he knew them by heart and must have told them in his own way. Arnold had estates in England and his courtiers were familiar with tales of English origin.[161]

Princely courts set standards in other respects too, though contemporary writers did not pay this much attention. In matters of dress, for example, Henry of Anjou, when he first came to England as a young man, was nicknamed Courtmantel because his clothes did not reach his ankles, as was then customary.[162] Adoption of fashionable dress was proof of sophistication; retention of local customary dress was remarked as odd. The Scots were mocked across Europe for their distinctive dress. In Spain, the peculiar garments of the Navarrese were likened to those of Scots; in Flanders, Philip of Harveng, abbot of the Premonstratensian monastery of Bona Spei, commented on the bare knees of the Scots. He was further scandalised to learn that Scots clerks dressed like knights and townsmen.[163] By the late twelfth century this had become a sign of cultural backwardness. Not all the remote parts of Scotland were lacking in dress sense. The *Orkneyinga Saga* paid considerable attention to sartorial elegance. Norse traders returned from overseas expeditions with smart clothes and duly impressed their compatriots. Earl Rognvald of Orkney, as a young man, cut quite a figure in Norway when he returned from – Grimsby.[164]

The clergy's greatest impact on secular society came about through their endorsement of warfare for religious purposes – the crusade. The situation of the crusading states in the Holy Land deteriorated as the Muslims regained the initiative. At Constantinople itself, the emperor Manuel sought to bolster his position by strengthening his ties with the west, calculating that it was the most likely source of reinforcements. In 1176, after his defeat at Myriocephalon, Manuel sent back some of Henry's own men who had been on the campaign to report in more detail and whip up support. The emperor's envoys were entertained in the south of England at the king's expense and the king sent back by ship from Norfolk some hunting dogs as a gift for the emperor. Two years later, on the departure of Robert, described as messenger of both the prince of Antioch and of the emperor, the king assigned him some money so that he could buy leaving presents: five ells of scarlet cloth, a leather hood and half a sable.[165]

Nearly ten years later, Richard of Limesia, former sheriff of Hampshire, was sent to Constantinople on the king's business. The situation in the east had become even more critical. All western rulers shared some general anxiety about the fate of the Christian communities planted in the Holy Land. In 1185, already anticipating that Jerusalem would fall to Saladin unless some western prince came to its rescue, Patriarch Heraclius himself came west and pressed Henry II above all to take on this task. Gerald of Wales was impressed by the patriarch's prophecy of disaster for the king if he declined this responsibility and thought the prophecy fulfilled by the grim events of Henry's last years.[166] Heraclius's appeal to Henry is understandable. Henry's grandfather had rescued the crusading kingdom in 1128 and Henry's own financial resources were known to be exceptional. According to Richard of Devizes, even the Saracens in the Holy Land had heard great things about Henry II. When Henry attempted to buy himself out of the running, the patriarch became angry; it was a prince, not money, that was required. All the same, an aid for the Holy Land was imposed in 1187. This was the first time the English had been taxed on the estimated value of their chattels and had it not been for such a worthy cause the imposition would not have been so readily accepted. Public opinion was being prepared. To foster enthusiasm for the crusade, Simon de Freisne, canon of Hereford, wrote a French verse life of St George, complete with anti-Muslim polemic. It was commissioned by the bishop of Hereford who, on his recent visit to the Holy Land, had acquired fresh information from Lydda about George, by then well on his way to being recognised as England's patron saint.[167]

To the discussion about how the crusading kingdom might be best assisted, Henry II had invited King William of Scotland. In the end the Scots did not pay up, William pleading the poverty of the kingdom and the Scottish bishops flatly refusing Henry II's request for contributions.[168] Two years later Richard I, preparing to depart for the east, began by raising money in England. When he offered William the chance to buy off the claims of English kings to the lordship of Scotland, William did find the money. In this way the Scots may be said to have made a substantial sacrifice for the crusade, though they got something more tangible than spiritual privileges. If William's refusal to make any direct payment for the crusade reflects a greater reluctance in Scotland to be swept along by crusading enthusiasm, this did not deter some of William's great men from setting out for the Holy Land.

The Welsh did not so easily evade crusading pressure. Archbishop Baldwin, accompanied by Gerald, undertook to recruit crusaders by making a preaching tour. Gerald's boasts about his own preaching in French and Latin suggest that the main thrust of the campaign was directed at the Anglo-Norman settlers rather than at the Welsh themselves. Even so, Gerald claimed that many common folk of Wales did sign up and the *Annales Cambriae* confirmed that some men from North Wales took the cross. On the other hand, the poet Cynddelw Brydydd Mawr actually commended the prince of Powys, Owain Cyfeiliog, for turning a deaf ear to Baldwin's preaching. The *Brut Chronicle*, which noted the departure of Richard I and Philip II for the Holy Land in 1190, significantly names no Welsh crusaders in their company. Gerald himself took no further interest in the Welsh contribution to the campaign and twice wriggled out of his own vow to go overseas.[169] Despite this evidence for Welsh indifference to crusading, at least one Welsh archer won renown by his prowess out east. The Norman jongleur, Ambroise, who wrote up a vivid account of Richard I's crusade, gave a graphic account of how a fearsome Turkish archer was so irked by the obvious talent of one Welsh bowman as to challenge him to a sporting context, in which the proud Turk was duly vanquished and slain.[170]

Detailed information about Richard's crusading expedition in English sources demonstrates the extraordinary scale of the operation and confirms what exceptional logistic resources went into the planning.[171] Over a hundred ships sailed down the Channel and round Spain, each carrying supplies for one year, forty horses and their equipment, forty infantrymen and fifteen sailors. Leaving in late March 1190, some arrived at Messina in mid-September, while others proceeded directly to the Holy Land. During the Third Crusade peoples from many different parts of the west were thrown together out east and in the process learned much not only about the lands concerned but also about their fellow Latins. The English experience of their French counterparts and some of the Greeks and Germans they met is reflected in the chronicles. Already the English are shown as totally careless about the effects of hearty eating and drinking in warm climates. They affirmed their national fellowship by rallying to their king at Messina, when Richard I called for drastic action against the perfidious Sicilians.

The importance to England of Richard I's crusade has long been recognised. The 'English' badge of the three leopards passant or the flag of St George's cross, now associated with public displays of 'national' pride, has been traced back to Richard himself though the king's battle standard, according to Richard of Devizes, remained that of the 'dragon'.[172] More important than the symbol used was the fact that the English clearly identified with the royal flag. The English chroniclers of the period give patriotic prominence to the military exploits of their king in the Holy Land where, by their reckoning at least, they outshone the French themselves. Richard's crusade was also important for introducing an English king to the advantages of borrowing from Italians. In the Holy Land, short of cash, Richard had no alternative source of supply: in Acre, he was able to secure funds from a Pisan merchant.[173] In this way, Richard gained first-hand experience of the commercial network in the Mediterranean that had kept the crusading states in the east afloat for several generations. The crusading adventure involved far more than the discovery of prejudice or the assertion of dominance; it was an introduction to an unfamiliar way of life.

In his narrative, the chronicler Roger of Hoveden duly included careful descriptions of the coastal cities of Spain for both its Christian and Muslim parts, and then of Italy; he also described the route for the return journey by water from the Holy Land through the Greek islands, expecting this precise information to be interesting or useful. Hoveden noted where the boundaries of political jurisdictions occurred, recognising the importance of distinguishing the lands of one prince from another, for both Christian and Muslim lands. Learned Englishmen had long been interested in Spain and access to the southern kingdom had probably become easier still after the marriage of Richard's sister Eleanor to the king of Castile. Such contacts probably explain how the English chronicler Ralph of Diceto, dean of St Paul's, obtained the text of a letter sent to the king of Valencia by Pope Alexander III in 1174. The letter is unremarkable except for the pope's valiant attempt to find common ground with this Muslim by stressing that all men owed respect to the same creator, a sentiment that might have seemed unusual enough at the time to attract Diceto's attention.[174] Military campaigns against the Muslims did more than foster religious hatreds. Crusaders prized secular as well as religious values, as shown by stories about the favourable impression made by Saladin on western crusaders. Participation in the crusade itself was at least as much an education about the world as wars became in the twentieth century.

Richard I, the absentee hero

The reign of Richard I drew English attention to the way 'foreign' affairs impinged directly on the kingdom. Richard's departure was not resented; it was the natural outcome of projects that had been discussed for several years. His careful arrangements for the government of the kingdom in his absence unfortunately gave rise to trouble after his departure, mainly because Richard's youngest and only surviving brother John made trouble for Richard's trusted representative, William, bishop of Ely. Richard, alerted in Sicily to the problem, responded promptly. Even at a distance, he commanded respect and was dutifully obeyed. Further trouble arose when Richard was taken prisoner on his way home from the crusade. Because of his treaty with Tancred of Sicily the year before, Richard was considered an enemy by the emperor Henry VI, so Richard travelled clandestinely through the Tyrol, hoping to escape recognition. In December 1192 he was recognised and detained by Leopold, duke of Austria, with whom he had quarrelled while on crusade. Richard's predicament was compounded when Leopold enhanced his satisfaction by selling his helpless captive to the German emperor. News of Richard's imprisonment encouraged his brother John to make a pact with the king of France, himself eager to take advantage of an unlooked-for opportunity to acquire some of Richard's Norman lands.

From this point until the end of the reign, Richard's affairs on the Continent became a major concern, first of the government acting on the king's behalf, then, after his release from captivity, of Richard himself. Contemporary writers were caught up in the excitement of events by the comings and goings of royal officials who were able to show them letters about the king's affairs and report what they had seen and done themselves. All this helped to focus attention on the way England was affected by foreign experiences.[175] Negotiations for Richard's release were protracted. In the meantime Richard received many visitors from England, including his aged mother. Letters were written on his behalf to persons of consequence in the empire. Whether the emperor Henry VI was in league with Philip II is not certain. Henry was wary of Richard's German relations, the Welf enemies of the imperial family, but his main motive in keeping Richard was in connection with his plans to topple the regime of Tancred, king of Sicily. By exacting a high price for Richard's ransom, Henry VI was able to afford his second and successful Italian campaign. He also demanded that Richard do homage to him as a sign of his subordination. Since Philip II had encroached on Richard's French lands in the meantime, Henry VI appreciated that Richard, on his release, would be far too busy nearer home to interest himself further in Sicily.

While Henry II had lived, Philip had already shown great skill in exploiting the rivalries of his sons and their belligerence against their father. Richard's succession reduced Philip's options. Richard's only possible family rival was his brother John, ten years younger, for whom he apparently felt a kind of benevolent contempt. Although Richard was born in Oxford, he was almost unknown in England at the time of his succession but experienced no difficulty in assuming control of all his father's lands. He did not seek Philip's permission to do so. The several questions outstanding between them were apparently settled, as between equals, while they were in Sicily together in 1191. Philip's claims on the Norman Vexin (granted as dowry for his sister Alice, whom Richard had never married) were bought off with cash. Philip concocted a different version of the Treaty of Messina, which he later used to advance his rights in Normandy, but even his intrigues with John aimed at no more than recovery of the Norman Vexin and the acquisition of border points along the eastern frontiers of Normandy.

Thanks to his acquisition of Artois in 1186, Philip was in a stronger position than his father had ever been to put pressure on Normandy, since it had become vulnerable to French military efforts on the north-east frontier as well as in the east and south. Even so, Philip may not have realistically aimed to conquer the whole duchy. He needed rather to protect his own lands by keeping Richard on the defensive.[176] Philip was well aware of Richard's military prowess and reputation, demonstrated when Richard made a whirlwind recovery of many places ceded by John or captured by Philip in Normandy. A truce was agreed and then a peace treaty in 1196. This still left Philip with the Vexin and some key places, but Richard did not expect to stop there. In the lull he negotiated alliances with the counts of Flanders and Boulogne, married his widowed sister Joanna to the count of Toulouse (to strengthen his Gascon possessions) and prepared for further campaigns against Philip, notably by constructing the powerful fortress at Château Gaillard.

The sudden death of his enemy, Henry VI, in September 1197, which released Richard from his formal subordination to the emperor, also precipitated a dispute in Germany about Henry's successor. Early in 1198 Richard's position was further strengthened by the accession of a new energetic pope, Innocent III, who was convinced of the dangers to papal interests posed by the imperial Staufen family. Duly encouraged, the enemies of the Staufen in Germany, particularly the archbishop of Cologne, looked to Richard for help and in June Richard's nephew, Otto of Brunswick, was elected and crowned king, much to Philip II's alarm.[177] Richard's support for the Welf king set English diplomacy on quite a new course, designed to isolate the king of France who had until this point been able to count on Staufen support. These hopes of using diplomatic alliances to put Philip II on the defensive were dashed by Richard's death in the Limousin.

Richard's multiple efforts had been supported from England by money and men. His absences and the heavy burdens his affairs had imposed on England had not provoked discontent with him or the Angevin regime. Admittedly, for the first time objections to the performance of military service abroad had been voiced by the bishop of Lincoln, Hugh of Avalon, not, however, for political reasons but on the grounds that it infringed the privileges of his church. Richard has been much criticised for 'neglecting' his kingdom but the reign is most remarkable for showing how little the king's presence mattered for an effective royal administration. After Richard's return from the crusade, the archbishop of Canterbury, Hubert Walter, was well able to manage affairs of state. Richard's death obviously left many problems for his successor, but the Angevin Empire had shown no sign of faltering in his lifetime.

At the end of the twelfth century English standing in continental esteem was considerable by any standard. Richard's intervention in German affairs alarmed the king of France; his involvement in Sicily and the Holy Land had thwarted the original plans of the emperor Henry VI. Their contributions to learning and literature confirmed the cultural reputation of the English. In the British Isles, English influence had been extended into Ireland. In Scotland, English lordship may have been renounced for cash but King William had himself assumed direct responsibility for refashioning his kingdom, largely along English lines. In Wales, a belated effort to do likewise eventually proved less successful. The Norman Conquest had brought England into close association with the Continent; in the Angevin Empire the English had become willing Europeans and were accepted as such from Lisbon to Jerusalem. The king of France felt threatened, as well he might, and in Richard's death perceived his opportunity to assert his authority over Richard's successor, whoever he might be. The 13-year-old Arthur, son of Philip's great friend Geoffrey, could hardly be feared. With John, Richard's youngest brother, Philip had already had enough dealings to know the score.

|5|

The loss of Normandy

When Richard I died in the Limousin of an infected wound (April 1199), there was some dispute about who should succeed him. Eight years earlier, in an agreement with Philip II at Messina, Richard had nominated his nephew Arthur, son of Geoffrey of Brittany, as his heir. Disregarding the 13-year-old Arthur's formal claim, Richard's only surviving brother, John, backed by the principal Norman lords, was promptly accepted as duke in Normandy and crowned in England as king. In Brittany, however, the Bretons took this opportunity to throw off Norman lordship and entrusted Arthur to Philip II who understandably seized the chance to exploit another Plantagenet family feud for his own purposes. John adroitly nipped these plans in the bud by coming to an agreement with William des Roches, seneschal of Anjou, Arthur's main supporter in western France. Instead of pressing on with a military campaign, John negotiated a truce with Philip, to be sealed by a marriage between Philip's heir, Louis, and John's niece, Blanche of Castile. By the time the peace treaty was agreed in May 1200, Philip had succeeded in extracting more land in France for Blanche's dowry and an unprecedented cash payment as the feudal 'relief' due for the succession. In return, Philip conceded that Arthur should hold Brittany of John, rather than of himself.[1] The integrity of the empire was thus preserved, only trimmed in Normandy by the loss of Evreux and by the cession of border lands in Auvergne and Berry. John may have paid a high price on Philip's terms, but the result appeared more satisfactory than persistence in family quarrelling. Nevertheless, within four years Philip had driven John out of Anjou and Normandy altogether. Henry II's Angevin legacy was never recovered by English kings. On the Continent, John retained only the lands of his mother, Eleanor of Aquitaine. French writers took great interest in these events.[2]

Historians have greeted the 'loss of Normandy' as though it snapped the English link with the Continent set up after the Norman Conquest. English kings were thereafter obliged to pass most of their time in England, learn how to live within the limits of what their English subjects would allow and compensate for their humiliation abroad by trying to impose their lordship on the Scots and the Welsh. The thirteenth century is accordingly presented as a period of English withdrawal from the Continent and recuperation from the damage done by the Norman yoke. This entailed royal engagement with domestic affairs and eventually brought into being a political society powerful enough by the end of the century to conquer Wales and occupy Scotland. Curiously, however, instead of thereafter concentrating on British affairs, the reinvigorated English kingdom turned, once again, to confront France. Leaving the Continent to its own devices was not actually on the agenda.

To interpret the loss of Normandy as a welcome relief from continental entanglements exaggerates the immediate impact of Philip's success. Far from accepting the Channel as a moat defending England from foreign intrusion, John became desperate to retain what he still held and, if possible, recover what was lost. This put his English subjects under unprecedented strain to satisfy his requirements. Instead of an absentee king busy with his French vassals, the English had to live with a king determined to make them shoulder the burdens of his dignity. The loss of Normandy introduced a new set of problems; it did not signify the separation of England from the Continent. At the end of his reign John was fighting for his crown against some of his barons who had invited Louis of France to England as their king, a situation without precedent. John's loss of Normandy entailed the possible loss of England too. Had Louis prevailed, England would have been even more closely bound to France than before.

The loss of Normandy made a deeper impression in England than the French occupation of Maine and Anjou. The association between England and Normandy had lasted so long as to have created expectations that were now called in question. One chronicler, Ralph of Coggeshall, apparently accepted the loss as definitive; others may have regarded the French conquest as more like a temporary setback, if only because, mentally, they could not adjust immediately to the new situation.[3] Had not Richard I promptly recovered much of what Philip had taken from him while he was held captive in Germany? Before 1199, Philip had not made much of an impression as a military leader and his success in 1204 was not fatalistically accepted as irreversible.[4] His occupation of the duchy did not necessarily make the separation between England and Normandy permanent. There seemed no fundamental reason for the catastrophe: John's indecisive and untrustworthy behaviour was obviously to blame for the slovenly defence of his rights in Normandy. His casual confidence that he could recover them easily enough at some future time could have alienated some Norman vassals. Did they conclude that he personally no longer deserved their loyalty? They may have harboured doubts about his right to rule. Years later, Louis of France alleged that an English court had found John guilty of treason against Richard for his devious dealings with Philip II in 1192 and declared him incapable of inheriting the crown.[5] But Louis's own hope of becoming king in England after the beginning of the civil war at the end of John's reign encouraged his English supporters to think they might rcover their Norman lands. Philip II himself remained unconvinced that the Normans had become willing Frenchmen ready to support him in his later campaigns against John.[6] After John's death some Normans continued to put their services at the disposal of Henry III and some English barons hoped that when Henry grew up he would prove a great warrior like Richard I.[7] On these grounds, Normandy did not seem in 1204 to have been lost for ever.

The loss of Normandy was after all not simply a matter of John's personal humiliation. He was not the only one to have suffered. Philip II had confiscated the estates of most of John's barons who continued to support him; those Normans who accepted Philip had their English lands sequestered by John. Some barons admittedly salvaged something for themselves, by dividing their estates between brothers or by negotiating terms with Philip II, as William Marshal himself did, while ostensibly remaining loyal to John. The Marshal and his friends were inclined to blame John for his misfortunes and saw nothing wrong with defending their interests as best they could. Less adroit barons became jealous of the Marshal's standing in France and professed to doubt his commitment to John. The great men of England who had remained loyal to John did not casually write off what they had lost. They expected the king to take action for the recovery of Normandy; if not, they looked for some compensation for what they had lost on his account. Philip II had disrupted the English barons' ties with their families, friends and neighbours in Normandy. It is implausible to suppose that they welcomed this change in the habits of a lifetime and did not expect, or hope, to repair their misfortunes. They were persons of great consequence in the kingdom. Fragmentary records of an enquiry into the English lands of Normans taken into crown custody by John identify only three barons of comital dignity who had accepted Philip.[8] Most of the Normans who stayed behind were of middling rank, without extensive properties in England. The king did not resign himself to permanent estrangement even from these minor Norman barons. The status of their lands was left provisional for nearly forty years. Only after the failure of Henry III's second French expedition in 1244 did Louis IX himself insist that any of his vassals who held lands of another lord must choose which lordship they preferred. He could not count in emergencies on men with dual allegiance. For his part Henry III, recognising that the Norman lords in Louis IX's lordship would now never revert to him, felt free at last to assign their lands to others.[9]

How did the rest of the kingdom react to the events of 1204? In the Tewkesbury annals for that year, pride of place was given to the Latin conquest of Constantinople. At Waverley, it seemed that John's Norman constable, William du Hommet, was personally responsible for the fall of Rouen. The Worcester annalist was inclined to blame the Normans as a whole for not putting up much resistance; John's losses regrettably entailed unwelcome demands for money in England.[10] John, who returned to England in December 1203, had already obtained some consent in England for taxation before asking in Ireland too for a contribution in February 1204.[11] Money was not everything. In expectation of an invasion of England by Philip in 1205, John ordered a mustering of forces. This may have generated enough alarm to excite a kind of patriotic anxiety, but as the danger receded so too did any national excitement.[12] The English themselves did not feel shamed by John's defeat. Chardri, a Norman poet living in England in the first decade of the century, sounded an unexpectedly confident note when he praised English knights and women, contrasting them with the French; according to him, England still surpassed all the kingdoms of the world for its pleasures and nobility.[13] A little later another Norman, Guillaume le Clerc, in French verses written for English patrons in the Coventry diocese, did not feel any need to hide his own French allegiance.[14] There were no national antipathies involved. It may seem perverse to praise England in a foreign language, but all that can be known about the sensibilities of the English laity of this period depends on a copious literature written in French, in many diverse genres. These writings allude to English legends, cite, even occasionally quote, English proverbs, but indicate that Englishmen who read and wrote normally did so in French. Such political hostility as surfaced between the English and the French was occasional rather than inveterate. If the French language served to express English pride in their own country and sharpen their determination to prove the equals of their enemies, it cannot have predisposed them to accept the loss of Normandy as being in the long-term interest of the English nation.

It had one inescapable consequence: the much greater prominence which Poitou came to enjoy in royal calculations. John's marriage to Isabella of Angoulême in 1200, like that of Richard to Berengaria of Navarre, was designed to bolster his position in southern France and in John's case to provide a better link between Poitou and Gascony.[15] Unfortunately, because the marriage abruptly put an end to the expectations of Hugh of Lusignan, count of La Marche, to whom Isabella had previously been affianced, any long-term advantage was immediately outweighed by the tensions it created between John and Hugh's family. The Lusignans' appeal to Philip II for justice in 1202 and John's refusal to acknowledge the jurisdiction of Philip's court had provided Philip with legal justification for stripping John of his French lands. John's quarrel with the Lusignans had some repercussions in Normandy (Hugh of Lusignan's brother, Ralph, was the Norman count of Eu) but the Angevin Empire was not shattered by any general disaffection in Normandy. Normandy rather than Poitou was lost because of John's inept defence of his position there and because Philip was able to apply greater pressure on John north of the Loire. Normandy was anyway a far more desirable acquisition than Poitou. Philip did hold Poitou briefly, but could not retain it when John made a determined bid for its recovery in 1206. The

Poitevins' local feuds in fact gave them no incentive to welcome incorporation into Philip's dominions. The Lusignan appeal had been a means of getting their revenge on John; it was not a bid for submission to the French king himself. The Poitevins found an English king who was French by parentage, speech and culture perfectly acceptable as their lord. With his greater, more distant responsibilities, he offered them an easier rein than Philip.

However, in England the prominence of Poitou in John's subsequent calculations rankled with barons who had been deprived of their Norman lands by Philip for their loyalty to John. Matters were made worse because Poitevins looking to John for advancement cared no more for English susceptibilities than they had for their part in John's misfortunes. John's concern to humour his Poitevin vassals is understandable: his hopes of recovering his lands in France depended on the retention of their loyalty. But nursing such hopes, John became ever more distrustful of English barons who did not give him the support he craved. Even English barons who remained loyal had no commitments of their own in Poitou. When the king demanded their military service there, some refused it. A rift therefore developed in John's own camp. Few of his Poitevins were absorbed into the English landed nobility. The most influential of them was the treasurer of Poitou, Peter des Roches, to whom in 1205 John offered the bishopric of Winchester, one of the richest sees in England. In 1214 Peter became justiciar, an appointment that affronted those who thought judges should be conversant with native laws. Personally, however, Peter was an able politician but, in a career that lasted more than thirty years, he aroused strong feelings in some quarters and made many enemies.[16]

The difference between the king and his barons over Poitou compromised efforts to recover the lost lands of the Angevin Empire. English critics made much of the Poitevin reputation for perfidy in putting their own interests before those of any lord. For their part, the Poitevins understandably supported John and did not sympathise with the English barons' grievances. By 1215, the barons' dislike of the king's Poitevin commitments was openly expressed by the proposal to limit their future military obligations to Normandy and Brittany.[17] Ten years after the loss of Normandy, no objections were raised to overseas service as such. Given their background, neither John nor his barons could have abandoned all expectation of eventually returning in force to the Continent. John took the optimistic view that an effective military campaign could easily recover what had been lost, as had been the case in Poitou in 1206.

Communication with Normandy did not cease in 1204. The many Norman religious houses with English property continued to exercise their rights in England. Though their acceptance of Philip II in Normandy meant that most secular lords could not expect favours from John, even so the counts of Eu, Perche and Meulan still did business with the king; likewise, Simon de Montfort, called earl of Leicester, later papal champion in the war against the Albigensian heretics, and father of Henry III's enemy, Simon. More unexpected are the visits of the mayor of Quillebeuf or Drogo of Dieppe's provision of siege engines in England.

John's somewhat fitful commitment to schemes for the recovery of his lost lands was matched on Philip's side. Having achieved so much by 1204, Philip might have been expected to press on and root out all the Plantagent holdings in his kingdom. Instead, after John had recovered Poitou in 1206, Philip made no concerted efforts to eat into John's surviving French dominions. It was only the pope's exasperation with John's defiance of papal authority that prodded Philip into acting as papal champion and working with disaffected English barons to carry the war against John into England itself.

Because of his fear of the Staufen and the need to provide support for Otto of Brunswick in Germany, Innocent III was predisposed to think well of John. As Otto's uncle, John was potentially Innocent's most powerful ally. When John had been arraigned before Philip's court in 1202, Innocent tried to intercede on John's behalf and was not pleased to be rebuffed on the grounds that a feudal dispute lay outside papal jurisdiction. John may have taken Innocent's goodwill for granted, but the pope could hardly overlook John's blatant offences against churchmen. John's treatment of the archbishop of Dublin and the bishop of Séez were judged so unacceptable by 1203 that the pope had even then threatened to impose an interdict. However, relations between John and Innocent were only seriously impaired by wrangles over the succession at Canterbury. Archbishop Walter died in 1205, just when John might have been expected to nurse what friends he had left. The king and the monks of Canterbury had different candidates for the post and the dispute, as was customary, went to the pope for resolution. Innocent, aiming at conciliation, proposed a compromise candidate, the distinguished English scholar Stephen Langton, whom John flatly refused to accept, either out of pique at not getting his own way or because he doubted the loyalty of Langton on account of his long residence in Paris. Innocent could hardly condone the flagrant rejection of papal authority but still had no wish to proceed to extremes. Only when the imposition of an interdict, the exile of the bishops and excommunication itself did not soften John's resistance, did Innocent realise that he needed to find a military champion if papal authority was to retain any credibility. He decided to make Philip II his instrument of punishment. Not only did the pope encourage Philip to plan an invasion and the conquest of England from an unworthy ruler, he helped to negotiate a treaty between Philip and Llewelyn of Gwynedd designed to stir up trouble in the Welsh borders. This in turn gave rise to a baronial plot for John's assassination.[18] When it was discovered the barons concerned fled overseas, arguing plausibly that they were motivated by their own abhorrence of John's crimes. The dangers were now so clear that John abruptly changed tack. His submission to the pope in May 1213 immediately deprived Philip of papal support. A few weeks later, in August, the fleet Philip had assembled for the invasion of England was destroyed in the port of Damme by John's naval forces.

Buoyed up by the sudden change in his fortunes, John concentrated on creating a new coalition of support against Philip II which meant finding considerable sums of money for foreign friends and armies. John expected that by joint campaigning with his allies, Philip II could be beaten and that he himself would then resume his former position without difficulty or resentment. The importance of his continental allies for his future was confirmed in 1214. Although John himself achieved some success in Poitou, the decisive rout of his allies at Bouvines was sufficient to ruin all his schemes and it gave his enemies in England their chance. This time they were not going to let papal support for the king thwart their determination to curb his exactions. John himself returned to England, unbowed and still confident of being able in time to recover his own, taking it for granted that England was rich enough to foot the bill, as it had paid up in the previous reign for the crusade and Richard's ransom. Nevertheless, he took some precautions, granting a charter of clerical liberties in November 1214 and vowing to go on crusade in March 1215, certain that the pope would see him through his continuing disputes with his barons.

English historical discussion of Magna Carta has traditionally concentrated on the domestic discontent brought about by John's contentious style of government, without allowing adequately for the international dimension of his situation. John's problems at home were intimately bound up with his standing abroad, all the way down the line. His demands for money arose from his heavy commitments to warfare and the cost of diplomacy, as well as a foolish confidence that success could be bought. John's difficulties were compounded by the stance he adopted, not so much towards Philip of France but to Pope Innocent III. Chroniclers abroad perceived that baronial grievances arose from John's oppressive government, but their interest in the dispute reflected their awareness of its further implications. It was papal fury at John's intransigence that created a tense international crisis, noted as far from the action as Denmark.[19] The barons really had no choice but to present their case against John to the pope. John was not fearful about Innocent's likely response, but before this arrived the defiant barons had secured their entry into London in June 1215. Seeing no other way of recovering their loyalty, John was cornered into granting them too a charter of liberties. The basic law of later English government was granted while England lay at the very centre of an international storm and would not have been granted in other circumstances. Although Innocent III, once informed of John's plight, did not hesitate to condemn the charter along with the baronial opposition, the barons were not to be fobbed off and turned for support instead to Louis of France, who came to England with an army as the baronial champion. After John's death the government, acting on behalf of the young Henry III, thought to win over the defiant barons by reissuing John's charter with only minor modifications. By then Innocent had died and the new pope and his legates in England raised no objections. The charter thereafter made the imposition of arbitrary taxation impossible. It was this that effectively hampered all later efforts to campaign in France.

When Louis of France was finally persuaded to leave England in 1217, the papal legate remained as a powerful member of the regency government. In his submission to the pope in 1213, John had actually gone further than was needed. Innocent had put him under no pressure to become a vassal of the papacy for England and Ireland, but by doing so John succeeded in flattering the pope and obliging him to remain a stalwart ally. John finally accepted that the 'moral' voice of the Church was not a negligible factor for his government. For the next fifty years, the papacy stood by the kings of England in their troubles. It was not gullible: England was well worth protecting. Innocent III's general sympathy for the Plantagenet family, his subsequent support for John against the barons in 1215 and the papal share in the government of the minority of Henry III provide ample evidence for the advantages England derived from the papal lordship. In the matter of English royal hopes for the recovery of the lost French lands, popes were by no means predisposed to favour France. Innocent III had been angry with Philip II for repudiating his Danish queen, Ingeborg, which flaunted his personal indifference to the magistracy of the Church in such a basic moral affair as his marriage. In the matter of the pope's overriding fears of the Staufen, Philip II had shown no inclination to abandon his former friendship with that family. On more than one occasion, Philip II had rebuffed Innocent III, showing himself to be single-minded in his determination to run his kingdom as he saw fit. English kings, on the other hand, through their foreign kinsmen, could help win friends for the papacy, notably in the empire, whence the papacy feared the worst. Papal perception of the value of the English connection ought to make it clear what an important role England then played in the overall scheme of European affairs. The size of the English king's continental dominions fully justified this. Moreover John pursued objectives on the Continent which were fully compatible with the interests of the Church. The papal lordship duly encouraged English kings to expect papal favour in their contests with the kings of France.

Despite its political merits, John's surrender of the kingdom into papal lordship struck some of his subjects as humiliating. It excited more comment from clerical contemporaries than the loss of Normandy. Archbishop Langton himself was believed to have deplored it as a major blunder. The Cistercian monk, Matthew of Rievaulx, who wrote Latin poetry in praise of England, considered the subjection of England to Rome to have turned things topsy-turvy and made 'free' Sarah into 'servile' Hagar. Other poets thought likewise.[20] What did laymen think of it? At a later stage, English barons claimed that they had not approved, but in 1213 most barons were given no opportunity to protest and some may anyway have appreciated the expediency of getting immediate papal protection from Philip II. Others may already have had 'constitutional' reservations. One of the accusations made against John in the manifesto Louis of France published in 1216 was that he had handed over the kingdom to the pope without consulting his barons.[21] The barons who supported Louis's own claims to the throne can hardly be considered 'patriotic' Englishmen, in any modern sense of the word, but the assumption of the manifesto that the status of the kingdom was not a matter for the king alone to decide has considerable interest.

John found no reason to regret what he had done. Just as he had bought the services of loyal vassals in the Low Countries with money rents, so in effect he bought the protection of papal lordship for an annual outlay of 700 marks for England and 300 marks for Ireland. As John's overlord, Innocent III not only blocked further French assaults against England itself, he backed the king against opposition in his own kingdom, even from his erstwhile protégé, Stephen Langton. It was the inflexible papal support for John that made the king's baronial enemies so desperate that, far from working for the defence of England, they invited Louis to lead their rebellion in 1216.

Louis's credentials for replacing John were respectable. He was the husband of John's niece Blanche. He already ruled the county of Artois across the Channel which he had inherited from his mother. On that account he was as much interested in English affairs as that long-standing royal ally, the count of Flanders. But Louis had not thought through his likely prospects as pretender to the English crown and his father, Philip II, was uneasy about Louis's involvement. In his father's lifetime, Louis simply took what chances he had to press the Plantagent enemy. After John's death, the papacy supported the new king of England against Louis and in 1217 ordered the excommunication of Louis and his party. This was not the only factor that finally induced Louis to leave England, but it was a very important one.

Historical records

Disagreements about how to deal with John, the loss of Normandy and the papal lordship brought about great confusion in England. The ability of historians to flesh out the character of English baronial society in the thirteenth century is considerably assisted by a number of narrative texts written in the vernacular. From them the activities of laymen can be perceived directly and no longer through the distorting lens of clerical preoccupations. In France, the vernacular was first employed in this way to write about the crusades for lay audiences, as in Villehardouin's account of the capture of Constantinople in 1204; in England it was used to provide a spirited biography of the great Marshal, earl of Pembroke, who had become regent of England in his last years. In his youth the Marshal, like other English sportsmen, had gone to France to test his combat skills in tournaments, which were not allowed in England until Richard I authorised the practice.[22] Richard I had given a new boost to English military enthusiasms and

England itself became a military arena at the end of John's reign. Another vernacular author, the anonymous of Béthune, provided eyewitness accounts of many engagements in which his fellow countrymen were involved in King John's service in his lands from Gascony to Ireland.[23] Never before have the historical records shown the English more deeply imbedded in the society of French speakers. In thirteenth-century England, French was the language of public communication, in the common law courts and in parliament. Most of the senior clergy had been educated in Paris. England was not a French colony, not even a French satellite. It was distinctively English, but culturally it was as much part of the same world as Flanders, Anjou and Savoy, more so probably than Provence and Gascony.

Our understanding of English society is further enriched by the quality of English chronicle writing in Latin. One of its peculiarities was the highly critical attitude taken of kings by the chroniclers. Whereas in France historical accounts of the kings' affairs were typically favourable, English monastic writers were more often suspicious of royal motives and resentful of any royal encroachments on vested interests. The chroniclers were not parochial in outlook. They took a very broad view of contemporary affairs. This makes them indispensable for showing how contemporaries themselves experienced the impact of events and government. Roger of Wendover, monk of St Albans, noted foreign events in which Englishmen were involved: the crusades, the expeditions in France, the affairs of the papacy. Occasionally Wendover's attention was drawn to other events with no direct bearing on England.[24] When Matthew Paris took over the writing of the chronicle in 1235, he became so interested in the world at large, not just in the British Isles, as to compile a chronicle of events between 1236 and 1259 which has value for the whole of Europe. It illustrates the extent to which Englishmen paid attention to what was happening outside their own kingdom. There is no reason to believe that the chronicler had to strain every nerve to pick up news. News arrived, sometimes in the form of letters which he carefully kept and copied; more often, he learnt from messengers, distinguished visitors to the abbey or from conversation with fellow monks about their occupations before taking to religion. Matthew may have been more diligent and more persistent in keeping account of what he heard, but it is unlikely that the news he recorded was not widely known to others. His accumulation of information appears to be motivated by the simple pleasure of knowing what was what and having some good tales to tell. He collected stories from all those parts of western Europe that were in touch with England and from the lands of crusading endeavour. Paris was more than a collector of tales. He was concerned to place his information geographically and this made him something of a pioneer in cartography. He chose to make his texts more attractive by adding drawings or other illustrations. He was not himself a notable traveller, but he did work for a time in London and undertook a mission to Norway on behalf of the pope and the king of France. As a monk he acquired a reputation as a historian in his own house, but he did not achieve high office there and never joined the managerial ranks. If ever there was a spokesman for the ordinary thirteenth-century Englishman, Matthew Paris has a good claim.[25]

He has been represented in a rather negative fashion as the member of a privileged order, but even in modern times those who presume to speak up for others need to be more articulate than most if they expect to do more than air their own prejudices. He has also acquired the reputation of being a 'typically' xenophobic Englishman, committed only to the defence of his own monastery. Yet because St Albans in Matthew Paris's time strove to defend itself against the diocesan, the bishop of Lincoln, by means of a papal privilege, Matthew could not be hostile to the papacy. Like the other monks, he thought his house merited papal protection, though it rankled that the papacy expected the monks to pay for their privileges. Paris also believed his complaints about excessive papal taxation in England were justified, but his criticisms do not amount to evidence for English restlessness about papal encroachments on English liberties. Although he denounced the Curia for abuse of powers in exacting money from English churches and for appointing Italian hangers-on to English ecclesiastical benefices, he did not aim to diminish respect for papal authority. Complaints about abuses in the system were addressed to the pope so that he should take remedial action. Like everyone else in his time, with the exception of the Roman emperor Frederick II, Matthew had considerable confidence that Christendom had to be ruled in all essential matters by the pope, if the highest possible goals for Christian people were to be achieved.

The scope of the chronicle proves that thirteenth-century Englishmen had not begun to withdraw into their shell in order to grapple with domestic problems. It provides a comprehensive conspectus of the way the world appeared in England to an unofficial observer. This impression, that England was well informed about what was happening in the contemporary world, is actually borne out by consulting other English chroniclers, who showed comparable curiosity, even if they did not sustain it over such a long period.

The interest of English chroniclers in public affairs is not the only advantage England offers to historians of thirteenth-century Europe. Although the period is marked everywhere in the west by a quite abrupt increase in the amount of written documentation available, the new importance of writing and written record was particularly striking in England.[26] From the beginning of John's reign, royal letters and instructions were regularly enrolled to provide the government with an archive. About the same time, similar papal records, which had been kept for centuries but carelessly preserved, received more scrupulous custody in the papal Curia. This sudden availability of abundant documentation brings the relationship between the kingdom and the Continent into much sharper focus. The royal government was so confident of its ability to obtain written records for its own purposes, even of commercial transactions, that in 1204 when John imposed a tax on the export of merchandise by foreigners, he required all the goods attracting the levy to be itemised and valued by six or seven law-worthy men and a record to be kept daily by their clerk. Two years later, he expected similarly detailed records to be kept by a clerk at sea when merchant ships were induced by a persuasive spokesman to enter his service.[27] Since such record-keeping provided the king with the means to scrutinise the affairs of his kingdom more closely and so exploit every device for getting money to fund his campaigns, it is hardly surprising that his subjects showed little willingness to comply with his demands. The king's attempt to interfere with every aspect of his vassals' lives was disapproved and resisted, the first sign of English political determination to keep the king's government as far as possible at arm's length.

Royal records may be unsatisfactory evidence for popular disaffection, but are sufficient to show that royal subjects were far from neglecting their own interests to serve the king's. The main problem for the historian of this period is finding documentary evidence not derived from government sources. To some extent English bishops kept pace with popes as keepers of written records and they had the institutional means to have their documents preserved. Parish priests, however, kept no records and were not expected to before the sixteenth century. This means that much more can be known about the episcopal administration than about the religious practices and beliefs of parishioners. For a few great cities, like London or Dublin, local authorities began to store their records or compile registers of important documents that have been preserved to the present. If the merchants or manufacturers of those cities kept comparable records of their own business affairs, they have not been saved. Glimpses of their activites may be gained from official records, but these are no safe guide to the nature of merchants' business as the merchants themselves perceived them. At Leicester, nevertheless, where the Merchant Gild Roll dated local records by reference to such distant events as the death of the emperor Henry VI (1197) or the capture of Damietta (1219), the burgesses must not only have kept informed about foreign news but expected such events to be remembered as guides to chronology. Not until 1234 did they make use of the year of the king's reign, a practice that became conventional.[28]

The official records of John's reign have not survived unscathed. The record is fullest for John's ninth year (May 1207–May 1208), from which some impression of the varied nature of contacts across the seas can be derived. Though their business is not made explicit, many royal messengers were despatched abroad. Ambassadors were sent to the pope, no doubt in connection with the ongoing dispute about the succession to Archbishop Hubert Walter. This year there was a papal legate in England who held a council in Reading Abbey and was entertained at the expense of the bishopric of Lincoln and the abbey of Ramsey. The earl of Chester, Ranulf de Blundeville, one of the most powerful barons of the kingdom, had business of his own at the papal Curia. Cardinal Gregory and some unnamed

Romans and Lombards made arrangements for the farming of their prebends at York to local clergy. The king of León, Alfonso IX, sent messengers to negotiate a treaty which was agreed in August 1207. Other Spanish business concerned his cousin of Castile, Alfonso VIII, John's brother-in-law. Compostela also appears in the records. At Bury St Edmunds, John received his nephew Otto of Brunswick, then at the lowest point of his fortunes since being elected king of the Romans in opposition to Philip of Swabia. Otto had slipped out of Germany with the help of his ally the king of Denmark who had sent him on to England. To help Otto, John was in touch with several princes of the Low Countries, the duke of Louvain, the counts of Alost (Namur), St Pol, Boulogne, Flanders and Holland. Merchants from the same region, like those of St Omer, were in England in order to buy wool. Flemings wanted to acquire supplies of English corn and had to get permission for export from the East Anglian ports of Yarmouth and Lynn; some corn, from as far west as Somerset, was shipped overseas from Dover. The Hospitallers of Jerusalem received a donation from the king and the bishop of Acre was welcomed in England, signs of English concern for the Holy Land. The sultan of Cairo, Saladin's brother El Adil, himself sent a messenger, a certain William, perhaps an Englishman; how he had become the sultan's agent is not known.

Concern for Poitou and Gascony naturally surfaces frequently in the record. The abbot of St Eparch of Angoulême came to inform the king about his negotiations with Poitevin lords for their return to John's lordship. He was entertained in England at Eynsham and Ramsey abbeys, where he must have kept the monks informed about Gascony. The bishop of Saintes too was engaged in this same business and had come in person to report. Large sums of money released from the royal treasuries at Oxford and Exeter were sent out to Poitou from Devon ports, escorted by burgesses of Exeter and others. The burgesses of Gloucester offered the king 300 lampreys to be excused the burden of housing some Poitevin prisoners who had been brought to England. The king was mindful of some of his own knights imprisoned by the king of France. Amphalus de Tilio had to pay a heavy ransom for his release. Mauversinus de Anoyl was allowed to come over to England and take service with the king. John's need of shipping to the Bay of Biscay meant calling on the services of even an east coast port like Ipswich. Horses were bought at Stowe fair for transportation to Poitou. William, earl of Salisbury, the king's half-brother, sent in command of a force to La Rochelle was obliged to borrow money there. The city of Bayonne obtained special permission to buy a specified quantity of corn along with peas and vetches and export them from Southampton and Sandwich.

In John's ninth year most parts of the kingdom were still exposed one way or another to people from the Continent. The government was apparently more actively engaged with continental affairs than it was with the rest of the British Isles. There is little sign of any interest in the Scots. Ireland appears only as a source of revenue. The recently appointed archbishop of

Armagh who had left Ireland on his way to Rome was detained in England officiating as bishop in the Exeter diocese, vacant since November 1206. An agreement was reached with the king of Man. Only the lack of comparable evidence for earlier periods makes it impossible to pronounce on the relative growth or diminution of such interests.

Foreign alliances

Under Innocent III, the papacy began to play a more active role in European political affairs than had been possible for his predecessors. The death of Henry VI in September 1197 followed by the election of Innocent in January created a wonderful opportunity for a fresh start in papal affairs. In Sicily, Henry's heir Frederick was only three years old; in Germany the election of Henry's brother Philip as king was countered by the election of an anti-king, Otto of Brunswick, in June 1198. Both parties needed and sought Innocent's approval. For most of his pontificate Innocent manoeuvred to make the most of the situation, mainly with a view to strengthening his position in Italy and careless of the consequences in Germany. Over the next half-century, these papal calculations had practical implications for England because it was drawn into papal plans, first for Germany and later for Italy as well.

Political understanding between England and the papacy had originally developed out of the pope's high expectations of English kings as crusaders, which Richard I's campaign in the east had done much to justify. Innocent hoped that Richard's successors would maintain this commitment to the future of the Holy Land. The pope also placed great hopes in Richard when Richard's favourite nephew, Otto of Brunswick, became Innocent III's preferred candidate for the empire. John had been less helpful and under the terms of his agreement with Philip II in 1200 had to renounce any support for Otto. Only when Philip turned against John could he resume support for his nephew.

John allowed his difficulties in the next ten years to turn the pope into an enemy but after the submission of 1213 the papacy resumed its benevolence. The papal legates had a place in the baronial government of the young Henry III and were influential in pacifying the kingdom and shaping future policy. The matter of John's lost lands in France remained on the agenda, particularly because Louis of France showed every intention of depriving Henry III of his remaining territories. In his father's lifetime, Louis simply took what chances he had to press the Plantagent enemy. Honorius III had to urge Louis to keep the peace with England in 1218; again in 1219 Louis's aggression was reproved, this time against Gascony. His father's death in 1223 at last gave him his head: as Louis VIII, he could no longer be held back. Nevertheless, his conquest of Poitou from the under-age Henry III still brought down on his head strong papal censure. Louis defended his action on the grounds that he was simply completing the task of repossessing the lands John had forfeited by decision of the French baronial council in 1202. As far as Louis was concerned, the inactivity of his father in his last few years had been due to his own advanced age rather than to any change of policy. Respect for the success of Philip II in Normandy and Anjou tends to diminish English appreciation of how relentlessly Louis VIII persevered with the humbling of the English kings.

The determination of French kings to give no ground to the pope's new English vassal explains why there was no formal settlement of the dispute between the two kings for over fifty years. Diplomatically, the two parties were not so unequal as may appear. During this period the papacy did what it could to restrain the French kings, arrange and prolong periods of truce and encourage renewed negotiations without losing hope of a settlement. The long-term objective was to secure a peace that would enable the war in the east to be prosecuted with greater vigour, though once the new emperor Frederick II, crowned in Germany (1213) and in Rome (1220) had assumed responsibility for activity in the east, the papacy became less anxious about securing English and French contributions to the crusade. Although the government of Henry III had to concede that crusading commitments had precedence, it continued to entertain expectations that in due course suitable circumstances would arise for restoring the king's lost lands or getting some compensation for his losses.

The sudden expansion of the French monarchy gave rise to some alarm outside Henry III's own domains. In the early thirteenth century, what is now the south of France was unfamiliar to French kings, whereas the children of Eleanor of Aquitaine were much more attuned to its particularities. Only the papal decision to unleash a war on the Albigensian heretics had drawn northern French barons, notably Simon de Montfort, into this other holy war and when Louis VIII, after his success in Poitou, also fought against heretics in the south, a royal presence was established there for the first time. Despite Louis's unexpected death, following a reign of only three years, the force of French royal power remained. In 1229 even the weakened government of the regent, Blanche of Castile, was still formidable enough to impose a settlement on the count of Toulouse whose dominions were the main breeding grounds of heresy. Committed to the repression of dissent, Blanche reckoned to secure the future reliability of Toulouse by demanding the marriage of the count's heiress to one of Louis IX's brothers. In this way, Gascony would be surrounded on all sides by French royal governments.

This novel demonstration of French royal authority threatened not only heretics but the interests of neighbouring princes. The monarchy was suspected of using heresy as an excuse for its irruption into southern affairs. Its political objective was plain, not only to Henry III but to the king of Aragon, lord of Montpellier, and his cousin, the count of Provence, who also had no son to succeed him. His four daughters were, however, considered desirable matches. With characterstic promptitude, Blanche made an effective bid for the oldest, Margaret, as a wife for Louis IX. They were married in 1234. The attractions of acquiring a stake in Provence seemed so important that in the end all four daughters became queens by marriage.

The rapid consolidation of French royal power in the south, so far from persuading Henry III to retire gracefully from the Continent, intensified his determination to make firm friends wherever he could.[29] Some of the best evidence for England's relations with the rest of Europe in the first half of the thirteenth century accordingly relates to the efforts made to create a family network of kings. Troubled relations with France threw the importance of connections with the German Empire into higher relief. The Saxon marriage of 1168 had created a close bond between the Welf and Plantagenet families, still cultivated on both sides in the generation after John. Otto IV's brother, Henry, duke of Saxony, wrote familiarly to the vice-chancellor, Ralph de Neville; Henry's nephew, another Otto of Brunswick, released from captivity by papal intervention came to England in 1230 where, as a favoured member of the king's family, he received formal permission to hunt at Windsor.[30] The king's German connections explain why so much care was taken with diplomacy there. The king's treasurer, the bishop of Carlisle, went on a mission to the empire in 1225 and his reports of how he fared are the oldest memoranda of an English ambassador to survive, vividly describing the hazards of his journey and the impression made on him by the leading princes he encountered.[31]

An early objective of embassies abroad was to find Henry himself a suitable bride. The departure of his tempestuous mother, Isabella of Angoulême, from England and her return to her own county in 1218 left the responsibility for Henry's personal affairs with the baronial council. It was in no hurry to introduce another disruptive element, in the shape of wife's kin, to precarious stability. The council did not worry about the succession. Henry had an indisputable heir in his capable brother Richard. After a suggestion about a Breton marriage in 1224, another proposal in 1225 came from Austria; between 1226 and 1228 the search was extended as far as Bohemia. Seven years later in the summer of 1235 a form of marriage with Joanna of Ponthieu was agreed but promptly vetoed by Louis IX because it would have given Henry control of the Somme estuary. Only a few months later, in January 1236, Henry III married Eleanor of Provence.[32] By then the king was nearly thirty years of age; his younger brother Richard had first married ten years earlier.

Eleanor brought Henry III no dowry and no powerful political allies, but his marriage proved to be an important turning point in his development as a ruler. The marriage of Eleanor's older sister to Louis IX even gave Henry III an advocate at the French court, where Margaret struggled unavailingly to diminish the hold over Louis of his mother, Blanche, Henry III's own intransigent cousin. Henry cannot have realistically hoped to get some share of Provence with Louis IX when Count Raymond died, but marriage gave him a valid reason to be concerned about a region of considerable importance for international diplomacy. The county of Provence nominally lay within the bounds of the empire, but from the 1230s the papacy encouraged any arrangement that would weaken Frederick II's authority there. This made the matter of the succession to Count Raymond crucial.

Provence was not the only county of the empire brought to Henry's attention. Eleanor's mother came from Savoy and one of her maternal uncles, William, bishop-elect of Valence, immediately became one of Henry's principal advisors in England; another, Peter, was assigned the estates of the earls of Richmond; Boniface was appointed archbishop of Canterbury and remained a person of consequence both within and without the kingdom for nearly thirty years. Two other brothers provided influential contacts between Henry III and continental politics. Philip was archbishop-elect of Lyon for several years and Thomas was successively count of Flanders (by virtue of his marriage, 1237–44) and then of Savoy. The Savoy brothers conveniently divided their loyalties between support of Frederick II and Pope Innocent IV, offering mediation in many different disputes. Eleanor's family interests in Provence and Savoy made Henry aware of the problems facing the sensitive western borders of the empire.[33] Both lands were French speaking and Henry's marriage accentuated the French element in his family connections. By diplomacy, if not battle, it helped to re-establish Henry III as a prince of consequence in the French kingdom.

The traditional English interest in building friendships in the German Empire had already brought about a resumption of diplomatic relations in the 1220s with the emperor Frederick II, nemesis of the Welf imperial ambitions. Quite fortuitously this connection suddenly blossomed. After Gregory IX reluctantly agreed to a rapprochement with Frederick in 1232, he hoped to keep Frederick in the right camp by negotiating for Henry III's sister Isabella to become Frederick's third wife in 1235.[34] Frederick was gracious. He sent one of his closest advisors, Peter of Vinea, the admired Latinist, to England and presented the king with a piece of gold cloth with eagles, which Henry offered on the great altar of Westminster Abbey. Henry III was sufficiently impressed by his new connection to offer Peter a pension and Peter's literary reputation won him influential readers in England.[35] After the marriage, Frederick reckoned to please Henry by sending him a present of three leopards in recognition of the king's heraldic device. As a result of this friendship, Frederick was able to recruit Englishmen to fight for him in Italy against Milan in 1238, when Henry de Turbeville, a Berkshire knight who had twice acted as Henry III's seneschal in Gascony, brought out 300 knights. So much was Turbeville himself at home on the Continent that when he died his heart was taken to Normandy for burial by his brother.[36]

The new friendship for Frederick was threatened when Gregory IX excommunicated the emperor for a second time in 1239. Henry III himself was reluctant to turn against Frederick. His family feeling for his sister and her husband had to contend with his sense of obedience to the pope. After Isabella's death, at the time of his second confrontation with Louis IX in

1242–43, Henry still turned to Frederick for support.[37] Alerted to the pope's intentions to depose Frederick from the empire, Henry authorised his embassy to the council of Lyon to press for a reprieve. When this was unceremoniously rebuffed, Henry found himself in a very awkward position. Innocent's aim, to suppress the rights of the whole Staufen family, threatened to deprive Henry's own nephew and namesake of any share in the imperial inheritance. English disapproval of the pope for pressing his case too hard in 1245 was clear. As late as 1248, Henry III was still friendly enough with the excommunicate emperor to send him four gerfalcons and the following year Frederick's son, Henry, wrote on his uncle's behalf to the king of France. Matthew Paris was well informed about Henry of Hohenstaufen whom he believed to be a convinced Anglophile.[38]

The quarrel between pope and emperor received critical attention in England. Matthew Paris evidently approved enough of the emperor's arguments to copy out many of the letters he sent defending his position. The English clergy had their own reasons for sympathising with Frederick's grievances. They had been forced to contribute money to Gregory IX's war chest in 1228 and, when the pope made peace before all the money was spent, dared to ask for some of their money back. For his later war against the emperor, Gregory also collected money in England. Some of this was actually captured by Frederick's Pisan allies at sea in 1241 and the irony was not lost on English taxpayers.

Henry's confidence in making friends abroad in order to bring pressure to bear on Louis was unwarranted but understandable. Just like his father, he was in no position to wage war alone. In France itself, his hopes were vain until he could find others with grievances against the French king who might be willing to accept Henry III as their lord. When Louis VIII seized Poitou in 1224 and threatened to advance on Gascony, Henry's brother Richard was sent as count of Poitou early in 1225 to thwart further loss. This campaign succeeded in its limited aim. The sudden death of Louis in 1226 then raised further hopes that disaffection in Poitou itself might be exploited in Henry III's interest, but Louis's widow, Blanche, took immediate steps to bring Poitou into line. She persuaded the Lusignans to submit, securing favourable terms for their defection. Gascony was indeed saved, but the loss of Poitou gave the French possession of La Rochelle, which presented thereafter a hazard for English shipping on its way to Gascony.

No further opportunity to renew campaigning against the French occurred until Count Peter of Brittany fell out with the French king and invited Henry III to join him in France. In 1230, therefore, Henry III himself crossed over. Count Peter agreed to become Henry's vassal and received the lands formerly held in England by earlier counts of Brittany as earls of Richmond. Henry won no battles, but he progressed through western France as far as Bordeaux and after an absence of five months sailed back to England having received some recognition of his 'rights'.[39] It did not last long. Peter came to terms with Louis IX in 1234 and the accord with Henry was dissolved. Warfare was not, however, resumed. The truce originally negotiated in 1231 was regularly renewed and still in force ten years later when Louis IX's brother Alfonso was formally installed as count of Poitou. At the ceremony, Henry's mother Isabella claimed to have been so slighted by her discourteous reception there that the Lusignans rashly decided to repudiate their submission to Louis and called on Henry for assistance.[40] His barons in England sensibly had strong misgivings about getting involved. By the time Henry actually reached Royan in May 1242, the Lusignan rebellion in Poitou had already collapsed. Henry tried to salvage something for his efforts by asking aid from Raymond of Toulouse, James of Aragon and the king of Castile, but the abrupt submission of the Lusignans and Raymond's loss of nerve by January 1243 left him standing. The truce was renewed in April and a despondent Henry returned to England in September 1243. This was his last attempt to risk military activity in France and it was clear to all that the French were not going to be dislodged from former Plantagenet lands. Henry's experience of dealing with various French lords ought to have opened his eyes sooner to their unreliability, but he had no alternative strategy, granted that to bow out gracefully was unthinkable.

For his part, since coming of age Louis IX had consistently shown restraint in his dealings with Henry III and appeared to have rejected his father's intention of pushing Henry out of the French kingdom altogether. If Henry III's marriage to Louis's sister-in-law in 1236 was intended as a way of creating a more friendly environment as a preliminary to finding a full settlement, it failed. National interests were not at issue between the kings themselves. In France, the Plantagenets were not foreigners, but Angevins who belonged there as much as they did in England. Louis was presumably baffled to know what to do. When he went on crusade in 1248, still no solution was in sight. Louis had no ambition at all to take a forceful line in the general affairs of Christendom. His preoccupation with the crusade rather irritated Pope Innocent IV who attached more immediate importance to defeating the insolent emperor, Frederick II. In the end, Louis's defeat at Mansourah and protracted, inglorious sojourn in the Holy Land hardly redounded at the time to French credit.

Whereas Henry learned from experience that his secular allies could not be relied on, he never lost his comparable faith in the support of the papacy. From the first, his outlook as king had been shaped by his awareness of what the pope could do to help him. As he grew up, the need for a permanent representative of the pope in England disappeared, but he still put his faith in his Roman friends. He felt that he had a right to Roman friendship and expected something tangible in return for his loyalty. In 1226, he chose to remind Cardinal Stephen of the 100 marks given him by King John (when his uncle, Innocent III, was still alive), suggesting bluntly that the cardinal had not so far done much for him.[41] Even the pope, Gregory IX himself, while bishop of Ostia had been in English pay. After he became pope, the religious house of Santa Maria di Gloria he founded at Anagni significantly attracted endowments in England, Wales and Ireland. Earl Gilbert of Pembroke, wary of Henry III after the suspicious death of his brother Richard, thought it worth securing papal goodwill by a judicious gift. The archbishop of Canterbury did likewise.[42] Throughout Henry III's reign, relations with the Curia were cultivated at many levels. When difficulties arose, the king naturally asked the pope to send a legate to help him. Cardinal Otto, who had acted briefly in England for Gregory IX in 1228, returned as a seasoned diplomat in 1237 and spent four busy years helping the English Church with the reform programme.[43] At the end of Henry III's reign another cardinal, Ottobuono, presided over the final settlement with his barons. Despite the problems the papacy eventually created for Henry, he never turned against his feudal overlord.

Henry's preoccupations with the recovery of the lost family lands in France and his reliance on the papacy for support both had implications for the rest of the British Isles. Not that Henry expected to compensate for his frustrations in France by flexing his muscles in Britain. Any success there would neither have salved his pride nor restored him to his family's homeland. The papacy was, however, instrumental in improving relations between the kings of England and Scotland. Alexander II had cooperated with the disaffected barons of the north, had recognised Louis of France's claims to the English throne, done homage to him and continued to support him after Henry III's coronation. Scotland was not defeated by military action but brought into line by the papal legate who induced Alexander II of Scotland to drop his support for Louis of France in 1217.[44] On behalf of a mere Scottish cleric, excommunicated for his active campaigns on behalf of Louis, Philip II was prepared to intercede personally with the pope: the Scots were not a contemptible quantity in international terms.[45] If their part in the troubles of Henry III's minority did not cause the English government grave disquiet, the peace settlement was sealed on something like equal terms by the marriage of Alexander II to Henry III's sister, Joanna.[46] This marriage helped to contain wrangling between the two kings in Britain for twenty years. The principal bone of contention, the Scottish king's claims to lands in northern England, was itself eventually resolved when another papal legate, Otto, presided over a meeting at York in 1237.[47]

In Wales too the papacy had a prominent role to play. John's expulsion from Normandy in 1204 attracted less notice in the Welsh annals than the dispute with Rome and it was only after 1212 when Innocent III absolved three Welsh princes from the oaths they had taken to King John that they were encouraged to make war against the king. Papal support for Wales proved opportunist. After John's submission to the pope in 1213, the Welsh princes were once more sidelined. The papacy gave Llewelyn no encouragement in his disputes with Henry III. At a time when papal recognition might have boosted Llewelyn's Welsh principality, Honorius III concentrated instead on upholding Henry III's rights. Papal mediation did broker a settlement with Llewelyn, who was by this time related to the king by his marriage to John's natural daughter Joan. Llewelyn in due course manoeuvred to secure the succession for his son David, in preference to his older half-brothers, a plan which upset traditional Welsh arrangements for division of inheritance. Llewelyn confidently expected Henry to endorse his nephew's rights and appreciated the importance of getting ecclesiastical support. Whereas the Welsh themselves could do little to resist pressure from Rome, there are few signs of the papacy taking much interest in Welsh affairs. In 1222, Honorius III, acting on the information of the prominent canonist, Master John of Wales, instructed some Welsh prelates to investigate whether the bishop of St Asaph was tolerating unfit priests in his diocese. The *Brut*'s only notice about Gregory IX was that he allowed the bishop of Bangor in 1236 to become a Cistercian monk at Dore. Like Honorius III, Gregory IX consistently endorsed the interests of Henry III in his dealings with Llewelyn and agreed to impose ecclesiastical penalties on Welsh rebels.[48] Henry III had every reason to appreciate papal support for his standing in the rest of Britain.

While Henry III kept his mind on his concerns overseas, the other regions of Britain were left to concentrate on what mattered in their own areas. In Wales, Llewelyn's ambitions and the rivalries of his sons for the succession prevented the Welsh princes from paying much attention to what was happening 'abroad' until 1256, when Henry III's difficulties revived their interest in foreign connections. But Wales was not completely isolated in this period. The Cistercian monasteries maintained their institutional links with the Continent and princely interest in the order was rewarded by the interest taken in their activities by the chronicler at Strata Florida. It was there that Llewelyn assembled the Welsh leaders in 1238 to secure recognition of David's rights to succeed him. From Strata Florida he secured monks for the foundation of a daughter house at Aberconway where he and David were both eventually buried. The links between the princes and the Church, though traditional, were reinforced in contemporary style and French, rather than English, example may have been influential.[49] French cultural influence no doubt made the Welsh familiar with other features of French life. Inasmuch as Welsh chronicles show any interest in continental affairs, it is more often in French events. The *Brut* chronicle briefly noticed the expeditions of English kings to the continent, as in 1214, 1230 and 1242.[50] That other information about remote events did reach Wales is shown by the *Brut* chronicle entry about the battle of Las Navas de Tolosa in Spain (1212), which was most impressed by the great number of men (10,000) and women (3000) slain.[51] True to type, the Welsh chronicle which noticed battles paid scant attention to the papacy.

Papal efforts to break up Scottish friendship with France did not deter Alexander II from negotiating in the summer of 1219 for the marriage of his sister Margaret to the young count of Champagne, Theobald IV, offering a dowry of 12,000 silver marks.[52] Although the plans did not materialise, they are revealing about Scottish financial credit and the continuing interaction between Scotland and the homeland of Alexander's mother, Ermengarde. Many years later, in 1239 after the death of the childless Joanna, Alexander II himself contracted a French marriage, to Marie de Coucy, the first Scottish royal marriage since 1066 made without consideration of any English interest. Alexander even felt free to offer Louis IX his alliance. Our information hardly does justice to the part Scotland was playing in Anglo-French relations, but is enough to reinforce the impression that the French connection mattered not only in England, but through much of Britain. Such a sign of Scottish autonomy was worrying enough in the long term for Henry III to try to limit its effects by securing the marriage of his own daughter Margaret to Alexander II's son and heir.

Whereas Henry III's policies were shaped by preoccupation with his continental lands, Alexander II, once he felt free to give the matter his full attention, was able to deal with the challenge presented by the king of Norway's influence in the western and northern territories of modern Scotland. His father had already established his credentials as a ruler against the semi-independent earls of the Norwegian diaspora by a notable victory over Harald, thane of Caithness and Orkney in 1199.[53] Alexander II himself had taken advantage of the murder of the bishop of Caithness in 1220 to show his power in the north and regain papal approbation. Scottish kings concerned to get recognition of their kingship within the whole area of the later kingdom had also intervened in the south-west, where Galloway had long been effectively autonomous. The first known reference to it as lying within *Scocia* at all comes in 1216.[54] Responsibility for bringing it into closer contact with the king lay initially with its lord, Alan of Galloway, who became constable of Scotland.[55] On his death in 1235 Alexander seized the chance to assert his own overlordship and divide his lands among Alan's daughters. Beyond Galloway, he also gave the affairs of the Isle of Man and Ireland some attention. In contemporary terms, both were areas of 'foreign' interest, even if they are now treated as constituent territories of the British Isles. In the Irish Sea, the king of Man had become so fearful of losing his independence that he sought to protect it by submitting to the overlordship of Honorius III in return for an annual payment. In practice the kings of Man continued to pay their respects to Henry III (who knighted King Harald in 1246 and Magnus ten years later) on their regular visits to Norway.[56] The papacy itself was in no position to prevent the eventual takeover of the island kingdom. With one lord for England and Ireland, Man ceased to be viable on its own. When the Hebrides passed into Scottish hands, Man too saw fit to acknowledge Scottish sovereignty. The thirteenth century marked a decisive phase in the development of the Scottish kingdom. The aggressive attitude assumed by kings in their dealings with the rulers of the territories to the north and west of modern Scotland shifted the focus of royal interest away from England and gave it a quite distinctive character. At the same time, the royal government, largely modelled on that of England, was determined to use its powers to keep its distance, not to become assimilated. Just as English royal government had pressed on its own neighbours in the twelfth century, so now the Scots kings turned their forces against the weaker, divided powers on their periphery.

Alexander II first made overtures to Haakon of Norway for the acquisition of the Hebrides in 1244. When these were rejected, he set out to assert his authority in the north-west by a military campaign, abruptly cut short by his death in 1249. Alexander II's temerity in choosing to challenge Haakon himself should not be underestimated. To eliminate Norwegian authority in the Scottish islands was not a simple matter. Orkney and Shetland remained outside the kingdom until the fifteenth century. In Alexander II's time, Haakon Haakonson (1217–63) was one of Norway's most imposing kings, with ambitions to have his power respected throughout Christendom. When Matthew Paris visited Norway in 1247, the king told him about a papal proposal to make him emperor, rejected on the grounds that Haakon might be prepared to fight the enemies of the Church but not those of the pope.[57] He naturally attracted many Hebrideans to his court and in his own time overshadowed Scottish kings. Despite Haakon's illegitimacy, the pope authorised a solemn coronation for him. Negotiations about this dragged on for many years. Haakon's crown was made in England and the ceremony was conducted by Cardinal William of St Sabine, who had sailed to Norway from England in 1247. The ceremonies attending the Norwegian coronation made a considerable impression in Scotland, where kings were not crowned. A description of the ceremony performed at Bergen for King Magnus, Haakon's son and successor, records how deeply one Scottish envoy was impressed by the occasion.[58] The relative importance of Scotland and Norway in this period is reflected in the historical sources. The Norse sagas, particularly Snorri's *Heimskringla* of the 1220s, provide much information about Scotland, revealing how differently England and Scotland interacted at that time with the Continent. The medieval culture of Iceland was reaching its peak in the early thirteenth century; in Scotland, there was nothing to match the literary accomplishments of Snorri Sturluson. Scotland lay halfway between Iceland and Norway and many Icelanders would have been familiar with the Western Isles. The storm-tossed journey of the bishop-elect of Holar, Gudmundr Arason, on his way to Norway for consecration was vividly described in the literature. The ship was able to put into port in the Hebrides before continuing the voyage, though the bishop was constrained to pay the customary dues for his reception. The Hebrides were situated on a maritime highway and well worth acquiring from Norway.[59] Scottish involvement in the maritime Norse world obliged the kings to pay more attention to their own coastal burghs. Ayr, with its commercial activities in the Irish Sea, comes to the fore at this point.[60] But there is some evidence of Scots seeking to establish links across the North Sea. One of Alexander II's sisters was married to Berman II, prince of Rostock on the Baltic. By 1248, when Innocent IV at the king's request allowed her to make two or three visits a year to her husband's Cistercian foundation at Doberan, she was evidently a widow.[61]

The king was not the only Scot to have foreign connections. Many leading Lowland families, like the Balliols, had French relations who provided them with their own direct access to France. In this respect they were no different from Englishmen. Several Scottish lords, by virtue of their tenure of lands from the English crown, fought in France for Henry III. From their own experiences abroad, if not in England, Scottish barons would have become familiar with the styles and fashions of the French royal court, as shown by surviving Scottish comital seals from this period.[62] The very close relations between the English and the Scots lords of the thirteenth century served to reinforce the 'Frenchness' of Scottish culture. Scottish interest in making firm friends outside the British Isles contributed to its ability later to preserve its independence from England. It was, however, rather because Scots were so familiar with how matters were arranged in England that they came to believe themselves as entitled to run their own kingdom as the English were theirs.

Ireland had no such native king to take charge of its affairs. The agreement reached at Windsor in 1175 had envisaged that Rory O'Connor would reign as high-king under Henry's lordship, an arrangement analogous to that devised the previous year at Falaise for Scotland under King William. Nothing came of this plan for Ireland and in 1185 Henry II proposed instead to set up his son John as king of Ireland. This plan too faltered the next year when John's older brother, Geoffrey of Brittany, died. Instead, under both John and Henry III Ireland became a mere 'lordship'. Some lands in the island were taken directly by the king; others were fiefs held of the English kings; some lands remained in the hands of Irish kings, some of whom acknowledged the English king as lord. Between 1172 and 1210 there were three English 'royal' expeditions to Ireland. Although no English king bothered to visit Ireland again until 1391, these earlier royal visits had the effect of throwing Ireland open to continental scrutiny. John's main purpose in going to Ireland in 1210 was to discipline his English barons, but he had expected at least some of the still independent native Irish to show due deference.

The chronicler of Béthune, who was a witness, records the impressions made by two native Irish rulers who proved more than a match for the king.[63] Cathal of Connaught and Aed O'Neill both managed their meetings with John to their own advantage. Cathal arrived with a large force, mainly on foot. John presented him with a fine warhorse, sumptuous saddle and bridle, for which he was courteously thanked. When he came to demonstrate his prowess in horsemanship, however, Cathal disconcerted the royal party by having the saddle removed and riding bareback and not in 'chivalrous' style. As for O'Neill, John intended to corner him into offering tribute, but was out-crafted. Moreover, having tricked John, O'Neill then stole up on John's camp just as it was being revictualled and made off into the mountains with the cattle, sheep and horses, along with their grooms. The chronicler was clearly fascinated by the unconventional aspects of Irish society, but was impressed rather than indignant that the Irish knew how to hold their own against John.

John's hold on Ireland had been sufficiently demonstrated in 1210 to make his surrender of its lordship to the pope three years later more than an empty gesture.[64] Indeed, the principal effect of papal lordship in Ireland was to reinforce the authority of the English king in the island, without kings themselves making efforts to assert their royal rights in person. Despite the new conditions brought about by the settlement of English barons and the long arm of royal government, English kings were content enough with acknowledgement of their formal lordship to leave some parts of Ireland to fend for themselves. Battle was waged only to defend what had been taken, not to proceed to systematic conquest. A few native rulers were therefore able to avoid making substantial changes to their style of rule. Irish resilience is noteworthy. By the fourteenth century, many of the settlers had themselves been absorbed into traditional Irish society and were denounced for going native, in speech, dress and manners. Had the native Irish ever been pushed to the wall by the colonists, this would not have been the case.

By the beginning of the thirteenth century, English barons had certainly established a firm basis for further encroachment and may have expected to 'complete' the task in due course. That they did not do this when they had the best opportunity has had a decisive effect on the island up to the present day. From the first, however, they had typically cooperated where they could with local rulers and advanced their own interests by exploiting the existing tensions between and within Irish families. They had also competed against one another. There was no consolidated 'English' drive to subdue the island. Although Henry III expected to secure recognition of his lordship from Irish kings and English barons, a separate royal administrative cadre was only provided for such lands as the kings claimed for themselves. Outside these, the king could not afford to alienate the barons on whose activities any extension of English authority would depend. At the same time, Henry could become agitated about the possible dangers to his own hold on the baronage from too much success across the sea. He was far from encouraging them to make ever greater headway against the surviving native princes and become potentially more powerful still. In fact, neither John nor Henry III could do much to restrain or encourage their barons in Ireland. Only the fortuitous extinction of several of the great Anglo-Irish families by the middle of the century left Henry III with the major responsibility for sustaining English enterprise. Royal officials sent to Ireland had no stomach for the task. A letter from Laurence de Somercotes expresses his relief that his tour of duty was nearly done; he hoped he would never set foot in the country again; he would rather go to prison.[65] Henry himself took little interest in the island; his major preoccupations lay elsewhere. As a result, both the native Irish and the settlers were left to struggle indecisively on their own.

The royal officials in Ireland themselves kept records in the manner of the government in England. Had their documents survived, thirteenth-century Irish affairs could have been as well understood as those of England. Unfortunately, their destruction in 1922, intended to blot out the shameful record of Irish subordination to the English kingdom, has made historians more dependent than ever on records of purely English provenance.[66] English royal interest in Irish affairs nevertheless has one considerable advantage, for Ireland features in English royal records to a greater extent than either Wales or Scotland. The lack of evidence from native Irish sources probably encourages a tendency to exaggerate the importance of the 'English' in Ireland. The stronger links established across the Irish Sea should not become an excuse for disregarding the more traditional ties of the regions formerly dominated by Norse sea power. The circumstances in which the king of Argyll died on an expedition to Sligo in 1247 are obscure but his campaign at least shows that the old links had not been broken.[67] But the success of the king of Scots in extending his power into Man, Galloway and the Hebrides had inescapable implications for the Irish rulers of the north and west and these began to impinge on them from mid-century.

The English and the aliens

The fresh problems thrown up for English interests on the Continent by the successes of Philip II and Louis VIII inevitably began to change perceptions of foreigners. John and Henry were the first English kings to be criticised, at least in some quarters, for showing greater favours to foreigners than to their native-born subjects.[68] After the loss of Normandy, the chief barons of England, for the first time since 1066, no longer themselves held assets on the continent and only their general obligations to serve the king drew them into affairs that were henceforward his, but not theirs. Objections to the influence of 'Poitevins', particularly in the early years of the reign to Peter des Roches, bishop of Winchester (actually from Touraine) and his protégés, reflected the dislike felt in England for John's henchmen. In the original version of Magna Carta, John also undertook to expel named Poitevin captains and their followers from the kingdom.[69] The reasons for baronial objections to them are not stated, but they were perceived as providing the king with staunch and unquestioning support. The Poitevins may have used their influence with John not so much in favour of a more energetic foreign policy as for their own enrichment at the expense of English barons. In that case the barons' disapproval expressed personal antipathies rather than political attitudes. When John was dead and Magna Carta reissued the Poitevins were reprieved. There can have been no sustained hostility to their presence in England.

The civil war and Louis's intervention created divisions of another kind. Those who had most vigorously opposed John were responsible for inviting Louis to take John's place. No longer champions of resistance to royal tyranny, they were discredited by their alliance with Louis's French forces who, not surprisingly, provoked some popular 'patriotic' resistance in areas where they prevailed.[70] In the king's own party, differences began to emerge between the barons with roots in England and those who came to join the king from the lands the Plantagenets had once held abroad. Such men not only expected to be appropriately recompensed for their loyalty and sacrifices; in exile their only hopes for the future lay with the king. Their loyalty to him was born out of desperation. Personal friendships between barons of different factions helped to blur the emergence of definable parties. In the confusion, calling enemies foreign born (*alienigenae*) became no more than conventional abuse intended to discredit not only Poitevins loyal to the dynasty but barons who had fought for Louis.[71] What was new was the notion that to be foreign born somehow disqualified a baron (though not a bishop or the papal legate) from exercising authority in England. In Henry III's early years, one of the chief victims of hostility to foreign-born men was the humbly-born Norman Fawkes de Bréauté, who had at one time performed great services for the king. Fawkes wrote to the pope making a detailed refutation of the charges against him.[72] According to this, he had been vindictively picked on, especially by Archbishop Langton. Fawkes still believed in the virtues of loyal service to his lord and regarded the baronial enemies of John, who had come into their own during the regency period, as treacherous rather than patriotic. The pope took up Fawkes's case, without success. Fawkes did not recover his English lands and died in exile. Judging from the warmth of papal support for him, it is unlikely that the case against him was clear-cut. Wendover at least acknowledged that he was an experienced soldier; Matthew Paris described him only as 'merciless'. More important than his Norman origin was the fact of his advancement from nothing to great power. He was personally hated and once he had left England there was no sustained campaign against remaining aliens. The barons' experience of sharing in government during Henry III's minority did, however, mould ways of thinking about newcomers over the next two generations. They concentrated on trying to rebuild confidence in England and, having no interests of their own on the Continent, viewed the king's rights there with more detachment than Henry III himself could ever do.

Partly because of the government's difficulties in England, Henry III's remaining lands in France had been further eroded in his early years. The campaign to save Poitou in 1225 had succeeded only in preventing the French occupation of Gascony, in the process showing up the Poitevins as fickle in their support. In 1230, Henry III's own martial efforts had exposed the vanity of any hopes he might emulate his warrior uncle Richard. Henry was so much aware of his military limitations that he tried to pin the blame for the unimpressive campaign on his justiciar, Hubert de Burgh. He made matters worse in 1232 when he appointed Peter des Roches, recently returned from Frederick II's crusade, as his new chief minister. Peter was glad of the opportunity to pay off old scores and favour his friends. The unpopularity of Poitevin influence with Henry in 1232–34 is explicable in purely personal terms. It is quite unconvincing to ascribe it to a gut reaction against aliens. The bishop of Winchester's origins may have predisposed the English barons to dislike him, but his own attitude to them was also at fault. His political insensitivity to the nature of relations between king and barons in England was the cause of the backlash against him in 1234. The objections may have been framed in general terms against foreigners; the real grievance was that these particular strangers had obtained disproportionate influence over the king and usurped the place of the king's 'natural', that is native-born counsellors. It was a long-established custom that free men should never be subjected to the authority of outsiders, but only judged by their neighbours and peers. Aliens accorded privileges detrimental to those of free men were heartily resented.

Another cause of discontent was the preferment of Italians to ecclesiastical benefices. For the most part they were offered prebends in cathedrals or churches in the gift of exempt monasteries. When the pope unwittingly appointed an Italian to a benefice in the gift of Robert Tweng, a Yorkshire knight, Tweng, aggrieved at this infringement of his own rights of patronage, noisily protested on the grounds that an alien had been intruded. He whipped up some popular support and his protest may have been orchestrated for political purposes. It created sufficient stir to alarm Henry III, who sent Tweng off to the pope with a letter of recommendation. After some delay, Gregory IX insisted that he had no intention of encroaching on the rights of lay patrons.[73] There were further incidents but the English barons were much more preoccupied about rights to present clergy to their livings than about alien clergy as such. Bishops sometimes protested about foreign clergy who could not speak English officiating in country parishes, but most Italians favoured in this way appointed vicars to serve the parish and simply had the revenues due to them paid over to their proctors.

A more serious problem, because it touched the king personally, was created by the arrival in England of foreigners with royal connections. When Henry married in 1236, his court became a magnate for his wife's family and friends. Over a hundred Savoyard relations and hangers-on of Queen Eleanor of Provence have been identified. The evidence that they aroused hostility comes mainly from Matthew Paris. He claimed that youthful magnates, like the earl of Lincoln and Richard de Burgh, were demeaned by being obliged to marry penniless Savoyard damsels.[74] Far worse was to come when the children of Henry's mother Isabella by her second husband, Hugh de Lusignan, arrived in 1247. They revived memories not only of earlier Poitevins, but of the recent fiasco when their parents had induced Henry III to campaign in France and then deserted him. The Lusignan brothers had nothing to offer the kingdom. They brought no useful diplomatic relations in their wake, yet expected substantial favours from the king. Henry welcomed them as members of his family, but in England impecunious Poitevins with claims on royal generosity were not welcomed by upstaged English courtiers. They were perceived as ill-mannered and undeserving.[75] Suspicions that they turned the king against his own subjects, once aroused, were aggravated by their conduct. Had they shown more political finesse, open hostility might have been averted. The barons could hardly impugn the king's relations as such. It was more tactful to denounce their foreign birth. Hitherto of no importance, this became a potential disadvantage, at least for those in close touch with the king.

Baronial disapproval of Henry III's foreign favourites has been treated as medieval evidence for an innate English hostility to aliens.[76] This goes too far. The barons resented Henry III's distribution of favours to relations with no roots in the kingdom and what appeared to them a preference for trusting foreigners rather than native-born subjects. These criticisms were not in themselves unreasonable, but Henry took the view that he was as entitled to please himself about whom he consulted and rewarded as his barons expected to be. The king's right to take advisors as he chose was not really in doubt and was confirmed in 1264 by Louis IX of France.[77] But Louis IX's situation was different from Henry III's and what was right was not necessarily expedient. A fundamental issue was at stake in England because the king was not just another great baron, even more free than the rest to please himself. In England, the barons knew that much of the king's foreign business had implications for themselves and understandably expected to be consulted about it, before and not after critical decisions had been made. It took a long time to establish the idea that the king could not be as free as his barons to please himself. He had to be more circumspect because of his duty to his people. Moreover, in practice, the success of his policies depended on their willingness to help him. That the new idea became accepted in England rested on the importance there of learning how to distinguish between what were properly domestic responsibilities of kings and those relating to his overseas lands, in which his English barons had no personal stake. The kings of France had no problem like this.

The proof of the opportunistic character of objections to foreigners was that they were taken up most vehemently in the circle of Simon de Montfort.[78] Simon was one of the most obviously foreign members of the English baronage in mid-century, with close family ties in the kingdom of France. He came to England in 1231 to make his fortune, asserting a right to inherit the earldom of Leicester. Henry III not only allowed this, but in 1237, without consulting the baronage, he connived at Simon's marriage to Henry's widowed sister Eleanor. Despite their new kinship, the relationship became the basis for a long-standing grievance about Henry's inadequate provision for his sister's dowry. This even held up the final agreement about peace with France. Simon's standing and abilities made him a suitable choice as Henry's seneschal of Gascony in 1248, but his self-confidence there stirred up opposition and the king was embarrassed to know how to handle Simon without alienating the Gascons. Henry III felt ill at ease with his abrasive brother-in-law and his resentment grew when it became obvious that his own son, Edward, was fascinated by his brilliant uncle.

The great men of the kingdom were not inherently more isolationist than the king, but their attitude differed from that of their predecessors. In the twelfth century many English barons had held substantial lands in Normandy; a century later they themselves had no estates in Poitou or Gascony. When they served the king overseas it was on a temporary basis. On their visits and campaigns abroad they were accompanied by their dependants; practical experience of foreign lands was hardly confined to a few. Some of the most remote parts of the king's dominions were affected. When Richard de Burgh, lord of Connaught, overlord of Irish kings and patron of Irish bards, participated in Henry III's expedition to Poitou in 1242 he almost certainly took Irishmen with him.[79] All the great barons accepted without question that it was their Christian duty to go on crusade, as they did in 1219 and 1241. It was more than obedience to clerical exhortation; it was expected of their rank. Their experience of the world was extended by the travels they made as envoys on behalf of kings. Many had more extensive and varied personal experience of foreign parts than their kings. Leading figures in England, like Henry III's brother Richard of Cornwall and Simon de Montfort, were of European importance. English barons were much travelled, not really any more nationalist in their outlook than the king. Their economic interests brought them into regular contact with foreigners. Richard of Cornwall, king in Germany, may have been exceptional among the barons as the principal exporter of English tin, but all great landowners sold surplus corn and wool from their estates and were able to obtain ready cash on the strength of their good credit from many different foreign merchant bankers.

Politically, no ties bound secular laymen to any 'foreign' power and because the lands they held owed obligations only to the king of England they respected him as their exclusive lord. Any new sense of 'national' commitment to the king developed naturally out of this. But their national duties to the king were not the only ones. They had other obligations which weighed even more heavily and immediately on them, as to their families, kin and vassals, without whose support and respect their own services to the king would have been valueless. They saw themselves as relatively independent agents, offering advice to rulers themselves, yet able to command and direct their own affairs, often enjoying considerable autonomy in regions where they were powerful. Ranulf, earl of Chester, for example, defended the clergy of his lands against papal demands for taxation when the king himself weakly gave way.[80] For many purposes some barons could act as they chose, whereas the king could not dispense with their services for his greater ambitions. When of full age they married and expected to make alliances with other great families for their own advantage. Although not

patriots in any modern sense, they tried collectively, when giving the king
counsel, to consider the interests of the kingdom as an issue distinct from
their own personal duties to their lord. Barons who were prepared to perform military service overseas for the king but refused to vote national taxation to meet the expense, perceived a difference between an interest of the
king in lands far away and a concern for the national safety of the kingdom.[81] For most of the thirteenth century, the conflict between the king's
personal interests and those of the kingdom as understood by the magnates
was unbridgeable.

It is convenient, if not really justifiable, to consider English treatment of
the Jews as further evidence of English attitudes to aliens. Edward I's expulsion of the Jews from England in 1291 is sometimes cited as another sign of
English xenophobia. However, most Jews in England were not technically
'foreign born'. The Jewish community, which continued to expand throughout the twelfth century, probably grew not as a result of steady immigration
from the Continent but mainly by natural increase.[82] The fact that they
became more numerous and more widely dispersed through the kingdom
indicates moreover they they cannot have been persecuted. Objections to
them arose, as elsewhere in Christendom, because they rejected the claims of
the Christian religion. This was not only seen as both unreasonable and
ungrateful; their attitude was resented. By scorning Christianity, Jews dis-
paraged what Christians thought most precious. Emotional effects apart,
the adherence of the Jews to their own religion precluded their acceptance
into contemporary society. At a time when sharing religious ritual was fundamental for cementing social relationships, the Jews themselves preferred
the claims of their religion to social acceptability by their neighbours.
Inevitably there was a price to be paid. Religious difference was not the only
matter to keep the Jews apart from their neighbours. Because the king
allowed them to settle their own disputes by their own laws, they did not
participate in the ordinary practices of the English courts.[83] Like other
townsmen they spoke French with their Christian neighbours and clients,
perhaps among themselves, but in writing and in the synagogue they also
used Hebrew, a language known outside their circle only to a tiny number
of erudite Christian scholars. This called attention to their strangeness.
Jewish resistance to the claims of Christendom puzzled pious and learned
theologians who felt duly challenged to understand and possibly subvert the
Jewish position, but this did not in itself encourage persecution.[84] The
papacy believed that the Jews would never be assimilated into the Christian
Church and actually ruled out putting them under pressure to convert. This
did not deter some zealous Christians from making strenuous efforts to do
just this and Jewish resistance excited some preachers to whip up popular
hostility to them. To survive in Christendom Jews needed effective protection.

No Jews are known to have lived in England before the Conquest. The
first Jewish community in England came from Rouen. Settling in London

under William I the Jews made a living from commerce. By the early thirteenth century, still under royal protection, Jewish communities had been established in about twenty other English towns with moneylending as their main business interest. The favour accorded them by the king could itself became a matter of grievance. At Bury, for example, Abbot Samson demanded that in his town the Jews should either be entrusted to his protection or expelled. Significantly, Henry II, rather than cede royal rights over the Jews, ordered the Jews to move elsewhere.[85] At that time, Jews were still free to move and settle in smaller towns, but as they did so other local authorities began to complain because Jewish enclaves under royal protection hampered the exercise of municipal jurisdictions. Henry III eventually issued an edict that Jews were not to reside in places other than those they had traditionally occupied. Royal supervision in the thirteenth century was designed to keep their activities within familiar bounds, often in response to demands made by barons, townsmen and clergy.[86]

Despite the impression sometimes given, Jewish communities in thirteenth-century England did not often suffer from mob violence. The notorious atrocities perpetrated in London after Richard I's coronation and then in York a few months later were not typical of Jewish relations with Christians in England. Nor did they deter Jews from promptly rebuilding their communities in those great cities. The chroniclers did not attribute the massacres of 1189–90 to the bigotry of young men arriving in the cities on their way to the Holy Land; they thought rather that the motive was to appropriate Jewish wealth for the crusading venture.[87] The king had no interest in condoning defiance of his authority. Although Richard I's officials could not save the Jews, some of the perpetrators were tracked down and fined.[88]

Most of the time Jews lived on good terms with their Christian neighbours. Gerald of Wales told the story of a Jewish fellow traveller who was confident enough to make jokes about the name of a Christian archdeacon; in Winchester, a Christian woman frequented the house of her Jewish neighbour, notwithstanding clerical rules forbidding this.[89] From the early thirteenth century, the drive to tighten up Christian discipline appears to have hardened attitudes towards the Jews. Regulations requiring Jews to wear special badges, as decreed by the Lateran Council of 1215, were, however, reissued so often as to suggest they were not much observed. Even as they stand, they indicate that without them Jews could not be readily distinguished from their neighbours. Jewish scholars abroad were scandalised that English Jews mixed so freely with their Gentile neighbours; they were not pitied for being persecuted.[90] Only English debtors who could not pay up and lost property to Jewish moneylenders understandably resented their presence. Social losers may indulge in abuse and violence but are not a powerful interest group. The price Jews really paid for a comparatively harmonious existence in England was being subjected to arbitrary royal demands for contributions to the king's treasure chest. In fact, they risked more from the king than from popular prejudice. John's extravagant demands on them in 1210 are thought to have prompted many to join a body of French Jews and emigrate to the Holy Land.[91]

The Jews were 'different' but not 'aliens' in the ordinary sense, for they occupied a recognised place in English society. Some Jews were extremely wealthy and owners of considerable urban properties. The more affluent may have travelled regularly to and from the Continent. English Jews certainly maintained close links with their co-religionists abroad. When Philip II expelled Jews from the Ile de France (1182–98) many came to England, confident of a welcome. Later, the wife of David of Oxford who wanted to divorce her in 1242 appealed successfully to a Jewish tribunal in Paris. The Jews belonged to an international community of their own and were proud of their connections. About 1268, Moses of London traced his ancestry back seven generations to a rabbi of Mainz. Rabbi Meir of England had studied with the Jewish scholar Samson of Sens. Benedict of Lincoln who was arrested in 1255 secured his release by the intervention of the English envoy of the king of Castile. That English Jews could have international reputations is confirmed by the efforts of Jean d'Avesnes, when he became sick in the late 1280s, to obtain the medical services of Master Elyas of London. Elyas, one of the most influential of London Jews, was not allowed to leave until he had obtained a royal safe-conduct.[92] The plentiful evidence about them in England does not actually provide much detail about their continental ties, but there is no reason to think that their foreign connections played any part in stirring up trouble for them. Whatever anti-Semitic prejudice may be detected can have nothing to do with alleged English xenophobia.

The loss of Normandy, Anjou and eventually of Poitou, had serious consequences for John and Henry III, as well as their barons and other subjects, but it was not greeted as a welcome release from burdensome commitments abroad; in some ways it intensified relations with continental neighbours and friends. John's English subjects do not seem to have regarded his expulsion from Normandy as a national humiliation. If poems in Latin and French (though not English) are anything to go by, the poets and their patrons who had been proud to be members of an independent kingdom did feel demeaned by John's offer of the kingdom as a vassal-state to the pope. A similar sense of humiliation seems to have been felt in Scotland when William was forced to do homage to Henry II in 1174. In both kingdoms, the reaction was similar: efforts to recover the kingdom's good name were indispensable. This loss of face itself may have been an incentive to find ways somehow of bolstering 'national' pride.

6

Making a living out of Europe

The well born and the well educated have little idea how most of their contemporaries make ends meet. Even if they give the matter any attention, they are badly placed to observe or understand it. On the other hand, those most preoccupied by the problems of everyday living will be those least likely to put pen to paper, or know how to do so. Before merchants, sailors and ploughmen became literate, what is known of their activities depends on royal records or ecclesiastical notice. However inadequate, this evidence is what we have to enlighten us about the life of the majority.

Historians are in no doubt that the population of England grew steadily from the Norman Conquest until the early fourteenth century, so conditions favourable for economic expansion were in place. Gerald of Wales believed that the regular revenues of English kings had plummeted from their peak at the time of Domesday and wondered how the Angevin kings could afford so much military activity. His answer was that they relied on expedients to supplement their reduced basic income.[1] Borrowing on a regular basis was one of these and easy access to credit in thirteenth-century England is another sign of a buoyant economy. The most widely consulted medieval reference book, written by Bartholomew, an English Franciscan, asserted that England was a rich land, needing nothing from elsewhere and supplying what others needed.[2] The relative wealth of the main kingdoms of Christendom was a topic of conversation at the French court. Louis VII assured Walter Map, archdeacon of Oxford, that although the way wealth was measured varied from one land to another, in his view the king of England lacked for nothing: he had men, horses, gold, silk, jewels, fruit and game for hunting whereas France was rich only in bread, wine and – (the sting in the tail) happiness.[3]

At the most basic level, England produced all the food it needed; normal grain yields were sufficient to allow for regular exports. Concessions on behalf of the Norwegian king, the archbishop of Nidaros and the abbot of Lysa show that this northern kingdom counted on good relations with

England to supply the grain it could not produce for itself: the Norwegian words for wheat (and for cloth as it happens) are both loan-words from English.[4] For similar reasons, Icelanders bought grain in England. Flanders also imported grain to feed its large urban populations. Landowners like the archbishop of Canterbury were important providers but the market was not monopolised by major producers. Smaller estates also profited from the demand. Merchants of Bayonne had royal permission in 1207 to make bulk purchases of grain in several Kentish manors. One Poitevin abbot came to England to sell his abbey's wine specifically to meet the cost of acquiring grain for his monks.[5] Grain was not the only foodstuff exported from England. English cheese was sold in Flanders and Norman monasteries were supplied with cheese from their English priories. The Winchester Assize of 1204 takes it for granted that bacon, meat, cheese, butter, herring and salmon would all pass out of the country to feed foreigners. The eagerness of foreigners to obtain English produce was only restrained under John by a royal order forbidding the export of corn, along with horses and arms, except under licence.[6]

The economic history of medieval England is chiefly remembered on account of the country's reputation for producing fine quality wool, most of it sold in Flanders where the manufacture of cloth was expanding rapidly.[7] From the twelfth century, the many Cistercian abbeys established in less populous parts of the country where hundreds of sheep could graze became a steady source of marketable raw wool. Wool exports were arranged privately between merchants and suppliers. The government made no efforts to regulate the traffic until royal customs were imposed in the late thirteenth century. Dues on the export of wool were then always coupled with dues on the export of hides, obviously at that time considered of comparable importance. Little, however, is known about the medieval English leather trade.[8]

England's reputation as a rich land was enhanced by its mineral wealth. The Flemings acquired not only wool, leather and cheese, but tin, lead, coal and iron from England. The tin mines of Devon and Cornwall had been exploited since Roman times, if not earlier, but written evidence for the export business only becomes available from the late twelfth century. By then merchants from Brabant made regular visits to Devon and Cornwall. The centre of the trade was Truro, which obtained a charter in the middle of the twelfth century when it was already flourishing. The new royal interest in Gascony after 1154 helped promote tin exports to southern Europe. Tin was exported via Oléron to Bordeaux; at the end of the twelfth century two merchants from Bayonne are known to have bought as many as 24,000 weights. Some tin travelled beyond Bordeaux, up the Garonne to Toulouse, thence to the Mediterranean. Merchants from Bayonne in 1198 also carried supplies of tin to Cologne, apparently as part of a three-way traffic via England between Biscay and the North Sea.

The expanding market for tin stimulated production and the perception that mining could bear a heavy rate of taxation attracted royal interest. The value of the royal impost at the mines rose from 25 marks *c.*1160 to 150 marks in 1194. Since this did nothing to discourage mining, the impost must have been an incentive to realise what private profit the industry could yield. The tin-men of the Cornish and Devon stannaries obtained a charter from John in 1201. The value of tin exports was appreciated by Matthew Paris. Reporting the discovery of new mines in Germany, he believed that this had reduced the market price for English ore and put an end to the earlier English monopoly.[9] Tin was not the only mineral sold abroad. Derbyshire lead was listed among the principal imports from England into Flanders. Copper and even English iron were also exported, though a nervous royal government tried to ban exports of iron for fear of its being made available to the king's enemies. Nor should the British Isles as a source of precious stones be overlooked. England itself was noted for the quality of jet found at Whitby and pearls, from both England and Scotland, were in demand.[10]

Quite apart from its export of raw materials, England supplied some manufactured goods for customers abroad. Since the time of Offa of Mercia, England had exported woollen cloth. Stamford gave its name to a type of material so much appreciated on the Continent that it was manu-factured elsewhere: for this reason, the 'stamfords' sold in Italy were not certainly of English provenance. Fine English cloth is mentioned in the *Orkneyinga Saga* and was distributed in northern waters: in 1171, Norse pirates seized an English ship in the Irish Sea, laden with cloth, wine and mead.[11]

The most luxurious of England's exported manufactures were elaborate embroideries. In earlier periods some of the women responsible for the needlework were identified by name and their skills rewarded proportion-ately. The Bayeux Tapestry, itself a work commissioned for export, is still on display to prove what they could do. There may have been a regular demand for decorative wall hangings. Earl Rognvald of Orkney was very proud of his set and challenged Icelandic guests to compete with him in improvising appropriate verses inspired by the narrative scenes depicted.[12] More is known about elaborate embroideries intended for ecclesiastical purposes. The demand for these luxury products had become so considerable by the mid-thirteenth century that workshops were set up to meet it, with most known embroiderers now men living in or near London. According to Matthew Paris, these embroideries were traded by London merchants.[13] Peter of Aigueblanche, bishop of Hereford, acquired vestments of English manufacture and the dean of his cathedral, another Savoyard, Anthelme de Clermont, did likewise. When Anthelme became bishop of Maurienne in 1262, he took back with him the red *capellam* with alba and stoles which he bequeathed to his cathedral on his death in 1269.[14] Other continental clergy with more tenuous English contacts, such as Archbishop Sancho II of Toledo, and Archbishop Pierre de Charny of Sens, possessed chasubles, mitres, buskins or other garments of English workmanship.

English needlework had been presented as gifts to popes in the twelfth century, but Innocent IV is the first pope known to have taken the initiative in obtaining such goods. The papacy's appetite for them proved to be insatiable. An inventory of 1295 lists no less than 113 items of *opus anglicanum*. Nicholas III gave St Peter's two chasubles adorned *frisio anglicano*; Nicholas IV gave a cope to the cathedral of his native town, Ascoli Piceno, where it may still be seen. The same pope thanked Edward I for his present of a cope, altar dorsal and other cloth worked with great variety in silk and feathers. Some of Boniface VIII's many English vestments have been preserved in the treasury at Anagni. Laymen also obtained luxurious garments from England. Otto IV acquired a coronation mantle of English manufacture, now preserved at Brunswick, and borrowed English ceremonial regalia comprising numerous costly pieces all carefully itemised on their return from Germany in 1208.[15] England had an established reputation for knowing how to celebrate public functions in style.

Ceremonial was also an incentive for English metalworkers to show their skill. In 1234–35, Henry presented gold circlets set with precious stones to the kings of Norway and Castile, and to his sisters Queen Joanna of Scotland and Isabella. The king of Norway turned to England when he needed a more elaborate crown. The craftsmanship of the one designed for him by Henry III's own goldsmith so impressed Henry that he insisted on getting a similar one made for himself. London's reputation for refined metalwork explains why Count Amadeus of Savoy had his privy seal engraved there in 1292, along with a gold chain and two silver seals.[16] English craftsmen prided themselves on keeping abreast of continental workmanship. The iron grille for Queen Eleanor's tomb in Westminster Abbey made by Master Thomas of Leighton (Buzzard) was almost identical to one at St Denis.[17]

Products from other parts of the British Isles were not as much in demand overseas as those of England. Nor were their economies so geared to trade. Even so, Scotland certainly exported some raw wool, mainly derived from the monasteries established in the Borders. To encourage the export of its wool Count Philip of Flanders exempted Melrose Abbey from the payment of tolls in his lands. Flanders also drew on Scotland for leather, cheese and tallow. Cattle was transported by sea from Inverness to Leith (1263). However, when William of Gley obtained permission in England to bring oxen and other livestock from Scotland into Lincolnshire, it is not clear whether the animals were to be driven or transported by water. Either way, livestock was on the move for some commercial purpose.[18]

The resources of Ireland too were appreciated by foreigners. Gerald of Wales called the attention of falconers to the superior quality of Irish hawks, but the more practical Henry II stipulated that the tribute he expected from the high-king of Ireland should be rendered in leather pieces certified by merchants, an oblique reference to the trade in hides. The only surviving Irish Exchequer roll shows that in those parts of the island where payments were not made in cash, debts were frequently discharged by offering large numbers of both cows and oxen which were then distributed to the countryside for improving arable, livestock and dairy farming.[19] In later years more diverse demands were met from Ireland. In 1258, Dublin sent out supplies of wheat and oats required by the king for Gascony. Other ports, like Cork and Youghal, sent horses, hogs, grain, even hay and beer. In 1291, corn was sent from Cork to Gascony. The stocks of local burgesses in Ross and Waterford were drawn on for wheat, oats and beans. Irish corn was taken to Chester in 1276 and the next year corn for the king's forces in Wales was supplied by Nicholas de Kolcloch, merchant of Carrickfergus. In 1297, Edward sent to Ireland for 400 horsemen with armoured horses, well equipped for the Scottish campaigns; the next year he called for wheat of various qualities, ground malt, hogsheads of wine, salt beef, fattened pigs and dried fish to be shipped to the Solway. Ireland also sent herrings, hake and eels. Even wine, acquired no doubt in the Dublin market, went to Scotland in 1290. Drogheda despatched prefabricated pieces of siege equipment with eighteen smiths and a carpenter to supervise construction. Apart from a report that impressive numbers of fleeces were exported from the Dingle (72,000 over thirty years, 1277–1302), details about Irish exports are only available for Dublin and Drogheda. Customs accounts list the export of all the native products: wheat, honey, wool, hides, cattle, sheep, pigs, bacon, butter, wax, boards and squirrel fur, as well as manufactures like linen and cloth, specified as Irish to distinguish them from both English and foreign cloth.[20]

The seas around these islands were also extensively fished. According to a mid-twelfth-century report, fishing grounds near the Isle of May in the Forth attracted many fishermen from the Continent. Sailors from Bayonne bought the rights to a monoploy of hunting whales between Mont St Michel and Dartmouth from King John and the exclusive right to buy, salt and smoke lampreys and whiting in Cornwall. Flemings coming to Yarmouth for the herring fishery kept the town prosperous. Irishmen from all around the coast between Waterford and Derry went to Man for the fishing. Englishmen, with others, went to Denmark and Norway for the same purpose. Fishing in foreign waters was apparently a new phenomenon, perhaps consequent to the demands made by the expanding population of western Europe, perhaps influenced by clerical exhortation to observe days of abstinence from meat-eating. Improvements in methods of curing fish made it possible to seek supplies from distant waters. The fish market was valuable and the Fishmongers of London were one of the earliest companies to receive a royal charter.[21]

Trade would have been very one-sided if the peoples of these islands had only sold and never bought. Imports most often mentioned were those of wine. Though a little wine was made in England itself, for centuries there had been a demand for foreign wine of various qualities. By the thirteenth century it arrived in huge quantities. Wine was drunk at all levels in English society and as far north as the Hebrides.[22] The king of Scots conveniently stocked his cellar by purchases at Ayr (red and white), at Aberdeen and at the fair of Dundee. Ireland imported wine from the south in return for the export of hides. Archaeologists have interpreted pottery from the Saintonge and Bordelais found in thirteenth-century Dublin sites as evidence for steady trade. Wine not only from the Rhineland and Gascony but from Auxerre, Anjou, Moissac, La Réole, or just 'France', entered England at several points. From Southampton wine was despatched throughout southern England; Bristol supplied Ireland and Warwick; Woodstock and Witney, like York, drew on Boston for their supplies. Judging from the care taken to specify their places of origin, English wine-drinkers were discriminating. Not much is known about retail prices of wine in England, but the men of Cologne were allowed as a special concession to sell their wine in the 'French' market, which offered more favourable terms of sale.[23]

Apart from wine, the Rhineland also sent other goods to English markets. According to a mid-twelfth-century statement of London customs, the king's chamberlain might come to ships in port and take for the king's use cloth of Constantinople, or of Regensburg, fine linen or coats of mail from Mainz.[24] Two picture-cloths of Cologne were acquired by Queen Eleanor of Castile by private negotiation, but her basins of Damascene work, Venetian vases, Limoges enamels and cloth from Tripoli were probably obtained through merchants.[25] Also from the east came a choice of silk, taffeta (Tartar or Chinese), Indian pearls, ebony- and ivory-handled knives and the goats' wool bonnets made in Anatolia for export to France and England.[26] Furs from the far north were considered indispensable, even for clergy, with Norway as the major source of beaver, sable, miniver and bear hides. Foreign merchants supplied exotic food: spices, cloves, saffron, aniseed, mustard, vinegar, even sugar. In 1290, a Spanish ship from Seville brought fruit, figs, raisins, grapes, dates, pomegranates, lemons and oranges as well as Cordovan leather, olive oil and rice to Portsmouth. This trade has implications for the elusive history of English gastronomy.[27] Information about the north is less detailed, but the currents of trade flowed as far as Scotland. Luke de Gisors, who supplied the king of Scots with harness in 1263, bought silk cloth and furs for him the following year at Ayr.[28] Supplies of silk acquired from middlemen possibly reached Ayr from Dublin or Bristol. Even if the sale of luxury goods was mainly for the benefit of the affluent, such trade had implications for humbler levels of the economy. The distribution of goods inland relied on the services of carters and bargemen.

Some imports, however, were essential. The ships of the Cinque Ports, for example, went regularly to Biscay, not only for wine but for salt.[29] The supply of raw wool for the native cloth industry could be met locally, but the dyestuff, woad, and the fixing agent, alum, both had to be imported from overseas. The chief source of woad was Picardy, across the Channel. Henry le Engleis supplied what was needed in Yorkshire directly, whereas merchants from Picardy themselves took their produce to many small English towns. The king calculated that woad was a sufficiently staple import to be worth taxing and from 1199 a royal custom of 5 marks for half a ship of woad and 10 marks on a full delivery was imposed in Lincolnshire. In London the cargoes of John de Croi and his partners, described as the king's enemies, were seized: a ship, four packets of woad and one cargo of alum. The woad was auctioned off for 47 marks. The crown also collected well over 100 marks from merchants who paid a levy to bring woad into England and sell it, presumably retail.[30] It was used in many parts of the kingdom. At the end of the thirteenth century, when woad belonging to foreigners in England was impounded, supplies were inventoried in the north (Newcastle, Yorkshire), Lincolnshire, the Midlands (Leicestershire, Northamptonshire, Bedfordshire, Buckinghamshire, Huntingdonshire) and parts of Norfolk. The poor quality, of the alum used for finishing English cloth is alleged to have impaired its quality, but matters improved when the Genoese began to bring alum from their recently acquired concession in the Crimea. The earliest known contract, drawn up in May 1278, arranged for two galleys to transport 1297 cantars of alum from Phocea in the Crimea to Seville and thence on to England.[31]

Other basic materials also came from abroad. Iron was mined in almost every county of England, but not in sufficient quantity to satisfy requirements at home.[32] Stocks were supplemented from several different sources abroad: France, the Pyrenees (some transported in Spanish ships), Sweden and Germany. The iron-working industry became sophisticated enough to combine iron of different provenance for different purposes, native ore being used for tools and Norman, combined with Spanish, for building siege-engines and weapons.

The English demand for animals was also intense. Horses were particularly important. Arnold of Lübeck was astonished at how the Danes had in his own lifetime become so rich. Apart from their valuable fishing grounds, it was above all thanks to their rich pastures where great numbers of horses could be raised for sale abroad. Ribe seems to have been a major port for this. When Danes brought palfreys to Yarmouth in 1226, the king promptly ordered some to be purchased for himself. In 1213 an enterprising merchant, Jakemyn of Parma, brought over horses from the continent. The next year a Bristol wine-merchant went to Spain specifically to buy horses. Judging from the way they were cosseted in England when they arrived, these were highly prized. Spain supplied large numbers of horses throughout the thirteenth century, no doubt entering the dominions of the English king in Gascony and travelling onwards by sea. Men were sent off to make purchases for the king but later Italian merchants were regularly engaged to buy up horses for military purposes. In 1276 Earl Henry of Lincoln was brought thirty by the merchants Benvenuto of Bologna and John le Gaunt. Roger Mortimer likewise sent a Florentine merchant to France to buy twelve destriers for his use in the Welsh wars. In the next six months the king's sergeant and several foreign merchants received specific instructions to go overseas and acquire nearly 200 horses for the king, his uncle, William de Valence, and others. Horses were not only sought abroad under pressure of war. While Edward I's ambassadors were in Aragon, they inspected stock there and bought fourteen fine warhorses. Spanish horses featured in the army Alexander III of Scotland mustered in 1263 for his campaign against the Hebrides. (The infantry was equipped with bows and Irish axes.) Horses were also bought for other purposes. To pay the monks of Westminster their due for the funeral of his brother Edmund, Edward I acquired two warhorses (at a rather low price) from Leonardo of Milan.[33] There is nothing to prove that horses were regularly imported for sale in the open market, but prospective buyers knew how and where to obtain what they wanted.

Men bought animals for sport as well as war. Various birds of prey could be bought at English fairs, chiefly from Norwegian traders. The most prized or rarest specimens were probably not available commercially. King John chose to send an agent to Denmark and Zealand specifically to buy hawks.[34] Others came as gifts. The most prized animals were exchanged by rulers as diplomatic gifts, *hors de commerce*. The king of Norway made a point of stressing the efforts he had taken to get rare hawks from Iceland as a present for Henry III. Norway may have been poor in some respects but it made up for this by offering many strange animals as gifts, like the *bestiam Helc* (elk) in 1222 or the polar bear which Henry III kept in the Tower of London and allowed out on a long chain to fish in the Thames. Some gifts were sent as mere curiosities, to arouse astonishment, like the whale's skull King Magnus of Norway sent to Edward I.[35] No doubt already aware of English interest in animals, domestic and exotic, so evident from the many books of bestiaries of the twelfth and thirteenth centuries, other foreign rulers clearly understood that gifts of animals to English kings would be well received. Frederick II flattered Henry III by presenting him with three leopards, a courteous reference to his heraldic shield.[36] Twenty years later, in 1255, Louis IX, just back from the east, presented Henry with an elephant, which was kept in a special house at the Tower of London and carefully drawn by a fascinated Matthew Paris. The keeping of exotic pets was not confined to kings. The bishop of Durham was kept amused by two apes, one young, one old, presumably from Spain since only Barbary apes were then known in Europe. More practically, when Richard of Cornwall was sent some male and female buffaloes, then unknown in the west, it was presumably to start breeding them.[37]

The giving of animals was reciprocated. Henry II made presents of *damas* to Philip II's new park at Vincennes; he sent others from England to the count of Flanders.[38] In 1212 King John offered the count of Holland some specimens of two different breeds of greyhound, possibly intended to improve the bloodstock of the count's pack, along with silver cups, gold rings and a silver belt.[39] These served the further purpose six months later of bringing the count to pledge himself in John's service. The possible consequences of giving such presents explain why Innocent III reproved Hubert Walter for accepting gifts of birds and animals from King Sverre of Norway when he was under papal ban for his persecution of the Church.[40]

Foreign trade was not confined to basic necessities or exotic luxuries, for quite humble products were regularly brought from overseas. Ships from Ponthieu detained at Branksea island in 1235 were laden with herrings and onions. Further west, ships from Normandy brought mixed cargoes to Exeter:[41] garlic and onions from Genêts, in the Bay of Mont St Michel; woad, iron, canvas, potash and candles from Port en Bessin; plaster, pitch, woad and potash from Barfleur; iron, potash and alum from Dieppe; woad from Abbeville. Apart from wine, ships from Bayonne brought iron, almonds, wax, cumin, liquorice, wool yarn, veil cloth and salt; from La Rochelle, salt; from Le Vivier, iron, almonds, anise, garlic and onions; some wine came from Santander.

Information about Irish imports is less specific, but rates set for paying murage at Dublin in 1250, and again later in 1278, at least indicate the great variety of goods handled in the city. Imports certainly included wine, woad, pepper, alum and perhaps unguents. Salt and herrings paid duty, both coming in and going out. Silk cloth without gold thread and reinforced silk could both be bought in Ireland. Millstones (*mola*) of both French and English manufacture are mentioned.[42]

With circumstantial evidence for exports and imports, there can be no question that commerce was important for the economy. The free movement of merchants in England, at least in peacetime, was specifically confirmed by Magna Carta. Trading as such was not normally subject to royal scrutiny, so royal records only attend to it at times of crisis. During the rebellion of 1173, for example, some Flemings, as subjects of a prince then hostile to Henry II, were accused of complicity and their goods impounded in nine different English counties. The merchandise impounded included silk and wine, as well as raw wool.[43] These goods had either been brought for sale or had been bought in England on their own account. The availability of goods on the English markets was itself an attraction for casual customers. In 1189 the Icelandic priest Ingimund was able to buy the wine and honey he wanted here. Another Icelander, Marcus, who got from Norway the timber needed for building a church *c.*1195, acquired church bells in England. The abbey of Sorø on Zealand, Denmark, had permission to export English marble for its church building, at a time when Purbeck marble was being obtained for Chichester Cathedral.[44] Marble as a decorative feature in building had recently become fashionable in England and may explain this otherwise strange-looking purchase.

Merchants

By the second half of the twelfth century, England occupied the central point in a trading system that stretched from the Bay of Biscay to the Baltic. Henry II's interest in securing marriages for his daughters at the political termini in Castile and Saxony reflects his appreciation of this fact. In the south,

Henry's possession of Gascony gave him the incentive to make friends in the Biscay region; in the north, the resumption of significant silver mining in mid-century Germany made it imperative to develop contacts in a region which supplied the royal mint with much of its raw material. The Angevin 'Empire' fitted easily into the economic framework of the Continent in the late twelfth century. Indeed, the far-flung character of Henry II's dominions played an important part in facilitating the movement of trade. Soon after he became duke of Normandy, Henry of Anjou confirmed the rights of merchants from Rouen to travel to all markets in England, a charter that had more importance at the time of issue for the Normans than the English.[45] Merchants from outside Henry's lands were also privileged. In 1155 Henry II allowed the men of St Omer to sell their own goods all over England.[46] Similarly, in 1173–75, Henry II granted those of Cologne, 'his faithful men', a royal charter allowing them to buy and sell anywhere in the kingdom. Cologne regarded the English trade as so important that it accepted the standard of the English mark for its own transactions. When Richard I was imprisoned by the emperor Henry VI, the city played an active part in negotiating his release. The king was grateful, confirming the rights of 'our citizens', the merchants of Cologne, to travel freely throughout his domains, with particular emphasis on their right to buy and sell in London *et alibi*; Richard also remitted the due previously paid for the Cologners' guildhall in London.[47]

Cologne was not the only place on the Continent to adopt the English mark as standard; it happened in Castile and Portugal, showing that Iberian merchants already did business in the English Channel.[48] Royal links with Aquitaine explain why merchants of Bordeaux and Bayonne so readily turned up, even on the eastern coast of England, as at Yarmouth for trade and fishing.[49] As to Italians, the names of a few craftsmen occur in early twelfth-century London records and the Guines chronicle refers in passing to Italian merchants in the county on their way to England. However, it was Richard I's borrowings to finance his Mediterranean activities and subsidise the candidature of his nephew Otto of Brunswick as king in Germany which were chiefly responsible for establishing Italian merchants in England. This is how men of Piacenza acquired English property in 1197, as security for the loans.[50] Exemptions from tolls on their goods had traditionally been accorded to monks. From this time merchants too began to acquire privileges allowing them to convey their merchandise freely and pay local dues only at the point of sale. Some of these applied throughout Henry II's dominions; others only in England or Normandy: there was room for bargaining.

Like Richard, John needed money for his foreign commitments. He borrowed regularly from Italian merchants, either to meet the cost of embassies to the Curia or to pay Otto IV's creditors. (The king's need for domestic cash could be easily satisfied in England itself.) The system was so well established that John sent his agents abroad with a wad of blank cover notes authorising them to borrow up to specified limits and promising that debts would be honoured by the king.[51] Roman financiers regularly supplied the immediate needs of Englishmen, not only of royal envoys, but of clergy. English crusaders borrowed money from them in 1204; some of their creditors were still trying to recover their money twenty years later.[52] In 1205, John borrowed from men of Bologna as well as of Rome. For a number of years thereafter, several different bankers from Bologna lent Englishmen money, perhaps because the established contacts between that city and English students had already created a network of relationships. Bolognese bought English cloth in 1208, so moneylending was only part of their commercial business. They obtained letters of safe conduct in 1220 and permission to attend the fair in Holland (that is, at Boston) in 1222, and again in 1226. In the 1220s their transactions were still impressive. In 1227 they were themselves at fault for not paying their debts to the bishop of Winchester, Peter des Roches. A royal letter was diplomatically addressed to the Podestà and commune of Bologna requiring them to settle the account.[53] Thereafter, Italians from other cities overtook the Bolognese as merchants in England.

Already in 1214 a merchant of Asti proposed to sell jewels, diamonds, rubies and emeralds in France and England, not deterred by war in both kingdoms.[54] The same year, traders from Piacenza more opportunely had horses for sale to the king, presumably as middlemen; ten years later, there is a note of others.[55] The next year Henry III was paying a pension to Ansaldus, a Genoese merchant with interests in the Levant, who, on the king's behalf, took various presents, including scarlets and fine cloth, to the sultan of Damascus. The sultan reciprocated and on his next mission to Damascus Ansaldus carried Henry III's plea for the release of any Christian captives he might have.[56] A few years later, in 1237, some Genoese were planning a commercial journey to France, Flanders and England. Only much later did the Genoese set up regular sailings round the coasts of Spain to England and Ireland, hoping to break into lucrative markets, not create them.[57] The specific city from which these merchants came is always named. In London the generic term 'Lombards' comprised Italian businessmen from many different places who had taken up residence, occupied a recognised space in the city and become part of its regular working structure.

Though a Sienese merchant is mentioned in royal records in 1213, only from the 1220s do references to Tuscans become more frequent. Henry III borrowed money from Sienese in 1229 and from both Florentines and Sienese in 1232. But these merchants were not mere moneylenders. In 1235 Florentine traders complained they had been robbed at Blythe in Nottinghamshire.[58] These merchants invoked powerful connections when they were in trouble. A Sienese merchant imprisoned in 1239 was released at the request of both the pope and the bishop-elect of Liège (William of Savoy, the queen's uncle) on whose behalf he was acting. Another, accused of rape in 1257, obtained a royal pardon. Their activities in England are best known in terms of their relations with the king, who borrowed heavily from them in the late 1230s, but he was not alone in this.[59] Protests from outraged borrowers about their terms of business prompted Henry III to publish a ban on usurers in 1240 and threaten to drive offending Florentines and Sienese out of the kingdom. This was mainly bluster but may have given merchants from Lucca the chance to break into the money market. In 1245 the king issued another decree against usurers, with the proviso that they might be allowed to stay if they were prepared to give him credit facilities.[60] Unlike John, Henry III found it more difficult to get the credit he wanted, but Italians in need of royal protection for their business were still prepared to offer him a service he could not do without. They operated on an international scale, buying raw wool in England for sale in Flanders or fine quality English cloth for Italian customers. They brought some goods from the Mediterranean to England. Handling bills of credit, they held deposits of specie in several major European cities. This equipped them to act as agents for the management of the papacy's finances, providing it with money on the basis of what would be collected in northern Europe. Their expertise in tax collection and financial management must have impressed English royal officials, themselves experienced accountants. Such business operations made it possible in the 1250s for the king and the papacy to cooperate in financial matters. Under Edward I, the many Italian business houses operating in England were used by the king to secure the best financial services available in his day. The Lucchese firm of Riccardi provided the king with instant credit for twenty years, on the security of the king's customs' revenues.[61] Lucchese were also well to the fore in Ireland where they farmed the king's Irish customs and used their advantages to trade on their own account. In 1290 they claimed to have merchandise deposited at several different ports, Waterford, Ross, Youghal, Cork and Limerick.

Though the king made use of them principally as bankers, these Italian merchants were businessmen, more concerned to make certain profit from trade than incur the uncertainties of moneylending. But their usefulness to the king gave them extra leverage, as in 1249 when they sought his aid in recovering debts due to them all over the kingdom. By the middle of the century, Italian merchants had either themselves become established in London and other towns or at least had permanent establishments with resident partners. Little is known about the family backgrounds of the merchants but some of them found English wives and settled down, if only for a time, in England. They may have acquired their English properties deliberately or as a consequence of landowners defaulting on their debts.

Italians were not the only merchant-financiers to find attractive opportunities in England. Henry III's interests in Gascony brought merchants from Bordeaux and Bayonne. His family connections in Provence and Toulouse opened the way for such southern French cities as Marseilles, Montpellier and Toulouse to trade with England. Montpellier, which had a famous school of medicine, was at that time the chief centre in the west for the distribution of spices from the east, as important for medicine as for gastronomy. Henry III's spicer, Robert, was a native of that city.[62] The southerners best known in England came from Cahors, and the word 'caorsin' became synonymous with usurer. They occur in the documents from the early part of the thirteenth century and eventually took up prominent positions in England. In 1246, Ernald Berand became royal chamberlain for London and Sandwich; he was succeeded by another Cahorsin, Poncius de Mora. Later another merchant, William Servat, undertook business for Edward I and was indispensable enough to receive a pardon for handling base coins.[63]

The closest of England's trading partners were, nevertheless, the Flemings, and by extension other peoples of the Low Countries. After the departure of Baldwin of Flanders on crusade, King John dealt with specific individuals or representatives of many different towns: Bruges (1205), Utrecht (1209), Douai and Louvain (1212), Damme (1213), Ghent (1215), Ypres (1217) and Antwerp (1231). The importance of identifying the merchant's place of origin became clear in wartime. In 1213, when the merchants of St Omer and Douai in Louis of France's lands had their merchandise seized, those of Ghent, Bruges, Lille and Ypres did not. To help identify themselves, merchants were expected to carry letters of credence from their city councils or local prince.[64] Sound commercial sense brought Flanders and England together but their very closeness challenged the king of France to try to extend his own influence over the county. Subjected to French pressure, the Flemings could be dragged into hostilities against England. Embargoes on Flemish trade were then expected to be sufficient to bring Flanders into line. Contrariwise, when Henry III himself went to war in France in 1229–30, he exempted merchants of Flanders and Brabant from restrictions on trade with French subjects. Those responsible for detaining ships deemed to belong to enemies were expected to recognise significant differences between merchants of adjacent towns and keep abreast of the fluctuating situations abroad. As in later centuries, Anglo-Flemish relations were integral to the international and domestic policies of English rulers.

England attracted merchants from all over Europe. Edward I's charter for foreign merchants (February, 1303) specified those of Germany, France, Spain, Portugal, Navarre, Lombardy, Tuscany, Provence, Catalonia, Aquitaine, Toulouse, Cahors, Flanders, Brabant and the rest without even mentioning those from Norway, Denmark and Sweden.[65] Some merchants remained in the kingdom for long periods and transacted business where they chose. Danes and Norwegians apparently enjoyed long-standing freedom of access and movement. Those who became resident paid local taxes, but otherwise escaped notice. Nevertheless, at a time when Denmark was Otto IV's chief ally, a Danish merchant from Ribe took the extra precaution of obtaining John's royal protection in 1208 for wherever he did business in England.[66] The advantage he probably obtained was an undertaking not to have his merchandise seized by way of reprisals against fellow countrymen indebted to English traders. In 1220 this befell Danes expected to have goods worth 200 marks, seized to compensate four London merchants who had had their own merchandise taken in Denmark.[67] Danish merchant shipping is attested in all the principal ports of the North Sea: Yarmouth, Boston, Newcastle and Tynemouth. Like Norwegians, Danes sought permission to export corn.

Despite traditional arrangements, trade with Norway too became subject to more formal regulations. In 1223, a treaty was agreed with the new king of Norway, Haakon Haakonson.[68] Scandinavia supplied highly prized commodities. From Norway, the English obtained not only furs, but also wooden boards, oil and wax, quite apart from birds of prey.[69] Swedes too entered the picture. Before 1226 merchants from Gotland had already obtained royal privileges which they claimed had been infringed that year at (King's) Lynn. Several other documents from the 1230s involve Gotland.[70]

Merchants from other specific parts of Europe were not so comprehensively privileged as Danes and Norwegians, but when in 1200 John issued instructions about trade the only condition laid down was that traditional dues were paid, both locally and to the king. Two years later, pressed for money, John imposed a tax of a fifteenth on exports. This was collected over the next two years. The returns indicate that, apart from Southampton, the ports contributing most to the king's Custom were all on the North Sea, from London as far north as Newcastle, and the merchants chiefly affected, those from Flanders and Germany.[71] Merchants with suitably impressive patrons had immediately sought exemptions from payment of the fifteenth and thereafter foreign merchants applied more often for individual letters of protection. They were not obliged to register for permission to trade; the initiative for obtaining royal safe conducts and privileges was left to them. Some sought individual permission to stay for some months, in order to cover themselves in case of legal proceedings concerning their commerce. General privileges were occasionally granted to all the merchants of some favoured cities. The men of the archbishop of Cologne had received one for London in 1173–75 and this was regularly renewed. As a consequence of Henry III's new friendship with the emperor Frederick, Cologne's privileges were extended to include the right to hold courts for their own merchants.[72] Men from Cologne appear as residents not only in London but at Boston and Lynn. So considerable were their commercial dealings with England that in the 1230s the Westphalian towns struck their coins as passable imitations of sterling.[73] Other north German towns sought comparable privileges to trade in England, invoking the king's friendship for their own Welf lords, like the men of Bremen in 1213 and Brunswick in 1225. When diplomatic ties were re-established with the empire in the 1220s, all the men 'from the land of the emperor' were treated as a national group, but individual cities still sought privileges for their own merchants, as Hamburg, Groningen and Stavere did in 1224. Frederick II referred to Lübeck's English trading interests in his charter of 1226, though no English privilege is known earlier than 1238 when Frederick's influence with his new brother-in-law was usefully invoked. After Richard of Cornwall became king of the Romans, he too interceded in England for the merchants of particular German cities seeking royal protection or confirmation of trading privileges.[74]

Competition between merchants for specially favourable terms of trade affected the towns of northern France too. When London agreed in 1237 that citizens of Amiens should enjoy the same freedom to travel and trade in the rest of England as Londoners, the terms were strictly interpreted to exclude other Picard towns like Corbie and Beauvais.[75] Merchants from those places had attended the fair at St Ives in Huntingdonshire in 1235 and were not deterred by discrimination, but it restricted their activities. Picards, principal suppliers of the woad, regularly petitioned for royal privileges. King John, who had borrowed money from a number of individual merchants from that region, could hardly refuse. After the loss of Normandy cross-Channel traffic continued. When Louis VIII made war in Poitou in 1224, both Dieppe and Barfleur obtained Henry III's permission to continue trading.[76] How peaceable the Channel really became in this period is arguable. John formally insisted that no obstacles should be placed on traditional fishing. Even so, Philip II had to write to the English government on behalf of some northern French merchants in 1220 complaining of the depredations against the men of Calais by seamen from the Cinque Ports. A few years later, a fishing vessel from Calais was detained on the grounds that it had fished without a royal licence, so that the government may have tried to restrain the Portsmen's more outrageous activities by this means.[77] It is difficult to believe that licensing can ever have been easily enforced or willingly accepted.

Royal efforts to take advantage of trade focused more narrowly on trying to force foreign merchants buying and selling in England to exchange their currency for sterling on their arrival. When official money exchanges were set up in 1279, it was expected that foreign merchants would arrive in Chester and Bristol as well as in Winchelsea, Dover, Sandwich, Hythe, Dartmouth, Southampton and Weymouth, the southern ports, and in Yarmouth, Tynemouth, Whitby, Scarborough, Hull, Grimsby and Newcastle on the North Sea. Even this was not an exhaustive list. In 1284 other east coast ports were also used for entering the country. In 1290 a Spanish merchant sold honey and wine as far away as Carlisle.[78] Foreign merchants might in fact be found almost anywhere in the kingdom, confidently moving in search of customers or produce, making their own arrangements and not necessarily dependent on the market place. They changed their money in anticipation of spending it up-country as required.

For many, the attractions of great fairs determined their itineraries.[79] From early in the twelfth century, fairs at a number of points like Winchester and Boston had become major occasions for substantial purchases. The legal rights to these fairs were held by private lords, like the bishop of Winchester or the earl of Richmond at Boston, so that the king himself could not issue exemptions from their local tolls. The fairs were a source of profit to their lords, but the provision of facilities, hospitality and trading booths also enriched local people. The most famous of these fairs was that of Boston, in July, a major occasion for the purchase of a variety of goods. Falcons were bought there for the king himself. The fair cycle stretched round the year from Lent to Christmas, and round the country from Stamford via St Ives, Boston and Lynn to Winchester in September, where the agent of John's queen acquired ermine along with pepper and cinnamon. The fair cycle then turned back through Westminster to Bury St Edmunds via Northampton. These locations were of most benefit to merchants from across the North Sea or the Channel, but Spaniards also took advantage of the possibilities to sell their own produce and buy goods from the north in England and spare themselves the voyage across the North Sea.

Commercial fairs were also found in Scotland, at Glasgow in the late twelfth century, at Dundee and at Haddington later, though what might be purchased there is not specified. About Irish fairs, we are somewhat better informed. Fairs lasting a fortnight were held at both Dublin and Drogheda, in summer and autumn respectively, and a fair was also held at Trim where three Flemish merchants bought cloth in 1258. The Dublin fair grant of 1252 anticipated the arrival of merchants from Elbeuf, Caen and Amiens. Richard de Burgh obtained royal permission shortly before his death for an eight-day fair at Kilfeakle, near Tipperary. If this grant was never implemented it was at least proof of baronial confidence in the economic opportunities available.[80]

The attractions of these fairs meant that quite apart from those foreigners who spent long periods in England there were even more birds of passage, visiting to discharge their cargoes and purchase goods which they either exported directly home or disposed of in other ports of call. Merchants who obtained letters of protection for more than one year at a time probably plied the commercial circuit. Records from St Ives for the late thirteenth century show that traders arrived from the Low Countries, Rouen, Caen, Paris, Provins, Bordeaux and Siena, each bearing goods to be sold in expectation of making purchases in return.[81] Competition between different cities to sell high-quality cloth was intense. There were so many different cloth-measures offered in English markets that for the benefit of consumers Richard I and his successors attempted to impose a national standard. The merchants were stronger than the government. As late as 1279, merchants of Douai still successfully protested that its cloth was distributed widely and its character could not be changed to fit English requirements alone.[82]

Foreign merchants who moved from fair to fair had every opportunity to visit and trade in other towns. Local trading brought Frenchmen to Coventry in 1216, Navarrese to Oxford in 1217, merchants of Ghent to buy wool at Gloucester in 1215. When Conrad of Brunswick accidentally killed another German in 1249, his goods at Northampton were seized by the sheriff. English records imply that foreign merchants could become familiar figures in several parts of the kingdom.[83] The ubiquity of cloth manufacture explains why Picards turn up in quite small towns. At Leicester, until the Leicester gild merchant intervened, foreign merchants used local agents to buy wool in the neighbourhood in order to get round the restrictive practices of Leicester town merchants.[84] Local restrictions usually reduced the abilities of merchants from outside the town to sell retail, but this did not confine foreigners to a few great commercial centres. Not until 1263–64 do the records provide evidence of foreign merchants being attacked or their merchandise damaged simply because they were 'aliens'. Far from endorsing the prejudices of a few, Simon de Montfort's government attempted to reassure foreign merchants that they had nothing to fear as a result of temporary disorder. Within weeks of the battle of Lewes, arrangements for the Boston fair took the resumption of trade for granted.[85]

Although there were limits to what kings could do to protect foreign merchants, royal encouragement and offers of protection must have helped to develop international commerce in England, but it was not disinterested. From the first, kings had seen how to take advantage of it for themselves. What precisely the king obtained in return for privileges before 'customs' were imposed is not clear because there is no information about what tolls were paid and what proportion of them was taken by the king. The most important of English exports on which the crown later imposed a profitable tax (customs) were wool, fleeces and leather. At what point the export of animal hides became a major factor is not known, but it was already important enough by 1199 when merchants needed a licence for the export of both wool and hides from England. Even the abbot of Clairvaux needed King John's permission to export leather for his house.[86] Wine did not yet attract any import 'duty', but the king claimed two barrels on each shipment as a royal privilege.[87]

The king's chief profit from English commerce came rather from his control of the coinage, which was struck as silver pennies. Numismatists estimate that the amount of silver currency in circulation more than doubled in the course of Henry II's reign, from £125,000 to £300,000.[88] This was made possible from the 1170s by greater output of silver after new mining operations had been opened up in Germany. Efforts were also made at home to meet demand by improving the extraction of silver from the Alston mines in Cumberland.

To guarantee the quality and quantity of the coinage, the king ordered foreign merchants coming into the country to exchange their own money for sterling at fixed points, and so keep English mints supplied with silver. Originally the exchange arrangements were left in the hands of the moneyers, but by 1180 the exchange of foreign for English coins had become such a major operation that the king set up an exchange under its own warden. This deprived the moneyers of their previous advantage and transferred the benefit to the crown. The same year, a new coinage of 'short-cross' type was issued under the direction of Philippe Aymar of Tours. Aymar was not a success and was soon dismissed for fraud, but the type of coin issued remained without change under Henry II's successors for nearly seventy years.[89]

Exchanging coins was a complicated matter. Notices of an order about the exchange in 1223 were sent to Ypres, Arras, St Omer and Ghent as places from which visiting merchants were most likely expected. Later discount rates anticipated the purchase of foreign coins from Spain, Pamplona, Montpellier, Ariège, Foix, Marseilles, Valence, Le Puy, Cologne, Brussels and Malines. The precise locations given for these coins show what a great variety of currencies the exchange was required to be familiar with, as well as giving some idea of where merchants came from. The contribution these coins made to the minting operation was impressive. By the 1240s, £50,000 of foreign silver was recoined in the English mints of London and Canterbury.[90]

The international nature of the money market may help to explain why the quality of the coinage itself was controlled by employing foreign moneyers. In 1247, when work began on the new English coinage issued the following year, Jordan of Brunswick was commissioned to bring over as many foreign craftsmen as he needed.[91] Likewise, in 1279, Edward I entrusted the engraving of a new coinage to William de Tournemire from Marseilles.[92] In mid-century, Henry III decided to experiment with striking a gold coinage at a ratio of one to twenty.[93] His recent dealings with the court of Castile and his new commitments to rule in Sicily (both kingdoms with a gold coinage) must have encouraged such a move but the experiment was not a great success. Sterling coins proved to be of greater worth abroad than in England because the official exchange rates paid only for the coins' value by weight and not at face value. This discouraged merchants from exchanging their coins in England. Abroad, sterling circulated freely. As early as 1177, merchants seized by pirates in Dalmatian waters were carrying sterling along with Sicilian taris and coins struck at Provins and Melgueil (near Montpellier). In 1204, Venetians lent crusaders money to be repaid in sterling at the Champagne fairs. At the other end of Europe, sterling was exported and used freely as currency in parts of Germany and Scandinavia. Even local prices in the Baltic were quoted in sterling.[94] Many imitations of sterling were struck across the North Sea. It was not as easy as the government expected to control the commercial movement of coins. It could not even enforce the exchange of all foreign coins for sterling. In the 1290s, when Edward I redoubled his efforts to prevent 'debased' coins from circulating in the kingdom, this only proved how easily such coins had in fact escaped scrutiny at the ports of entry.[95]

After the establishment of the English lordship in Ireland coins were struck from John onwards at Dublin and Waterford in the name of the king. These provide further evidence for the importance and prosperity of Irish commerce in the thirteenth century. Such coins were distinguished from

English ones by having the royal head placed in a triangle and these too were imitated on the Continent, as by Rudolf of Habsburg and the counts of Lippe and other neighbouring rulers, particularly at Dortmund. They have been found in coin hoards in Lower Normandy, Montpellier, Brussels, Bruges, Liège, Koblenz, Bremen, and in towns of Denmark, Norway and Sweden, indicating, if not how far Irish merchants themselves travelled, at least how far Irish coins inspired confidence. Irish coins were evidently accepted as sound currency on the Continent and their international accept-ability was guaranteed by entrusting the mints of Dublin and Waterford to Alexander of Lucca in 1281. Foreign money brought into Ireland was assayed, as in England. The goldsmith, John of Ely, was charged in 1299 for neglecting his duty, but acquitted by the jury. Less is known about the inter-national circulation of Scottish coins but, after the new English coinage of 1247, Henry III threatened to take appropriate action if the Scots did not keep to the same standard of silver.[96]

The livelihood of many people in the kingdom was dependent in some way on the regularity of foreign trade. The demand for corn and wool made producers, who included most of the great men of the kingdom, aware of economic considerations. When Richard of Cornwall became king of Germany in 1257, he immediately perceived the commercial disadvantages of the many tolls on the Rhine and negotiated for their removal.[97] There was no conflict of economic interest in England between merchants and mag-nates.

Townsmen

Already in the eleventh century about one-tenth of the English population is estimated to have lived in towns. The number of towns greatly increased in the period considered here and some towns grew considerably in size. Not only did urban expansion depend in the first place on immigration from the countryside, or indeed from abroad; because of higher rates of urban mor-tality, immigration was needed to sustain expansion. As a consequence all flourishing towns had mixed and shifting populations. Newcomers, if not always welcomed, could expect to be accommodated and find employment. Urban records, written in French, show that English townsmen of this period were familiar with that language. This was not the result of any cul-tural pressure from a 'feudal' aristocracy nor even to the constant influx of French townsmen. French had become the ordinary language of public com-munication, used as a matter of course by the Englishmen most often exposed to contact with foreign visitors: the chief citizens and burgessess of the towns. Despite their apparent sophistication, these men were intensely local in their loyalties and held themselves responsible for securing the best possible terms for their communities. In most towns, business flourished in proportion to the amount of commercial activity, so townsmen had no reason to tolerate hostility to foreign merchants. They were sufficiently aware of urban institutions on the Continent to borrow from them the idea of the sworn commune and the office of mayor. For several towns, Henry III happily confirmed that mayors should be as under his father and allowed more to be instituted.[98] They managed their own business interests. At Leicester and Warwick the town authorities took it upon themselves to obtain special permission to import woad for their industry.[99] Many flourished to the point of acquiring charters from kings which guaranteed their liberties and entitled them to pay their dues to the crown directly, and not through the sheriff. They paid for autonomy, not for royal interference. At the most, if their merchants were ill-treated abroad, they asked the king to bring pressure to bear in order to secure compensation or reprisals. Such intervention was intermittent and exceptional. English towns were keenly aware of the privileges of their own place; they did not collaborate as a class or a commercial interest with other towns in the kingdom. Until they were required to send spokesmen to royal councils, they had no opportunities even to consider such matters.

Trade was a major factor in the growth of English towns in this period, as contemporaries appreciated. In his life of Becket, William Fitz Stephen began with a eulogy of London as more glorious than all the other noble and celebrated cities of the world. Fitz Stephen deliberately drew on his familiarity with Latin authors to praise his own city. According to him, London was an even older city than Rome, since it had been founded by Brutus the Trojan. He firmly attributed London's importance to its trade, sending wealth and merchandise into distant lands and gladly receiving merchants coming by water with costly produce: the Arabian, gold; the Sabaean, spice and incense; the Scythian, arms; oil of palms from Babylon; precious stones from Egypt; purple silk from China. This was not mere persiflage, for such commodities were certainly available for sale. When he referred to imports of fur and sables from Norway and Russia, he drew not on literature but on contemporary experience. In London, foreign produce could be bought at any time in the year. Thirteenth-century cordwainers, for example, could expect to find the leather they needed in the city. When a Spanish ship foundered off the coast near Abbotsbury in 1277, the most valuable part of its cargo, 100 bales of cordovan leather, was valued at £1600. Fitz Stephen's praise of London is echoed by his contemporaries, Thomas of Britain and Richard of Poitou. Urban prosperity naturally had its downside. Like Fitz Stephen, Richard of Devizes drew on classical Latin poets to enhance his effect, this time to deplore the kind of cosmopolitan society he recognised London to be.[100]

London already welcomed immigrants from Germany, Gascony, southern France and Italy. At the time no distinction was drawn between Londoners who were native and those who were 'foreign'. The operative factor for London merchants was whether the city authorities treated them as 'citizens' entitled to the privileges of Londoners, or not. The city, not the king, decided their status. It recognised Dentayt, a Florentine, as citizen in 1252; Arnold Giffard, from Cahors, in 1259; in 1280, Thomas Romano, in 1289, Dono de Podio, both from Lucca; Servat, also from Cahors, in 1292. Just as casually, one sheriff of London slipped away to become a burgess of Harfleur, leaving debts behind him.[101] Apart from those who made their own way in the city, arrangements could be reached to accord some collective privileges, as in 1260 when the merchants of Ghent, Ypres, Bruges, Douai and St Omer secured exemption in London from payments of murage. The German Hanse asserted their rights to comparable exemptions in 1282. In 1284 London agreed reciprocal rights with Toulouse.[102] The city's autonomy in such matters particularly displeased Edward I because the city declined to admit his subjects of Bordeaux en bloc to citizenship. Edward I took the view that those who submitted to his authority ought to be distinguished from those who owed allegiance to a 'foreign' prince. Such an idea was, however, not generally shared in the thirteenth century.

London was already more of a cosmopolitan city than an English one and its very independence made it a power in the kingdom kings had to come to terms with. The victor of Hastings had to bargain with Londoners to be crowned at Westminster; Stephen owed his crown to Londoners, who drove out his rival, Matilda. When London joined the barons in 1215, John was cornered into granting the Great Charter. Between the Tower and Westminster the city of London might look vulnerable to royal pressure; in fact, kings teetered on the periphery of a community they could not master. No wonder Becket came to symbolise resistance to royal bullying. Tom was never a popular name in the Plantagenet family and no Tom ever became king.

London was not the only town to attract foreigners to England. William of Malmesbury noted the presence of German and Irish ships at York in the early twelfth century.[103] Apart from resident Danes, York was reported to be full of Scotsmen. French Jews, said to have been attracted to England on account of its wealth, built up a large colony there. If not as cosmopolitan as London, York had its own foreign residents. But all towns must to some extent have been accustomed to finding strangers in their midst.

Trade also began to assist the growth of urban societies in Scotland from the reign of King William and the king himself may have deliberately promoted this development.[104] Most Scottish towns were on the coasts and estuaries of the kingdom, facing east, west and north. Foreign elements stand out from the start. When the bishop founded a burgh at St Andrews *c*.1144, the provost he installed was Mainard the Fleming, a burgess of Berwick.[105] Berwick was the major point of embarkation for the Continent. It was there that King William's messengers found appropriate transports to Flanders in 1173 when he sought urgent intelligence about the Young King's proposed rebellion. It was the principal port of the kingdom, flourishing enough in the thirteenth century to be the only Scottish burgh with separate houses for all the new orders of friars. Berwick was a cultured centre. In

1291 one of its burgesses, Roger Bartholomew, had the rare distinction of being a graduate *magister* (master). Berwick had its own international connections. A merchant of Florence who lent money to Augustine of Nottingham, archdeacon of Dunblane, while he was studying at Bologna in 1269, stipulated repayment at Berwick. Its merchants travelled far. In 1263, a burgess who complained that one of his ships with its cargo had been seized by the crew, obtained a mandate from Henry III ordering his officials in Wales, Ireland and Gascony to look out for it. In 1272 the authorities in Berwick themselves summarily executed some pirates, including a man with property in London.[106]

Some idea of the value of Scottish commerce is conveyed by the extent of Alexander III's indebtedness for wine and corn to a Gascon merchant – over £2000. As security he offered his tolls at Berwick, though nothing was actually paid before 1286.[107] (For comparison the whole of the English king's Custom revenue was worth about £8400.) Already, before the end of the twelfth century, the Scottish economy was strong enough to support King William's offer to English kings of large sums of money. On the occasion of his agreement with King John in 1209, William was able to offer a payment of as much as £5000. Whereas the interests of merchants were not even considered at Falaise in 1174, their right to trade in England was specifically reserved in 1209 and confirmed when peace was made with Alexander II in 1217.[108] As so often, not until the papacy took an interest in securing equitable assessments for crusading taxation were Scotland's financial resources closely scrutinised and only parts of the papal valuation for the tenth imposed in 1274 have been preserved. By then the pope's financial agents, the Italian merchants, were becoming familiar with Scottish clients. Robert, archdeacon of Ross, borrowed money from a Florentine merchant in 1269. William Fraser, dean of Glasgow, authorised his agents in 1279 to borrow as much as £200 from certain merchants to meet the costs of his urgent business at the Roman Curia. In 1281, the earl of Carrick borrowed £40 from a merchant of Lucca. The bishop of Glasgow repaid his debt to a Florentine house in 1283. Italian creditors were not necessarily found in Scotland itself but, either in Italy or at home, Scots in need of money knew where to find it and their domestic assets became proper objects of interest abroad.[109]

The commercial interests of the Welsh are more elusive. According to Gerald of Wales, they paid no attention to commerce, shipping or industry, devoting their energies entirely to military training. Gerald also asserted, however, that they imported stocks of cloth, salt and corn from England and that if steps were taken to patrol the seas and prevent these imports the English conquest of Wales would be easily completed.[110] Long before Edward I did apply himself to this end, new towns had been founded. Norman settlers appreciated what advantages might flow from urban development. The earl of Warwick founded a new town at Swansea and conceded regular grants of oak trees for house- and ship-building though his charter refers only to fishing boats rather than commercial trading. By the early thirteenth century there were merchants at Haverford who got permission to take their ships to any part of Henry III's dominions.[111] Later towns founded inland by Welsh princes like Gruffudd ap Gwenwynwyn at Welshpool in 1247 and Rhys ap Maredudd at Lampeter in 1271–77 did not become great trading centres but Wales was being drawn into commercial activity.[112] A murage grant at Crickhowell (Powys) in 1281 lays down the rates of payment on goods brought into the town for sale. Most of the items listed were for local produce: corn, livestock, fish, game, animal skins, honey, nails of various kinds and cartloads of iron. Other items must have been brought from some distance, like silk cloth with gold samite, diaper linens and perhaps baldrics (bandekyn), silk cloth without gold, cendal, silk caps, wine, salt itself, Irish cloth, alum and probably the horseloads of garlic.[113] If such a variety of produce could be expected, even if only rarely, for such a small town as this, the availability of foreign produce in much larger places must be taken for granted. Urban communities were sufficiently developed to attract Dominicans to Cardiff (before 1242), Haverfordwest, Bangor, Rhuddlan and Brecon. Franciscans occur not only at Cardiff but at Carmarthen. Edward I's own urban foundations after the final conquest of 1284 are better known, but only reinforced a development already under way.

The readiness of some Welsh clergy to contract heavy loans at Rome implies that the Welsh economy was stronger than it seems. The coin hoard found at Llanfaes in Anglesey has been interpreted to show how Gwynedd, just before the Edwardian conquest, was opening up to foreign trade.[114] The only Italian to have left evidence of his activities in Wales is Jakemyn of Pavia who, unsurprisingly, was the papal proctor for the collection of the crusading taxes. As a sideline, in 1284 he lent 10 marks for the purchase of a horse bought at Nevyn, stipulating repayment in London with the significant proviso that any delay would incur a penalty for the benefit of the Holy Land.[115]

By contrast, there is no doubt about the intensity of Irish commericial activity. The chief ports had long-established foreign contacts. English lordship not only gave the principal Irish ports a new political significance but did much to promote the prosperity of the ports best placed geographically to profit from it, like Drogheda, Dublin, Wexford, Waterford, Dungarvan and Cork. Henry II initially offered Dublin to the men of Bristol, a pointer to its chief English trading partner, but very soon the town was taken directly into the king's hands: it was too valuable to be granted away. Henry's second charter, issued at St Lô, assumes that Dubliners will trade in Normandy.[116] Traders from Ireland were ready to exploit all their chances across the seas. The names on the roll of Dublin merchants (1256–57) included men from Bayonne, Besançon, Le Huy, Bruges, St Omer, Douai, Angers and as many as six from Rouen.[117] On another Dublin roll (1190–1265) the names indicate equally diverse origins: Ypres, Antwerp, Dixmunde, Bordeaux and Cordova.[118] When the mayor of Bordeaux sent messengers to Dublin in 1252, he could expect them to be well received. Other merchants who were more than transitory included William le Kyteler of Ypres. In 1277, as the merchant of the Irish justiciar, Robert de Ufford, he acquired a royal safe conduct for English and Irish trade. Two years later Arnold Johannis of Ponthieu had an agent to manage his men, lands and merchandise in Ireland. In 1281 the London merchant, John de Briland, himself of German origin, nominated Hermann le Jovene of Almain as his Irish attorney. Among the local burgesses of Ross and Waterford who provided supplies for shipment to Gascony was one Fermin of Abbeville.

The commercial and cultural resources of these Irish ports are made more explicit by a poem in Norman French, composed to celebrate the building of the town walls of New Ross. The work had been accomplished by local craftsmen working in relays, changing day by day, according to trades (with women doing all the work on Sundays, the craftsmen's day of rest). The numbers of workers are not specified, but the trades involved are. There were vintners, mercers, merchants, drapers, sailors, tailors, trimmers, dyers, fullers, saddlers, leatherers, tanners, butchers, bakers (who were numerous enough on their own to provide Thursday's workmen), porters (Fridays) and finally the construction workers, carpenters, masons and smiths.[119] At least on the east and south coast, Irish commerce was in a flourishing condition. Already in 1218 the receipts of the king's customs at Wexford were considerable enough to discharge his debts to the merchants of St Omer.[120] Less is known about the northern ports, but as Scottish commercial interests in the region grew, northern Ireland must have been increasingly exposed to trade. The abbey of Furness often turned to Ireland for supplies of corn and, after the Isle of Man had passed into Scottish hands, the monks of Dundrennan in Galloway thought it prudent to obtain Henry III's permission for their purchases of wheat, oats, flour and wine at Dublin and Drogheda. Chester too bought wheat in Ireland. The town of Liverpool obtained its first charter from King John. Commerce across the more northerly stretches of the Irish Sea may have been quite common.[121]

Shipping

Coming and going between England and the Continent rested on the availability of adequate shipping arrangements. In the eleventh century, the miracle stories of St Edmund refer casually to ships already capable of carrying more than sixty passengers; one of them also found room for 16 horses and 36 other animals.[122] Exchequer records shed further light on how the king and his officials crossed the Channel. At Bosham in Sussex the king kept a swift transport vessel (*esnecca*) of his own for his messengers; the king's agent in 1177 was assigned £14 for the passage of six great persons across the Channel and £12 for the fares of lesser passengers. At Southampton in the same year, apart from the king's *esnecca*, the ships of six separate shipowners were hired, not only for favoured messengers, but for others. In 1187 the king engaged seven shipowners to provide him with vessels. There were also professional sailors without vessels of their own. In 1183, when the king's treasure was taken to Normandy, a steersman and sailors had to be found and ten extra sailors to guard it. At Dover sailors, specially hired, became responsible for the safe transport of the king's falcons.[123] The Exchequer accounts are unfortunately short of detail about the navy men on whom the sound working of the Angevin Empire depended. Like some of his barons and prelates, the king had a few galleys of his own, but even for these he had to engage professional sailors as crew. He certainly had no fleet and expected to hire or commandeer what he needed in exceptional times.[124]

From the same period comes the earliest reference to the men of the Cinque Ports, known thereafter by this French name.[125] They claimed privileges dating from before the Conquest and the Domesday inquest confirms that some particular ports already owed specific services to the crown. Dover, the most important, then owed twenty ships with a crew of twenty-one each, for fifteen days service a year; by contrast the service due from Sandwich was only five ships. Each of the original five towns belonged in different lordships. Sandwich belonged to the archbishop of Canterbury, Rye and Winchelsea to the abbot of Fécamp; only in 1247 did Henry III, recognising that he had no hopes of ever recovering possession of Normandy, buy out the abbot's interest. Henry soon discovered that the port of Winchelsea was in danger of silting up and had to ask one of Fécamp's monks, the prior of Coggs, to give advice on the matter.[126] The abbey may have been relieved to be spared further expense itself. But the monks were no slouches at sea. Thanks to the abbey's records, we have a unique statement setting out the abbot's dues from several sizes of fishing vessels at Rye, the most with twenty-four oars, the least with less than ten. The presumption must be that there were many ships in each class. Some of them must have been substantial vessels. In 1264 even a ship with no more than five or six oars was deemed capable of crossing from Sandwich to Flanders.[127]

It is not known how the several ports came to operate as a unit when called for royal service. In practice, there were soon more than five because some individual ports began to find difficulty in fulfilling their obligations and took on subsidiary members to help them fit out and man the vessels needed. The only collective interest of all five ports was in the herring fishing at Yarmouth where they asserted comprehensive privileges, including the right to hold a court for their own men. Yarmouth contested this in vain. The king was far too dependent on the goodwill of the Cinque Ports to think of offending their interests.[128]

Most of the information about the Portsmen comes from royal records, but the services they owed to the king took up very little of their time and they should not be regarded as constituting a royal navy in embryo. Rather, the king made occasional use of seamen with full-time activities of their own, as sailors, traders and transporters, not necessarily on their own account. Sometimes they were hired by Flemish or Italian merchants to transport their merchandise. They were accustomed to defending themselves and their cargoes from aggressors. Violence at sea must have been commonplace. The Portsmen were an independent force and though the king reckoned to make it worth their while to serve his purposes they were not always immediately willing to act as loyal subjects. When Honorius III wrote to William Marshal and other English magnates in 1217 putting his weight behind their efforts to restore effective government in England, he had clearly been advised to despatch similar letters to the 'barons' of the Cinque Ports, recognising that they needed to be approached separately. Thirty years later, they were still independent enough to send their own delegation to the papal council of Lyon in 1245.[129]

The Portsmen could be both truculent and unruly. In both 1216 and 1264 they fought for the king's enemies. Rulers had to conciliate maritime forces they were in no position to control and whose interests were not necessarily identical to those of the crown. Whereas Henry III was desperate to conciliate the men of Bayonne, the hostility of the Cinque Ports to them, first mentioned in 1236, was implacable. They did not encourage royal interest in their affairs. Royal records suggest that the king was powerless to bring them to heel.[130] Efforts to secure legal redress for their exactions at the Shipway, the Cinque Ports' collective court, were frequently frustrated. In the summer months, when the Portsmen were at sea, court proceedings had anyway to be suspended. In the autumn courts were simply prorogued *sine die*. Their independence made it difficult for kings to deal with complaints against them and throughout the thirteenth century their outrages continued to excite ineffective protests. Their enterprise at sea made them feared in Normandy as well as in Bayonne. Nor did they neglect to quarrel with rival English portsmen, such as those of Poole and the western ports. In 1266, still committed to the baronial cause against the king, they burnt the royal dockyard at Portsmouth. Henry III had to call on Flemish, Norman and Spanish mariners to help him make the seas safe for commerce. The Portsmen were ready to fight in the North Sea, in the Channel and in Biscay, particularly after the loss of La Rochelle to the French in 1224.

The king's interest in maritime belligerence might be only occasional, but when he did go to war he was confident of finding ships capable of transporting soldiers, supplies and considerable numbers of horses. For continental campaigns, horses might be moved long distances, as from Bristol to Bayonne in both 1214 and 1225. Ships capable of taking as many as sixteen horses were highly prized and must have been available for use even in 'peacetime'.[131]

After the loss of Normandy, the Cinque Ports of Kent and Sussex mustered the principal force able to protect England from raids across the north French coast. If they had not already been familiar with routes beyond Brittany, John would also have lost Poitou and Aquitaine. In 1205, to secure their loyalty, John immediately confirmed an earlier charter given by Henry II, and in effect licensed their acts of piracy in return for half the profits. This device was tried again by Henry III, ostensibly to encourage them to concentrate on fighting pirates who preyed on shipping, but probably more in order to derive a cut for himself (now of only one-fifth) rather than for securing control of the seas.[132] Their advice was sought on how the coastal defences might be best provided for. When Philip II assembled a fleet for the invasion of England in 1213, a force was quickly found to attack and destroy it in harbour at Damme. The Portsmen were capable of putting up a fight against a possible invasion fleet, intercepting it at sea, as happened at the battle of Sandwich in 1217 when the fleet sent to support Louis of France's campaign in England was destroyed. They could even intercept ships of hostile princes on the high seas and bring them into English harbours.

The king's main concern was to make use of their pugnacity when he needed to. In 1242, he urged his sailors to do their utmost to ravage the coasts of French lands loyal to Louis IX. On occasion they might welcome this royal approval and lend their support to his plans but, even without royal sanction, acts of 'piracy' still occurred. Ships might be seized under the impression that merchants or merchandise came from lands of the king's enemies. This might be offered in justification, even against those who had received individual royal permission to trade. In 1235 they disregarded a royal safe conduct issued for the men of Barfleur and snatched it away. Not all 'mistakes' were made inadvertently. Some shipmen had grievances against merchants from particular foreign ports on account of damages they had themselves incurred there. They felt entitled to exact compensation from fellow countrymen of their oppressors. Merchants from the Low Countries who suffered from such outrages often asked their princes to intercede for them with the king, who was certainly expected to give them satisfaction. In cases where the king's own officers were responsible for impounding merchants' goods, disregarding their privileges or treating them as royal enemies, the king either diplomatically investigated the claims of injured merchants or ordered restitution of their property, but over matters of complaints about English shipmen the king was hardly ever in a position to secure compensation or retribution. English shipmen themselves made no known use of royal diplomacy; they reckoned to be self-sufficient.

The Channel Islands were briefly overrun by Philip II's men in 1204, but rapidly recovered for the English crown.[133] The islands remained something of a law unto themselves: after all, the king had no navy of his own to defend them. Royal officials there acted as they pleased. In October 1224, Geoffrey de Lucy was ordered to restore the barrels of wine he had seized in Guernsey if Elyas Marthese of Bordeaux would swear that the wine was his property and not belonging to anyone at war with the king. Geoffrey was instructed to order his men to allow all merchants and shipping from Bordeaux to bring their merchandise to England and not do them any harm.

But the very next year Geoffrey's men detained a ship belonging to Richard Marshal of Loyre because the ship had taken on its cargo in Poitou, by then in French hands. The merchant pleaded that he had a personal privilege from the king, but the officials ignored this. The merchant had to make a special case to the government, all of which took time. In 1226, when the Channel Islands were committed to Richard de Gray, it was taken for granted he would be taking prizes at sea, half of which the king claimed for himself. Some islanders wrote to the king protesting about his condoning of lawless men, but others made their living out of preying upon merchants. At Guernsey, Eustace of Lesvianein (Lisieux), a 'man' of the archbishop of Rouen whose ship was loaded with rushes in the lands of the king's enemies, and the ships of Peter the Englishman from Caen and William de Odimere of Winchelsea, who had loaded cargoes of wine at Nantes, also in enemy hands, were detained. Peter (but not his vessel) was released because he was from Normandy; William, though English, was still required to give sureties that he would proceed to Winchelsea with his wine and stand trial there. The connivance between Portsmen and the Channel Islands explains why Stephen of Rye took the wine cargo of a merchant of Périgueux at sea and carried it off to Guernsey in 1235.

The notoriety of the Cinque Ports may obscure the fact that there were many other English ports, engaged maybe in local trade by water, rather than long distance, but still liable for royal service in emergencies. In 1173, when Henry II, fearing an invasion from Flanders, summoned naval forces to Sandwich, ships were sent from unnamed ports in Yorkshire, Lincolnshire and Norfolk as well as from Dunwich, Orford and Colchester. Shipmen from other places could be as bellicose as the Portsmen. In September 1264 the government ordered an enquiry into the violence at sea between the men of Lyme Regis and those of Dartmouth, though, given the year, this may have had more directly political causes.[134] The availability of shipping was expected all along the coast. Gerald of Wales when he was denied the use of the 'public crossing for everyman' at Sandwich in 1202, crossed the Thames from Faversham to Tilbury, expecting to find a ship as he moved up the coast towards St Osyth.[135] The later thirteenth-century Custom accounts for the port of Exeter name local ships from Plymouth, Dartmouth, Teignmouth, Topsham, Exmouth, Sidmouth, Weymouth and Portsmouth, most bringing in wine, presumably from the Biscay ports. There is no comparable information for the ports of the Thames estuary, but if so many southern harbours were engaged in commercial traffic, provision must have been in proportion. Most ships were in private hands and some shipowners traded on their own account; others were certainly for hire. English sailors transported goods to and from Bordeaux in the English king's duchy of Gascony, but also further away to the ports of northern Spain and round to Lisbon.

The Welsh too occasionally ventured into Biscay, providing direct sailings to Bordeaux for pilgrims bound for Santiago, but most Welsh traffic by sea appears to be local. When Lord Edward, exasperated by the rebellious Welsh in 1256, threatened to bring over Irish forces to deal with them, the Welsh claimed to be ready to intercept any Irish forces at sea. Just what naval resources could the Welsh muster and what ports might they have used? Gerald of Wales refers to ships which came into Caerleon on the tide and the use of a ship sent from Margam to Bristol to buy corn in time of famine.[136] In 1254, merchants of Carmarthen had a ship in harbour there which was attacked, presumably from the sea, by burgesses from Tenby. Welsh ships no doubt went more often across to Ireland than to the Continent. There is no need of speculation in the case of Scotland. There were shipbuilding yards at Ayr (1260, 1264), Rothenek (Speymouth?), Perth, Forfar and Inverness.[137] How far afield Scottish sailors or fishermen were prepared to go is not indicated by such notices, but some contact with the wider world is implicit.

Ireland already had substantial shipping resources before it was brought into the Angevin Empire, but English lordship did much to enhance them. Already in 1216 there was enough Irish shipping in the vicinity of Normandy for the government to think it worth commandeering.[138] There were also Irish shipbuilders. In 1222 and 1233 Henry III commanded ships to be built in Dublin, Drogheda, Waterford, Cork and Limerick and in 1256, when he sent to Ireland for supplies for the Welsh campaign, he expected to find ships at Arklow, Wicklow and Wexford.[139] At Waterford as many as twenty-three ships were hired to transport 600 horses and a military force. The Irish ports acquired enhanced significance after Henry III set about reinforcing his ties with what remained to him of his lands in France. Ships proceeded directly from Ireland to Gascony. When Henry III made provision for the newly-wed Lord Edward in 1254, the prince was given Ireland and Gascony, with Bristol as the nodal point of his regular administration. The connection between Ireland and Gascony was responsible for the fact that evidence for Irish business turns up in the so-called Rôles Gascons, the records of Edward's administration.[140] Ireland was frequently called on to send supplies for the king's forces in Gascony. In 1291, corn was sent to Gascony from Cork in the *Snake*, master, Simon the White, and from Youghal in the cog of the *Holy Cross*, master, Peter of Paris. Ross and Waterford also sent supplies to Gascony. For the transport of these many different products a variety of ships both great and small, including *farcoste*, for coastal traffic, were available. But in 1298 grain sent to Gascony was probably shipped by men from Bayonne.[141] The carrying trade was not an English-Irish monopoly.

Sailors from Bordeaux and Bayonne may have been principally engaged in the importation into Britain of wine, but they were not particular about their cargoes. Ships from Bayonne also engaged in the carrying trade, transporting goods from Ypres in 1225. In 1224, shipping in English ports included those of both Spaniards and men of Toulouse. In 1226, a Spanish merchant docked as far north as Beverley. The attraction of England for southern merchants was enhanced by the certainty of finding merchants from the northern seas in English ports. Frisian ships are recorded in London, Orwell, Yarmouth, Lynn and Portsmouth. At Yarmouth, in 1224, there were ships from Scotland, Norway, Iceland, Frisia, Cologne and Denmark. At Lynn, in 1256, there were as many as eleven Norwegian ships in port.[142] The commercial activity of the waters between Biscay and the North Sea attracted so much shipping from all over the region that King John was tempted in 1205 to try to exploit this on his own account. To augment his fleet of transports, he encouraged English sailors to detain 'foreign' ships and persuade their crews to join the royal contingent, in effect authorising them to seize vessels belonging to 'subjects' of his enemy, usually those of the king of France or the count of Flanders. In 1226–27, when the king detained French ships for his proposed Gascon expedition, some had come from Barfleur, Caen, Dieppe and Dinant. Henry III's naval contingent for the French expedition of 1230 included ships not only from England and Ireland, but from Germany, Spain and Normandy itself.[143] This practice was not peculiar to the English. King Haakon of Norway pressed English ships into serving on his campaign in Scotland in 1263, a course which Henry III then chose to deprecate.[144]

Some Custom accounts provide detailed information about the variety of foreign shipping in English waters. Apart from the Exeter records, those from Hull for ten months in 1275–76 offer a glimpse of the bustle created by the great number of ships from many foreign ports.[145] Some returned two or three times within the ten-month period. Twenty-six separate ships' captains from Barfleur paid dues, fourteen from Amiens, twelve from Corbie, five from Calais, three from Abbeville, with singletons from other northern French ports. About a dozen ships are described as from Lübeck, nine from Ghent and four from Bruges. Ships belonging to five Cahorsins, three Florentines and a single merchant from Bordeaux extend the connections of the Yorkshire seaport beyond the limits of the North Sea and English Channel. The record was made in French, the lingua franca of this international depot. English sailors must have spoken some French themselves. Their ships often had French names.

Placed midway between the Baltic and Biscay, England enjoyed an unrivalled geographical advantage. Preserving favourable conditions for trade was an obvious concern of government. Disputes of various kinds could not easily be resolved by appeal to terrestrial courts. Violence might secure some sort of temporary resolution, but recognition that arbitration would provide a more satisfactory outcome encouraged the development of maritime law. Significantly, these attempts to establish some justice in trading operations and suppress piracy at sea were enshrined in the so-called Laws of Oléron, where judgments were given not by any royal officials but by the seamen themselves.[146] These regulations came into effect at a time when both shores of the English Channel were still in the hands of the English king, that is before 1204, though no text is older than the mid-thirteenth century. Oléron

was a valuable island which was offered as part of the dowry for the proposed marriage of Henry's sister Joanna to Hugh of Lusignan. After this
proposal fell through, Oléron was recovered by the king in 1230 and
retained thereafter.

Given the variety of purposes and destinations involved, it is not very
important to consider how the balance of interests between native and foreign shippers worked out. It does seem probable, however, that the bulk of
the maritime services required to maintain links between these islands and
the Continent was provided from native resources. There are few ways of
measuring the relative strength of local as distinct from foreign shipping,
but licences to export wool in 1271 were issued for 284 English merchants
as against only 44 Italians, mainly from Tuscany.[147] These latter, at least,
had no vessels of their own and must have made use either of English or
Flemish transports. The handling of commerce in the British Isles had not all
fallen into the hands of foreigners.

Coming and going

The counterpart of foreign merchants in England was that English merchants did business abroad. The king took it as axiomatic that foreign merchants could only trade in the kingdom on condition that English merchants
enjoyed reciprocity in their home countries. If English merchants lost goods
or suffered damage, they petitioned for reprisals against merchants of that
land in England, not to get vengeance but to get compensation. A merchant
of London who had £200 worth of goods seized by Lübeckers in Denmark
secured a letter from king Christopher to Henry III in order to justify his
request for getting reparations. If Christopher's 'secretary' was often called
on for help with commercial diplomacy, his nationality may have been an
asset: he was an Englishman called Luke.[148]

Royal documents which show so many merchants from foreign parts
doing business in England cast scarce light on the comparable activities of
English merchants abroad. Exiguous foreign records hardly make up for
this. The occurrence of English merchants at Montpellier and Alexandria in
mid-twelfth century is mentioned casually as though this were unremarkable.[149] A description of Bergen about 1200 in the time of King Sverre
notices the presence there of men from all over the northern seas –
Icelanders, Greenlanders, Swedes, Goths, Danes, Germans and English –
trading in wheat, wine, honey and cloth.[150] English fishermen are reported
to have flocked to the Scania herring fair. Traders from Lynn and Yarmouth
turned up in Norway (1224) and Hamburg (1251); they also went to La
Rochelle (1226). Hugh of Selby traded from York to Anjou (1235); the seamen of Shoreham had chattels detained in Poitou (1200) and had permission to go overseas to purchase salt (1228–31). Men of Hartlepool lost
merchandise in Bremen (1279); William of Doncaster, merchant of Chester,

was robbed of goods in Antwerp.[151] Merchants of Norton on Tees went to Bayonne in 1215.[152] More predictably, perhaps, men of Bristol went to Biscay for wine and salt in 1226. English wool-traders and craftsmen also surface in foreign records: Wiles of Pontefract and John Setentor of York at Amiens; Nicholas of Ludlow, or Shrewsbury, and Laurence of Ludlow occur at Ypres (1277); at St Omer, there were many; Walter de Anglia had a house in Brussels (1263); John the Englishman was a dyer for Lübeck who figures in the Ypres accounts.[153] The existence of a *vicus Anglie* at Lagny must surely be a quarter for English merchants attending the Champagne fairs, even if the *vicus Anglorum* in mid-thirteenth-century Acre does not similarly imply commercial activity.[154]

Not all commercial transactions abroad were left to merchants. Paris was a favoured destination for those looking for luxury goods. Occasional visitors took their chance. A royal chancery clerk, Roger of Doncaster, sent on an official mission and probably already familiar with the city, wrote home to report his safe arrival and a reunion with mutual friends at a jolly dinner party. To cheer up his correspondents for what they were missing, he expressed his intention of looking out for a suitable tapestry (*tappetum*) with a fringe to brighten the Chancery *aula* back in London.[155] Henry III himself took advantage of his visit to the city in 1254, when he bought two embroidered copes and an altar cloth for Westminster Abbey from a citizen of Paris, Geoffrey de Curton (himself of English or Norman origin).[156] Steady recourse to Paris for high-quality products made it sensible for Edward I to maintain an agent there to buy on his behalf. For the great tournament at Windsor in 1278 many items were needed. The royal accounts show how the real cost mounted up when not only the separate articles but also the packaging and the transport to the port and further freight by barge across the Channel and up the Thames were itemised.[157] Less bulky to transport were books. William de Valence, earl of Pembroke, had a Book of Hours based on a Worcester cathedral calendar painted and decorated in Paris as a gift for his daughter at the time of her marriage to John Comyn *c*.1292. Such luxurious Parisian manuscripts were fashionable accessories in England. Some of them had a wealth of droll figures in the margins, features which appealed to English taste but were unusual for Paris illumination, making it look as though they were deliberately designed for prospective English buyers.[158]

Some of those who went abroad stayed or worked there for long periods. Several Londoners took up residence in Genoa from 1179, where they carried on business as goldsmiths. The later Scotti family of Genoa probably owed their origin to Scottish or Irish tradesmen who had likewise become established in Genoa.[159] In 1242 the Venetian doge settled a case of breach of promise involving a citizen, formerly resident in England, who seems to have been English.[160] At quite another social level was the English masterbaker in Rome who allegedly incited a sedition in Rome for the release of Brancaleone, the former Senator. That Matthew Paris was well informed about events in Rome and the presence of an English baker there, however improbable this may seem, has to be taken seriously. A baker could have attached himself to the household of one of the Roman clergy who were frequently in England. Several English bakers certainly worked in Paris, for they are listed in the taxation returns of 1286, alongside other men of many different occupations described as 'English' or more occasionally as 'Londoners'. There were some 200 men in all, scattered across the city. Parisians must have been familiar with the sight of quite humble visitors from the British Isles.[161] The allusion in Parisian sermons to the English wrestler who, when thrown, unexpectedly sprang from the ground to defeat his opponent, refers to what must have been a familiar street entertainment.[162] Likewise, the mean Scot was already proverbial, mocked for carrying his shoes and walking barefoot because the skin of his feet would grow again without cost. Preachers did not draw these illustrations from their books. When Robert la Chievre of Reims compared himself to a poor Scots vagabond, he obviously invoked a familiar stereotype. What circumstances brought enough Scots to the continent to establish their national reputation as poor and mean?[163]

The provision of 'services'

Economic considerations may be expected to feature somewhere in any social relationship but there are limits to what buying and selling can explain on their own. When John despatched a hundred Welshmen to fight for King Sverre in Norway, was it the pay or the adventure that attracted volunteers? The king could not have sent men from his own army, for he had none. England is not normally thought of as a recruiting ground for mercenaries, but they could apparently be found easily enough when asked for. English soldiers fought under Henry de Turbeville for the emperor Frederick II in Lombardy; Edward I thought of sending contingents to help Alfonso of Castile fight the Saracens of Andalusia. The king of Norway hired soldiers in England for his war with Denmark. There may have been some English interest in fighting for others. When Henry III mustered his forces for an attack on the Welsh in 1257, he expected the sheriff of Sussex to be able to send him one hundred good archers and the sheriff of Northampton one hundred good lancers from their respective counties as though experienced soldiers could be found there without strain. Was this a fair indication of English military resources? English sailors were also available for combat when called on. In 1226 Henry III asked the barons of the Cinque Ports to send him as many as 180 good and choice sailors with two master mariners able to take the king's galleys to Gascony. For a ship taking treasure to Gascony in 1253, the king demanded forty proven sailors as crew, stipulating that twenty of them should be crossbowmen equipped with bows, bolts and other armaments.

If sailors are not known to have found foreign patrons, they did at least see service overseas.

The king of England, for his part, received offers of military service from comparative strangers, presumably in expectation that they would be well rewarded. A Milanese noble, Jacobus Amarotus Lancevegia, asked Edward I to confer knighthood on him and offered his services as soon as he was no longer required by the captain of imperial Lombardy, William, marquis of Montferrat. Lancevegia had only the most remote connection with Edward: Montferrat's recently deceased wife, Isabella, was Edward I's cousin.[164]

Hardly 'foreign' in thirteenth-century terms were the Gascon subjects of the Plantagenets. Halengrat, burgess of Bordeaux, described as the king's crossbowman, was a wealthy man who lent the king money and had a house in London, at home therefore on both sides of the sea. Henry III himself kept a small force of Gascon soldiers in England. Otto de Grandison, Edward I's trusted *familiaris*, brought over thirty crossbowmen from Gascony to serve in the Welsh war. The rulers of Flanders had long-standing obligations to provide the king with knights, so there was nothing unusual about Henry III's demands for soldiers from Countess Margaret in 1260. From the same region, the count of Louvain took part in the royalist siege of Kenilworth in 1266. Foreign soldiers could easily be brought over to fight for the king in England. Henry in fact obtained many knights from Louis of France in his confrontations with his barons. The practice of using 'foreign' soldiers against native subjects was not disapproved as unnatural. The important difference was between those who served the king loyally, of whatever ancestry, and his enemies. If his enemies were native born, they were not favoured on that account. Rather, their hostility made them 'unnatural'. And barons fighting the king also used foreign soldiers against the king, as in 1173 and 1216. Against Henry III they had Teutonic forces at their disposal. Military kings helped one another to deal with their enemies. Though Henry III declined Alfonso's help against the Welsh in 1262, the offer itself was well meant. At war in 1294, Edward received offers of military help from some noblemen of Aragon and secured a promise of 1000 troops from the archbishop of Cologne. In no sense can military confrontations in this period be considered occasions for the display of national ardour.[165]

On both sides of the sea, men with professional skills at their disposal could attract commissions, which were as likely accepted for the interesting challenges they presented as for the monetary reward offered. We have very little to go on. Craftsmen in the building industry are certainly to be included among English professionals who worked abroad. Presumably the closer links between England and Savoy after Henry III's marriage were responsible for the departure of the Englishmen, Bartlet and Philip the carpenter, to work in Savoy, but at whose initiative?[166] English masons are also believed to have worked often on the continent. Did they go as a matter of course to hone their skills or gain wider experience, or did only a few take rare opportunities to refine their art?

The many great cathedrals of thirteenth-century England were all raised by master masons with obviously English names, yet their technical achievements were in no way inferior to those of France. Lincoln and Wells are as distinctive as Paris and Chartres, different, not inferior. But these buildings were not erected in ignorance of what was done abroad. So, far from reflecting quintessential English originality, the building at Lincoln Cathedral initiated under Bishop Hugh of Avalon owed its distinctive features to the truly cosmopolitan character of culture at Lincoln in his time. How did English masons themselves keep in touch with foreign developments? The experience of English masons working on continental building sites is the most likely reason why, for example, the nave at York cathedral resembles that of Clermont-Ferrand.[167] The king himself and those responsible for the rebuilding of Westminster Abbey were obviously attentive to the work being done on the great French churches of the period, Reims Cathedral, Sainte Chapelle in Paris and St Denis. Both builders and patrons must have kept an eye open for what was fashionable. When Edward I decided to have his wife commemorated by the erection of Eleanor crosses along the route of her funeral cortège, he followed a French precedent. Twenty years earlier, Philip III of France had memorials put up along the route taken for the burial of Louis IX, some of which Edward would have seen on his return from the crusade.[168] English art itself could inspire foreigners. At Nidaros, masons borrowed motifs from the angel choir at Lincoln Cathedral. Englishmen may indeed have worked in Norway. Scandinavian art was open to English influences, either because English artists carried out commissions there or because those from the north visited or studied in England. If no English masons are known to have made careers abroad, it was because England itself offered them more than enough opportunities. As they built up experience, they branched out in their own distinctive way. Just as Durham Cathedral had been at the forefront of the development of 'Gothic' architecture (by no means an exclusively French invention), so by the end of the thirteenth century English architects had begun to elaborate a distinctive new Decorated 'style' of architecture, which was soon taken up on the Continent and helped launch the new Rayonnant style.[169]

One foreigner who appears in the comprehensive list of architects working in thirteenth-century England is James of St George. This military architect was brought over from Savoy by Edward I because of his experience in constructing castles in mountainous country.[170] Apart from the Savoyards' work at Conway and Beaumaris, they were probably responsible for the so-called 'Burgundian' influences at St Werburgh's, Chester (now the cathedral), the headquarters of Edward I's Welsh operations.

Using foreigners to supplement England's own impressive resources is understandable when patrons insisted on work of an unfamiliar kind. Foreign masons were not needed to build Westminster Abbey itself, but workmen were brought over from Italy to lay the Cosmati pavement and to sculpt the tombs of King Henry III and members of his family.[171] Their tasks completed, such workmen returned home. The use of foreign experts to supplement English native talent was not a sign that for most purposes English craftsmen were not among the most accomplished in Europe. It was rather proof of determination to take advantage of the best professional work wherever it could be found.

When London's first stone bridge was found to be in need of repair in 1202, King John naturally recommended Isambert, the engineer responsible for the bridge which had so impressed him at Saintes in Poitou.[172] Although London is not known to have adopted John's suggestion, the king himself drew extensively on workers from overseas with skills not otherwise available in England. John had acquired a number of crossbows in 1204 from Genoa; he also employed Peter Sarracenus to make them. Twenty years later, Henry III employed several Navarrese to make crossbows of different qualities, of ivory or wood at the Tower of London.[173] In 1207 John engaged the carpenter, Drogo of Dieppe, to make siege-engines for his campaigns, a skill no doubt much valued in Normandy over the years but previously of little practical application in Angevin England.[174] Six years later, when John made Peter of Douai his royal treasurer, this was probably connected with John's extensive borrowing in Flanders: Peter's contacts would have been useful and his appointment reassuring to creditors.[175] The complications of curial diplomacy explain similarly why Henry III took the famous canon lawyer, Henry of Susa, into his service, and why Edward I made Master Francis Accursius one of his counsellors.[176] In Accursius, who went to the Curia on Edward's behalf, Edward I had found the best man available. Edward had no difficulty about retaining him in England. In 1275 Accursius, his wife and household were established in the royal manor of Oxford on condition that the county court continued to meet there on the appointed days. Had he desired to do so, Accursius was well placed to observe local justice in operation. Accursius even acquired his own property in Berkshire. In both 1276 and 1277 he received from the royal forests an impressive quantity of oak, presumably intended for building work, along with separately specified kindling.

To help with his diplomatic correspondence with the papacy, Edward I took into his service Master Stephen di S Giorgio, a papal chaplain. He was not only himself granted four English churches; he secured a post in the royal household for his brother Peter, a monk of Monte Cassino.[177] The king's example was followed by Archbishop Peckham who engaged the notary, Master John of Bologna, to smarten up the style of the archbishop's letters to the Curia. John thought the English were dragging their feet over attempts to introduce notarial practices familiar on the Continent.[178]

Foreign professionals were summoned to England for a great variety of special purposes. In 1246, when Henry III wanted to provide gold ornaments for Westminster Abbey, he engaged Landulf the German to turn the royal collection of gold dust into ingots.[179] To help with the discovery and exploitation of his Devon mines Henry III several times turned to Germany, bringing over men from Hamburg, Brunswick and Goslar.[180] Henry also did his best to keep the prolific courtier poet Master Henry of Avranches, who had many patrons across Europe, in England.[181] Such patronage was expected to redound to the king's prestige. At the other end of the social scale, Henry III had rewarded the talents of two of the king of Castile's entertainers in 1257.[182] His daughter-in-law, Eleanor of Castile, had gardeners brought all the way from Aragon for some unspecified purpose, who returned when their task was completed. On a more permanent basis she found a use for the services of a carpet or tapestry-maker (*tappetarius*), no doubt an aspect of domestic living characteristic of her homeland. Matthew Paris reported on the amazement Spanish taste in domestic luxury had aroused in London when Eleanor had first arrived.[183] To what extent England offered occasional or seasonal employment to foreigners is not measurable, but in the large establishments kept by English magnates there was always room for an exotic extra, like the Gascon 'fool' Martinot de Gascoigne.[184]

Even foreign 'beggars' could expect to be well received in England. Cologne Cathedral was confident enough of respect in England for the city to send agents to collect contributions towards the cost of repairing the building after a conflagration.[185] In 1247 the pope urged English bishops to help finance the completion of Lyon Cathedral, perhaps with the expectation that English clergy who had sat in it at the council of 1245 would want to make donations.[186] When the hospices of San Bartolomeo de Monte Gorman in the Appenines and of Altopascio near Lucca sent agents to England to collect alms, they must have counted on English appreciation of the services they provided as resting places for travellers.[187] The house of St Antoine in Vienne, famous for its care of travellers and the sick, is frequently mentioned in the records, receiving royal permission for their agents to stay for some months in England while they collected money.[188] In Rome itself, the ancient Saxon hostel, which had been re-established by Innocent III, was another regular recipient of English largesse. King John had added the church of Writtle in Essex to its endowment in 1204 and authorised its agents in England to collect alms in 1213.[189] The hospice at Roncevaux in the Pyrenees possessed a house in London.[190] The Teutonic order maintained a house there too.[191] More opportunistic appears to be the mission of the prioress of Bellevaux near Beaubec in 1226, who brought over three nuns to help her collect alms from Englishmen still mindful of their Norman past.[192]

The nature of the historical record for this period frustrates any attempt to provide a realistic account of informal contacts between Britain and the Continent. But it should not be assumed there were none. Some allowance must be made for those who took advantage of the common facilities for crossing the seas to come over for reasons of their own. Like many later

French writers, the author of the romance, *Jehan et Blonde*, travelled as a young man in England and his work appears to have been inspired by his *Wanderjahre*.[193] Foreigners who made no name for themselves must also have visited or worked in England, quite apart from the stream of messengers and distinguished foreign visitors seeking out the king. What impressions did the country make on the count of Artois's barber who seems to have been his emissary in England?[194] The followers and servants of foreign magnates will have been sources of much everyday gossip abroad about medieval England. What they related will never be known, but they will not have been unimpressed. The kingdom was wide open to foreign contacts and interaction with foreigners was a familiar fact of thirteenth-century life. To suppose that only kings and magnates were concerned with foreign affairs would be mistaken. People from many different parts of these islands had their own concerns outside the kingdom and managed these interests without deferring to any national considerations. The British Isles were part of the same cultural complex as the Continent itself. People and objects of all kinds found their way in and out of the country. It is worth considering what impact such diversity had upon the inhabitants.

|7|

The papal lordship of England and Ireland

The papal programme

The French king's lordship of twelfth-century English kings for their continental lands had given him no rights in England itself. The papal lordship effected by John in 1213 introduced an active and formidable player into English affairs. The pope could not, however, act simply as a benevolent overlord. He had problems of his own and expected his English vassal to assist him with their resolution. For this reason, forty years later the pope offered Henry III's second son the kingdom of Sicily, and so precipitated the domestic crisis for which Henry's reign is chiefly remembered. If in the end papal support did not bring about the hoped-for restoration of former Plantagenet lands to English lordship, it nonetheless had the effect of binding England more closely than ever to the continent.

The longer-term disadvantages should not be allowed to obscure the immediate domestic benefits of the arrangement. After John's death, Pope Honorius III gave Henry III's government unqualified approval and papal legates shared the responsibility of government with leading magnates in England.[1] Papal influence in the British Isles reached its apogee in the first half of the thirteenth century. Though in England both the king and the clergy discovered there was a price to be paid for papal protection, the best educated and best placed men of the kingdom did not seek to throw off papal lordship. In 1213, John's need to escape from a situation (largely of his own making) may explain how it came about; the succession of Henry III as a mere child, admittedly one loath to seize adult responsibilities, turned papal lordship into a positive advantage. There were, however, other important factors which explain papal ascendancy.

The self-confidence of the new pope Innocent III would have astonished the beleaguered Alexander III and his short-lived successors. The dominance achieved by the emperor Henry VI in both north and south Italy, if only for a brief period (1194–97), had been perceived at the Curia as threatening the institutional independence of the Church. When Innocent was elected pope in 1198 at a surprisingly young age, he seized the chance opened up by the death of Henry VI four months earlier to recover the initiative in Italian affairs for the papacy. Innocent rose to the challenge. He was the first pope to assume confident direction of the affairs of Christendom and to achieve some remarkable successes. His pontificate had the further effect of inspiring the better clergy of his time to make a more determined effort to transform the spiritual life of the Latin Church. Clerical concern about the woeful state of religious observance may now seem hysterical, but the clergy felt they had just cause for alarm. In the east, the crusade of kings had not rescued Jerusalem from the Muslims in 1192; the Fourth Crusade did not even manage to reach the Holy Land in 1204 and Innocent strongly disapproved of the outcome. He had, however, to make the most of the new situation and since there was no longer any chance of getting help from the Greeks, sole responsibility for the welfare of the eastern churches devolved on Rome. The crusade thus became not an occasional obligation but a steady commitment. Major campaigns were launched in 1202, 1219, 1229 and 1248, with minor expeditions in between. Financial contributions for eastern affairs were demanded even more often.

Closer to home, Innocent was perturbed that so many regions of Italy and southern France rejected the Church's ministry and defied attempts to win them over by persuasion. After the papal legate Pierre de Castelnau was murdered in 1208, Innocent declared war on inveterate heretics. England itself was not rife with heresy, but some of the king's lands in the south of France were affected and reports about its ravages were noted anxiously by English chroniclers. Alexander Neckham wrote his *Speculum speculationum* to confute heretics. Raymond of Toulouse, the prince held responsible for allowing heresy to flourish in his dominions, was King John's brother-in-law. Simon de Montfort, who led the orthodox forces against the Albigensians, was nominally earl of Leicester, and his death in 1218 attracted notice in England.[2]

English prelates may not have worried about the problem of heresy at home, but they were uneasy that the imposition of the papal interdict and the exile of most bishops had left laymen so indifferent.[3] Everywhere in the west, it seemed, Christian fervour was feeble and ecclesiastical institutions under attack. Criticisms varied. Some contrasted the riches of the ecclesiastical establishment with evangelical simplicity; some found the bishops ignorant and idle; laymen resented ecclesiastical privilege which removed clergy from the jurisdiction of the public courts, but subjected laymen to church discipline in matters as important to them as marriage, contract and testamentary bequests. Innocent III could not compromise with doctrinal error but recognised that abuses in the Church had to be remedied. To this end he summoned a great Church council to the Lateran in 1215, where he promulgated a series of resolutions that set a reforming agenda for the Church, the most important before the sixteenth century. Even the Irish annalists were impressed and reported that the council was attended by over 400 bishops and 800 abbots, with Ireland represented by the archbishops of Armagh, Cashel and Dublin, along with one bishop, Killaloe. No doubt because, exceptionally, Irish attention was drawn to Italy in 1215, the annals also notice an extraordinary natural phenomenon in the Tyrrhenian Sea.[4] The eagerness of leading Latin clergy to implement Innocent III's programme was not merely due to dutiful obedience. They were disturbed themselves by the shortcomings of their own body and conscientious enough to accept that reform was desirable. The clergy accepted that they had a duty to win over the lay majority and needed to make better preparations for the task ahead.

While churchmen rallied to the defence of orthodox Christianity, the pope and the Roman Curia had to cope with the problems which arose in the political vacuum created by the death of Henry VI. When Innocent III assumed the leadership of Christendom, he resolved to do his best to prevent the Staufen family ever again acquiring such power in Italy as Henry VI had gathered into his own hands. At the beginning of his pontificate, Innocent III encouraged the Welf opponents of the Staufen family in Germany to help him in this objective.[5] Thinking along the same lines fifty years later, Innocent IV offered Henry III's son the kingdom of Sicily to keep out another Staufen prince. The papacy cherished great expectations of England and few aspects of papal policy did not have implications for the people of the British Isles.

This was true even for the crusading ventures. After Richard I, Edward I was the only other English king to depart on crusade, but both John and Henry III took the cross. In the middle of the civil war, as late as 1216, John ordered a ship to be made ready for his departure to Jerusalem.[6] Henry III's brother Richard did actually fight in the Holy Land in 1241.[7] English commitment to the crusade should not, however, be assessed in terms of the royal family alone. When the archbishop of Canterbury asked the pope for advice about the acceptability of would-be crusaders, Innocent ruled against allowing the poor and destitute to take the cross, but pointed out that some craftsmen and farmers (*agricolae*) would find suitable opportunities out east, though not too many of them. A scrutiny conducted in a score of parishes between Boston and Spalding at this time discovered that some thirty countrymen had taken crusading vows there, most of whom could not afford the journey. Some had departed and got no further than Rome, where they obtained authority for returning to England. How many Englishmen actually left cannot be stated but there is no denying the eager, if not always realistic, response to the call. The names of a few are known from the royal letters authorising their departure in 1202.[8] In Rome, some discovered that they would need more money for their journey and contracted loans; years later, sanguine creditors were still hoping to recover the principal. Their numbers were probably not sufficient to have significantly weakened John's own forces of resistance to Philip II, but their departure proves that fighting for the survival of an English Normandy was not the only preoccupation of the English baronage in those years. Philip II appreciated what advantages he himself would derive from the departure of John's ally, Baldwin of Flanders and other crusaders. Recruitment for this notorious crusade in the British Isles was not confined to England. The Scottish share in these expeditions always remained marginal, but was enough to bring Scotland closer to the preoccupations of the rest of western Europe. When the papal legate held a council at Perth in 1202, David Rufus of Forfar took the cross; about the same time, lands in Ayrshire were assigned for the endowment of St Thomas's Hospital in Acre.[9] The names of no Welsh crusaders are known, but the *Brut* chronicle kept sufficiently informed about the east to report an earthquake in Jerusalem in 1201.[10]

The capture of Constantinople in 1204 was not without real implications for Britain. When Baldwin of Flanders remained in the east as Latin emperor, this left a vacuum in the Low Countries which John and Philip II competed to fill. Philip's military success at Bouvines in 1214 sealed his political victory over John and seriously compromised future English policy in the region. Later counts of Flanders never recovered their former independence. Baldwin's daughters and their various husbands who ruled Flanders for the next seventy years were no match for the Capetian monarchy of Philip II and his descendants. It is hardly surprising therefore that the conflict between Philip and John over the next decade was closely followed by a lay witness, perhaps combatant, from Béthune who fully appreciated the repercussions across the Channel of John's own misfortunes.[11] As the leading barons of England, France and Flanders became embroiled together, the author was under some strain to keep abreast of events in the east as well as nearer home. For contemporaries, all engaged with their immediate problems, it was difficult to take in the full implications of Latin occupation of the greatest city of Christendom.

While the crusaders themselves recouped the vast expenses they had incurred by their military efforts on behalf of Alexius V, the west was chiefly rewarded by the dispersal of the saintly relics stored up in the holy city for centuries. A relic of the True Cross in a precious reliquary eventually found its way to Bromholm in Norfolk. An English priest who had served in Baldwin's chapel until the emperor's capture in 1205 returned to East Anglia and decided to sell the relic to raise money for the education of his sons. The royal chancellor, Richard Marsh, bishop of Durham, gave marble to the priory of Bromholm in its honour and the relic began to attract many pilgrims, including Henry III who took a solemn oath of some political significance there in 1232.[12] The Latin occupation of Constantinople also brought the Latin west into much closer contact with the Greek cultural world. English clergy already interested in scientific works in Greek proved to be among those most eager to take advantage of this to acquire a knowledge of that language in the following generation.

The capture of Constantinople had not, however, been the initial objective of the Fourth Crusade and in no way compensated for the failure to attack the Muslim power bases in the east. When in 1215, at the Lateran Council, Innocent III called for a further military expedition, he aimed to secure the liberation of Jerusalem. Nevertheless, four years later the projected crusade took the form of an attack against Egypt, the most powerful of Muslim states in the region. England had by then barely recovered from the civil war, but the earls of Chester, Winchester and Lincoln all departed for Damietta. English participation explains why so much information about the affairs of the east at this point was available to English chroniclers. The conversion of two mosques at Damietta into churches dedicated to St Edmund and St Thomas at the behest of John's former henchman, Robert de Argenteuil, was welcomed as evidence for English prestige in the east.[13] Scotland too had been involved. Saher de Quincy, the earl of Winchester, had a ship built in Galloway, though it was fitted out in Bristol for the journey. Another Scot, William de Somerville, accompanied the English contingent.[14] The Melrose chronicler who recorded crusader campaigning entered verbatim a letter reporting events from Hermann de Salza, master of the Teutonic Order.[15] At last, the Irish annals noticed the crusading activity. In Wales, the *Brut* chronicler made a brief reference to the Christians at Damietta, the Nile flood and the eight-year truce negotiated in 1219.[16] No part of these islands stood apart from this campaign.

When the next crusade was announced, its leader designate was the new emperor, Frederick II. Wendover asserted that from England alone as many as 60,000 fine men, not counting old men and women, set out by sea and reached Italy in 1227. Since Frederick was then taken ill and his departure delayed, most of these 'pilgrims' turned back. Despite being excommunicated by the pope for his tardiness, the emperor did sail the following year, still attended by some Scots and Irishmen along with English lords, including the bishops of Winchester and Exeter. The part played by the bishop of Exeter, William Brewer, in negotiating the peace treaty with the ruler of Damascus was singled out for praise by the (Welsh) Margam annalist. Wendover reported the initiative taken by an English Dominican, Walter, in the liturgical celebrations after Jerusalem was reoccupied. The personal contributions made by a few individuals were followed at home with pride and satisfaction.[17] The English continued to give some attention to eastern affairs throughout the 1230s. In 1241 Henry III's brother, Richard of Cornwall, went to the Holy Land and earned some military and diplomatic credit. On his return, he paid a visit to his brother-in-law, Frederick II. Matthew Paris, like others, enjoyed hearing about Richard's travels.[18]

Evidence for Irish participation is more significant. Whereas there was nothing very unusual about Henry de Lacy releasing his prisoner, the Anglo-Irish baron John de Courcy, in 1204 on condition that he went to the Holy Land, it is much more interesting to hear of an Irishman who participated in Frederick II's crusading expedition of 1229 and died in captivity. An Irish pilgrim died at the Jordan in 1231 and Amaury of St Amand, who died on a crusading expedition in 1240, had property near Dublin. The Anglicised parts of Ireland were not the only ones affected; the Irish also went to the Holy Land. After spending the autumn on the Mediterranean, Gille Brigde Albanach wrote an Irish poem at sea near Greece to invoke the help of the saints, Mary Magdalen and Brigid, on his way to Damietta, apparently in connection with the Fifth Crusade about 1218. Another Irish poem addressed to Cathal, king of Connaught, before June 1224, refers to one of his relations who had died on the way home from a pilgrimage to the river Jordan in a party of four. The poet himself, returning by sea through the Adriatic, completed his journey overland through Italy.[19]

Alongside Richard of Cornwall when he took the cross in 1236 were John the Scot, earl of Huntingdon and Gilbert Marshal, brother-in-law of King Alexander II of Scotland. Alert to the requirements out east, the king of Scotland asked the pope in 1238 to allow his nephew, Richard de Toni, treasurer of Angers, who had taken the cross, to convert the value of his ecclesiastical benefices into a subsidy for the Holy Land.[20] Ten years later, Louis IX's crusade aroused considerable enthusiasm in the British Isles. The links across the North Sea between Flanders and Scotland explain how it was that Hugh de Châtillon, count of St Pol, had a great ship built at Inverness to provide the transport of his men from Blois and Flanders.[21] Earl Patrick of Dunbar raised money for his journey by selling his stud farm at Lauder to Melrose, but died at Marseilles on the way out. Probably with the fate of some particular Scots in mind, Patrick's wife set up a house at Dunbar for Trinitarian brothers, an order founded for ransoming Christian captives from the Muslims. Several other Scots lords and knights are known to have left for the Holy Land at this time. Though the Melrose chronicler bluntly attributed the failure of Louis's campaign in Egypt in 1250 to French pride, he was happy to report that Louis IX had been impressed by his Scots recruits. The good relations then established may help to explain why so many of the Scots participants on Louis's second crusade in 1270 remained with the French contingent at Tunis rather than proceeding directly with the Lord Edward to the Holy Land. The *Brut* chronicle which thought that Louis had recaptured Damietta after the disaster at Mansourah, at least shows that the Welsh were aware of Louis IX's campaign against the infidel.[22] In 1250 a ship was hired at Messina to take 453 persons to join Louis IX's forces at Acre, but failed to deliver them as planned. They sued the company for breach of contract. Among the named plaintiffs were two Templars, messengers of Richard of Cornwall, travelling with nine men and three named Englishmen, Thomas and William, and Roger who was travelling with his daughter.[23]

Crusading in the east was far from being regarded in Britain as a lost cause in the first half of the thirteenth century. There was some justification for this. The emperor Frederick II had actually succeeded in restoring Jerusalem to Christian possession, at least on a temporary basis. Since it was achieved by negotiation rather than combat some clergy gave the emperor no credit for this, but Frederick II himself took a practical view of the problem and wanted something to show for his efforts. These did in fact keep Christian hopes alive longer than might otherwise have been the case. Richard of Cornwall was equally alert to the political realities crusaders had to cope with. Military men accepted that they had to negotiate with the Muslims and find effective allies where they could. Some of their ideas proved impractical. They were aware that the Mongols who broke into eastern Europe in the 1230s and caused great havoc there were no less hostile to their Muslim neighbours than they were themselves. In the west, this encouraged the idea that these marauders might be converted to Christianity and used as allies against the Muslims. Matthew Paris, the chronicler of St Albans, collected an impressive amount of information about the Mongols though they offered no direct threat to any English interests. Matthew was not unusual among Englishmen in thinking that the Mongols deserved careful consideration. He knew of an English exile in the east who had been used by the Mongols as a envoy, thanks to his knowledge of several languages.[24] When Innocent IV decided to send an embassy to the Mongols two English Franciscans, John of Stanford and Abraham de Larde, were originally named as members of the company, though in the end they did not leave with John of Piano Carpini.[25] One way or another, the papacy experienced no difficulty in keeping interest in the crusade alive in the British Isles.

The papacy and the British Isles

The weight of the papacy's new responsibilities could never have been borne from its own resources. As vicar of Christ, the pope claimed legal justification for asking the whole Church to help him meet the costs of running it effectively. The English clergy were particularly susceptible to demands from the papacy. They had for centuries made an unsolicited, annual offering of Peter's pence to Rome as a token of their gratitude for the original Roman mission. Individual English churches, mainly monasteries, had paid modest annual pensions to Rome in return for papal protection. Since 1213 England and Ireland, as vassal states, had become substantial contributors to papal finances. The self-confessed subservience of the English Church to the papacy made it difficult for clergy to evade papal demands. This never made them willing contributors. In this they were not alone. In 1225 when Honorius III asked each cathedral to help support the burden of papal administration by assigning two prebends for curial officials, he provoked uproar not only in England but in France as well.[26] No agreement was reached about regular subsidies for the curial administration, so the papacy resorted to expedients. Historical attention has focused on the number of Italians connected with the Curia who were assigned revenues, mostly as prebends in the English secular cathedrals. The pope did not normally expect Italians to be appointed to serve parochial churches. In England, many of these were in the gift of laymen well placed by common law to defend their property, even if canon law itself did not admit that laymen had rights of presentation to churches. Popes made no attempt to overthrow lay rights of patronage, but incidents did occur which infringed lay interests and aroused strong protests. Baronial grievances on this matter were presented to Innocent IV at the council of Lyon in 1245 and the Curia recognised the need to humour complaints. The bishops were in a much weaker position to resist papal pressure. In 1253, an English delegation at the Curia alleged that the papacy's demands on the English Church amounted to a payment of 50,000 marks a year, for which they begged relief. There is no way of assessing the true scale of papal demands, but Innocent IV, protesting that he had already begun to moderate his demands, offered to settle for a mere 8000 marks.[27] The records we have suggest that the main burden fell on a comparatively small number of cathedrals, York, Canterbury, Lincoln and Norwich, and that it had grown totally out of proportion only in the first ten years of Innocent IV's pontificate, that is while he was out of Italy and desperate to protect his papacy from Frederick II. Norwich, though it had a monastic cathedral chapter, had been obliged to provide benefices for Italian clergy after the legate Pandulf had become bishop there, and particularly through the efforts of the Italian archdeacon of Norwich, John of Ferentino.

Italians were not the only foreigners to profit from the availability of prebends. On a much more modest scale clergy from other lands were assigned revenues in cathedrals by bishops. Three Hungarians, Henry, Hugh and Peter, are recorded as prebends at Lincoln in the first half of the century and Frenchmen too held English prebends.[28] Foreign clergy connected with the king's relations also became beneficiaries of such arrangements. Bishops and abbots were not blind to the advantages of ingratiating themselves with well-placed curial clergy. It would have been foolish to do otherwise. Conceding personal favours gave satisfaction to both giver and receiver; being put under institutional pressure to grant out benefices was not so agreeable. But even those who were indignant to have been excluded by Italians still sought papal intervention on their own account.

Papal taxation in England did not bear down heavily on an impoverished nation. Quite the contrary. Money had been made available from England for Richard I's crusade and ransom without ruinous consequences. John's impositions were also heavy: the new demand for customs in 1202, the fifteenth in 1203–4 and the thirteenth in 1207.[29] During the interdict, John had used church revenues to subsidise his government. However, it was not just a matter of being able to pay up. It was a question about whether taxation was justified. Financial demands had been heavy enough in England to encourage thinking about how to distinguish between demands that could be justified as necessary and those that could not. To pay for Richard's energetic enterprises was one thing; asked to pay for John's unsuccessful military campaigns, taxpayers had already baulked. Hence Magna Carta's attempt to block arbitrary royal impositions. Difficulties about getting consent for royal taxation sabotaged all Henry III's subsequent efforts to renew warfare on the old Plantagenet model. It was to get round the problem of finding the money needed to put royal government on its feet again in 1217 that the pope had asked the English clergy to pay a subsidy.[30] The king may have surrendered his right to tax without consent; the pope's right to tax the clergy in times of crisis could not so easily be called in question.

Papal agents in England were not slow to appreciate that the English economy was soon once more in a flourishing condition. In 1225 Honorius III felt no scuples about asking for a subvention. When Gregory IX asked for another, he diplomatically offered to share the proceeds with the king, at that time preparing a campaign against France. Careful that nothing should be lost, the pope sent Master Stephen to supervise the collection of the money.[31] The activities of determined Italian financiers in both England and Ireland soon aroused protests. The king might allow his clerical subjects to be taxed by the pope, but they themselves were not prepared to leave it at that. If the papal right to tax could not be contested, the means and excuses offered for it might be honourably doubted. Henry III did little to screen his clergy from papal demands; in fact, papal taxation alerted Henry not only to the financial resources of his kingdom, but to the advantages of working with the pope. Over the next forty years, pope and king generally cooperated to get the money they wanted, the pope offering the authority and the king smoothing the practicalities of the operation, until such time as the king felt confident enough to dispense with papal sanction altogether. To secure the distribution of the tax burden as equitably as possible, successive efforts were made to evaluate the values of clerical property. These provide the first comprehensive evidence about English property values since 1086. The king appreciated the advantages he himself derived from papal authorisation of clerical taxation and kept a careful record of the documents concerned.[32]

The resources of the other parts of Britain were not perceived to be comparably abundant, but they did not escape papal demands for money altogether. In connection with its efforts to raise money for the needs of the Holy Land in the winter of 1263–64, the papal chancery sent letters addressed to the archbishops, bishops and other beloved prelates established in Wales, clearly in some confusion about the actual organisation of the Welsh Church.[33] In fact, the Welsh bishops remained so certainly under the jurisdiction of the English archbishop of Canterbury that they had little room for manoeuvre with Rome on their own account. They did their best. Richard de Carew, bishop of St David's, obtained consecration from Pope Alexander IV in 1256; he was also in Paris in 1271 and stayed at Rungy, though the reasons for this are not stated. Richard, described in his local chronicle as a theologian and fine philosopher, was treated as though he were the senior Welsh bishop. If he deliberately misled the papacy about the true position of his see, he would have had to pay heavily for courting

Roman favours.[34] A later bishop, David, was in 1296 authorised by Boniface VIII to borrow 1000 marks from Florentine merchants in order to pay the Curia various *servitia comunia* he owed. The next year David borrowed more money at the Curia from five tradesmen, a butcher of Viterbo, a Florentine spicer, a Lombard innkeeper, a fishmonger from Orvieto and a poulterer, all businessmen attendant on the Curia (*curiam romanam sequentes*), an unusual glimpse of how petitioners at Rome had to find the ready money they needed by calling on several different creditors.[35] One way or another, those who did business at the Curia were made to subsidise the work of the papacy.

Scotland's relations with the Curia were much more assured. The kingdom paid no Peter's pence, but a number of Scottish churches were in close enough contact with Rome to receive special protection in return for the payment of an annual *cens*: 2 gold coins apiece from three houses of the order of Tiron (Kelso, Arbroath and Lindors), 1 *maravedi* from Augustinian Jedburgh, 3 marks (after 1216) from Glasgow Cathedral, with a couple of payments of 2 shillings apiece from the diocese of Aberdeen. The number of diverse currencies assumed to be familiar to Scotsmen is unexpected.[36] The earl of Orkney had also offered Pope Alexander III a penny on the hearth from his possessions in mainland Scotland, that is Caithness. In 1184, shortly after the pope's death, John, the new bishop of Caithness, suspended these payments. Innocent III, on his accession, lost no time in instructing the bishops of Orkney and Ross to remind John of his obligations to Rome. John's attempts to collect what the pope asked for provoked a cruel reaction: the bishop had his tongue cut out and lost at least one eye. The layman forced to commit this atrocity was sent to Rome by the bishop of Orkney so that the pope might impose condign penance. Innocent III sent him back to Caithness with a letter prescribing painful scourging, followed by six years' service in the Holy Land. Caithness was still not cowed. When the papacy insisted that Bishop John's successor, Adam, a former abbot of Melrose, should persevere with the unpopular collection of tithes, he was actually murdered. This time the outrage against the Church gave King Alexander II a useful excuse to assert himself in the far north of the kingdom.[37] He fully recovered papal favour by exacting brutal punishment on the large number of those involved.

Papal interest in claiming benefices for Italian clergy in Scotland concentrated on the sees of St Andrews and Glasgow. Since these bishops were regular rivals for Roman attention, they accepted that they had to offer something in return. Glasgow claimed in 1248 that of the nine prebends in the cathedral, four had been assigned to Italians. Innocent IV promised to spare it further impositions until at least one of the Italians had died. At St Andrews, the papacy offered its legal support for the suppression of the traditional rights of the Culdees and the annexation of their assets to the cathedral.[38] Another Scottish church eager to secure papal benevolence was the royal abbey of Dunfermline which was also asked in 1246 to find a benefice of 20 marks for Peter son of Ingembald, a Roman citizen. When the bishop of Moray claimed that the church offered actually belonged to him, the Curia, not to be put off, demanded an alternative. Dunfermline could not wriggle out; it needed good friends at the Curia if it was to secure formal canonisation of its foundress, Margaret of Scotland.[39]

Papal legates sent to Scotland achieved little. The Melrose chronicle noted the holding of legatine councils as at Perth (1221) or Edinburgh (1239) to enforce ecclesiastical discipline, but sour comments that legates were mainly interested in obtaining money from Scottish churchmen and leaving before they had accomplished what they promised do not give the impression that legates served as useful a purpose as they did in England.[40] In 1221, the conduct of Honorius III's legate, Master James, was closely observed in Scotland and swiftly reported to the pope by a third party. The pope was forced to remonstrate with James about his poor choice of companions; this had given the papal mission a bad name. The legate had also succumbed to blandishments from the king who wanted a formal coronation ceremony to be introduced into Scotland, a suggestion that Honorius III promptly swept aside as an infringement of Henry III's rights.[41] Rome's unhelpful attitude did nothing to diminish Scottish interest in a formal coronation. In 1249, for the inauguration of Alexander III, a novel ceremony was devised at Scone to remove any doubts about the autonomy of uncrowned Scottish kings.[42] Innocent IV still hung back, though he rejected Henry III's counter-claims that the king of England should determine the nature of the Scottish ceremony.[43] Innocent IV appreciated the advantages of royal goodwill. In the spring of 1248 he allowed Alexander II to eat eggs, butter, cheese and meat during Lent, as both his confessor and his physicians recommended.[44] Five years later, the pope released money collected for commuting crusaders' vows to kinsmen of the king setting out for the Holy Land.[45] Good relations with Scotland were sealed when Innocent IV at last approved the cult of the king's ancestress, Queen Margaret. Her body was ceremoniously translated in 1250, though no bull for her formal canonisation is extant.[46]

The papal protection of the Scottish Church as a special daughter of Rome brought the bishops into regular touch with the Curia. Some travelled willingly to the Curia, if only for their initial consecration. The king raised no difficulties about this, provided he approved of their promotion. Innocent IV consecrated Master Abel as bishop of St Andrews in 1253. Abel's successor, Gamelin, the former royal chancellor, quarrelled after his election with the king and spent three years at the Curia pursuing his grievances (1254–57). The next year Nicholas, bishop-elect of Glasgow, went to the Curia for consecration as bishop. When he declined to pay the curial fees, he was deposed. William Wishart, a much more pliable prelate, used his good standing at Rome to secure first the bishopric of Glasgow and then that of St Andrews.[47] At Gregory X's Lyon council in 1274, as many as five bishops put their seals to documents issued there: Glasgow, St Andrews and

Dunblane, but also, less predictably, Argyll and Man from the 'Celtic' lands.[48] Other Scots also took their problems to Pope Alexander IV, not only the abbot of Melrose but William earl of March. Notorious abuses in churches were naturally drawn to papal attention. The papacy could also be appealed to for securing concessions from the rigours of canon law. Alexander IV allowed the monks of Kelso and of Lindors to wear furs as a protection against the cold, a concession renewed by the Franciscan pope Nicholas IV in 1289.[49]

Only a handful of papal letters relating to Ireland are known from before Strongbow's invasion of 1169 and about forty for the rest of the twelfth century. From Innocent III's time papal letters become extremely numerous. He himself wrote to bishops of nineteen dioceses in those parts of the island dominated by King John; in mid-century, Pope Innocent IV had correspondents in twenty-six dioceses, so that the fullest information about contacts between the bishops and the papacy concerns his pontificate.[50] John's surrender of Ireland, as well as England, into papal lordship did not actually have the same impact on secular Irish affairs as it did in England. Although Innocent III wrote directly to several Irish kings urging them to conform to best ecclesiastical practice, he was more inclined to trust King John than Irish rulers committed to local traditions and indifferent to such practice.[51] They themselves had little incentive to heed papal counsels; nor did their influence extend very far. In 1220 when a new legate was sent, Honorius III still recommended him to four Irish kings, those of Ulster, Cork, Limerick and Connaught. At that time, only Cathal Crobderg of Connaught was of much consequence. With a show of goodwill, he posed a series of questions to the pope about rights of sanctuary; to ingratiate himself with reformers, he tried to force his people to pay the unpopular tithes.[52] His efforts to establish a kingship acceptable by papal standards could not be sustained. Already threatened with more English encroachments, Cathal perceived the potential advantages of good relations with the English government for bringing pressure to bear on ambitious English barons in his vicinity. He wrote to the English king expecting him to intervene, if only to deal with vassals of the crown the Irish king was not confident of domineering for himself.[53] After his death in 1224 the native kings of Connaught counted for little; effective lordship was exercised by the Anglo-Norman baron, Richard de Burgh. Thereafter, the papacy had little direct contact with any Irish rulers.

Where Angevin lordship was established, Ireland experienced the same kind of ecclesiastical government as England. Papal judges-delegate settled disputes. Appointments to bishoprics proceeded much as in England. Initially, neither the king nor the barons in Ireland aimed to bar the promotion of Irishmen acceptable to themselves. Before Innocent III's death, out of thirty-six episcopal appointments only nine were not of Irishmen. After John's death, a nervous government attempted to bar the further promotion of Irishmen in the Church because this was alleged to have encouraged dis-

turbances. Nor did Irish clergy seem very deserving to English patrons.[54]
Already by 1220 Honorius III took up the cudgels for learned and honest
Irish clerks who were not getting the preferment they merited.[55] Ireland does
seem to have been short of ambitious, idealistic clergy eager to carry forward a reforming movement. There is still only fitful evidence that any of
them trained abroad. The archbishop of Tuam who died in 1249 was
described as both a *magister* of canon law and a palmer (i.e. having been on
the pilgrimage). On his return from Rome in 1237 he had summoned a
synod, spurred on, perhaps, by his visit to the Curia.[56]

By the second half of the thirteenth century the wishes of Henry III in the
matter of ecclesiastical appointments had come to prevail in twenty-seven of
the thirty-two Irish bishoprics: only in parts of the province of Tuam did the
king of England count for little.[57] The king might have a preference for
appointing Englishmen to Irish bishoprics, but Irishmen were promoted and
generally turned out to be loyal. When David MacCarwill, dean of Cashel,
was elected archbishop in 1253, it was not only Henry III who objected to
him (on the grounds that he had sided with the king's enemies); the bishops
of his province were aggrieved that they had not been consulted. While the
merits of the case were weighed up at the Curia, Innocent IV was encouraged to condemn certain practices of the secular courts in Cashel that
unfairly discriminated against Irishmen. Another year passed before the
pope approved David's appointment but the king then bowed to the papal
decision. David's long service at Cashel, over thirty years, is most notable
for his efforts to secure for Irishmen the same rights as Englishmen in the
courts. He spent three years in England (1277–80) negotiating this and cannot have been any serious opponent of English rule in Ireland. His only
known dispute with the royal authorities was about building a royal gaol at
Cashel.[58] Some Irish bishops took the view that the interests of the Church
would be better served by cooperation with the English government than by
encouraging patriotic resistance. Most of MacCarwill's province lay within
the English sphere of influence and the example of the Church in England
must have shown what advantages the Church in Ireland might derive from
good relations between Church and State.

The papacy was in no position to give the Irish much help in any difficulties they had with the English lordship. Alexander IV made one or two
fitful attempts to speak up on behalf of Irish bishops. He was induced to
protest to Henry III about the persistent unwillingness of Englishmen in
Ireland to recognise the rights of the Irish to their own laws with regard to
the succession of property. His intervention in a dispute between the bishop
of Kilfenora and the Irish justiciar over the hearing of ecclesiastical cases in
a secular court was blocked at the Curia by the king's own representatives.
The papacy could not raise effective objections to the way the English lordship affected the Irish Church.[59]

The presence of four archbishops in Ireland ought to have multiplied
opportunities for contact with the papacy as archbishops applied to the

Curia for their pallium. How regularly they themselves went to Rome is not known. Cashel obtained Henry III's permission to do so in 1224, but the pallium for his successor in 1239 was brought by a clerk. The expense of visiting the Curia may have deterred the archbishops.[60] Several naturally paid their dues to the papacy by borrowing from Italian merchants, but when they did not repay their creditors on time the pope duly intervened. Armagh had to be reminded of his debts to Italians in 1261; the archbishop of Tuam forestalled further trouble by repaying his Florentine creditors in 1263; Dublin repaid his in 1266.[61]

The papacy was not much involved with Irish episcopal appointments. An exception was the promotion of Master Albert Swerbeer of Cologne as archbishop of Armagh in 1239. Albert, whose nomination to the see of Riga had been rejected some years earlier, was a distinguished man then serving on the staff of Cardinal Otto, the influential papal legate in England. After his appointment he went to Rome, returned with relics for his see and held a council for his province, but he failed to hold his own in Ireland. On his arrival at Armagh he had discovered that the church there was racked with debt and had lost much of its endowment. Albert was so disturbed by what he learnt that he went to Gascony to get Henry III's authority for an investigation into losses of its property. However, his attempts to pursue claims against the prior of Llanthony in the ecclesiastical courts caused him to fall foul of Henry III. Innocent IV rescued him from his difficulties in Ireland by transferring him to Prussia in 1246 and immediately appointing his successor. Little is known about Reginald except that he took possession in October 1247, left Ireland for Rome in July 1252 and died there four years later, possibly without ever returning to Ireland. His sojourn abroad appears to have been disapproved in England and, at the very beginning of his pontificate in January 1255, Alexander IV wrote to Henry III beseeching him to not to believe all the malicious reports circulating about Reginald.[62]

Serving the Irish Church was a very exacting task, even for Irish bishops. Several obtained papal permission to resign their charges, employing the formula that they despaired of the people they lived among: Cloyne in 1235, Ossory in 1250, Ardagh and Raphoe in 1252. Even Christian observance seemed at risk in some places. Alexander IV remonstrated with the bishop of Raphoe in 1261 about the laity of his diocese who not only still worshipped idols but persisted in their abhorrent marriage customs.[63]

How Ireland's long-standing relationships with Germany might have been affected by its closer connections with the papacy is not apparent. That they still counted for something appears from the confidence with which Frederick II sent his clerk, Master Walter, to Ireland in 1236. Frederick's purpose is not known but Henry III's suspicions were immediately aroused.[64] There is no sign of Irish interest in the papal-imperial struggle. At the first council of Lyon where Frederick was deposed, the only Irish bishop known to have attended was the bishop-elect of Elphin and that specifically to get Innocent IV's confirmation of his appointment. He was sent back to

Tuam for consecration.[65] The Irish annals paid the council scant attention. After 1245 the dispute between pope and emperor must have caused some disruption of Irish communications with Germany, or the priors in Ireland of the Irish house at Regensburg were allowed to receive novices and spare them the distance and dangers of the journey to Germany, a practice presumably maintained until then. On the other hand, the abbot himself retained his powers to correct the Irish monks subject to his authority and the pope reminded him that monks should not be allowed to wander off into remote places to escape supervision. References to Irish connections with the dioceses of Constanz and Vercelli help to show that Ireland was not quite so isolated as it might seem at first sight.[66]

The travails of the papacy did not concern the Irish clergy and it was no part of Irish tradition to turn to the pope when in trouble. Admittedly in 1206 Eugenius, the new archbishop of Armagh, was sent by the Irish bishops to Rome to complain about English activity in the island, but he seems to have been detained in England and John's quarrel with the pope rendered further action impossible.[67] Papal discipline was anyway not very effective. In 1227 Gregory IX demanded an enquiry into the appointment of the bishop of Limerick, accused of illegitimacy, ignorance, simony and disobedience to his metropolitan. Hugh de Burgh was not only a member of a baronial family powerful in Ireland; he had been prior of the Austin house of Athassel. Nothing came of the slanderous accusations; he was still in office twenty years later.[68] The ineffectiveness of papal intervention in Ireland was apparent at Mayo where a decision of Innocent III was still being contested in 1240.[69] Papal legates occasionally visited Ireland, usually after discharging similar duties in Scotland, but they left no mark. In 1221, one legate's activity was reported simply as that of raising money. When the papal legate Ottobuono arrived in England in 1268, he gave Ireland some attention, ordering the crusade to be preached there, but he did not himself cross over.

Some Irish bishops cultivated connections outside the island. The deaths of bishops in England, as at Bristol in 1247 and 1256, are bare signs of movement, but Irish bishops also occasionally served as suffragans in English dioceses for reasons not explained. Thomas, bishop of Elphin, was a Cistercian exceptionally well connected who secured letters of support from the kings of France and Castile in his dispute with Henry III.[70] Making foreign friends was not easy for Irish bishops. In 1258 Abraham, archbishop of Armagh, was presumably trying to curry favour with the pope when he gave a church in the diocese of Meath to the convent in Anagni founded by the pope's uncle.[71] Another church in the Meath diocese was held by a papal chaplain.

Irish bishoprics were an unattractive source of prebends even for papal hangers-on. Dublin, the only Irish see well endowed and staffed in the manner expected in England, offered a prebend to one of the clerks of Cardinal Otto, while legate in England.[72] Lewis of Savoy was given a prebend at

Dublin (1271–79). At Armagh, Innocent IV's appointee Reginald was asked in 1248 to find an Irish benefice for a kinsman who was a papal notary. Much more is known about John de Frosinone, Innocent's resident agent in Ireland, for whom the pope asked Archbishop Luke of Dublin to provide a benefice. Frosinone was excommunicated by Irish bishops at the instigation of the bishop of Limerick, but this controversial papal agent left Ireland only in 1261/63. He received periodic instructions to find Irish benefices for curial officials but his main task was financial, collecting money for the Holy Land. By 1252 he was said to have amassed 40,000 marks, from which he had taken 3000 marks on his own account and had deposited them at the Cistercian monastery of Mellifont. Not surprisingly the archbishop of Tuam became suspicious about Frosinone's honesty; Innocent IV defended his agent from this criticism and warned the archbishop to drop his enquiry. There is more to this affair than meets the eye. Frosinone may have been trusted by Innocent IV for personal reasons; the papacy as such was not necessarily the better for it. In 1266, when Clement IV ordered the archbishop of Armagh and the bishop of Meath to investigate what had happened and hand over what they recovered to the pope's special envoy Master Sinicius, the money collected for the crusade by Frosinone was still not accounted for.[73] Despite what looks like a decline in papal interest in the Irish connection, Innocent V in his brief pontificate had some reason to send a special envoy, Manseronus de Spoleto, to Ireland.[74] The native Irish Church was sufficiently aware of papal policy in 1295 for an Irish king to have dutifully accepted Boniface VIII's bull *Clericis laicos*; unlike Edward I, he had not normally collected taxes from his clergy anyway.[75] Was his compliance politically motivated?

Whatever its limitations in practice, the papal programme made some impact all over the British Isles, thanks to its own powers of organisation and the willing cooperation of native rulers and clergy.

The bishops' programme

While the papacy became preoccupied with what it regarded as its responsibilities for the universal Church, the bishops themselves concentrated on pastoral reform. Nowhere in Christendom did thirteenth-century clergy make greater efforts to bring laymen to a more religious way of life than in England.[76] They welcomed new ways of realising religious vocations. They sought to improve their own intellectual understanding by further study, even from such unlikely sources as the pagan philosophy of Aristotle and the scientific learning of the infidel Muslims. They undertook arduous journeys into Greece or Spain for such purposes, spending years mastering the languages and the difficult texts. Others pursued studies for several years at the new 'schools', the universities. The reformed Church was based on sound learning and personal commitment.

Once peace returned to the English kingdom, the bishops threw themselves into the task of restoring the condition of the Church which had seriously deteriorated since the death of Archbishop Walter of Canterbury in 1205. There was much to do simply to repair the damage caused by the interdict and the civil war. The new archbishop, Stephen Langton, unlike Walter, had no administrative experience. As a prominent teacher of theology in Paris, he had been called to Rome as cardinal before his appointment at Canterbury. His experience and talents made him an able advocate of the Lateran reforms which he promulgated in England at the Oxford council of 1222. On his return to England in 1218, he set about trying to relaunch the spiritual life of the Church. He took advantage of the fiftieth anniversary of Becket's death in 1220 to dedicate a new shrine at Canterbury and welcome an imposing number of foreign as well as native clergy.[77] In this period, a number of English bishops were formally recognised as saints. The process began under King John with Wulfstan of Worcester; Hugh of Avalon, bishop of Lincoln was canonised in 1220. The claims of Birinus of Dorchester were investigated in 1224, those of Edmund of Abingdon approved in 1246 and of Richard of Chichester in 1262. Ireland too benefited when the sanctity of Laurence O'Toole was approved (1225).[78]

Thanks to bishops who began to keep orderly records of their activities, the implementation of Innocent III's great reform programme can be more closely monitored in England than elsewhere.[79] Unlike their counterparts abroad, most English bishops had gained their earliest experience of administration in royal service, so they probably knew how to get results. Langton himself appreciated what university training could do to prepare graduates for high office and great responsibility. Episcopal commitment to further study was focused on the need to find suitably competent men for the bishops' administrations.

Their main pastoral concern was to ascertain that religious services were properly provided in every parish, which required bishops to make personal visitations of the parishes and arrange for regular supervision by alert archdeacons. They checked on the fabric of the local churches and their furnishings, their provision with altar plate and service books. The duty laid on all Christians to make an annual confession to a discreet and celibate priest obliged reforming bishops to ensure that every parish had a resident incumbent, but not that he should be educated beyond the most basic level. Not even preaching was expected of him. His duties were to perform the sacramental mysteries and teach laymen to say their prayers. For this purpose, bishops calculated that an income of 5 marks a year was sufficient to provide for a suitable priest, a 'vicar' who stood in for the rector. The rector, the nominal holder of the benefice, received the greater part of the income from his church's endowments so that he could pursue other activities considered more valuable than the care of mainly rural parishes.

This may now seem a very curious state of affairs, but the bishops were not being irresponsible. For centuries, individual English churches, monas-

teries, cathedrals and parishes had been accumulating substantial endowments for their own benefit. There had been no provision for financing
ecclesiastical management of the kind now required for the reform programme. It was necessary to consider how this expense might be met. In the
new order of things, bishops saw no harm in diverting most of the churches'
revenues into funding their own administrations. If rectors were not immediately assigned senior responsibilities, they studied to acquire qualifications
for service in the administrations of the bishop or of other great lords,
including the king.

The bishops' need for highly qualified clergy to manage a reforming
Church could only be satisfied by redistributing the wealth of local churches
from the purposes for which it had been assigned originally. Any frontal
attack on vested interests would have been resisted by patrons whose rights
of property were protected by royal courts. Instead, bishops concentrated
on getting papal support for arrangements designed to satisfy as many parties as possible. In this way they were able to subsidise the establishments,
not only of the bishops but also of the papal Curia itself. These became the
principal patrons of ambitious clergy. To implement the reform programme
close cooperation between the bishops, the Curia and the universities
became normal. Its dependence on getting papal support and intellectual
stimulus from the Continent is undeniable. Without these, the management
of the Church would have been organised differently.

Two main issues required attention. First, the rule that clergy must themselves be celibate was difficult enough to enforce, but many clerks of this
period suffered from a further liability: born into clerical families, they were
deemed illegitimate and therefore ineligible for the clerical life. To proceed
to holy orders, they needed papal dispensation. Second, rectors who did not
intend to reside in their benefices sought papal approval. The most ordinary
business of the parish thus came to concern the papal administration.
Bishops were also troubled by all sorts of other issues, many of which were
contentious enough to attract the attention of the Curia. Bishops needed to
know whom they could rely on for support there and their letters reveal
how much they cultivated these connections in the interest of their own
office. The pope was not necessarily consulted in person, nor did every
parish priest have to take his own case to the Curia, but the intermediaries
who became an indispensable part of the Church's management needed to
be completely au fait with the workings of the Curia.

In other parts of the British Isles, bishops cannot be shown to have taken
up the task of reforming their churches with comparable enthusiasm. With
no metropolitan to coordinate their efforts, Scottish bishops obtained papal
permission in 1225 to hold their own provincial councils, but little is known
about whether they met or what they did.[80] The best evidence for episcopal
innovation at this time comes from Dunblane, the smallest Scottish diocese.
When Clement was brought over as bishop in 1233 from Paris, the Church
was in a sorry state and Clement's plans for reorganising the cathedral chap-

ter needed papal approval. For twenty-five years, he was one of the most energetic of Scottish bishops. He was the first Dominican to be appointed bishop anywhere in the British Isles and he owed his zeal to his order.[81]

Had the reforming programme of the bishops been confined to administrative efficiency it would not have resolved the more intractable problems facing the Church in the early thirteenth century. The spread of erroneous doctrine and the refractory character of the faithful were signs that the Church had not succeeded in winning the trust of laymen. In the past, the Church had taken the view that the truly devout would enter the cloister or seek ordination and that the spiritual hopes of those who remained laymen would be realised vicariously through the clergy's prayers. By the thirteenth century, many laymen were inspired by a spiritual idealism they did not reckon to satisfy by entering formally into the clerical life. Abroad, but not in England, some espoused the views of zealous preachers denounced by the authorities as heretics. Others found inspiration and ideals which could not be stamped out by mere anathemas. More direct ways of satisfying laymen's aspirations had to be found. The clergy did not conclude that there might be something faulty with the Christian message. Rather, they assumed that the principal reason for disaffection lay with the failure to articulate orthodox belief with adequate conviction. What was needed, above all, was better instruction about Christian faith and discipline. To be weaned from false doctrine laymen were to be taught how to live as Christians in the world, and if the clergy were to do their duty properly, they had to be better prepared. To succeed in these tasks, English bishops also called upon continental resources.

Preaching

The most dynamic force in the thirteenth-century reform programme was provided by the friars. These entered England from the continent in the period of initial reform in the 1220s. The Order of Preachers founded by Dominic, canon of Osma in Castile, and the Order of Minorites, founded by Francis of Assisi, needed papal support for their initial survival, but owed their early drive to the exceptional visions of their founders. Dominic's purpose was to provide preachers so well versed in theological disputation as to go openly and confidently among heretics in order to confound them and win them back to the Church.[82] The Dominicans, as persuasive exponents of sound doctrine and clever critics of heretical demagogues, served the purpose perfectly. The south of France and Italy were the main regions where wrong theological opinions were openly canvassed. In England, however, where there were no heretics and no existing audience for controversial theology, the bishops immediately welcomed the Dominicans when they arrived in 1222. Their dedication to sound learning brought them to Oxford, where they helped to reinforce the reputation of its school of theology. They soon found willing recruits to the novel concept of a preaching order, like Robert Bacon and Richard Fishacre, original thinkers whose ideas made an impact on the theological teachers at Paris itself.

Francis's personal charisma originally gave a very different character to his order. Not intended as an order of clergy, and certainly not designed to offer any preaching services or require any educational qualifications, the Franciscans had aimed initially to bring orthodox religion and piety to the most destitute sections of the Italian cities, where mercantile wealth had driven a social wedge between rich and poor. Their stress on an emotional commitment to the simple, wandering life of the human Jesus offered a totally new interpretation of Christianity. The order's potential attractiveness everywhere is now so much taken for granted that it is difficult to realise what an impression its weird devotees originally made.

The popularity of the order in England owed nothing to the existence of any social deprivation comparable to what was known on the Continent. English towns were neither exceptionally large, nor riven by feuds; there is no independent evidence for the corrosive effects of wealth on the social order. Yet, within its first decade, Englishmen were already found among its most prominent adherents. When the first group of Franciscans reached England in 1224, three of the four ordained friars were Englishmen who had joined the order abroad, probably in Paris. The Franciscan message and mystique were fresh enough to impress even the monk-chroniclers of St Albans and must have gained the order English adherents in considerable numbers.[83] At the time, Robert Grosseteste was the most distinguished teacher in Oxford and the Franciscans in England asked him to provide a teaching programme for them. This attracted idealistic and highly educated clergy to become Franciscans and English friars played a leading part in making study central to the work of the order and encouraging the friars to develop their skills as preachers. A number of English Franciscans eventually took up posts as teachers in houses of the order abroad, as they did in Lyon and Genoa.

An educated English Franciscan, Thomas of Eccleston began to accumulate notes about the success of the order in England as early as *c*.1230 and took obvious pride in the praise heaped on the fervour and learning of English friars by senior members of the order.[84] English influence helped to shift the objectives of the order in a more conventionally ecclesiastical direction. When Brother Elias, the minister-general of the order, was deposed for resisting the pressure to greater discipline, the part played in this by Haymo of Faversham is noteworthy; in 1241, Haymo became only the third minister-general.[85] The English reception of the friars illustrates how membership of the universal Church could provide unexpected blessings, which were not strictly necessary but put to good use as ways of enriching the English Church's religious offerings. Eccleston's account also makes it clear that English Franciscans took up responsibilities wherever the order flourished, and as far away as Syria. They moved without hesitation to Scotland and

Ireland, of course, but also to France, Germany, Spain and Italy. Eccleston showed proper patriotism (though the vernacular speech of English friars he recorded was always in French), but he cannot be described as nationalistic.

The international ramifications of the order as they were felt in England can be gauged from the letters of Adam Marsh, the well-connected and most influential of the early Franciscans. He had joined the order in 1229 while still in Paris where he was a prominent teacher. After his return to England, he kept well informed about events abroad through the Franciscan network. In this way he became aware of some of the prophecies of Abbot Joachim of Fiore which he passed on to Grosseteste for copying. Because they kept their ears close to the ground, Franciscans picked up rumours and gossip very rapidly. Marsh received information about the extraordinary Pastoureaux movement in France from a French Franciscan and passed it on to his bishop. News of Louis IX's defeat at Mansourah in Egypt reached Marsh before Simon de Montfort had heard of it. Marsh's contacts with the provincial of the French Franciscans enabled him to ask Queen Margaret to reconcile Alphonse of Poitiers, her brother-in-law, with Simon de Montfort, to whose interests Marsh was devoted. Marsh also had other foreign correspondents outside the order: bishop Erland of Roskilde, the abbot of Vercelli, Peter of Savoy. Marsh remained a figure of international standing who attracted some students from abroad. He sought Grosseteste's permission for a young French Franciscan to perfect his study of literature (*studium literalis*) in Oxford, because *alibi quam in Anglia* he did not think it possible to do so.[86] Marsh's surviving letters show how the international character of the order helped to strengthen English involvement in the affairs of the universal Church.

England was not the only part of these islands that benefited immediately from these innovations. The friars rapidly established themselves throughout Britain. In Ireland there were Dominicans at Dublin and Drogheda by 1224 and the other east coast ports soon followed suit, already reaching Youghal in the south in 1224–25, and Cork a bit further west in 1229–30.[87] Wales, with few real towns, offered less scope for friars who depended on the daily collection of alms. Only two Dominican houses were established before the middle of the century, at Cardiff and Haverfordwest. A very unusual foundation for Franciscans was Llewelyn ap Iorwerth's house in Anglesey, where he wished the friars to pray for the soul of his late wife Joan, Henry III's sister.[88] Princely patronage was also the principal reason for the presence of friars in Scotland, where King Alexander II was at the time actively promoting the growth of royal burghs. In this context, the friars became essential, possibly because mendicant friars offered an economical alternative to the endowment of parishes.[89] The Melrose chronicler noticed the arrival in Scotland of Dominican friars in 1230, calling them Jacobins because, like Clement of Dunblane, they came from the order's house in Paris of that name.[90]

For whatever reasons they were patronised, the two orders of friars between them succeeded in changing thirteenth-century expectations of religion. The friars moved deliberately among laymen, stimulating their thoughts, encouraging their devotions through confraternities, providing devotional manuals for their use. Preaching became a regular rather than an occasional feature of religious experience. The Church made it a prime objective to instruct the laity in all matters the clergy decided were necessary for them to know, giving them a new sense of purpose and a direction for their aspirations. From this time forward, the Church became committed to the painful task of making laymen improve their chances of salvation after death by reform of their own lives and conduct. It encouraged examination of conscience, preparation for confession and amendment of life, without insisting on total renunciation of the world or commitment to a regular religious life. This had implications for matters not hitherto of much concern to religion. In the early part of the century a campaign to stop Sunday trading had been launched by an enthusiastic French abbot who went on an extensive preaching tour in 1201. This cause was taken up later by Henry III, who issued a formal decree that markets should no longer be held on Sundays.[91]

There were limits to what the authorities reckoned they could reform. Whereas in France, for example, Louis IX tried to stop gambling with dice, no such reform was attempted in England. The most important change in English public life forced through by church reformers came as a response to a decision of the Lateran Council in 1215. For centuries, intractable judicial problems had been settled by ordeals, considered as the appeal to God. When the council forbade ecclesiastical participation in these rites as an intolerable superstition, an alternative form of judgment had to be found. In England, juries had hitherto been responsible only for making public accusations of crimes, or judging civil cases brought by royal writ. Seeing no alternative to hand, English courts simply took over trial by jury in criminal cases. In this matter, the significance of church reform for daily life is undeniable.[92]

The exhortations of preachers were followed up by reading. Literacy, which had once been a mark of clerisy, became a requirement for civility. Laymen did not need to be won over. Many were already eager to read and write. Perceiving their opportunity, the clergy wrote not in Latin but in the vernacular, namely French. Now clergy aimed to do more than entertain lay courtiers. They wrote serious and improving works to realise their moral purpose.[93] Nothing comparable was written in France itself before c.1280. The English were precocious; in this respect, by using French they set an example, they were not imitating continental practice. Religious teaching was expected to show results: more loving relationships between spouses and more justice in social relations. How much did thirteenth-century criticism of royal government or papal abuses owe to the religious inspiration of the friars? To discount all influence would be unwarranted. Several bishops supported the baronial reform programme in the 1250s and 1260s in spite of their sense of duty to the king and pope. To do this, they can only have drawn on religious convictions remarkably akin to those expressed by the preaching orders.

Unlike earlier religious movements which expected monks to live in stable communities, the friars were committed to moving about to meet the people. In principle they had no property and lived from day to day by begging alms, putting themselves in the same demeaning position as the most destitute members of society. Their ability to do this on an international scale reveals something important about the changed outlook of Europe by the thirteenth century. Their way of life would not have been been possible at any earlier stage nor their approach to religion valued. Their prompt expansion throughout the Latin west and its crusading adjuncts in the east proves how much they filled a perceived gap in religious provision. The willingness of men to join these truly transnational orders, which took many of them overseas without any prospect of return, even now seems somewhat disconcerting. There is no way of estimating the relative importance of these religious exiles, but it was not only at the highest level. The Franciscan Bartholomew Anglicus, after study in Paris, was assigned responsibility for his order in Saxony and never returned to England. He wrote a compendium of knowledge, a kind of encyclopaedia, a work so useful that it was frequently consulted in the Middle Ages. It offers gratifying proof of general appreciation of one Englishman's erudition.[94]

The universities

Preaching to laymen was taken up by the new orders of friars; improving the qualifications of the clergy was the responsibility of the 'schools'. Bishops concerned to secure better management of the diocese or enforce discipline on their clergy found it desirable to keep abreast of Church law: for this they relied on engaging recent graduates in canon law. In the early thirteenth century the smartest of these were trained in Italy where the discipline developed rapidly as decisions given by the papal court on contested points were avidly collected and arranged in orderly fashion. Probably because English royal legal institutions had impinged so effectively on episcopal courts in the twelfth century, English clergy had shown an early and earnest determination to defend their jurisdictions by invoking canon law. They pressed the papacy for decisions on abstruse problems in order to eliminate every possible doubt and systematically collected such papal decisions.

Several scholars from Britain became respected teachers of canon law at Bologna. One of them, John of Wales, assisted in the work of gathering the many judicial pronouncements of Innocent III into a useful compendium *c*.1213.[95] A few years later, Magister William Scotus, a doctor of canon law living in Oxford, was appointed by the pope to look into an ecclesiastical dispute.[96] The most eminent English canonist, Robert de Summercotes, had studied at Bologna with the patronage of the abbot of Peterborough and was later given the church of Croydon by Archbishop Langton before entering papal service and becoming cardinal in 1239.[97] Even before Gregory IX issued the first official collection of papal decretals in 1234, when the formal teaching of canon law was begun at Oxford, England already had skilled practitioners of canon law.[98] The number of canon law manuscripts written in Italy and surviving in England shows how attentively the English followed amendments to the law of the Church. In England the operations of the king's own courts, where clergy frequently acted as judges, could not be ignored and common law cannot have remained unaffected by the judges' canonistic learning. Bracton's attempt to codify English royal law was obviously inspired by the civilians and canonists.[99] That English law did not subsequently build on Bracton's foundation followed from the fact that, unlike popes, English kings were not empowered to pronounce on legal questions. English law grew from the decisions of the courts. Even statutes needed judicial interpretation.

Medieval students of learned law were extremely influential, not so much as lawyers, except in church courts, but in royal administration, particularly as diplomats. Such specialised government servants acquired increasingly arduous responsibilities. The careers open to law graduates made it certain that the numbers of students were not small. The Bolognese registers provide ample indications about the presence of students from the British Isles in that city in the second half of the thirteenth century. Only the lack of documentation prevents us from knowing whether they had been less numerous in the earlier part of it. From the 1260s, however, the general situation appears striking. For 1265–66, there are ten named Englishmen in the registers, including Bernard, *anglicus, civis Bononiensis*, and a Petrus de Ibernia; the following year, 1267–68, there are fourteen names, including two Scots and, again, Peter of Ireland. In 1269, no less than fifty-five names of men from the British Isles appear in the registers, seven certainly Scots and four Irish. Sometimes it is not clear whether the same man does not appear in the register in different places under slightly different forms, but even allowing for a little duplication the numbers remain impressive. Possibly the end of the troubles in England in 1268 had made it easier for students to resume study abroad; if so, the lower numbers of 1267–68 may represent the falling off from higher numbers before 1258. Some of these students seem to have become resident in Bologna, others lodged with Bologna masters; those with greater resources took out annual leases on a house for their own use. Some are described as archdeacons or rectors, perhaps to establish their creditworthiness. Some were affluent enough to loan money, at least in the short term, to fellow students.[100]

Whatever the source of their income, they needed to be supplied with cash by their agents or bankers and there are records of how the money was transferred to Italy, both through channels in Paris and through Italian merchants. The evidence for so many students, however sparse for individuals, is sufficient to establish the importance of relations between the British Isles and Italy in this period. There was even a long-distance haulage service: a canon of York arranged for six law books to be transferred for him to Paris by the Bonaventura company of Siena. The flow of cash was such that several payments noted in the Bologna registers were made in sterling, even by students without connections in England. In 1269, two Irish students received money from a Florentine banker which had originally been paid by their proctor to the Florentine company in Ireland itself.

The influence of learned law in Scotland was considerable in the first half of the century because royal courts were not able to offer comparable facilities for settling quarrels at law and, unlike those of England, did nothing to inhibit the activities of church courts. With no archbishop to take account of, Scottish clergy dealt directly with the papacy when need arose. The impact of learned law from Italy in Scotland was direct.[101] Law graduates must have been at least as useful to Scottish bishops as their counterparts in England, if not more so. The evidence from Bologna is sufficient to identify at least thirty different qualified Scots lawyers, but only about one student, Simon the Scot, do we learn something personal. With others he was accused of forcing his way into the room of Hugh, an English *scolaris*, in 1235 and making off with all his property. When summoned by the authorities to answer the charge, Simon absconded and was put under the ban.[102] Unfortunately nothing else is known about this incident of hostility between rival Britons, but without this record the presence of Scots students at Bologna so early in this period would have gone totally unremarked.

The early history of all university institutions remains obscure. In the late twelfth century, a few English scholars who had previously achieved distinction in the schools at Paris returned to England to teach, as William de Montibus did at Lincoln or Alexander Neckham at St Albans. In their day, Oxford had still not become a magnet for advanced study. This changed rather suddenly. By the early thirteenth century, Oxford had already acquired a distinctive reputation. Its independence was shown in John's early years when Edmund of Abingdon became the first western scholar to lecture there on Aristotle's *Sophistici Elenchi*.[103] The oldest western commentary on Aristotle's *Posterior Analytics* was also composed there by Grosseteste about the same time.

Teaching was resumed at Oxford after the end of the civil war. A ban imposed in Paris on the teaching of Aristotle's scientific works, first issued in 1210 and in force for over twenty years, gave Oxford the opportunity to build up its own reputation in this field while Parisian masters were under restraint. This may have attracted students from abroad. In 1225 Henry III offered a bursary to a clerical brother of the count of Auvergne so that he could study at Oxford. Strangely, however, when the university in Paris was (temporarily) closed altogether in 1229, Henry III urged students and teachers there to come to England, 'to any place they chose'.[104] Unlike Paris, Oxford did not obtain any formal recognition of its independent university status. Nevertheless, it was soon recognised as a reputable place of learning in the Parisian mould. Thus in 1246, Innocent IV approved a proposal made by Grosseteste that to qualify as 'masters' at Oxford candidates would have to be examined *secundum morem Parisiae*.[105] In the course of the century, two 'universities' became established in England at a time when Germany, for example, developed no university institution at all. Both remained closely connected with the great schools abroad.

In the early part of the century, the foreign schools where Englishmen went to study were not necessarily any more formal than Oxford itself. Students went to learn from distinguished teachers or simply in search of scientific works which they translated with the help of local savants. One of the most important motives for the pursuit of scientific learning was to gain better understanding of medicine. To do this involved study abroad, in Salerno, Montpellier or Spain, where students could become familiar with Arabic and Greek science. Little is known about the organisation of such studies. Only the survival of some medical manuscripts and the reputations of a few outstanding physicians shed any light on the matter.[106] An English doctor, Hugh de Milaburne, studied at Bologna; another, Gilbert of Aquila, at Salerno and Montpellier, where he became chancellor *c.*1250. The oldest known manuscript of his compilation, *Compendium Medicinae c.*1240, was copied a generation later when it was still considered useful enough.[107] He provided the best medieval description of leprosy. Master Bernard Gordon, who may also have been English, occurs in Montpellier *c.*1283 and wrote his *Lilium Medicinae* in 1303, which is still notable for its early mention of spectacles, an invention dependent on the development of the study of optics in the thirteenth century. In the south, English doctors were respected by the famous Catalan doctor Arnold de Villanova for a number of their medical 'recipes'.[108]

That they had something of an international reputation in this field explains how some English doctors came into the service of the papal Curia. Richard of Wendover, later canon of St Paul's, attended Gregory IX on his deathbed and was given an ivory crucifix by the pope.[109] Twenty years later, the French pope Urban IV had a Scottish physician, Adam of Kirkcudbright, who later returned to his homeland in the service of the Bruce family. King Alexander III's son, Alexander, later wrote on Adam's behalf to Edward I praising his skill, which had been responsible for saving him when his life was despaired of.[110] The most distinguished of all English doctors on the Continent was John, a Cistercian who became physician to the pope and a cardinal of great influence in the Curia for over thirty years.[111] He left a number of influential medical writings, was himself a patron of learning and maintained a large household where several prominent clergy began their careers, including Richard Gravesend, bishop of Lincoln, and pope Honorius IV. Cardinal John's prominence made him much valued. He was frequently called on, not only by English suppliants at the Curia, but by Scots and Irishmen. His sobriquet 'of Toledo' is usually interpreted to mean that he had studied medicine there; it is the most likely place for him to have learnt Arabic. Later, in 1280, another English doctor, Hugh of Evesham, was summoned to the papal Curia, where he was made cardinal and became physician to Pope Martin IV.[112] Where Hugh studied medicine is not known, but it is difficult to believe that adequate facilities had not by his time been developed in England.

English records yield the names of nearly 250 doctors, equally divided between both halves of the thirteenth century, without giving any information about their places of training.[113] Nor is there evidence about the development of medical study in Oxford or Cambridge. Further study of surviving medical manuscripts in England would make it easier to understand the nature of medical training in this period. Medical texts, including a Latin translation of Rhazes's *Liber Almansoris*, were copied, possibly in East Anglia, as early as 1200; and before 1230 an Anglo-Norman translation of Roger of Salerno's *Cirurgia* was provided with instructive illustrations. The Latin version of Abulcasis's *Cirurgia* was transcribed in late thirteenth-century England and about the same time medical works by Galen and Avicenna were given to Canterbury Cathedral. All these works were useful for training doctors.[114] The early fourteenth-century physician John of Gaddesden, who wrote a widely consulted medical manual the *Rosa Anglica*, has been described as the first English doctor to have received all his medical training in England, but the position of his predecessors in this respect remains too obscure for certainty.[115] By the late thirteenth century the training of physicians in England was apparently sufficient to make it unnecessary to go abroad for further study or to coax foreign practitioners into the service of English patrons.

Nearly a score of doctors are described as being in the service of Henry III, but the only ones of obviously foreign origin were Peter de Joinzac from Gascony, Peter de Alpibus from Provence, and Master William of Fécamp, also named as a clerk of Richard of Cornwall. Of Edward I's dozen physicians, Peter of Portugal stands out as anomalous, since Simon of Beauvais and William of St Père were not necessarily of French origin. Though Eleanor of Provence is known to have been attended by English doctors, in her later years she also employed two from her homeland, Raymund de Bariamondo and William le Provençal. Eleanor of Castile's two known physicians in her final years were both Spaniards. Master Gerard of Parma is the only Italian doctor named.

English students had been going to Spain to improve their understanding of science since the twelfth century and Michael 'Scotus' was doing nothing unusual when he went to Toledo in 1215.[116] Here he acquired his knowledge of Arabic and translated al Bitrogi's work on the sphere, and three parts of Aristotle's '*de animalibus*' from an Arabic version. Where Michael's interest in science had first been aroused is not known, though Oxford is the most likely place. From there he would quite naturally have proceeded to Paris: somewhere, at least, he became a 'master'. Unlike his English predecessors in scientific work, Michael never returned to Britain; perhaps as a

'Scot' he had no powerful patrons at home. By 1220 he was in Bologna and impressed the pope enough to be offered appointment as archbishop of Armagh. Michael turned this down on the grounds that he was ignorant of the Irish language so Honorius III secured for him instead four benefices in England and Scotland. Later he entered the service of Frederick II as court savant and magician. Scot's major and lasting contribution to learning was to translate the comprehensive Arabic commentaries on Aristotle's scientific works.

In the early thirteenth century the intellectual challenges presented by the pagan Aristotle and the Muslim Averroes were chiefly responsible for the great expansion in formal university institutions in the Latin west.[117] The teachers of the twelfth-century 'schools' had become committed to an extraordinarily ambitious project. Until then, religious teachers had elucidated the holy scriptures within the conventions of the literary education bequeathed them by the ancient world. The new scholastic learning aimed to rearrange biblical texts in a systematic way in order to construct an intellectually coherent theology. In this task they found themselves confronting contradictory statements which they attempted to reconcile, making use of ancient writings about logic, particularly those of Aristotle. His unassailable reputation as a logician disposed scholars to accord comparable respect to Aristotle's other works on the natural sciences when they later came to scholarly attention. Unfortunately, being of pagan origin, they seemed incompatible with religious teaching.

As it happened, Muslim thinkers in their own commentaries on Aristotle had already struggled to reconcile his opinions with their religious beliefs. Latin scholars recognised what benefit they derived from consulting Muslim works on Aristotle. However useful, these commentaries remained deeply suspect on account of their origin. What with Aristotle's paganism and Muslim exegesis, scientific studies provoked understandable disquiet in circles of traditional learning. Undeterred, many believers in the Christian revelation did not flinch but saw that new ways of justifying what they believed to be the revealed truths of religion had to be found.[118] In the pursuit of this end, western thinkers came to believe in their ability to benefit from alien learning, yet at the same time refute unacceptable conclusions drawn from both pagan and Islamic systems of thought. The development of university study in the thirteenth century can be regarded as another indirect consequence of the interaction between the east and west. Whereas the crusades ultimately failed in their military purpose, intellectually scholasticism prepared the way for the global triumph of western-style rationalism.

The intellectual challenge was nowhere taken up with more brilliance than in Paris, but not only by French scholars. Since the mid-twelfth century many clergy from the British Isles had chosen not only to study there but, as teachers, to build up its reputation as Christendom's main intellectual centre. When the first formal statutes were published for any medieval university, this was done in 1215 at Paris by an Englishman, Cardinal Robert

Curzon, then papal legate in France.[119] Englishmen continued to play a leading part in the activities of the university of Paris throughout the thirteenth
century. Most archbishops of Canterbury and of York, from Stephen
Langton onwards, had themselves been both students and professors at
Paris earlier in their careers. The attractions of Paris were in no way diminished by the brief closure of the university in 1229. As soon as it reopened,
several English masters happily returned. John of Garland, who had taught
in the meantime at Toulouse, returned to Paris where he spent the rest of his
long life teaching within the older tradition of Christian humanism against
the more innovative claims of the scholastics. Nevertheless, he composed a
lament on the death of his compatriot, Alexander of Hales (August 1245), a
pioneer of Parisian scholasticism.[120] In 1231, when Hales himself returned
to Paris, possibly from Angers, he became a Franciscan and began his
Summa Theologiae. This work created a new genre of theological writing,
the commentary on the *Sentences* of Peter Lombard.[121] Another treatise
composed in Paris by an Englishman in the 1230s or 1240s remained a standard work for three centuries. *On the Sphere* was written by John of
Sacrobosco (either from Halifax or from Holyrood), who had acquired his
original scientific training at Oxford. He completed other mathematical
works indebted to Arabic learning and wrote a prose commentary for
Alexander of Villedieu's verse treatise on arithmetical calculations which
extended knowledge of 'Arabic' mathematics in thirteenth-century
Christendom.[122] He too had probably studied in Spain.

The prominence of the English in the university of Paris is made clear by
the way responsibility for university discipline was divided among the four
'national' communities, French, Norman, Picard and English. This last comprised all 'foreign' students, though the English predominated. Its statutes
were the earliest of the four to be drawn up (1251) and the 'nation' had its
own seal by 1252.[123] Shortly after this the English abbot of Clairvaux,
Stephen of Lexington, established a college dedicated to St Bernard so that
Cistercian monks could study at Paris. The English links of the new college
were strengthened when the abbot's brother John, lord of Eston, endowed it
with half the Yorkshire church of Rotherham.[124] The first Cistercian to
graduate as a university doctor was James '*anglicus*'. The English presence
at Paris was one of the most self-confident. This underlines the intensity of
English interest in securing opportunities for learning.

In mid-century, John Romeyns acquired a house in Paris while he was a
student and is not likely to have been the only Englishmen to do so. Later,
he did his friends a favour by allowing them to use it, first the nephews of
Cardinal Matteo Orsini (a canon of York) and then those of Bishop Bek of
Durham. His house was even furnished with copies of the decretals and
other things relating to Parisian study.[125] Nor were these the only students
with excellent connections to smooth their way at Paris. Peckham's letters
refer in passing to the three sons of the earl of Oxford who were studying
there in the 1280s.[126] With many sons to provide for, the earl sensibly

thought of possible careers in the Church, but saw to it that they were adequately educated and did not expect birth alone to secure their advancement.

Scottish students at Paris as early as 1213 are the most likely source of the report in the Melrose chronicle about the measures taken by Robert Curzon to deal with the Amalric heretics. In mid-century, several letters from W. de Bernham, nephew of Bishop David of St Andrews, show how even a wealthy and well-connected student at Paris had problems about getting ready money. For fifteen days he was obliged to economise on his food; in order to pay for a journey to Rome, he had to pawn his books to the Jews. He expected to be able to raise money if necessary by disposing of his horses, but found when the time came that the best of them were missing. Money sent from England was weak and illegal. His mother was the chief recipient of news about his material problems. As a gift he sent back to Scotland four pounds of *alba pulvere*, possibly sugar, or at least confectionery.[127] Two Scottish masters, William of Scotland and Adam de Gulayne, archdeacon of Lothian, taught in Paris well before the most famous of them all, Duns from Roxburgh, arrived towards the end of the century.[128] Another slight indication of Scottish links with Paris is provided by a document from the (Cistercian) Bernardine college which bears an impression of the seal belonging to Simon, bishop of Sodor and Man.[129]

A few names of Irish clergy in Paris are also known. In 1253 the pope asked the bishop of Ferns to find a benefice for Richard 'Chancellor' who had long studied there. Two Irish preachers, William and Reginald Scotus, also occur there. Maurice, an Irishman, became proctor of the English nation in 1275; Patrick (1281) and Robert (1284) were other Irish members of the English nation.[130] More is known about Jofroi of Waterford, a learned Dominican, who had travelled in the East and learnt Greek and Arabic to supplement his Latin. He had probably acquired his intellectual interests in Paris. He made several translations into French from works in those languages and is notable for his appreciation of the different French wines he identified: those of Provence, Gascony, St Emilion, La Rochelle, Reims, Champagne, Auxerre, the Ile de France, Orléans and what he calls *vin vernache*, grenache.[131]

Paris was not the only place on the continent where Irishmen studied. In 1257 Master Thomasius, canon of Dublin, son of the noble Maurice Gherold, was said to be living in Orléans; that he was there to study is a reasonable surmise.[132] Others occur in south Italy. An Irish scholar, Peter of Ireland, had the honour of teaching grammar to the young Aquinas at Naples and of answering questions put to him by Frederick II's son, King Manfred (1258–66). Peter may have been attracted south originally by his compatriot, Michael Scot. Another Irishman working in the southern kingdom was Thomas, a Franciscan who occurs at Aquila in 1270.[133]

Where precisely other Irish scholars had studied abroad is often obscure. Malachias, a learned Franciscan who had probably been educated abroad, was chosen by some of the clergy as archbishop of Tuam in 1279, but failed to convince the Curia of his merits. Though not heard of in Ireland, a treatise he wrote on poison later became popular on the Continent. Bede had believed that Ireland had been spared poisonous beasts; Malachias was convinced it still suffered from poisons of the soul and denounced what he considered Irish shortcomings. He referred to the damnable marriage customs of the Irish and the boast of King Rory that he would not exchange his six wives for the grant of a papal crown. In Malachias's view, however, Irish priests were more lascivious than the laity. He also strongly disapproved of despicable *carmina* and the activities of *histriones* and *adulatores*, a reference to the familiar entertainments of Irish secular courts, which other Christians of his time found very strange.[134] Given his attitude, the papacy's rejection of his election as a bishop is understandable. Notices of Welshmen on the Continent are also rare, but John of Wales, a Franciscan, had studied in both Oxford and Paris. His compilation, *Summa Collectionum* (1283), useful for preachers but lacking any individuality, was much admired by contemporaries.[135]

One of the reasons why so many Englishmen achieved distinction in Paris is that they had been well provided at home for more advanced study. They went abroad already convinced of the value of learning. University studies had such great impact on the development of English diocesan organisation that in retrospect the promotion of universities may look like a calculated response to the papal reform programme launched in 1215. This was not so. The Lateran decrees had rather laid down that every diocese should have its own resident teacher of theology to provide what training parish clergy might require. There is no evidence that the Lateran proposal for a diocesan theologian was taken up in England. Neither of the two English universities was even sited in the episcopal sees of their respective dioceses. Nor are university teachers in England and France known to have encouraged their students to think of the needs of the pastoral ministry. Although university teaching expanded enormously in the thirteenth century, it had the least impact at the level of the parish. Like other patrons, bishops took advantage of the availability of graduates to improve the quality of their administrations, but the universities did not reckon to turn out graduates even for this purpose.

In England, the most prominent teacher at Oxford in the early years of Henry III was Robert Grosseteste, who may never have studied abroad but had a profound effect on the development of learning in the kingdom.[136] Though his own scientific work, on optics, is indebted to his Muslim predecessors, he was chiefly notable for his active encouragement of the study of Greek in England. As bishop of Lincoln he sent to Greece itself for manuscripts and gave a canonry at Lincoln to a Greek scholar, Nicholas of Sicily, who assisted with his translations. Grosseteste made a substantial contribution to Christian thought with his Latin translation of Aristotle's *Nicomachean Ethics*, of which over 300 manuscripts are known. Grosseteste's intellectual work as bishop was done at Lincoln rather than

Oxford and the lack of any obvious relationship between the schools at Oxford and the bishop's base at Lincoln indicates how informal the development of learning could still appear in the first half of the thirteenth century. Grosseteste did his best to attract distinguished scholars to his service as bishop and no doubt encouraged them to keep up with their studies. But he also engaged learned men for the administrative work in the diocese. His archdeacon of Leicester was John of Basingstoke, himself distinguished for his knowledge of Greek. He had learnt this in Athens from an erudite young lady (as Matthew Paris has it). He translated a Greek grammar into Latin for the benefit of future students and was responsible for introducing into England a knowledge of Greek numbers.[137]

Another scholar drawn into Grosseteste's circle was John of St Giles (Flamstead, Hertfordshire) who became archdeacon of Oxford. At the time, John was probably the most famous physician in England. Where he had studied medicine is not known.[138] Subsequently he turned to theology and taught in Paris, becoming a Dominican in 1230 when the university was closed. He went to teach at Toulouse but returned to England in 1235 and was immediately engaged to accompany Henry III's sister Isabella to Germany for her marriage to Frederick II. He gave Henry III the news of her first pregnancy and on his return to England joined Grosseteste's staff. His distinction was appreciated by Matthew Paris. His most dramatic public appearance was at the execution for treason and piracy of Walter de Marisco, whose final confession he heard. John's versatility as teacher, confessor, preacher, doctor and administrator as well as his experiences of France and the royal courts of Germany and England make him one of the most notable men of his age.

Only during the latter part of the thirteenth century did Oxford effectively become capable of providing all the education necessary for university students. This made resort to Paris a matter of choice, rather than one of normal progression. The two greatest scholastic teachers from Britain, Duns Scot and William of Ockham, both still went on from Oxford to Paris, not to sharpen their edge but to advance their influence. Quite how Oxford developed this independence from Paris is elusive and currently subject to investigation. Political tensions do not seem to have had the effect of making Paris any less attractive for study, or France any less welcoming to English students. Oxford simply became more confident of its own powers and began to benefit from the provision of establishments for study, halls and colleges, three of these by Edward I's reign and two more under his successor. Many Scots went to Oxford, where Dervorgilla de Balliol set up a college for northern students in 1257. Before the effect of college foundations for seculars to study became felt, the university's best known teachers had been friars. Thanks to papal patronage two of their most distinguished teachers, Kilwardby and Peckham, became archbishops of Canterbury in succession.

The most independent English teacher of the late thirteenth century was the Franciscan, Roger Bacon, whose scientific interests have made him famous in modern times. Even in his own day he acquired an international reputation. His *Opus Tertium* was written for the French pope Clement IV, at the pope's request.[139] Bacon's insistence on his own independence of mind may reflect a tendency at Oxford to harbour suspicions about the views of Parisian masters. One of the difficulties about discussion of these intellectual debates is that information about the movements of masters between the two universities is so casual. What has been established is that the style of teaching in Oxford began to change in this period. Instead of composing the traditional commentaries on set texts, Oxford teachers preferred to raise general questions in less structured works called '*quodlibets*', which aimed to tease out the meanings and implications of texts. This encouraged a more speculative approach to learning and sharper argument. Oxford became most famous for the study of Logic. In practice, as the number of students at the university rose, the number who went on to Paris may have remained steady. In the last decades of the century, the Oxford teachers had become much more confident of their powers to hold and defend opinions not necessarily accepted in Paris, without incurring accusations of heresy. The scholars there no longer held Paris in awe. When the bishop of Carlisle asked Boniface VIII to allow Oxford graduates the privilege of lecturing anywhere, as enjoyed by Paris graduates, he assumed parity of esteem for the two universities.[140]

The close relationship between Oxford and Paris is borne out by surviving manuscripts of the new Aristotle. The Latin translations were accompanied by commentaries to make them intelligible and wide margins were left for readers to make additional annotation and glosses. The model for the complicated page layout came from the legal textbooks of Bologna, an indication of how academic disciplines could interact.[141] Whereas legal books seem to have been copied mainly in Italy, however, Aristotle was in such demand that his works were copied in both the northern universities and scholars are often uncertain whether such texts were written in Paris or in Oxford. Competent scribes were attracted to both university towns; teachers and pupils in both universities required copies in similar form.

Religious orders

University study in this period looms so large in historical accounts that it obscures the continuing importance of the regular religious life in thirteenth-century Britain. As with the friars, the international character of the religious orders explains how some Englishmen became prominent members of continental houses. The English chronicler of Prémontré did not explain how he came to be living in a monastic community abroad. Most likely it has something to do with his abbot, Gervase, who was also English. Abbot Gervase had not wandered into international responsibility. Before becoming a regular canon he had studied in Paris, and his election as abbot was not the culmination of his career, for he eventually became bishop of Séez (1220–29), well after the king of England had been expelled from Normandy.[142] The career of Gervase abroad shows how well connected an Englishman could become in his day. His surviving correspondence focuses on his efforts to revive the fortunes of his order on a truly international scale, from Norway to eastern Europe, southern Italy and the Holy Land. He was on familiar terms with Innocent III, several cardinals, Stephen Langton and other English clergy. Many of them were probably old university friends. He corresponded with prominent laymen, like King Ottokar of Bohemia and William des Roches, seneschal of Anjou. Despite his preoccupations elsewhere, he kept a close eye on the political affairs of his native land, fretting about John's relations with the barons, the attitude of the pope and of some clergy, like those who invited Louis of France to intervene.

Because of the close involvement of its English houses with Prémontré itself another Englishman, William, abbot of Dale, became head of the order in the 1230s. He had been entrusted by Gregory IX with a mission to Norway and was much respected. The Frisian chronicler of the house at Mariengaarde commended his zeal and commitment to the ideals of the order. Under William, however, the order became much divided. French abbots were accused of being slack about discipline, but they proved strong enough in the end to force William out and he retired to the Premonstratensian house of Bayham (near Tunbridge Wells).[143]

Like the Premonstratensians, the Cistercians had their own institutional framework for keeping all the houses in touch with the order's main continental centres. From the late twelfth century, the surviving records from the annual chapter meetings of the order at Cîteaux enable us to see what problems had to be addressed. The most serious challenge facing the order in these islands was presented by the breakdown of discipline in Ireland. Even in the east of the island where the Cistercians were first established in strength, enthusiasm for the new order waned: Irish monks were accused of failing to live up to Cistercian requirements. Though critics blamed the Irish for their lack of discipline, from their side the Irish felt let down by the new monasticism. Whereas traditional Irish monks had been devoted custodians of Old Irish learning, Cistercians showed no interest in the Irish past and aimed to serve as channels for the transmission of continental practice. By 1228 the situation had become so serious that the Cistercian general chapter entrusted Stephen of Lexington, then abbot of Stanley, with the delicate mission of reforming the Irish houses. Stephen was deeply discouraged by the conduct of several monks and his attempts to remedy the situation encountered resistance. But he discharged his duties conscientiously and was rewarded by election to the abbacy of the great Norman house of Savigny; from there he became abbot of Clairvaux itself. Within a few years he incurred the hostility of his monks. They appealed to the pope against him for infringing the constitutions of the order. With evident reluctance, the pope felt cornered into asking for his resignation. It can only be sur-mised that their foreign background contributed to the difficulties experi-enced by William at Prémontré and Stephen at Clairvaux or that their (maybe) autocratic style of abbatial rule ran counter to continental expecta-tions. It is worth recalling that Ralph, the English dean of Reims, had had similar experiences. The most likely explanation is not national antipathy, but the simple difficulty of being an outsider in communities that were basically very local.[144] What is more to the point is that in the first half of the century Englishry was no impediment to advancement in their orders. As Englishmen, they had won high reputations and were called accordingly to great responsibilities.

Cistercian abbots from Britain expected to attend the annual chapter at Cîteaux in person and matters of discipline were normally raised and cor-rected on those occasions. Without evidence from elsewhere as corrobora-tion, the Cistercian chapter statutes offer some idea of how Welsh houses kept in touch with their continental brethren. Some houses attracted more attention than others. Whereas Neath, Margam and Gratia Dei appear sev-eral times in the records, other houses such as Caerleon, Aberconway, Llantarnan, Strata Florida, Basingwerk and Valle Crucis hardly figure at all. The Cistercian chapter agreed to include the name of Llewelyn's brother David in their prayers. (Such prayer fellowships clearly counted for much. The abbey of Prémontré similarly accepted the name of Rhys ap Maredudd.[145])

The records of the Cistercian general chapters occasionally cast inci-dental light on Welsh affairs. In 1217 the abbot of Strata Florida was deposed for writing to a Roman cardinal, without permission from the abbot of Cîteaux. Unfortunately there are no details of what was written to help explain what seems like a drastic punishment. Forty years later the resources of the same abbey had become so slender that it petitioned to be excused its religious obligation to offer hospitality for three years. In 1247 Neath Abbey, also bewailing the collapse of its revenues on account of the disturbances caused by frequent and widespread warfare, asked permis-sion to celebrate the feast of St Margaret, hoping to restore its fortunes by attracting pilgrims. The Cistercian records have more to say about the Welsh houses in the first half of the century than the second, but they are never very illuminating. Neighbouring Cistercian houses seem to be in regular disputes with one another, which other near abbots of the order were expected to resolve. The plans of Madoc ap Gruffydd to found a house at Valle Crucis were held up while commissioners discovered if he had a legitimate title to the property (1218). The Cistercian chapter's con-cerns were often extended to the economic problems of the houses. Strata Florida was in dispute with a citizen of London. A conversus of Neath was in trouble for selling hides, but so insolent that, to the scandal of the chapter, he mocked his judges. The Welsh give the impression of operating on the periphery of the order's affairs, but the order itself paid more attention to Welsh needs than the Welsh themselves gave to the affairs of the Western Church.

One Welsh Cistercian with continental experience was Cadwgan, abbot of Strata Florida, then of Whitland, whom Llewelyn ap Iorwerth made bishop of Bangor (1215–36). A colourful figure of some learning, he wrote several works, including a Latin treatise for the clergy of his diocese on how to hear confessions. He showed familiarity with the similar work of Robert Curzon, written at Paris 1208–13, and Raymond of Penyaforte's *Summa de Penitentia*, which was known in England soon after 1222. Cadwgan was said by Gerald of Wales to have been born in Pembrokeshire to an itinerant Irish priest and to have been an effective preacher himself in Welsh. In his retirement at the abbey of Dore, he was criticised in 1239 for not keeping the rule of silence. One of his merits, however, was that in his time he aimed to keep the clergy of north Wales abreast of recent affairs on the Continent.[146]

The Cistercian network must have provided much of the information about continental events noted in Welsh annals. At Margam, the annalist provided a very full account of the Spanish battle of Las Navas derived from the letter sent by the Cistercian archbishop of Narbonne, Arnaldus Amalricus, to the general chapter of Cîteaux. Probably from Cîteaux, the Margam annalist obtained the story of the Swedish abbot with miraculous powers of healing the sick. Less easily explained is the notice of an earthquake at Brescia on Christmas Day 1222 where 2000 men perished. The importance for a monastery of contact with its lay founders is apparent from the Margam annalist's vivid account of John's coronation, with its reference to his formal ineligibility for the kingship, to the rights of Arthur and the consequences of Arthur's murder.[147]

The chronicle kept at the Scottish Cistercian house at Melrose also derived much of its information about events abroad from its contacts in the order.[148] The annual chapters were obviously the main source of its information about foreign appointments, like that of the abbot of Cîteaux made archbishop of Narbonne. The reports in the chronicle about the heretics of the Albigeois were surely derived from the same source. An agreement that the regular sums due from the monastery at Coupar to Cîteaux should be paid at the Troyes fair in Champagne hints at other advantages attaching to these annual visits. This payment was something of a thank offering for the good offices of the abbot of Cîteaux in 1218 who had helped to get the interdict lifted from Scotland.[149] A letter inserted into the chronicle about the interception and imprisonment by Frederick II's sailors of Cistercian abbots on their way to the proposed papal council of 1241 may have provoked a more general interest in the nature of the quarrel between the pope and emperor. When the final showdown occurred at the Council of Lyon in 1245, no Scottish bishops are known to have been present. The chronicler who copied out Innocent IV's letter explaining why he had excommunicated Frederick and called for a fresh election to the empire, then simply appended

Frederick's own refutation of the papal case, covering this apparent incon-
sistency by referring to the emperor as 'reprobate'. Though Scotland was
informed, it was much more detached from this great dispute than England
could be.

Preoccupation with its own order more than any general interest in
Scotland rather defines the character of the Melrose chronicle. Mainly
because a few Cistercian abbots were promoted to Scottish bishoprics,
episcopal elections were noted. These often involved appeals to Rome,
not only because there were rival candidates but because the king
remained imperious about getting his own way. As in England, such
domestic squabbles had their international repercussions. The chronicle
also noticed the arrival of papal legates for Scotland and Ireland. One
legate took the opportunity to promote an abbot of Melrose to the Irish
see of Down. Melrose appreciated the importance of maintaining close
contact with the Curia. Cardinal Otto, who had long resided as papal
legate in England, visited Scotland in 1239 and after his return to the
Curia interceded in 1245 with the Cistercian chapter on behalf of
Melrose. The very fitful references to the affairs of the wider world show
that information was jotted down when it seemed interesting, like the
alarmed notice about the arrival of the Mongols, but such lines are not
pursued subsequently. Of foreign affairs, only those of the Holy Land
received regular attention at Melrose.

Responsibility for keeping the record up to date was assumed by several
different writers until 1263, with only occasional notices for another dozen
years. This was probably another consequence of the troubled phase of
Melrose's history shown up by the Cistercian general chapter statutes. At
Melrose the abbot was deposed in 1266 for himself unjustly deposing the
abbot of its daughter house at Holme. In 1275 a monk of Melrose, Brother
Thomas, had caused his abbey much grief by obtaining false letters for a
loan in the Roman Curia. All the abbots of the order were ordered to be on
the lookout to catch him and invoke the help of the secular authorities if
necessary. The next year, the abbot of Melrose was excused attendance for
one year, probably for reasons of economy after its difficulties with Brother
Thomas. That links between the Scottish houses and Cîteaux itself might be
rather fitful is indicated by the report in 1250 that a previous decision about
the penance imposed on Coupar for its shortcomings had not been delivered
as it should have been by Newminster, so communication even between
Scottish houses themselves cannot have been very effective. Monks were
not, however, the only ones to visit the leading Cistercian houses abroad.
On his return from the crusade in 1273, Robert Bruce, for example, paid his
respects to the shrine of saint Malachi at Clairvaux and gave land in
Annandale to the abbey for the provision of a light to burn perpetually at
Malachi's tomb.[150] The patchy quality of information about Scottish links
with foreign religious houses is nowhere more obvious than in the case of
the hermit monks of the order of Vallis Caudis from Burgundy who arrived

in Scotland in 1230. They were installed in three priories in the outlying regions of the kingdom recently brought under royal control: Argyll, Ross and Moray.[151] In a psalter copied and illustrated in Paris for the Argyll house at Ardchattan, the names of some early Irish saints have been inserted into a predominantly English calendar, evidence for the Burgundian monks' wish to identify with the local religious tradition. This Burgundian house never had English priories and how the Scots became involved with Vallis Caudis is a mystery.

The Burgundian congregation with the most enduring interests in these islands was Cluny, from whose archives have survived several accounts of visitations made of the English priories, usually by one prior of an English house accompanied by a prior from one of the French houses.[152] Thorough visits might take more than three months to complete, either in summer or winter, and could not therefore be annual occasions. At Lewes many problems began after the priory was caught up in the civil war of 1264. In 1266 several monks had to be removed to Cluny itself for starting what was described as an insurrection in the priory. Most Cluniac priories were found to be in good spiritual order by the visitors. The most common criticism of the priors was that they rode abroad without cruppers or ate meat with laymen. Criticism of the management of the temporal properties was confined to a few individual houses, though by the 1290s visitors everywhere found the priories mismanaged and burdened with debts. But it was not all criticism. Some visitors went so far as to praise the church at Barnstaple Priory and describe the church and cloister at Thetford as 'beautiful'. Most of the monks must have been English, but it was expected that the priors would be French. The occasional English priors could, however, be commended: at Carswell the prior was *bonus, sapiens, humilis, et discretus, licet Anglicus*; at Monks' Horton, the prior was of *vite honeste et redolentis fame*. At Wenlock, when the visitors took advantage of the absence of a prior suspected of being untrustworthy to question the monks more closely about the state of their debts, the monks were still very reluctant to tell tales about him. Some French priors made sufficient impression to secure the headships of prominent Cluniac houses back in France, like Milo, prior of Lewes, who became abbot of Vézelay in 1274.

Even without being affiliated to a religious order, Benedictine houses, like St Albans, had their own contacts abroad, though such relations remained occasional rather than regular.[153] When Cardinal William was sent by Innocent IV to Norway for the belated coronation of Haakon Haakonson in 1247 he paused in England on his way.[154] The chronicler Matthew Paris also went to Norway at the pope's behest and this provoked reflections about unfamiliar people and places. English contacts with Norway remained important on both sides of the North Sea. The Englishman, Abbot Lawrence of Hovedo, in Norway helped in the negotiations for the coronation. Monks who were frequently abroad, especially in Rome for their affairs, like those of Canterbury, cannot have remained unaware of the major events even if they confined their own written comments to immediate business.

Religious motives are also likely to have prompted considerable numbers of laymen to move about in Christendom, given that there were far more of them than there were clergy. Pilgrimage remained a popular reason for travel and pilgrims probably always preferred to do so in company. On their behalf, the royal envoy in Castile negotiated special concessions in matters as important to pilgrims as freedom to choose their own lodging and the right to buy food without consulting their hosts. He is unlikely to have done so for a minority interest.[155] Far more people went to Spain to visit the shrine of St James at Compostela than ever went to study. The cockleshell mementoes of these pilgrimages were the foreign objects most commonly introduced into medieval Britain. In Scotland, the priory of St James had been founded at Paisley in 1159 by William Stewart. His descendant, Alexander, is the first Scot known to have made the pilgrimage to Compostela in 1254, probably in connection with Prince Edward's marriage at Burgos in October that year. He was followed by Walter de Lindsay in 1260, in 1263 by the justiciar, in 1291 by the earl of Atholl, all visits known for reasons incidental to the journey itself.[156] Such journeys had become commonplace and scarcely aroused chroniclers' interests; the cult had clearly spread to Scotland by then, though the name James itself did not become common until later. From Ireland too, by 1220, enough pilgrims for Santiago were expected at Dublin for Archbishop Henry to establish a hostel for those awaiting ships bound for Spain.[157]

The easy movement of clergy and devout laymen within the Christian community was guaranteed by respect for the ecclesiastical order over which the pope presided. The reigns of only four popes between 1198 and 1254 gave the medieval Church a stability and coherence unparalleled before or since. Looking back, historians point out that these popes had many grievous problems to deal with: the crusade, heresy, the quarrel with the emperor, disputes between religious communities themselves. The popes were not always successful in their policies or wise in their decisions. The difficulties experienced by their successors were in large measure the result of excessive papal confidence earlier that the Church of Rome had the right and the power to impose its will on others. Whatever historians may see now, at that time western Christians believed that the papal order was divinely ordained to help men attain salvation. In this period the people of these islands embraced the new opportunities for cultivating their spiritual lives with supreme confidence.

8

Coming to grips with France

In mid-century, Matthew Paris intended to lay down his pen and conclude his chronicle appropriately with a summary of the events of the previous fifty years (effectively his own lifetime). He reckoned this had been the most eventful of the twenty-five half-centuries since the beginning of the Christian era.[1] However dramatic the first half of the thirteenth century, Paris would surely have been even more impressed by the unpredictable turn of events in the second. Most worrying were events in the east. After the Greeks recovered the city of Constantinople from the Latins (1261), the lands of the former empire, far from serving any longer as a base for sustaining more effective crusades, became a battleground between rival statelets. Louis IX's efforts to put fresh heart into Christian resistance in the Holy Land (1250–54) may have kept crusading ardour alight in the west for another generation, but failed to prevent the steady recovery of Islam. The new Mamluk sultans of Egypt pressed on with the reconquest of the Holy Land; Acre, the last outpost, fell in 1291. The Mongols who destroyed the caliphate of Baghdad in 1258, themselves eventually became Muslims, dashing earlier hopes of converting them to Christianity.

The Mongols still did not lose all their attractions for westerners. Venetian merchants saw how they might benefit commercially from the Mongol Empire. When Marco Polo's father and uncle returned from their visit to the Mongol court, Edward I was in the Holy Land and surely conversed with them, for Marco Polo himself later carried a letter from Edward to the court of Hulagu's son. This was the first of several letters Edward despatched to eastern rulers in the next thirty years.[2] Marco Polo's reminiscences of his time with the Mongols were written up by a professional writer, Rusticiano of Pisa, who had himself met Edward I and been lent by him a book of Arthurian romances.[3] Edward continued all his life to maintain contact with eastern rulers. In 1275 he wrote to the Mongol Khan, Abaga, in connection with a letter originally addressed to the pope. Three years later Edward received envoys from the king of Armenia. From Burgos, in 1279, the king of Castile sent on to Edward a certain Henry Bartlet who had been in 'Tartary'. In the next decade Edward was putting questions to the pope about the situation in the east and himself being urged to take action. As late as 1292 Edward was in touch with King Andrew of Hungary about the crusade. Towards the end of the century, he was still sufficiently optimistic about getting a Muslim alliance against the Egyptian enemies of the crusading states to send an embassy for this purpose to Persia.[4]

Western concern for the east was sustained not by any serious assessment of what could actually be achieved, but by a religious fervour for the holy places and a sense of duty to serve on crusade. Henry III himself had been moved to take the cross in 1250. Though he never departed on campaign, he was eventually allowed by the pope to convert his vow into the Sicilian project, for which he was granted crusading taxes on the English Church. This crusading taxation was exacted even during the period of his troubles with the barons. After these were resolved, the crusade was preached again in 1268 and Cardinal Ottobuono imposed a papal tenth to help meet the costs. Edward I, who had left for the east in 1270, was still there when his father died in 1272 and did not hasten back to England. After his return, Edward intended to resume crusading when his problems at home gave him an opportunity. Meanwhile he subsidised the Latin outposts in the Holy Land. While out east, Edward had contributed to the defence of Acre by building a tower, then entrusted to the Provost and Confraternity of St Edward which remained a continuing obligation. Edward also supported the house dedicated to St Robert of Knaresborough, which Richard of Cornwall had given to the Trinitarian brothers, to help them in the work of ransoming Christian captives in Muslim hands. In 1279 Edward renewed a grant to the Teutonic Order in Jerusalem of an annual pension of 40 pounds. In 1281 he took the Canons and Brethren of the Holy Sepulchre into his protection. The king's *familiaris*, Otto de Grandison, was actually in Cyprus in 1292 when he asked his friends in England to despatch one of his yeomen with a horse laden with cloths and other things he needed.[5] When the Muslim revival drove the hermits of the order of Carmelites from Mount Carmel, they received a sympathetic welcome in England. The first western minister-general of the order was Henry, an Englishman; a later English minister, Simon Stock, was canonised.[6]

The Scots had also been drawn more deeply into the crusading movement. At the time of Louis IX's first crossing, the papacy had imposed a tax of one-twentieth on ecclesiastical revenues. In Scotland, the Dominican bishop of Dunblane, the collector designated, raised as much as 3000 pounds tours from this tenth and from the commutation of crusading vows, all of which was to be handed over to named Scottish crusaders. Two and a half years later Richard Giffard, a kinsman of the king who was going east with five knights, got 400 marks from this same fund and suitable sums were paid to his three cousins. The marriage of Alexander II's widow, Marie de Coucy, to John of Acre, son of the king of Jerusalem, in 1257 may have stirred fresh interest in the crusading movement.[7] The Templars and Hospitallers received benefactions in Scotland and the Holyrood chronicler was sufficiently intrigued by what he heard to make a reference to the Hospitallers' carrier-pigeon service in the east.[8] When Ottobuono had imposed a papal tenth for the Lord Edward's crusade, he treated Scotland as though it were a mere adjunct to England and expected the Scots to pay up. Alexander III surprised the legate by declining to subsidise his brother-in-law's campaign and sending the cardinal's envoys back empty-handed.[9] The king did not deter Scots from going on crusade. The earl of Athol joined Louis IX at Tunis, where he died in 1270 along with Ingram de Balliol and perhaps others; the earl of Carrick instead served with Edward's party. The Melrose chronicle followed events closely, giving a story about a squire Nicholas attending the Scottish knight Alexander of Setun there and how Edward himself escaped an assassination plot. Edward's aims on crusade were said to have been thwarted by Charles of Anjou's truce with the Saracens, hinting at the tension between those who participated in the two different campaigns and implying some sympathy for Edward's reaction.[10]

The fate overhanging the crusading enclave in the east became the principal concern of Pope Gregory X (1272–76), but the pope concentrated on securing regular funding to subsidise its defences rather than on recruiting military contingents. This was no easy task. Master Baiamund de Vitia, canon of Asti, chaplain of Cardinal Ubert, was sent to Scotland to collect the tenth of ecclesiastical revenues voted for six years at the Council of Lyon II in 1274; after eight years in the northern kingdom he asked to be relieved of his post in 1282. The king himself declined to take the cross as the pope urged and was said by Baiamund to have forbidden him to pay over the crusade money to the Italian merchants. Baiamund was then accused of lending the money he had collected for his own personal advantage and was summarily recalled in disgrace.[11] That there was still money to be got out of Scotland, however, is confirmed by Edward I's pleas to the pope for a say in the nomination of the Scots collectors. He claimed, already, to have inside knowledge of Scotland.[12]

Worries about the Holy Land were not the only problems facing the Church in the second half of the thirteenth century. The effective disappearance of the medieval Western Empire as a force in Christendom had created a political void it proved difficult to fill. After his formal deposition in 1245, Frederick II had still remained the pre-eminent ruler of the west until his death in 1250, but thereafter no Roman emperor until Charles V two and a half centuries later enjoyed comparable distinction among the rulers of their day. The efforts of the Staufen heirs failed to arrest the crumbling of imperial power. Innocent IV had been warned of the potential dangers of his policy towards Frederick II by both Louis IX and Henry III. The papacy's right to excommunicate the emperor was not in doubt but to depose him was controversial. It was provocative to do so in an ecclesiastical council and the decision was undoubtedly injudicious. Innocent IV did not reckon with the political problems created by his decree of deposition. In Germany, the papal partisans supposed that minor princes could be hoisted into the saddle and that as long as they discharged their political responsibilities to ecclesiastical satisfaction all the troubles created for churchmen by Frederick would be resolved.

None of these German kings ruled in Italy and without Italy no German ruler could give the imperial concept of the past any substance. Although the coherence provided by the Staufen dynasty for over a century had lapsed, the Western Empire nominally survived in Germany. Even so, at a time when only dynastic monarchies proved capable of holding kingdoms together everywhere else in Europe, the survival of elective kingship in Germany prejudiced its future development. Whatever satisfaction the papacy derived from seeing the power of the Roman Empire shrivel away, the practical outcome for European politics was disastrous.

The direct cause of this eclipse of the empire was the implacable opposition of the papacy to Frederick II, who had shown himself to be effective enough as a ruler to make the papacy fear both for its own independence in Italy and for its aspiration to direct European affairs in the Church's interest. The papal triumph over the Staufen did not, however, bring about the expected benefits. Not all the clergy of Frederick's own kingdoms were sympathetic to the papal programme and were anyway, on their own, not sufficient to secure general acceptance of the pope's candidates for kingship. Spiritual sanctions were inadequate to terminate Frederick's rule, so the papacy was obliged to find secular allies prepared and able to do the dirty work on behalf of the Church. This involved taking the interests of its champions into account. The task set them was considerable. Military resources had to be mustered from outside the Staufen territories and would have to be paid for. It is symptomatic of the papacy's political naivety that it believed it could not only buy what support it needed on its own terms, but that its alleged right to tax the whole Western Church would provide it with inexhaustible funds. The clergy of England and France are known to have been reluctant contributors, not in the main because of their sympathy for the Staufen, but because they had no wish to pay taxes at all. Taxpayers have been grumbling ever since about governments whose authority they dare not challenge.

The clergy's recognition of the pope as God's vicar on earth made it impossible for them to challenge papal taxation in principle. Popes were anyway not disposed to listen to grievances. In the hands of obedient, well-educated clergy, the resources of churchmen were accordingly assessed and attempts made to distribute tax equitably. In England, these assessments provide the earliest official evidence for the valuation of every church and chapel in the kingdom.[13] Because the money raised from the churches was eventually spent on military contingents, secular rulers became as interested as the pope in this then novel device for funding warfare. Within two generations, all European rulers had begun to impose regular taxation not only on their clergy but on laymen as well. They drew from Roman law the justification that in cases of urgent necessity they too had a 'right' to tax and might indeed demand money from their 'own' clergy without prior papal approval. So far from exalting the power of churchmen in secular affairs, the papacy had shown kings the way to stake out a claim to a share of ecclesiastical riches. Once this had been accomplished, the papacy's own power to restrain royal ambitions was diminished. The apparent triumph of papal principles against imperial pretensions had actually called into being a number of smaller states, some strong, some weak. The empire was gone, but the 'secular state' had arrived and popes found that kings within their own territorial limits could be as intractable as emperors.

If the fortunes of the Church did not improve as much as Innocent IV had anticipated from the collapse of the Staufen family, one of the reasons was that after Innocent's death, a succession of short-lived popes deprived the Church of resolute direction. Cardinals were themselves too divided and confused to advise on policy and some long vacancies in the papal office ensued (1268–72, 1291–94) when they failed to agree on a suitable candidate. Celestine V, who was chosen for his holiness in 1294, lasted only months before his incompetence to deal with the problems needing papal decisions brought about his enforced abdication. This raised some doubts about the validity of the election of his successor, Boniface VIII, whose authority was challenged and his person finally insulted by officials of the king of France. In the first decade of the next century, the papacy began its long absence from Italy altogether. The papacy admittedly remained indispensable to the well-being of Christendom, but it could no longer count on the submission Innocents III and IV had secured.

In Italy, the long-term consequences of papal policies were even more dire, but initially Germany was hit hardest, since Innocent IV's deposition of Frederick II had immediately unleashed civil war. Successive papal candidates, Henry of Thuringia (d.1246) and William of Holland (1247–56), confronted Frederick II's son, Conrad IV. By 1256, Conrad IV himself was dead and his heir Conradin a mere child. The princes of the Rhineland who took the lead in imperial elections perceived that the most powerful rulers they had to deal with had become the kings of France and England, long-standing rivals for dominance in the Low Countries of the Rhine estuary. In 1246 Louis IX had settled the dispute over the succession rights of the sons of Countess Margaret of Flanders by her two husbands, separating Flanders from Hainault, taking Flanders into his kingdom and leaving Hainault to the empire. This did not in fact settle the matter. William of Holland had understandably taken a keen interest in the dispute. Warfare over this had brought Louis's youngest brother Charles of Anjou into the region and the troubled outcome had finally persuaded Louis IX to return from the Holy Land.

The English with their traditional political and commercial interests across the North Sea were naturally concerned about these events. The cultivation of good relations in Flanders had been a point of English royal policy since the eleventh century and the subjection of Flanders to French royal interests was not welcome. This helps to explain why, after William was killed in Frisia in 1256, the English responded positively to the proposal of the German electors that Richard of Cornwall be chosen as their king.[14] This election redressed the balance in England's favour over France. From mid-century, efforts were made to confine French influence to French-speaking Flanders and bolster English contacts in adjacent lands like Hainault, Brabant, Holland and Guelders. This policy had some success in hobbling French ambitions until the Valois dukes of Burgundy brought all these diverse territories under their control in the fifteenth century. The legacy of Anglo-French rivalry in the Low Countries has reverberated for centuries and may, even now, enjoy a kind of afterlife at Brussels.

The consequences of papal opposition to the Hohenstaufen in Italy became even more dramatic for England. Frederick's southern kingdom, like England itself, was a vassal state of the papacy: there were no electors to take account of and Innocent IV considered himself entitled to appoint which ruler he chose. Initially he planned to rule this papal fief directly. When Conrad IV, unabashed by papal anathemas, came south in 1252 to claim his inheritance, the pope realised he had to find a secular prince with ambition, money and forces at his disposal to resist the Staufen. In practice, he had a choice between an English or a French prince. While Henry, Frederick's son by Isabella of England, was still living (he died early in 1254) there could be no question of English princes trying to deprive their Staufen nephew of his rights. Matthew Paris shows that Henry of Hohenstaufen kept in close touch with his English relations, even writing on behalf of his uncle Henry to Louis IX himself. Richard of Cornwall properly declined papal offers of the kingdom. Nor did Louis IX give the papal proposal his blessing; it was more than ten years before Louis's brother Charles was tempted to try his luck in the south.

In the meantime, the papacy's prospects had brightened before Innocent IV's death in December 1254 because Henry III had committed himself to the idea of his son Edmund becoming king of Sicily. The offer appeared to confirm his own importance to the papacy; it promised his second son a kingdom; by accepting for Edmund, he also pre-empted the expectations of any French prince to act on the pope's behalf. From Henry III's point of view, the Sicilian venture would enhance his general credit. Innocent's successor, Alexander IV, accordingly prepared for Edmund's installation, counting on English money to meet the cost. Henry III failed to see the dangers ahead and though baronial misgivings about Henry's plans were reported to the Curia in 1256 and 1257, the pope brushed aside the warning signs. How Henry III could ever have fallen for a scheme his own brother had refused was ascribed by Matthew Paris to the king's natural gullibility (*simplicitas*). However unwisely, Henry was tempted to assume this charge because the times seemed propitious for reviving the long-standing Plantagenet commitment to a European role. He was not merely tricked by popes; he nursed ambitions beyond his personal capacity for action. The Sicilian business precipitated a disastrous domestic upheaval from which Henry III's reputation as a ruler has never recovered.

In the European context, Henry III's commitment to Sicily, however unwise, still made a kind of sense. In the early 1250s, with Louis still abroad, Henry III's confidence owed something to the temporary absence of serious competition and was not altogether without substance. His own dominions were wealthy and he enjoyed the favour of the papacy. His main preoccupation since taking on responsibility for government in England had been to make peace with France on condition that he recover at least some of the lands lost in France by John. Despite his diplomatic and military efforts, nothing had been settled by the time Louis left for the east. On crusade, Louis enjoyed papal protection from attack at home. The ignominious failure of Louis's Egyptian campaign and his apparent determination to stay in the Holy Land presented Henry III with an opportunity to assert himself on the diplomatic front. The death of the regent Blanche in December 1252 had plunged the French kingdom into such disarray that, according to Matthew Paris, the French nobles even tried to persuade the earl of Leicester, Simon de Montfort, to become seneschal of the French kingdom.[15] To bolster his position Henry had already set about making friends all over Europe. He had some reason to hope that if ever Louis did agree to return to France, his own position would look much stronger than it had done some years earlier.

After the failure of his Poitevin campaign in 1243, Henry III had to concentrate his efforts to rule in his continental lands on Gascony. He soon realised that to do this he needed to reach agreement with the new king of Castile who himself had claims on Gascony going back fifty years. This was arranged with exceptional rapidity and Henry's heir, Edward, was married to Eleanor, half-sister of King Alphonso X, at Burgos in October 1254.[16] The basis of the alliance was mutual interest in the good order of Gascony and peaceful navigation of Biscay where Castile had interests of its own. The alliance offered something more than political friendship. It seemed to herald a new breakthrough in policy. By then Henry had accepted the offer of Sicily for Edmund. With one problem solved, Henry felt ready to take on another, gratified to be considered capable for once of a great enterprise.

That autumn, on his return from the east, Louis was sufficiently impressed by Henry's position to feel uneasy about his intentions and took appropriate measures to deal with a possible renewal of hostilities. Some Poitevin captains inspired enough distrust to be deprived of their posts in the kingdom; the defences of Normandy were reinforced.[17] Louis may have considered making some territorial concessions as a kinsman to Henry III. If Henry III cherished hopes of forcing Louis's hand, the favourable moment quickly passed. As soon as the Welsh began to cause major disruptions on the English border in 1256, English barons were so uneasy, they begged Louis not to take advantage of English vulnerability at this juncture.[18] Henry III was less anxious. Indeed, his brother's election in Germany encouraged him to think his political strength had been augmented because it would restrain any interference from there in Sicily. However slight the danger to France from Germany may seem now, Louis was himself perturbed by Richard's election and refused to allow Englishmen to cross his territory on their way out to Richard in Germany, a petty gesture that Henry III resented. In France, Richard's kingship may have strengthened the arguments of those who thought it sensible to secure a formal settlement with England, but terms of peace were elusive. Henry III was unwilling to sign away his lost lands without compensation and Louis's barons refused to contemplate the restoration of any of the conquered provinces. What brought England and France to a settlement was, in a sense not intended or appreciated, the Sicilian project.

To the surprise of both Henry and Alexander IV, the Sicilian kingdom showed an astonishing determination to resist papal domination. After the death of Conrad IV, the resurgence of the kingdom under his half-brother, Frederick's son Manfred, caused such alarm in Rome that the pope put Henry III under pressure to honour his obligations in Sicily. This precipitated a stormy encounter between Henry III and his barons in the spring of 1258. At this point, Henry's obvious weakness encouraged Llewelyn of Wales to propose a formal alliance with the Scots.[19] As Henry III floundered in the difficulties created by the Welsh, the pope and his barons, his inability to defend his own state in his own kingdom made it imperative to secure an agreement with Louis.

English historical accounts of the 'Sicilian' business invariably focus on the domestic issues, but neither the king nor the pope viewed the situation in this way.[20] For them, it was not so much Henry III's disputes with the barons as his difficulties with Louis IX that held up Edmund's arrival in the south. The interaction of papal policy, English relations with France and domestic disputes between the king and his barons immediately became highly intricate. The effects of domestic politics proved more serious for Henry III's plans than he had anticipated. Henry III's own weakness, not the numbers of kings on his side, eventually made peace with France possible. Henry accepted what he could not change and Louis graciously declined to take unfair advantage of the hapless Henry's predicament at home. The two kings were married to two sisters and sensitive to the claims of family. Agreement about the terms of the treaty was hard to secure, even under the pressure of political circumstances in Italy and, by that time, in England. That the treaty effectively kept the peace between the two kingdoms for thirty-five years is even more remarkable. But the character of English relations with the Continent was thereby totally transformed.

By the treaty of 1259, Henry III finally renounced his claims to the lands in France which Louis actually held. Any remaining ambiguity about the status of Gascony was removed by defining it as a fief of the French king-dom.[21] The role of the English king as duke of Gascony now seems both anomalous and unsustainable, but in 1259 neither Louis nor Henry considered that it would cause any more difficulties than that of king-duke in the twelfth century. The treaty that prescribed the relations between the king of France and king of England as duke of Gascony was also flexible enough to lay down different rules for other disputed territories comprised within the terms: the Agenais, the Saintonge and the three bishoprics, Périgueux, Limoges and Cahors. Settlement of these various issues was not considered urgent and was left for the future.

According to Louis IX's biographer, Joinville, the king justified the treaty as a means of improving their family relationships.[22] This explanation seems designed to deflect criticism from the saintly king for a decision that by the time Joinville wrote (he dated his book October 1309) made no sense. Changing perceptions of the treaty within two generations have caused the treaty to be picked over ever since for its inadequacies. Its merits have been disregarded. Henry III could not conceivably have renounced Gascony outright and the treaty gave formal satisfaction to both kings. Criticism that the treaty did not provide a permanent solution is misguided. No form of words can ever be found to last for ever. Treaties settle differences that are already clear and represent the best terms available at the time of negotiation. Even if they do successfully resolve the most pressing problems, they thereby create new situations that throw up other, unforeseen complications. The more obstinately the parties then attempt to deal with the new problems within the old framework, the more difficult it becomes to appreciate the novelties of the new situation. After 1259, the changes brought about by the treaty did not all become obvious at once. It seemed that outstanding difficulties could easily be settled by narrowing the focus to precise legal questions. Professional lawyers came to play the chief role in diplomatic negotiations. This had not been foreseen in 1259 and it was not the fault of the treaty that persistent efforts to resolve political problems by legal means ultimately exasperated both parties. The confidence of lawyers in their own ability to settle disputes made them obstinate.

By the time the treaty of Paris was finally agreed in May 1259, Henry III was in deep trouble at home with his barons, but he still did not regard this as more than a temporary inconvenience. Neither Henry III nor the pope yet realised that Edmund had effectively lost his chance of becoming king of Sicily. As late as the spring of 1261, Richard of Cornwall was negotiating with some of Alexander's cardinals and others for his entry as king of the Romans into Italy. Richard was actually elected Senator of Rome.[23] Then abruptly, in August, with the election of a new pope, the Frenchman Urban IV, Richard's plans collapsed. Urban decided that the papacy had a better chance of achieving its objectives if Charles of Anjou, count of Provence, became the papal champion in Italy. Urban arranged for Charles's election as Senator of Rome for life in 1263. Louis IX was still opposed to the idea, but Charles's Italian ambitions were given fresh impetus in 1265 when Louis's former counsellor, Guy Foulques, was elected to succeed Urban as Clement IV. Only at this point was Edmund formally deprived of his title on the practical grounds that in over ten years Henry III had honoured neither his financial nor his military commitments to Sicily. When Charles eventually invaded Italy he was in no better position financially than Edmund had been, but contrary to all reasonable expectations his risky enterprise paid off. Manfred was killed at the battle of Benevento in 1266 and Charles found his acquisition to be valuable beyond his dreams. Charles not only took the kingdom; as champion of papal interests, he was accorded uncontested respect throughout the peninsula. Henry III had accepted the offer of Sicily as part of his programme to establish his credentials with Louis IX. Charles's triumph became a demonstration that it was France, not England, the papacy would turn to in its need. The subordination of England's king to France's had a profound effect on the way European politics developed thereafter.

The French hegemony of Europe at first encountered no serious obstacles. Charles's success was promptly followed by an unprecedentedly long delay in electing a new pope (1268–72), a symptom of disarray in the Curia which left Charles arbiter of Italy. To serve Charles's own interests, even Louis IX's second crusade was diverted at the last moment to Tunis in 1270. The French pleased themselves about how they conducted their affairs. The defeat of the Staufen interest in Italy in 1266 was confirmed in 1268, when the young Conradin's attempt to recover his inheritance was defeated and the young prince brutally executed. Charles now had the whole peninsula at his mercy. This did not give total satisfaction, but it was not until the insurrection in Palermo, known as the Sicilian Vespers, in 1282 that a new force capable of countering French supremacy was introduced into Italian politics. The Sicilians induced the king of Aragon, husband of Manfred's daughter Constance, to come over as their champion. Provoked by their defiance, another French pope, Martin IV, unreservedly threw his weight behind France.

So far from liberating Italy, the death of Frederick II had therefore offered up the peninsula to the rival interests of the remaining great powers of the Continent, France and Spain. Competition between them took centuries to resolve. The southern kingdom, which had been the strongest political state of Italy, was fatally weakened. None of this was of any benefit whatever to England. Yet the way European affairs began to develop was in part the result of English domestic events. When the barons took advantage of the king's embarrassments over Sicily for their own purposes, they naturally did not concern themselves about the likely consequences abroad. Not that they were blind to international affairs, but understandably they put domestic issues first. 'Foreign' affairs were not their direct responsibility and Henry III had no wish to have the barons make an alternative policy on his behalf; all he asked of them was financial and military help to implement his own. He originally accepted baronial restraint only in the expectation that this would advance his plans for Edmund.

Henry's ambitions may now seem absurd, but had Henry been in as commanding a position at home as he thought he was entitled to, they were not as fantastic at the time as they soon appeared. Edmund's presumption was no greater than that of Charles of Anjou. Charles's success shows what Edmund's might have been. Henry's disappointment required a major readjustment of English policy. In the course of the second half of the thirteenth century, the political relations of England with the continent were accordingly transformed. As a result of the Treaty of Paris, the English too had become caught in French toils. The treaty had turned Louis IX into Henry's firm and dependable ally. Louis was prepared and able to supply him with a force of soldiers, originally so that he could carry out his commitments to the papacy in Sicily, but subsequently to help him with his domestic troubles. Louis's willingness to stand up for Henry III signalled that the two kings' old differences had definitely been put aside. It made it clear, however, that Henry now flourished only thanks to the backing of his French overlord. When in 1264 the English barons sought a trusted arbiter of their disputes with the king, they appealed not to the pope as in 1215, but to Louis. Their disappointment with his award brought them to the point of open confrontation with their own king in battle, but their victory at Lewes brought only ephemeral success. Henry, even as Montfort's prisoner, still had the pope and the king of France on his side. As Louis correctly perceived, the barons could not persist in their intransigence. The restoration of royal power after the defeat of Simon de Montfort at Evesham in 1265 brought about an accretion of royal strength in England for the first time since 1215. This gave Henry III's successor the confidence to behave in Britain as a sovereign ruler. As such, however, he (unrealistically) expected to be treated by the king of France as a royal ruler in charge of a loyal kingdom and not merely as his formal vassal for Gascony. The incompatibility of these roles eventually led to a great showdown with France and the beginning of centuries of hostility between the kingdoms.

The policy of Edward I

When Henry died in 1272, Edward I was still in the Holy Land, so the royal administration dealt only with routine business and postponed difficult problems until the king could deal with them himself. On his return to England in 1274 Edward, unlike his father on his accession, was already a man of great experience in public affairs, in peace and war, married with children and able to move confidently abroad with his foreign relations. The Treaty of Paris had made the king of France his friend rather than his foe. The troubles of the baronial wars had been resolved in favour of the monarchy and Edward was able and willing to provide the decisive direction of affairs his father had never mastered. Edward intended that he should never be hounded as his father had been. He would listen to grievances, but he would not tolerate insolence.

The character and intentions of Edward I have been been discussed endlessly; conclusions about him have differed widely, mainly because our sources of information are not of a kind that enables us to answer modern questions about personal motivation. For Edward, the problem is complicated by centuries of denigration from Scotland and Wales on account of his alleged intentions there. Recognition of his merits in England has not been sufficient to rescue his reputation. It is at least arguable that Edward only reacted to particular situations and had no long-term ambitions at all. He held firmly to what he believed to be his rights and could not tolerate the idea that these were in any way negotiable. On his return in 1274, Edward was most concerned about the obvious reluctance of Llewelyn, prince of Wales, to do the homage undoubtedly due. There is no reason to think that Edward was then bent on the subjugation of Wales. Given the disparity of their forces, it was reckless of Llewelyn to give Edward occasion to make war, but Llewelyn's attitude left Edward no alternative. Even then, after the first Welsh war which brought about Llewelyn's submission, Edward did not seek to suppress his principality. Such a course was no part of any long-term plans. Only when Edward decided that he could not rely on Llewelyn, or his brother David, to respect the terms of peace did he set about systematic conquest of what remained of independent Wales.

The absence of any long-term plan for Wales is replicated in Edward's dealings with Scotland. In the lifetime of his brother-in-law, Alexander III, Edward made no moves to subordinate the kingdom. After Alexander's death, Edward's proposal to marry his own heir to the Scottish heiress, Margaret of Norway, in 1290 carried no implications of disparagement for the northern kingdom. After her death, the Scots still had no misgivings about accepting Edward's adjudication for determining the succession to the Scottish throne. The elaborate precautions Edward took with his choice did not apparently threaten the kingdom he awarded to John Balliol in 1294. Only after the Scots made a formal alliance with Edward's adversary, the king of France, in 1295 did Edward invade Scotland and force Balliol to abdicate. At that time, he still had no premeditated scheme of government ready for Scotland. The various proposals made for it in the last decade of his reign only serve to show his continuing uncertainty about what might be the best solution. He accepted that the responsibility for resolving the problems rested with himself, so it is captious to think he was merely concerned to get his own way every time. But his changes of plan make it hard to detect what might be called settled 'policy'. Edward had become entangled in a conflict that he never understood to be incapable of resolution as he wished. In the process he provoked the Scots into finding not only an unexpected will to survive independently of England, but an ability to do so against all the odds and in the face of persistent English hostility. The formal Scottish alliance with the kings of France against Edward created a situation without precedent. For the next three centuries, indeed until the eighteenth century, Scottish enmity in the north continued to hamstring English ambitions on the Continent and to affect the course of English domestic government as well. In the early 1290s, such importance for Scotland and Wales in the affairs of England and Europe was totally unpredictable. Yet the evidence is clear. Edward's conduct of his war with France for the recovery of Gascony after 1294 was seriously hampered by his need to campaign in both Scotland and Wales. They may now be regarded as domestic, 'British' problems, but from Edward's point of view they were on a par with his French ones. Had there not been a war with France in 1295, the Scots would not have found an ally in their resistance to Edward. Edward's relations with France were as much part of the history of the British Isles as those with Wales and Scotland were.

If Edward's approach to Wales and Scotland is seen in such terms, it is easier to grasp the nature of his dealings with France itself. As a result of the baronial wars, Henry III and his family had grown closer to Louis IX. Louis had proved not merely an overlord but a dependable ally and the French could no longer be considered as enemies. Friendship with France replaced the previous reliance of English kings since John on papal support. Unlike his father, however, Edward had no need to feel personally so indebted to his French kinsmen as to lose sight of his own assets. He had been exposed at an early age to military experience and had no fear of engaging in warfare when he felt it necessary. His credentials as a crusader in the Holy Land gave him credit with popes, increasingly anxious and desperate about the deteriorating Latin Christian positions in the Near East. Edward accordingly figured prominently in the affairs of the whole Latin west, as conciliator of secular quarrels and potential leader of further crusading efforts. Not since Richard I had an English king enjoyed such prestige abroad and, as a full royal cousin of King Philip III, Edward was not prepared to treat Philip, still less his son Philip IV (1285–1314), with the deference expected by French kings of their other close relations.

Edward's political stature rankled sufficiently with French kings to make them counter Edward's independence by reminding him of his proper place in their kingdom as duke of Gascony. Edward felt, therefore, that in France he was not treated with adequate respect. He suspected that he was deliberately subjected to harassment in his efforts to get all that he was entitled to under the Treaty of Paris. Some issues had surfaced as early as 1260, but Henry was then too preoccupied with difficulties at home to treat them as substantial grievances.[24] The real problems for the English king in France only became inescapable under Edward I. He strove to resolve them, not by military confrontation or diplomatic pressure, but by legal arguments in the courts, case by case.[25] Because the most contentious issues arose from his own commitment to proceed within the strict limits of the law, he was nettled when the judgments of his ducal court were questioned and appeals launched against them in the courts of the king of France. This obliged him to keep a watchful eye on the legal situation lest any neglect of his duty as a vassal might cause more trouble. The Lusignan appeal to Philip II against John was an ominous precedent for what could happen.

Edward did not try to wriggle out of his obligations altogether. Indeed they were actually increased when his wife inherited the county of Ponthieu in the kingdom of France from her mother in 1279.[26] In no way did Edward's continental commitments diminish, even as the French kings' ambitions soared. By the time of Philip IV, the French king felt confident of his pre-eminence in Europe provided the king of England was kept trapped, as duke of Gascony, within the French kingdom. Edward's status as feudal vassal undoubtedly compromised his freedom to act internationally as king. Like his father before him, Edward accepted that if he was not willing to give up his own rights he had no alternative but to cultivate as many friends elsewhere as he could find.

Simply as duke of Gascony, Edward could not be blind to the effects of French dominance in European affairs, not merely for himself but for his neighbours, friends and relations. While he did his best to treat the French king respectfully in France, it is possible that he hoped his other foreign connections would help him contain further French ambitions. Edward's appreciation of the advantages of diplomatic friendships had begun with his own marriage as lord of Gascony to Eleanor of Castile. Edward understood the desirability of extending his influence by improving his connections with his other southern neighbours. At the beginning of his reign he undertook to marry his oldest daughter to the heir of the king of Aragon, a project that he persisted in despite papal disapproval after 1282. The hapless princess, married by proxy, never met her husband, King Alphonso III, who died childless in 1294. English relations with the other Spanish kingdom of Navarre improved after Edward's brother Edmund married Blanche of Artois, widow of King Henry. Edmund then ruled Champagne-Navarre until Henry's heiress, Jeanne, was old enough to be married to Philip IV of France.

Cultivating good friends in the south was prescient. In the longer term, the most powerful adversary of French ambitions to lord it over Europe came from Spain under the Habsburgs. The origins of this enmity can be traced to the thirteenth century and the kings of France were already aware of the possible implications for their own political dominance of competition from the Spanish kingdoms of Aragon and Castile. These had only recently emerged victorious from the centuries-long conflict with the Muslims. The boundaries of Castile had been extended as far south as Seville in 1248 and those of Aragon to Valencia in 1238. These kingdoms were far more formidable than in the past: stronger, richer and battle-hardened. Philip III was so confident of his clout in continental affairs as to send an army to settle a succession dispute in Castile on behalf of French interests in 1285. To his surprise, this campaign was unsuccessful. The

Spanish kingdoms had, however, been fully apprised of their French neighbour's ambitions.

The implications for English foreign policy of distant events had been starkly demonstrated over the Sicilian business. The fallout from Charles of Anjou's eventual success continued to create difficulties for Edward I, albeit of a different order. Edward had originally negotiated the marriage alliance with Aragon before the Vespers and was loath to abandon it despite papal opposition. Edward's relations with Aragon were more seriously strained by the imprisonment of his cousin, Charles of Salerno, negotiations for whose release cost Edward much trouble in the years 1288–91. In this region Edward I regarded himself as a natural go-between and popes appreciated his diplomacy. Edward I spent three years in Gascony (1286–89) shoring up his southern connections and trying to discharge what he thought of as his responsibilities for making peace between his various relations.[27] His eagerness to play such an active role in disputes to which he was not himself a party stretched his diplomatic skills to their limits.

Throughout his reign Edward I was regularly engaged with negotiating for the marriages of his large family of sons and daughters, not all of whom even lived long enough to be married. His expected heir, Alfonso, who died aged twelve, was nevertheless betrothed to a princess of Holland in 1281. When still only four, in 1276, Edward's daughter Joan was sought in marriage by Rudolf of Habsburg for his prospective heir, Hartmann. Edward agreed on condition that Rudolf procured the election of Hartmann as king of the Romans in order to provide for some continuity to Habsburg power. Arrangements were made to receive Hartmann in England, but before this could happen he was drowned in the Rhine.[28] In 1278 Edward began proceedings for a marriage between the three-year-old Margaret and the three-year-old John, heir of Brabant. The young people were married twelve years later and John spent many years both before and after his marriage in England before succeeding to the duchy in 1294.[29] The marriage of Edward I's youngest daughter Elizabeth to the count of Holland, planned at an equally early stage, was only celebrated in 1296. By that time, Edward I himself had become a widower, but one with plans for a second marriage. These had to be shelved because of war but eventually he did marry the king of France's sister Margaret as part of the peace settlement in 1299. At the age of sixty Edward then started a second family of two boys and a girl.

Never before had the rulers of the west been so closely related or so familiar with one another, person to person. Creating family relationships between rulers became a significant aspect of the way foreign affairs were conducted. These arrangements took for granted a system of hereditary rule throughout Christendom that offered some hopes of continuity in policy from one generation to another. It also assumed princes were effective masters of their dominions and that what princes promised as family men would be honoured by their subjects. Only in Germany did hereditary monarchy not emerge. The affairs of the empire had been comparatively straightforward as long as the Staufen had commanded respect. From the second half of the century even the smaller German princes began to behave independently. The frustration of Richard of Cornwall's Italian plans and papal support for Charles of Anjou thwarted hopes of giving the empire a new boost and left France with undisputed political influence. This was the situation confronting the Milanese Gregory X, elected pope in 1272 (the first non-French pope in over a decade). Gregory worked to provide for more stable governments in Germany and Italy as a necessary preliminary if effective assistance was to be offered from the west for the Christian Holy Land. The death of Richard of Cornwall in 1272 gave Gregory the chance to negotiate for the election of a new ruler in Germany: Rudolf of Habsburg. At the time, Rudolf was himself only another minor count, but he quickly confounded expectations by defeating the most powerful prince of the empire, Ottokar II, king of Bohemia in battle (August 1278) and making himself master of Austria. In this way, from a new base, he prepared for the eventual restoration of effective kingship in Germany. The significance of Rudolf's military victory was immediately apparent to the bishop of Verdun when informing Edward I about it, but Edward had already identified Rudolf as a prince worth cultivating.[30] Rulers needed to keep informed about one another's successes and problems if realistic calculations were to be made. Diplomacy came into its own.

Long before regular diplomatic relations between secular rulers became the norm, the papacy had been in the habit of sending representatives to the various parts of Christendom. The papal Curia had attracted some of the best educated men of the day to its service and their experience of how to arbitrate or judge intractable disputes among the clergy themselves and of composing letters of various kinds to settle grievances had already created a diplomatic resource on which secular rulers drew later. Because all the rulers of the day were related by marriage to one another and fresh marriages for the next generation were constantly in prospect, papal dispensations to marry within prohibited degrees of kinship had to be sought rather frequently. Permission was easier to obtain if popes were well disposed to the proposed alliance. Despite its own political weakness, therefore, the papacy could not be overlooked as a factor in international affairs. Independently of diplomatic negotiations with rulers, papal oversight of all the churches in the west gave the pope inside knowledge of all the European kingdoms. He was exceptionally well placed to mediate between rulers if necessary and regarded this as a natural extension of his role as head of the Church.

Secular princes could not be induced to do papal bidding, unless it was to their obvious secular advantage, but they were not predisposed to resent papal advice and they worked to keep the Curia on side. The writing styles and diplomatic language in Latin of the papal Curia influenced secular chancery practice. Bishops and abbots familiar with diplomacy at the papal Curia on their own account took naturally to the task of serving as envoys between rulers. But laymen too came to be closely implicated in diplomatic affairs. When royal marriages were in question, it was courteous to send distinguished members of the nobility on missions to the foreign ruler. Other laymen also began to take part in these exchanges, initially as mere couriers, but then with confidential missions. The greater finesse expected in diplomatic relations in the second half of the thirteenth century affected all rulers and the eventual preponderance of laymen in the exchange of confidential communication made French, rather than Latin, the language most frequently employed, both for written instructions to envoys or letters of introduction, and in the personal conversations of diplomats with the rulers to whom they were credited. This presented no difficulties for English spokesmen.[31] Some intimate conversations between English laymen and the pope might also be conducted in French. Only in Spain or Germany was French less commonly spoken, which is why envoys from those countries who had formerly been students at Paris made useful diplomats. France or Paris did not, however, in this respect offer superior advantages for diplomatic exchange to England where French was also the language of public discourse. In 1282 Spanish envoys to Germany passed through England and sought English diplomatic introductions to ease their path since it was more common for Iberian travellers to reach the northern lands by sea than overland across France. When Haakon IV of Norway negotiated a marriage for his daughter Christine with the king of Castile's brother, messengers on both sides passed through England. England's place at the centre of the northern waterways gave it a pivotal, not a peripheral role in diplomatic affairs.[32]

The nature of the contacts between rulers and the delicacy which was required by envoys for dealing on their master's behalf with foreign princes called for men of exceptional distinction and experience. Some envoys became so practised that they may be considered career diplomats. John Mansel and Roger Lovel under Henry III were already identified as experts. When Henry, abbot of Shrewsbury, was chosen to go as royal ambassador (a term first attested in 1280) to Castile, Mansel was asked to give him some tips about the country, though Henry may have had Spanish contacts of his own, having previously seen service at Rome with the English cardinal John of Toledo.[33] Later, Edward I and Alfonso X both depended on Master Geoffrey of Eversley as their go-between. After several years working in the papal chancery, Geoffrey had been recommended by the curial vice-chancellor to Spanish friends who introduced Geoffrey to Alfonso. As the king's emissary, Geoffrey travelled back to England on several occasions and became a trusted advisor in both kingdoms. For Alfonso 'the learned' Geoffrey wrote an 'Ars scribendi epistolas' and in it quoted letters from popes and kings, including the Muslim rulers of Murcia and Granada. Geoffrey was an international diplomat, well informed and much experienced.[34] English interest in Spain was fostered by Edward's consort, Eleanor of Castile, who kept in regular contact with her family. Most of the information about foreign embassies in the public records is limited to more public aspects, like the despatch of envoys. Though the nature of the business they transacted is not often set out, it is possible to gather a variety of information, including evidence about itineraries and expenses; by the second half of the century the practice of diplomacy had become a normal and indispensable part of relations between European rulers.[35]

Whereas Edward consulted widely in England about his domestic affairs, the management of foreign affairs was his; for the most part, they were matters of his own family relationships. In his dealings with the kings of France, his close kinsmen, Edward was far better informed than his own subjects could be. Of his nobles, Edward expected only that they would loyally support whatever course of action he decided on. The personal reactions of kings are very likely to have swayed them in issues of policy, but our sources do not make it easy to detect these in action. Edward I's envoys reported one incident bearing on the question. Their insistence on Edward acting as mediator between France and Castile gave Philip III the impression that he was being kept in the dark about the real intentions of Alfonso X of Castile. Philip took this as a slight to his dignity. He was under no obligation to consult his vassals, but appealed to his barons for advice as a useful ploy to avoid committing himself.[36] Rulers' personal feelings also mattered because they took advice, as they took service, from any persons they found useful or agreeable, irrespective, for example, of their 'nationality'. Edward I found it to his advantage to take into his service foreigners from Spain, Italy and Germany who were well informed about their native countries and often served their own rulers in a similar capacity. National allegiance was not required and double-dealing was not suspected.[37]

The great range of Edward's contacts round Europe complicated Edward's own relations with the kings of France, but still he did not aim to renounce his feudal status in the French kingdom. Even when Edward realised it had become almost impossible to work with Philip IV within the spirit of their feudal relationship, he remained willing to repair the damage in traditional style by arranging two more royal marriages, his own to Philip IV's sister Margaret and that of his heir (later Edward II) to Philip's daughter Isabella. Through Isabella, her son Edward III was to claim a right to the French succession itself. None of this suggests any long-term plan to break with France or renegotiate the status of Gascony. As in Wales and Scotland, Edward conducted his affairs with France on the hoof. He defended his own rights and had no intention of allowing the status quo to deteriorate. His confidence that his affairs in France could be resolved within the terms of the Treaty of Paris may even have induced a false sense of security that there would not be any major showdown. It could, however, have had the effect of encouraging him to think he might in his turn consolidate his own political ascendancy in Britain by comparably formal agreements. In that case, assertion of monarchy across the continent would have had a direct impact on English constitutional development.

Scotland

In mid-century, Scotland had been ruled by a minor, Alexander III, Henry III's son-in-law. Henry was eager and able to intervene several times in Scottish affairs, in what he judged to be the young king's best interests. Many Scots resented Henry's intrusion into their affairs and suspected his motives. Such friction did not really spoil harmonious relations between England and Scotland. The Scots had long been cultivating their own relations with continental powers. Well before the formal alliance of 1295, the French connection had already become important to Scotland. Alexander III's mother, the widowed Marie de Coucy, who went back to France across England in 1250, returned the next year with her brother and an imposing retinue for the marriage of her son at York. She tarried in England longer than was expected, receiving many precious gifts from Henry III. In 1256 she made another visit to her home country, where she remarried. Her second husband, John of Acre, had become a courtier of Louis IX and butler of France. Newly-wed and wanting to return to Scotland, they asked Peter of Savoy to intercede with Henry on their behalf for getting a safe conduct through England, anticipating an even longer spell in England than in 1251. Henry III gave only a grudging consent to this, grumbling because Louis IX would not allow English subjects to travel through his lands on their way to Germany, where Richard of Cornwall had just been elected king. A year after Marie and John had returned to Scotland, the arrangements for the regency set up by Henry III were overthrown, and the queen mother with her new husband became leading members of the new regime at a time when Henry III could not interfere. After John's return to the Continent, he remained an influential figure, acting as governor of Champagne for Edmund of Lancaster, nominal ruler as stepfather to the heiress.[38] Throughout his reign, therefore, Alexander III had his own good connections in the kingdom of France, quite apart from those he owed to his Francophile English relations. His first wife Margaret was herself a niece of Queen Margaret of France after whom she was probably named. Anxious about the succession after the death of his heir in 1284, Alexander III took a second wife, this time from France: Yolande of Dreux. Despite Henry III's earlier efforts to guide his son-in-law, Alexander III in his maturity proved quite capable of diplomatic independence from England.[39]

The Scottish kingdom was still only in the process of being put together in Alexander III's time, taking on a new shape by the successful acquisition of the king of Norway's lands in the west, the 'Isles' (though not Orkney or Shetland). King Haakon was loath to surrender any of his outlying dependencies, but his attempt to shore up his Scottish interests in 1263 produced only an inconclusive campaign, brought to an end by his death in Orkney. The Norwegians then accepted Scottish terms. Negotiations were protracted but themselves prove that Alexander III had a clear sense of his diplomatic objectives and could count on a number of skilled envoys.[40]

There were no hard feelings. Friendship with Norway was guaranteed in the next generation by the marriage of Alexander's daughter Margaret to Eric in 1281. Margaret is said to have taught her husband the idioms of France and England and to have effected changes in Norwegian styles of cooking and clothing. Diplomatic relations had cultural implications not reflected in the written sources of information. Embassies went to and fro between Norway and Scotland. When Alexander died in 1286, the Scots raised no objections to the succession of his granddaughter, the Maid of Norway.[41] After her death, when a number of candidates declared an interest in the succession, King Eric himself put in a bid. Scottish acquisitions in the former Norwegian territories clearly added a new dimension to the responsibilities of the crown and gave the kingdom a new centre of gravity. This helped to accentuate its differences from England. Not only did Scotland begin to seem less like a northern annexe to England; it was confident enough of its position to contend with England for control over the Isle of Man. Later it would dispute with the English in Ireland itself.

A region of important interest to Scotland were the lands closest across the sea in the Low Countries where the Scots were already well known. William, dean of Glasgow, is described in 1252 as a kinsman of the king of the Romans, William, count of Holland, himself a descendant of King David of Scotland. William's son, Florent V, was one of those who claimed the Scottish succession in 1291. In 1281 Alexander III's heir apparent, also Alexander, was betrothed in Flanders to strengthen good relations there, though his death three years later thwarted this intention.[42]

For negotiating the Flemish marriage Alexander sent the earl of Dunbar, probably along with graduates to serve as his diplomatic staff. The deployment of graduates on diplomatic missions is a further sign of growing sophistication in Scottish royal government. To Norway or Man Alexander sent not only bishops or abbots, but Dominicans and secular graduates. Walter of Glasgow went in 1261 and 1281; John of Keith accompanied Bishop Mark of the Isles to Norway in 1289. Alexander III nevertheless offered graduates fewer opportunities of attractive employment than the kings of England could. Some Scottish graduates accordingly made careers elsewhere. Weland Sticklaw went on an embassy to Norway in 1292 and, along with his brother Henry, subsequently entered the service of the king there. This may have been another consequence of the collapse of Balliol's kingship, but exile did not always mean that contacts with Scotland were severed. Scottish graduates are also recorded in the service of the English cardinals, Robert of Somercotes and Hugh of Evesham; other graduates went out to the Curia on behalf of prelates at home. But graduate careers could be advanced by political contacts. When Henry III was in Bordeaux negotiating his son's marriage, he befriended the king of Castile's brother Philip, bishop-elect of Seville, whose clerk was Master Simon le Scot. Nothing more is known about how this enterprising Scottish graduate had made his way, but through Henry III the kings of Scots and Castile had become related. A Scottish lord, Alan Durward, accompanied Edward to Burgos for his marriage in 1254.[43] Added together these details still fail to fill out our picture of Scottish relations with the Continent, but even separately they indicate that contact was more than occasional.

The failure of the royal line after 1286 has overshadowed the signs of Scottish self-confidence in the preceding generation. For this period, Scottish historians have tended to focus attention on the way Edward I's involvement in Scottish affairs degenerated into an attempt to suppress Scottish independence altogether. Alexander III himself successfully resisted Edward I's claims. When he did homage to Edward at Michaelmas 1278 for his several English estates, Alexander was able to postpone *sine die* further discussion of what this meant for Scotland.[44] In one respect, Scotland was more autonomous than England, since there was never any suggestion that the kingdom was in papal lordship, even if the papacy had taken the Scottish bishops into its special protection. The very ability of the Scots to defeat English ambitions in the long term, whatever it may owe to Robert Bruce, rested on the foundations of Scottish autonomy laid down before the death of Alexander III in 1286. The kingdom had by then acquired sufficient confidence in its own integrity to survive for the next twenty years without continuous and forceful royal leadership and despite some uncertainty and wavering about the right course to follow.[45]

The issue of the succession itself was never perceived to be a matter of exclusive interest to the Scots and English. It had an international dimension from the beginning; among the candidates were the count of Holland and the king of Norway. Edward I himself consulted various legal experts about the rights of the various candidates and the opinions of the lawyers in Paris have survived. In later discussions about the implications of homage to Edward I and his jurisdiction in Scotland, Scottish graduates and learned law were involved.[46] It was only when Edward's troubles with France became serious in the autumn of 1293 that he began to try to assert himself in Scotland, either imitating the French by insisting on his rights as sovereign lord or in order to consolidate his strength in Britain. It was war with France in June 1294 that encouraged the Welsh to revolt in September and by the summer of the following year the Scottish royal council felt emboldened enough to break with Edward and seek an alliance with Philip IV. Those who went to Paris to negotiate were the bishop of St Andrews and the abbots of Jedburgh and Melrose. This act of defiance provoked Edward's first military campaign in Scotland and by his success at Dunbar procured the abdication of Balliol (July 1296). Wallace's revolt of May 1297 brought Edward to Scotland again the next year and led to the establishment of a new form of government in Scotland against which the Scots called for papal support. In 1299, accordingly, Boniface VIII ordered Edward to desist, brazenly claiming Scotland as a fief of the Holy See. For over a decade, the issue of Scottish independence was therefore far from being of interest only within the island of Britain. The survival of the kingdom in the fourteenth and fifteenth centuries owed something to English preoccupations with France, as well as to Scottish patriotic campaigning in the borders.

Wales

In 1256 disturbances in Wales caused the first hitch in the realisation of Henry III's grandiose projects for Sicily. Llewelyn ap Gruffydd, who felt sufficiently independent to propose an alliance with the Scots in March 1258, may have also hoped for a better understanding with Louis IX, then negotiating a peace settlement with Henry III. Even if there was little chance of any French diplomatic support, the Welsh may have looked on France as potentially sympathetic. The *Annales Cambriae* have enough entries relating to France to show that events there attracted some attention. The record of the Lord Edward's sporting activities in France with the flower of English youth in 1260 takes obvious pleasure in the three victories of the French in the tournaments which drove the English from the field, leaving the victors in possession of their noble steeds. (The English chronicles refer to Edward's exploits as victorious.) When Edward I went as king to see Philip IV in 1286 he was said to have been received in Paris *nobilissime*, but there is a hostile edge to the bare report that Edward afterwards executed many of the burgesses of Bordeaux who opposed him.[47] The *Brut* pays little attention to events abroad but such notices as there are usually relate to French affairs. If the reference to Louis IX's death in 1270, 'on his way to Jerusalem' rather misrepresented the Tunis campaign, it more reliably noted Henry III's visit to Bordeaux in 1252, his conference with Louis in Paris in 1258, the election of the French pope Clement IV in 1265 and Gregory X's election on the feast of St Denis in 1272. The French connection explains its interest in Charles of Anjou's campaign against Conradin (misdated by a year to 1267) 'in a battle on the plain of Apulia'. The comment that the grandson of the emperor Frederick II was killed by Charles suggests some sympathy for the Staufen cause, rather than plain endorsement of the papal policy. The only other notice for the same year was that the sultan of Babylon (that is Baybars of Egypt) took Antioch and ravaged Armenia.[48] The Welsh could actually have been even better informed about distant affairs than the chronicle entries might suggest, but the little inaccuracies of its brief notices indicate that there cannot have been much determination to get the facts right. On the other hand, the French paid Wales no attention at all and perceived no more advantage for themselves from encouraging Llewelyn ap Gruffydd in the later thirteenth century than they had in supporting his grandfather earlier. That neither of the Llewelyns was able to cultivate French friends probably betrays a lack of confidence on both sides that the French could provide the Welsh with any practical help. Openness to the French-speaking world must nevertheless explain why the French *Chronicle of Turpin*, relating the wars of Charlemagne in Spain, a popular work in chivalrous circles, was translated into Welsh prose by Madog ap Selyf for Gruffydd ap Maredudd, that is during the period of Llewelyn of Snowdonia's success (1265–82).[49] It proves that there were thought to be enough Welsh speakers with a taste for stories of chivalrous conflict to justify the translation. No motive for it is advanced. It may be explained on purely literary grounds; possibly there was a political purpose – the hope that it might inspire martial ardour in the continental mode.

If, by mid-century, those parts of Wales still subject to native rulers remained somewhat aloof from continental affairs, where Wales was subject to lords with strong English connections access to the Continent was no more difficult than it was for the English. For centuries, the Welsh and English had lived cheek by jowl. When some of the older Marcher dynasties broke up, a number of fresh English families (Bohun, Valence, Verdon, Giffard) brought new interests into Wales. After the Edwardian conquest, seven of the ten English earls had acquired estates in the March, all helping to remove any surviving barriers to the penetration of influences from outside Wales itself. Some Welshmen were forced out of their homeland by their own family feuds, or exiled in England by their own princes. Dafydd Benfras, from north Wales (d.1257), wrote a lament 'from exile', where he regretted his inability to speak English, with only a smattering of 'passionate French'. That he knew any French at all and no English provides an interesting insight into the languages spoken in thirteenth-century Wales. That his ignorance of English was a handicap for him proves that when driven into exile he had ventured no further than England.[50] The reason for his own exile is not explained, but the popularity of the poem no doubt owed much to the familiarity of the experience.

The attitude of the papacy to Welsh aspirations for autonomy had never been very encouraging. Nevertheless, the Welsh had reason to be grateful to the papal legate Ottobuono, responsible for negotiating the treaty of Montgomery in 1267. This recognised Llewelyn as 'Prince of Wales' and allowed him to keep the lands he had acquired during the baronial wars.[51] The Welsh could have misread this treaty as a sign of papal support for their cause rather than a desire to be rid of a side issue as quickly as possible. Between 1273 and 1275 Llewelyn was in correspondence with Gregory X, but if Llewelyn was seeking papal sympathy in his stand against Edward, Gregory, who had known Edward as a crusader in the Holy Land, would anyway have given Llewelyn short shrift, even had he not died shortly after.[52]

Ireland

If Llewelyn did at least achieve some temporary advantage from Henry III's difficulties, no Irish king was able to do likewise because Irish princes did not create as much disquiet in England as the Welsh could. The parts of Ireland most resistant to English government were in the north and west which still looked to the Norse regions of Scotland for allies. In 1259 a marriage at Derry between Aed O'Connor and a daughter of Douglas MacSomerled of Galloway brought together a great company of eightscore warriors.[53] The year before, English government records refer to a raid on Connemara made by a Hebridean fleet which seized a merchant ship laden with wine, cloth, copper and iron. These incidents reveal that the peoples of these northern seas were in contact with one another and that they operated effectively beyond the range of English government. In these same years the Irish king, Brian O'Neill, attempted to revive the native office of high-kingship, a scheme that foundered at the battle of Down in 1260.[54] In the next few years, the transfer of authority over the Hebrides from the king of Norway to the king of Scotland must have sapped Irish hopes of recruiting any free spirits in the region to bolster their chances against the English. Alexander III had no motive for encouraging Irish disaffection and so offending Edward I gratuitously. Only after England was at war with Scotland did the old sympathies between the Scots and Irish resurface, when Edward Bruce carried the Scottish fight against the English into Ireland.

Where the native Irish remained in control, they left few records of their activities. By virtue of their own position, Irish rulers had little reason to cultivate relations outside Ireland. The visit to Edward I in England of Domnall Ruad MacCarthy of Desmond, in 1285 was reported as an unusual event. The Irish vernacular annals provide the only glimpses of what was known of the wider world in the remoter parts of Ireland. Some interest was taken in Henry III's expeditions to France. His visit to Gascony in 1254 was described, Irish style, as a raid into Castile. The deaths of some kings and popes were duly recorded. The belief that an emperor Charles was killed in battle in 1268 is difficult to account for except as a very garbled version of the fate of Frederick II's grandson, Conradin, after his defeat at Tagliacozzo by Charles of Anjou. When the *Annals of Loch Cé*, noting his death in battle (1281), described Domnall O'Donnell, king of the North, as 'the general guardian of the West of Europe', just what did the writer mean to imply by this?[55] At least as far as secular affairs were concerned, the native Irish were in most respects still out of touch with the ways of the Continent.

Edward I's own interests in Ireland had been created nearly twenty years before he became king, when Henry III had entrusted him with the government of his lordship of Ireland. Henry had qualified his grant by declaring that Ireland was never to be separated from the crown of England which by that time had acquired much greater direct responsibility for government there. Unfortunately, it was at a time when Henry's attention was focused on resolving his continental problems that the estates of some great baronial families established after 1172, like the Marshals and the Lacys, were split up by division among heiresses. This brought the momentum of English expansion into the north and west of the island to a halt. The crown was then in no position to confront the difficulties faced by the Anglo-Norman barons in Ireland and the further problems arising from Henry III's domestic affairs after 1258 prevented him assuming the initiative. After 1274, not even Edward I spared much time for Ireland. Any general expectation that the whole of Ireland would eventually accept royal government without sustained military activity receded. The unsatisfactory nature of the outcome as it was by the late thirteenth century had a lasting impact. By 1300 there were two kinds of political authority in Ireland. The lesser part was ruled by various Irish 'kings'; the greater, by officials of the English royal government operating from its Irish headquarters in Dublin. Royal officials accepted that they were powerless in some areas, but the island as a whole was not lawless. Geoffrey de Joinville, who arrived as justiciar in 1273 and settled down there as lord of Meath, was not dissatisfied with his lot. Robert Muscegros, seneschal of Queen Eleanor of Provence, acquired a lordship west of Limerick. A Poitevin, Maurice FitzGuy of Rochefort, founded a family in Ireland: not all the settlers were English. Nor did English lords in Ireland fail to take Irishmen into their own service. When the earl of Norfolk returned to England in 1280 he brought with him several Irishmen, some of whom he claimed as kin. It was hardly possible for English government to have worked as well as it did in thirteenth-century Ireland without a general acceptance of the new settlement. Many Irishmen must themselves have taken the view that there were opportunities for them under the new dispensation. The government proposed to extend the benefits of English law not merely to specially favoured Irishmen who asked for it, but on a more general basis, a natural corollary of its own conception of how the lordship should work. Not all English settlers agreed. At Cork, for example, in 1279–81, the appointment of an Irishman as keeper of customs was opposed by the citizens on the grounds that Irishmen were the king's 'natural enemies'. The situation in the south-west was perhaps more unsettled than in Leinster, but anyway the king was not concerned about 'nationality' in official appointments. In 1278 he made two Lucchese responsible for the collection of the king's Irish customs on wool and hides. Whatever violence occurred, the English and native Irish were not at this period in a constant state of war and the Irish gave the English little trouble. Only in the bishoprics of Ross and Killaloe was warfare held responsible for causing damage (1274–75, 1281–82).

The international commitment

Royal involvement in diplomatic relations abroad necessarily concerned the large number of persons engaged in various ways on royal business, but in a more general way also exposed all those who lived in the kingdoms to the repercussions of events far away. The best educated were inevitably those best placed to be aware of what was going on. In many respects the continental dimension of the English clergy's concerns still remained far broader than the king's own. The fact that so many senior English clergy had their own experience of living abroad, sometimes for several years, particularly in Paris as students, often prepared them to serve as suitable diplomatic agents of the king, able to make use of their student contacts in the French royal service; some were even personally acquainted with members of the French royal family. Though the clergy's periods of study at Paris proved of incidental value to rulers, the students did not go there with the intention of entering the diplomatic service but in order to advance their own careers in the Church. English clergy also regularly did business with the papal Curia though, as the college of cardinals grappled with the immediate problems of Italy and discounted future help in that quarter from England, the English exercised ever less influence at the Curia than the French. To what extent the clergy of the British Isles fully appreciated the seriousness of the problems facing the whole Western Church is hard to gauge. As the papacy became increasingly dependent on the goodwill of the French kings, could the English clergy have anticipated what problems this might create for them in the future? The special relationship created by John's submission in 1213 certainly now counted hardly at all in international affairs. The last important contribution made by the papacy to English domestic politics was in 1267 when the final settlement between the barons and the king was arranged by the papal legate, Ottobuono. One of his clerks (after his own election to the papacy, as Boniface VIII) was kind enough to recall how the legatine party had been rescued from the Tower of London by the young Edward I, but as king Edward had no need of papal legates to settle his problems at home and, as the papacy itself became more dependent on French support in Italy, he could no longer expect to find the papacy a source of strength.

The confidence of churchmen in their own power to influence events was also shaken in the intellectual sphere. The middle years of the century had been marked by the stupendous achievement of mastering the difficult new science of Aristotle and making use of it to propound a coherent natural theology, intended, as in Aquinas's *Summa contra Gentiles*, to show rational grounds for the Christian religion rather than exclusive reliance on revelation. By the late 1270s, after his death, faults were being found with his teaching. The bishop of Paris condemned 177 propositions defended by Parisian masters, including some by Aquinas, in 1277. Only ten days later Kilwardby, the Dominican archbishop of Canterbury, rushed to Oxford and made a similar denunciation of erroneous opinions. Some of Aquinas's arguments were forcefully rebutted in England, particularly by Franciscan scholars. Aquinas's fellow Dominicans were generally disposed to defend him against his detractors and were expected to rally to his defence. Curiously, the general chapter that met at Milan in 1278 sent two lectors to punish some English Dominicans who had criticised Aquinas, though the only ones now known to have expressed opinions on the matter were ardent

Thomists. Contrariwise, an English Franciscan, William de Mara, wrote a commentary on Aquinas which was recommended by the Franciscan general chapter at Strasbourg in 1282 as necessary reading. Mara's profound knowledge of Greek and Hebrew was respected in his time and this learning he gained entirely in England. In the last decades of the century, the Oxford teachers had become much more confident of their powers to hold and defend opinions not necessarily accepted in Paris without incurring accusations of heresy. Nevertheless, the period of intellectual discovery and optimism was over. In its place, there was argument, contrary positions and attempts to contain controversy lest heresy get a foothold.

Ambitious clergy still went to Paris and even taught there, but the most distinguished could expect high office in England and their careers were shaped by English requirements. The reordering of government after the turmoil of the barons' wars had its parallel in the Church. By the second half of the century, the survival of episcopal registers for most English dioceses enables us to show how they set about their tasks. To conclude that they were already becoming somewhat detached from the Continent would be going too far, but the security of their English bases simply gave them a different perspective. They studied abroad to hone their competence, not to discover new learning. At a superficial level, little may seem to have changed.

Our information about individual English clergy concerns mainly the most senior prelates, whose eminence anyway gave the English Church its sense of direction. About eighty men served as English bishops in the second half of the thirteenth century. Of these, only the careers of thirteen cannot be traced. A handful had been monks, regular canons or friars before their elevation; only seven could have counted on their high social rank; a mere eight made their careers by starting in the lowly ranks of the king's clerks and rising by their ability or servility. More than two-thirds of these bishops owed their careers to an initial period of university study at Oxford (only one from Cambridge); several are also known to have studied in Paris, Orléans, Montpellier or Bologna. Even to continue their studies for long periods, these men needed patrons able to provide them with benefices, usually more than one, and for this canon law required them to obtain appropriate dispensations from the papacy. Clerical careers were therefore made in England by the ability to combine the possibility of obtaining favours from English patrons, secular and ecclesiastical, with permission from the papacy to hold benefices concurrently. To what extent it became necessary to go to Italy for papal permission is not certain, but ambitious clergy were in no doubt of the importance of securing curial backing for their careers. Particularly at the final stage, disputes about the processes of episcopal elections invariably involved taking their cases to the Curia in person, for long periods and at great expense, both in travel, lodging and bribery.

Some English episcopal careers were made by serving at the Curia as agents for certain English churches, Canterbury, Lincoln, York, or for the king himself. Some English clergy even entered the service of cardinals and were nominated as papal chaplains as they built up their connections and expertise.[56] Senior English clergy appreciated only too well how much they needed to pay attention to the formalities of the international Church for their own purposes. International commitments did not deter them from becoming involved themselves in the troubled years of the baronial rebellion. In no other period of English history did the bishops, as a body and as individuals, play such an active part in public life, confident of their calling in a truly universal Church.

Like scholars of any period, many of these bishops associated their success with influential teachers whom they venerated. Edmund of Abingdon was held in great respect by Oxford students and his shrine at Pontigny was both visited and enriched from England. After the death in exile of Thomas of Cantilupe, his successor as bishop of Hereford, Richard Swinfield, worked tirelessly for Thomas's canonisation, hoping to hear of miracles performed at his tomb in Italy.[57] In these circumstances, the sense of loyalty to particular persons was not confined within the kingdom.

All the archbishops of Canterbury in this century from Langton to Winchelsey had long-standing personal contacts abroad, Boniface of Savoy by birth, the others mainly through experience as students and teachers at the university of Paris. Among the most illustrious of these late thirteenth-century archbishops were the Dominican Robert Kilwardby who was called away as cardinal to the Curia, and his Franciscan successor John Peckham who, after studies in Paris, was invited to teach theology at the Roman Curia itself. There he not only impressed the Franciscan pope Nicholas III, but made friends with whom he was able to correspond later about his difficulties. Some of them subsequently became cardinals; a few became popes in due course: Honorius IV, Nicholas IV and Boniface VIII. Peckham wrote separately to some twenty-five different cardinals in his eleven years as archbishop, looking to them for advice and comfort; some even helped in financial matters. All were as well informed about his affairs in England as Peckham and his agents could make them. In building up such relationships, Peckham's own experience at Rome stood him in good stead in his necessary confrontations with the Curia. Peckham refers bitingly to certain curial officials he considered enemies, but he was not at a loss as to how their intrigues might be circumvented. The purpose of his correspondence was to smooth his own administration.[58] He did not seek to rally papal support for his difficulties with the king. He wanted not conflict but results and his practical approach was typical of the new spirit of the ecclesiastical order.

In his monastic cathedral, without canonical stalls, Peckham had reason to regret that he had so few benefices at his disposal to offer as douceurs to his supporters. By contrast York, with its four minster churches (York, Beverley, Ripon and Southwell), had many prebends with attractive endowments. Rome was naturally very interested in obtaining some of them for cardinals and their dependants. For this reason York itself became familiar, if not with the principals at least with their Italian proctors, including the many Tuscan merchants from Florence, the Amanati of Pistoia, the Bonaventura of Siena and the Riccardi of Lucca. But these were not the only foreigners involved in the affairs of York Minster. There were Savoyard relations of the king, James of Spain, nephew of Queen Eleanor of Castile, and members of the Saluzzo family allied by marriage with the earls of Lincoln. All these often competing interests had to be looked after in York by the archbishop's own staff. Because of the rivalry with Canterbury, there was no way of securing even cooperation among clergy for devising a general strategy or setting up a 'national' office for dealing with the Curia. The archbishop was obliged to deal with his problems from his own resources in money, contacts, friendship and reputation. International experience from an early age was a valuable asset for such purposes.

The archbishops of York of this period were scholars as distinguished as those of Canterbury. John le Romeyns was the son of an Italian clerk of good Roman family who had himself made a successful career in England. The later archbishop had studied and taught theology in Paris long enough to have acquired house property there. As archbishop he was several times on the Continent, first for his consecration at Rome in 1286; second, two years later, for five months travelling with Edward I to Gascony and accompanying the king of Aragon back to his own kingdom. From Jaca in September he wrote in some agitation to Cardinal Matteo Orsini when he first heard of the cardinal's proposal to appropriate the York prebend he had received for the benefit of the Hospital of the Holy Spirit in Rome. Even so far from home and Rome, Romeyns still had to keep up with the business of his church. On a third trip to the Continent lasting nearly a year, December 1291 to November 1292, Romeyns continued to manage English affairs brought to his attention. The problems and people of York pursued him to Italy and back. A papal letter requiring him to summon a provincial council to raise money for the crusade reached him on his way out to Italy and his vicar-general was instructed to act on his behalf. When, at St Martin's near Viterbo, he heard about an unfortunate turn of events in his dispute with Durham, he was obliged to provide different instructions as to how to proceed according to the various ways that the dispute might have developed before the arrival of his messengers.

His foreign tours were anything but relaxing. Thought had to be given to the most mundane business: instructions had to be issued to secure the release of one of the archbishop's horses for which a citizen of Pavia had provided stabling. From England, Romeyns had to rely on agents to see his business through the Curia. For this purpose he maintained separate establishments of English and foreign envoys. Labro of Lucca was entrusted with one piece of business that he was on no account to divulge to the English envoys but only to his own 'colleagues', Master Geoffrey of Novara and Bernard of Carcassonne. What this business might be is not disclosed, yet the episode is instructive. If the archbishop himself in effect employed two different agencies in Rome, the English at the Curia obviously could not act as a united force. One of Romeyns's most urgent early pieces of business was his attempt to get Roman approval for his right to raise his episcopal cross in the province of Canterbury, which Peckham bitterly opposed. In his search for allies at the Curia Romeyns was obliged to get his agents to represent his case in slightly different ways with different cardinals. He tried to insist that his business be pushed through with the connivance of officials rather than have it openly debated in the public courts where objections could easily be raised. Romeyns's register provides invaluable evidence for the care needed in the conduct of affairs. His short-lived successor, Henry of Newark, too old and sick ever to visit Rome again, had in earlier years also acted in the Roman Curia as an envoy for Edward I.[59]

Kings and clergy had commitments and interests overseas about which we are tolerably well informed, but royal documents are not of exclusively political interest. English relations with the Low Countries, for example, were deeply influenced by Flemish dependence on supplies of English wool for the manufacture of cloth.[60] There had been occasional disputes involving this commerce in the past but serious difficulties arose during the barons' wars in England, when the commercial affairs of many merchants in England were disrupted. In 1262, merchants from Rouen got Louis IX to intercede with Henry III on their behalf about the non-payment of debts due to them, though there is nothing to show that Henry III ever paid what he himself owed.[61] Flemish merchants had no such powerful advocate. They were assaulted or lost merchandise as 'aliens' in the period of Montfort's dominance between the battles of Lewes and Evesham. Reprisals in Flanders created further complications. They caused damage not only to English traders there, but also to German burgesses of Lynn whose wool exports were seized at Bruges.[62] After Lewes, Montfort's government itself sought to reassure foreign merchants that it was safe to return. Persecution of alien merchants was no part of baronial policy. At Southampton, the local authorities were reluctant to interfere with commerce on political grounds and the government had to make it clear that it was only against the king's enemies that it wished to proceed, not against all alien merchants. Disorder was not, however, the only obstacle to trade. After Evesham, the royal government had to find ways to meet its obligations to its wartime creditors. One of the measures taken to this end had far-reaching consequences for commerce. Early in 1266 Henry III provided for the financial support of his son Edward in England by granting him authority to license imports and exports, in effect putting foreign trade in his hands. This grant guaranteed Edward £4000 a year, the fee initially paid by Italian merchants for acquiring the sole rights of administration. Within a year, Edward had negotiated to farm out the customs of Bordeaux for almost as much (15,000 pounds bordelais) to a consortium of Cahorsins.[63] The way to financial solvency had been found.

This was the first stage in a remarkable change in royal exploitation of commerce which settled into the parliamentary grant of royal customs duties in 1275. This discovery of how the king could himself profit from the commercial activities of his kingdom had great importance in a number of ways. It affected English relations with foreigners and the king's dealing with native taxpayers, and gave the king confidence that he had adequate financial reserves to persist in lines of policy which might result in costly warfare. Well before all the implications became clear, objections to royal control of English commerce were raised, not least by the king of France himself on behalf of his merchants.[64]

Whereas Henry III and Edward thought it prudent not to reject the pleas of such a great friend as Louis IX, they were less conciliatory in their dealings with Countess Margaret of Flanders when she similarly rallied to the defence of her merchants. With the countess there was a further problem. Payment of the customary fee-rent of 500 marks due had been irregular. The deficit was supposedly made good after the battle of Evesham from the fines imposed on the rebellious Cinque Ports for their support of Montfort. By 1270 Margaret, still unpaid, concluded that more forceful measures than diplomacy were called for. The goods of English merchants in Flanders were suddenly seized. This was countered in England by a comparable measure and all Flemish merchants were expelled. A ban on all export of wool to Flanders, in a bid to cause a crisis in the Flemish wool-cloth manufactures, inevitably hit English exporters of wool who did their best to circumvent government policy. Resolution of the impasse was delayed by Edward's absence on crusade, but even after his return a settlement of the financial terms dragged on for years and was not reached until after Margaret's death in 1280. Payments of the regular pension to the new count, Guy, were resumed only in 1288.[65] The changing character of political authority everywhere in Europe had direct impact on trade and finance. In the meantime, Italians had taken the opportunity to improve their own trading position in England.

Apart from merchants, no other sections of the population appear to have had pressing reasons for cultivating foreign contacts, but this may be because the right kind of personal evidence is not available about the leaders of society. The English baronage, powerful men in their own right, receive a certain amount of historical attention, but given their social and political influence the evidence for their activities and outlook is meagre. Reliance on royal records for most precise information about them distorts rather than enhances our understanding. The barons appear there simply as royal vassals, campaigning in France for the king or serving on embassies sent to other princes. Little is known about their own personal affairs, friendships, enmities or political interests. At best, a few surviving household accounts show what they spent their money on. Modern rejection of the traditional values of aristocratic society and disdain for the routines of rural life have compounded the difficulties of trying to gauge the range of its mental horizons.

The secular English baronage comprised the 'top' few hundred families in the kingdom. For some, family interests might stretch outside the kingdom proper. After 1244, they had been deprived of what lands they had continued to hold in Normandy, but many had lands in Wales and Ireland; some in Scotland too. When considering such men, it is appropriate to take Scottish lords into account also, for many of these had lands in England and moved as easily in the same kinds of society as English tenants-in-chief. Bruce and Comyn both fought for Henry III at Lewes in 1264; Guy de Balliol fought for Montfort at Evesham the next year. Simon de Montfort's final campaign is described very sympathetically by the Melrose chronicle in an exceptionally long passage devoted to affairs outside Scotland. Several Scottish lords with lands in England, owing service to the English crown, served Henry III in both Wales and Gascony. These connections, which tended to blur the distinction between what might be due for English estates and what from Scotland, also helped to give something of a non-national tone to the baronage as a whole. Barons swore oaths to their lords, not to their country.[66]

There were as yet no gradations in the 'peerage'. All barons were tenants-in-chief of the crown and the small number of men entitled earl enjoyed no obvious advantages of rank. At any one time, there were never more than a score of these, some royal kinsmen. More is known about such men. They might be much travelled. Henry III's brother Richard, earl of Cornwall, had personal experience of conditions in the Holy Land before his election as king of the Romans in 1257. This alone helped to make Germany, particularly the Rhineland, familiar to those noblemen who served in Richard's entourage. In the next generation, Edward I's brother Edmund, earl of Lancaster, though disappointed of the kingdom of Sicily, nevertheless became a figure of great consequence in France as regent of the county of Champagne. The international standing of Simon de Montfort was an embarrassment to Henry III, who felt ill at ease with his abrasive brother-in-law. The effect of the clash of their personalities in domestic affairs is fully appreciated, but Simon's grievances helped to drag out negotiations for the Treaty of Paris. From Henry III's point of view, his foreign relations and his French lands touched him as closely as his domestic interests and he did not invoke different principles to deal with them. Because the dispute between Montfort and Henry III came to involve the king of France and the papacy as well, it naturally attracted contemporary notice on the continent. The high point was reached when Simon's son Guy murdered his own cousin Henry of Almain at mass, not in England, but in Viterbo Cathedral. There was an international outcry. Guy fled to escape capture and was looked for everywhere. Even the king of Norway detained someone suspected of being Guy.[67]

Those of Henry III's relations by marriage who came to England did not sever their continental links. His wife's uncle, Peter of Savoy, who acted effectively as earl of Richmond for many years, eventually returned to Savoy when he succeeded to the county. At Richmond he was replaced by John, duke of Brittany, whose ancestors had held the earldom in the twelfth century. John married Henry III's daughter Beatrice and though John supported Philip IV after 1294 their son, also John, spent most of his life in the service of his English relations. One of Henry's half-brothers, William of Valence, earl of Pembroke, was frequently abroad: in Aquitaine on royal service; fighting at Tunis in 1270; and negotiating in Castile in 1279. Three of Henry's Lusignan sisters married English earls, Robert of Derby, Gilbert IV of Gloucester and John Warenne. Baldwin, earl of Devon, married a cousin of Queen Eleanor of Provence. The links established by the marriage of Edmund, earl of Lincoln, with Alice, daughter of Manfred III of Saluzzo, in 1247 were reinforced in the next generation by the marriage before 1285 of Richard Fitz Alan, earl of Arundel, to Alasia, daughter of Tommaso I of Saluzzo, Earl Henry of Lincoln's cousin.[68] It was not only the king who had interests in the Alpine region; these comital marriages introduced at least some English barons to its complications.

Although Matthew Paris opined that English lords were demeaned by being forced to marry Henry III's kinswomen, royal influence is not always detectable in the marriage of magnates. Humphrey de Bohun, earl of Hereford, married Maud of Eu, and his namesake, grandson and heir, also married abroad, Maud de Fiennes from Hainault; Roger Bigod, earl of Norfolk, married a daughter of King William of Scotland. The earl of Winchester, Roger de Quincy, who in his twenties had accompanied his father on crusade to Damietta in 1219, became hereditary constable of the kingdom of Scotland by his marriage to Helen, heiress of Galloway. Little is known of his experiences of foreign travel, but in 1259 he went to St Omer on behalf of the English barons to intercept Richard of Cornwall on his way home for the first time since the Oxford parliament of 1258. Many earls are known to have gone to Santiago de Compostela on pilgrimage. Richard, earl of Gloucester, one of the most powerful men in mid-century England, made the pilgrimage to both Pontigny and Compostela, visited the pope at Lyon, was sent by the king as ambassador to Germany and Castile, and was frequently in France, both for tourneys as sporting occasions and for diplomacy. Of all the earls, only those of Aumâle and Warwick had no evident foreign connections. This may be the fault of the evidence, for William of Aumâle died at Amiens in 1260, probably while serving on some mission, and William of Warwick at least served in Gascony in 1297. Unfortunately, we cannot from such information draw any conclusions about how these great men viewed their experiences.

The counterpart of this was the willingness of foreigners, many of different social standing, to come to England to settle. The most distinguished was probably the German widow of Richard of Cornwall, Beatrice of Falkenburg, sister of the archbishop of Cologne, whose substantial dower enabled, or obliged, her to live on in England, for twenty-five years after her husband's death.[69] How did she adapt to a country she hardly knew and where she had no kinsmen of her own? There are numerous examples of well-born men from abroad entering royal service. Not all the foreigners in the king's service played politics with the barons. Geoffrey de Joinville (brother of the seneschal of Champagne, who wrote the famous life of Louis IX) came to England as a young man and married an heiress who brought him estates in England and Ireland. He acted for Edward I as his ambassador, notably in Paris. As Lord Geneville, he entered the 'peerage' and died at Trim (1314), aged over eighty in the Dominican house there.[70] Occasionally he returned to his estates in Champagne, but to what extent he remained in touch with his more famous brother is not known. Their separate careers in France and England illustrate what little part national sentiments had to play in the activities of thirteenth-century nobles.

War

When the breach with France came in 1294, it was not because of any breakdown over interpretation of the Treaty of Paris, but as a result of a confrontation at sea between the Normans and the Cinque Portsmen (with Spanish and Dutch ships on their side). Edward attempted to forestall escalation of the violence by offering Norman sailors satisfaction in his courts, but Philip IV's uncompromising rejection of all his proposals brought war with France. Philip chose to make the maritime dispute a test of his rights as feudal suzerain. Alleging the need for a face-saving device, Edward was tricked into allowing a purely 'formal' French occupation of Gascony in 1294, Edward's brother Edmund, who acted for the king at Paris, being assured by his aunt Queen Margaret and his step-daughter Queen Jeanne that Philip IV had no intention of keeping the confiscated duchy. Only when Edward realised that Philip had no intention of handing it back did warfare become the only option left to him.[71] Not that he recovered his losses by military success, but hostilities opened the way for further negotiation under papal aegis. Diplomatic wrangles between England and France became a regular feature of politics; warfare, though recurrent, was by contrast only intermittent.

In retaliation for the French occupation of the duchy of Gascony in the spring of 1294, Edward I ordered the sheriffs to arrest the wool and merchandise of all foreign merchants in June, and banned all exports to France. Before the end of July these orders had to be modified to allow for the release of all non-French goods but arrangements for selling off the goods seized from French merchants were in hand by mid-August. An inventory of the goods of foreigners in London was ready by October. At the end of the year further measures for the defence of the coast against invasion were published and over the next few months the king tried to assemble a fleet of his own and recruit sailors for his force. In the meantime the pope had despatched two cardinals to England to negotiate a truce and though

Edward I was prepared to accept this by August 1295, the French were more hesitant. A French attack on Dover in that month caused casualties. The death of Thomas de la Hale, a monk, was treated in England as martyrdom.[72] The French enemy was being demonised. The king had by then become convinced that many goods of French merchants had been kept hidden from his officials. He ordered a more searching enquiry. So far, the purpose of these measures was clearly financial, to get compensation for damages done in Gascony. However, in November the order to move all aliens at least thirteen miles inland from the coast indicates that the king had begun to suspect that resident aliens, even French monks, might sympathise sufficiently with Philip to assist his invasion forces. Frenchmen flushed out by these enquiries were required to present themselves at the Exchequer by late January 1296, to give sureties. Such an unexpected reaction caused protests; exemptions, exceptions and special favours began to appear. Some Frenchmen long resident in England were able to find local Englishmen friendly enough to stand as warrantors for their good behaviour.

To protect foreign-born residents in England pursuing legal claims in the courts, the king was prepared to issue letters deeming individuals to be 'denizen' which enabled them to continue with their litigation in the courts without prejudice. By this means the notion of 'naturalisation' came into being.[73] It is possible that their adversaries had alleged their 'foreignness' in order to deny them legal standing, but there is otherwise no other evidence of hostility, or eagerness, for example, to denounce French neighbours as potential spies. Yet royal fears of an invasion by sea were still rife in June 1296. Negotiations dragged on about the terms of truce throughout much of the year. Despite the uncertainty, the English were neither particularly alarmed nor persuaded by the king's arrangements for defence. Rather, they complained about the extortionate measures royal officials had taken for coastal defence. Thanks to the king's worries, however, his officials were obliged to compile a very detailed dossier on the foreigners in their midst. From this some surprising facts about the foreign community emerge. Many had lived in England for years without molestation. Foreignness became worthy of remark only as a consequence of war with France.

The outbreak of hostilities in 1294 quite suddenly prompted an unprecedented flurry of diplomatic activity as Edward consulted allies and sought new ones. By this point, the political forces that would dominate European affairs for centuries to come are clearly discernible. France had become the major state and England was determined to circumscribe French influence. The Anglo-French confrontation threatened to divide the Iberian kingdoms and the Low Countries. The German Empire having lost its hold on Italy had ceased to have any notable impact on the affairs of the other western rulers. Rather the reverse: some princes on its western borders became susceptible to the growing attractions of friendship with France. In the longer term, successive French governments were able to push the eastern frontier to the Rhine itself. Southern Italy was fatally split by the Sicilian rebellion of

1282. This was a very different Europe in the making from the one that had existed in 1200, or even in 1250.

The notion of sovereign power has been appropriated by whatever state has been able to defend its independence and has spread worldwide.[74] Sovereignty asserts exclusive power at home and invites conflict abroad. This shift in the moral balance of power between the spiritual and the material worlds upset the earlier confidence of the best educated clergy in their own social destiny. It showed that they were not in fact the persons best fitted to assume direction of human affairs. Innocent IV and his clerical allies in Germany had so little understanding of the operations of secular government that they thought any minor prince they endorsed could discharge the functions of the king of the Romans. Matthew Paris, who followed their efforts with close attention, correctly judged that Innocent IV's hostility to Frederick II and his family not only deprived Germany, Italy, Apulia and Calabria of a ruler capable of controlling disorder, but exposed 'the Church' to many troubles. By 'Church' was still meant the whole body of faithful Christians and not just the clerical hierarchy, but in a narrower sense the long-term interests of the clergy also suffered.

The troubled last years of the thirteenth century did not prevent many people holding sanguine expectations of the century ahead. For the first time ever, the end of one century and the beginning of another became the occasion of official celebration. Pope Boniface VIII decreed that for the year 1300, and every hundredth year thereafter, the fullest possible indulgence should be granted to all confessed penitents who visited the churches of saints Peter and Paul in Rome. The idea seems to have come to the pope a little late, for he did not publish his offer of a plenary indulgence until 22nd February, awkwardly making it effective retrospectively from Christmas 1299. The jubilee proved a great success in attracting visitors to Rome, not least from England, where the jubilee was enthusiastically reported by the Guisborough chronicler.[75] The idea of linking the celebration to a plenary indulgence arose from the recent promulgation of the doctrine of indulgence at the Council of Lyon in 1274. Although Boniface VIII has been remembered historically for the outrageous treatment he received at the hands of the French king's arrogant envoy at Anagni in 1303, the horror this insult aroused throughout Christendom points rather to the continuing respect felt for the pope as God's vicar on earth. There was no eagerness to throw off allegiance to the papacy. For all its faults, the papacy still appeared to offer the only hope of containing the wilful ambitions of secular rulers. It took more than another two centuries before some kings were prepared to dispense altogether with submitting their spiritual and moral problems to the papacy for adjudication. Only historians can detect the fissures in the great monument that would eventually bring it down to earth.

Conclusion

Pre-Conquest England already had steady contact with its continental neighbours. The English acknowledged that their ancestors had come from overseas and that Germans were their kinsmen. They had received the Christian religion from Roman missionaries and no medieval church was more respectful of Roman authority than the English. As the great surge of enthusiasm for a renewal of Christian practice, reorganisation of ecclesiastical structures and a totally new kind of education flooded over the continent from the mid-eleventh century, it would inevitably have reached England. The Norman Conquest did not mark a breach with the English past in bringing about close contact between England and the Continent. It intensified the relationship and in a sense completed the process of integrating England into Europe. The political union of England and Normandy became so familiar to Englishmen that the enlargment of the political framework to include Anjou and Aquitaine created no disquiet on this side of the Channel. But the success of Henry II could not be accepted as permanent by the kings of France and efforts to undermine the Angevin Empire became their major preoccupation. The success of Philip II in taking Normandy and Anjou became a challenge that could hardly be ignored. A settlement of a sort was reached but Edward I and his successors concluded that the French would not be satisfied until the king of England accepted the implications of his inferior status as a French vassal. With the first outright war between the two kings, a new period of international interaction opens. Thereafter the English accepted that they would have to fight hard for acceptance on the Continent. The natural consequences of the Norman Conquest of 1066 which had brought the English on to the mainland were now at risk.

English involvement in continental affairs at almost every level had implications for those parts of the British Isles not themselves already much affected by what happened on the mainland and innately indifferent to its concerns. The pace of change there was for the most part set from England, but it was slower and more variable according to local circumstances. To understand how things turned out, a closer reading of each local situation is required. Unfortunately, this is often attempted without paying enough attention to the wider context, so that accounts of what was happening in Scotland, Wales and Ireland focus entirely on English responsibility for events of much greater significance. Even though in many respects our information about the three centuries discussed here is inadequate, it could still be explored in greater depth, given a disposition to take a broader view than British attitudes normally allow.

The familiar preoccupation of British public opinion with how to relate to the mainland has blinded us to the effects in Europe itself of British policy. After all, even in modern times it is thanks mainly to Britain that French or German attempts to dominate Europe have been checked. The resultant divisions and squabbles of European politicians are in some measure the result of British insistence that the Continent not be united to our disadvantage. If the smaller nations of Europe are aware of what their independent survival owes to British policy, German or French resentment of Britain should also be understood. Even by non-engagement with the Continent, yet intervening on suitable occasions, Britain has helped to make Europe what it is and create the problems it does not want to help solve. Britain has had a charmed life and owes this in part to being an offshore island to a divided Continent. This enviable position has been appreciated for what it is on the Continent. What Britain itself owes to the Continent is not widely appreciated here.

Considered overall, it would be difficult to explain the main lines of domestic development in the twelfth and thirteenth centuries without taking the foreign commitments of English kings into account. It is impossible to know how the great events of continental history would have affected England if kings had not had continental dominions. The condition of France offered an opportunity for English intervention that could hardly have been resisted, as the counts of Flanders, Normandy and Brittany began to act independently of their own king. The close links between the papacy and French monastic and scholastic centres would have necessarily attracted English interest, even had the French connection lacked a political dimension. Such contacts produced more than a few additional elements. The character of the English Church was deeply marked by these experiences and the grandiose ambitions of royal government endowed the monarchy with a lofty and enduring conception of its purpose. The powerful monarchy of mid-eleventh-century England might have subjected the rest of the British Isles to its dominion had it not preferred to throw its energies into displays of power abroad. The continuing divergences of England, Wales, Scotland and Ireland are one of the legacies of this period. Scotland learnt most directly from England how its monarchy might be transformed to defend Scottish independence rather than prepare for union with England. In time, it began to cultivate its own foreign friends. Wales and Ireland were both badly placed geographically to make direct contacts abroad and both were disposed to look for ways to preserve their own traditional cultures, rather than welcome changes thrust upon them from outside.

The English were not only the principal conduits for these continental influences in these islands; they provided some of the star performers of the new arts. Their most surprising originality lay with their determination in the fields of science and mathematics. Their belief in the value of education took many of them to senior positions in the schools of Paris, and in the thirteenth century led to the development of not one but two universities in England. The English were pioneers in using the vernacular for non-literary purposes and so encouraged the spread of literacy among the laity. The first English 'national' history written in the vernacular was Gaimar's French *History of the English*; stories taken from their neighbours in the island about Arthur and the Other World provided inexhaustible material for the new 'Romance' literature. The quality of English book illumination was highly regarded on the Continent and had a decisive impact on the development of the art in France. Even after Paris itself acquired a reputation in this field, English artists held their own by dint of their imaginative gifts and their technical expertise. These were displayed most dramatically in many English illustrations of the Apocalypse produced in the late thirteenth century. Church reformers were more successful on the Continent in securing independence from lay interference than they were in England, but by virtue of the challenge the English clergy mounted to royal autocracy they set a benchmark for 'constitutional' opposition. Without Innocent III's successful stand against John over the appointment of Langton at Canterbury, and John's grant of a charter of ecclesiastical liberties, there could have been no Magna Carta. The logic of opposition to the king induced the barons to invite Louis of France to take John's crown. The foundation stone of English liberty could have been enforced by a foreign ruler. Similarly, without the Sicilian question, there would have been no barons' wars and perhaps no parliament. The contribution its foreign connections made to English development could be both indirect and unintended.

The interactions of the parts were not easily affected by conscious acts of policy on either side, and it is inappropriate to try to assess the outcome by weighing the advantages against the downside. The English benefices showered on Italian clergy in mid-thirteenth century may have been out of proportion to the benefits received in return from networking at the Curia, but it is a difficult equation to measure. The desperation of Innocent IV at the height of his quarrel with the emperor Frederick II brought the pope to Lyon for six years, closer to English petitioners than at any other time in papal history, and at least offered Henry III greater hopes for the success of his future foreign policy. Whereas it may be easier to show that, economically, the balance of foreign trade was in England's favour, it is not possible to adduce agreed ways of measuring the profit and loss account in matters of politics or culture. If the dominance of spoken French in England is deplored for its disastrous effects on writing in Old English, its part in simplifying the grammatical structures of the language and preparing the way for Chaucerian English must be considered a positive benefit. The only choice open to the inhabitants of the British Isles in their dealings with the Continent was to resist what arrived with all their strength or to learn to make the best use of it they could. Even before the Conquest, English culture was receptive to foreign influences. Elsewhere, traditional cultures with much less experience of coping with novelties reacted against change. Confidence in familiar routines meant that their inadequacies for satisfying new expectations in ecclesiastical and secular affairs were not perceived.

During the historical period reviewed here, England's place in Europe was not considered a problem up for discussion. England, under its kings, clergy, men of education and enterprise, played a significant role in the public affairs of the Continent, in shaping its culture and commerce, in devising viable forms of government and in bringing the princes of the time into a diplomatic network. The English rarely attempted to filter out any continental elements suspected of contaminating the purest waters of the island. Kings who were touchy about papal encroachments on their sovereignty got little support from their clergy. It took the Hundred Years War to make king and parliament wary of popes who were by then all 'French'. Only towards the end of the wars did the English language reappear in official publications. For the period discussed here, the use of French as a lingua franca across the Europe known in these islands did assist with cooperation and friendship at an international level. What is even more remarkable is that such an environment did not produce uniformity but fostered distinctive styles of government, as in England and Scotland. In education, or architecture, there was scope, not only within Christendom but within the British Isles themselves, for the development of local traditions. Belonging to Europe was not like wearing a straitjacket. It was an invitation to show off before an appreciative audience, living in what all recognised as a society with common interests.

The most elusive aspect of this whole question has to be the attitude of the great majority of the population. Their opinions were not formally consulted at the time; it is not certain that ideas about it were ever formulated, let alone written down for posterity's consideration. In principle, much attention is devoted to what the views of the majority might be, but even now they are at best ascertainable only in the form of answering yes or no to questions devised by governments and explained by educated spokesmen. The majority are bound to be guided by what they are told about matters of which they themselves have little personal experience. For the period discussed here, we do have information about governments and about the well educated. Neither of these interested parties hung back from acceptance of England's role in Europe. Because the English economy prospered by trading with its continental neighbours, the enlightened self-interest of producers, manufacturers, merchants and townsmen might have secured a yes vote even from the unconsulted majority. The prevailing assumption that the majority were downtrodden, ignorant, even brutish, refuses to recognise the real character of medieval English society. Its lords were not absentee rentiers but familiar figures on their estates. The peasantry were regularly in local courts settling disputes, stating local custom, answering royal enquiries, meeting officials, paying taxes for crusades. Some of them travelled far. They may not have been often called to give their opinions or have thought enough of themselves to suppose their opinions of much value or interest, but they were probably at least as alert and public-spirited as is now believed desirable. Islanders have more choice than those living on the mainland about how much contact they make with their neighbours. There will be those who prefer to keep aloof and self-sufficient. Others will welcome the possibility of going to sea at will, picking what they value, rejecting the rest. The Norman and Angevin rulers of England provided a political umbrella for the operations of the islanders, but they were not responsible for stimulating them in the first place and when the umbrella was discarded, the English found other ways to make their way in the world. The violence inflicted on some aliens in brief moments of public disorder was not representative of a society permeated with 'foreigners' and cannot be used to argue for any natural reluctance to have dealings with people from abroad. The medieval wars with France, when they came, were not fought to preserve the kingdom's independence but to retain an English foothold abroad. The high point was reached when Henry V was recognised as heir to the French king, Charles VI. Only when English ambitions to hold on in France were finally blocked was compensation sought for this by turning to the New World. Only after the loss of empire did the British think again about entering into Europe. It is not possible to recreate situations long since changed, but there is something to be said for taking a fresh look at the one period of our history when England really did behave like a European power and dragged the rest of the British Isles along with it. The Norman Conquest is always treated in England as a foreign intrusion into a traditional society. Its long-term effects, however, were to make England a continental power. Only with the greatest reluctance did the English finally abandon their efforts to retain their place on the mainland of Europe.

Abbreviations

A	Annals
AASS	*Acta Sanctorum* (Antwerp, 1731)
AB	*Analecta Bollandiana*
AC	*Annales Cambriae*, ed. J. Williams ab Ithel (RS 20, 1860)
AConnacht	*Annals of Connacht*, ed. A.M. Freeman (Dublin, 1944)
Adam	Adam of Bremen, *Gesta Hammaburgensis ecclesiae pontificum*, ed. W. Trillmich, Quellen des 9. und 11. Jahrhunderts zur Geschichte des Hamburgische Kirche und des Reiches (Darmstadt, 1973)
AFM	*Annals of Four Masters*, ed. J. O'Donovan (Dublin, 1851)
AI	*Annals of Innisfallen*, ed. S. MacAirt (Dublin, 1951)
ALC	*Annals of Loch Cé*, ed. W.M. Hennessy (RS 54, 1871)
AM	*Annales Monastici*, ed. H.R. Luard (RS 36, 1864–69)
ANS	*Anglo-Norman Studies*
Anselm	Anselm of Canterbury, Epistolae, *Opera Omnia*, ed. F.S. Schmitt (Edinburgh, 1946–49), vols iii–v
ASC	*Anglo-Saxon Chronicle*
AU	*Annals of Ulster to AD 1131*, ed. S. MacAirt and G. MacNiocaill (Dublin, 1983)
BEC	*Bibliothèque de l'Ecole des Chartes*
BIHR	*Bulletin of the Institute of Historical Research*
BNJ	*British Numismatic Journal*
Brut	*Brut y Tywysogion, The Chronicle of the Princes, Red Book of Hergest Version*, ed. T. Jones (Cardiff, 1955)
CChR	*Calendar of Charter Rolls*
CCM	*Cahiers de Civilisation Médiévale*
CCR	*Calendar of Close Rolls*
CDI	*Calendar of Documents Relating to Ireland*, ed. H.S. Swetman *et al.* (London, 1875–86)

CDS	*Calendar of Documents relating to Scotland* I, 1108–1272, ed. J. Bain (Edinburgh, 1881)
Church	*King John: new interpretations*, ed. S. Church (Woodbridge, 1999)
CLibR	*Calendar of Liberate Rolls*
CM	Matthew Paris, *Chronica Majora*, ed. H.R. Luard (RS 57, 1872–84)
CPL	*Calendar of Papal Letters*
CPR	*Calendar of Patent Rolls*
CR	*Close Rolls*
CS	*Chronica Scotorum*, ed. W.M. Hennessy (RS 46, 1886)
Davies	*The British Isles*, ed. R.R. Davies (Edinburgh, 1988)
DB	Domesday Book
Devizes	Richard of Devizes, *Chronicle*, ed. J.T. Appleby (Edinburgh, 1963)
Dialogue	Richard son of Nigel, *The Course of the Exchequer*, ed. C. Johnson (Edinburgh, 1950)
Diceto	Radulph de Diceto, *Opera Historica*, ed. W. Stubbs (RS 68, 1876)
Dip. Docs	*Diplomatic Documents preserved in the Public Record Office 1101–1272*, ed. P. Chaplais (London, 1964)
Dip. Pract.	*English Medieval Diplomatic Practice*, I, Documents and Interpretation, ed. P. Chaplais (HMSO, 1982)
EcHR	*Economic History Review*
EHR	*English Historical Review*
Exchequer Rolls	*The Exchequer Rolls of Scotland* I, 1264–1359, ed. J. Stuart and G. Burnett (Edinburgh, 1878)
Flores	*Flores Historiarum*, ed. H.R. Luard (RS 95, 1890)
GC	*Gallia Christiana*
Gerald	Gerald of Wales, *Opera*, ed. J.S. Brewer *et al.* (RS 21, 1861–77)
Gervase	Gervase of Canterbury, *Historical Works*, ed. W. Stubbs (RS 73, 1879–80)
Gesta	*Gesta Henrici Secundi*, ed. W. Stubbs (RS 49, 1867)
GP	William of Malmesbury, *De Gestis Pontificum*, ed. N.E.S.A. Hamilton (RS 52, 1870); trans. as *The Deeds of the Bishops of England*, by D. Preest (Woodbridge, 2002)
GR	William of Malmesbury, *Gesta Regum Anglorum*, ed. R.A.B. Mynors, R.M. Thomson and M. Winterbottom (Oxford, 1998–99)
HA	Matthew Paris, *Historia Anglorum*, ed. F. Madden (RS 44, 1866–69)
HF	*Recueil des Historiens de France*
HH	Henry of Huntingdon, *Historia Anglorum*, ed. D. Greenway (Oxford, 1996)

HMC   Historical Manuscripts Commission
HN   Eadmer, *Historia Novorum*, ed. M. Rule (RS 81, 1884),
               trans. as *History of Recent Events* by G. Bosanquet
               (Philadelphia, 1965)
Hoveden   Roger of Hoveden, *Chronica*, ed. W. Stubbs (RS 51,
               1868–71)
HP   John of Salisbury, *Historia Pontificalis*, ed. M. Chibnall
               (Oxford, 1986)
HR   *Historical Research*
IHS   *Irish Historical Studies*
Jaffe   P. Jaffe, *Regesta Pontificum Romanorum* (2nd edn,
               Leipzig, 1885–88)
JEH   *Journal of Ecclesiastical History*
JMH   *Journal of Medieval History*
JRSAI   *Journal of the Royal Society of Antiquaries of Ireland*
JWCI   *Journal of the Warburg and Courtauld Institutes*
Lambert   Lambert of Ardres, *The history of the counts of Guines
               and lords of Ardres*, trans. L. Shopkow (Philadelphia,
               2001)
Littere   *Littere Wallie preserved in Liber A in the P.R.O.*, ed. J.G.
               Edwards (Cardiff, 1940)
MARS   *Medieval and Renaissance Studies*
MC   Magna Carta 1215
Melrose   *Chronica de Mailros*, ed. J. Stevenson (Bannatyne Club,
               Edinburgh, 1835)
MGH, SS   *Monumenta Germaniae Historica, Scriptores*
MTB   *Materials for the History of Thomas Becket*, ed. J.C.
               Robertson (RS 67, 1875–83)
Municipal   *Historic and Municipal Documents of Ireland
               1172–1320*, ed. J.T. Gilbert (RS 53, 1870)
Munimenta   *Munimenta Gildhallae Londoniensis*, ed. H.T. Riley (RS
               12, 1859–62)
NEMBN   *Notices et Extraits des Manuscrits de la Bibliothèque
               Nationale*
Newburgh   William of Newburgh, *Historia rerum anglicarum*, ed. R.
               Howlett (RS, 1884–5)
OV   Orderic Vitalis, *Ecclesiastical History*, ed. M. Chibnall
               (Oxford, 1969–80)
PatR   *Patent Rolls*
PBA   *Proceedings of the British Academy*
PL   *Patrologia Latina*
PMLA   *Publications of the Modern Language Association*
Potthast   A. Potthast, *Regesta Pontificum Romanorum* (Berlin,
               1874–75)
PR   *Pipe Rolls*

PRIA	*Proceedings of the Royal Irish Academy*
PRS	Pipe Roll Society
PSAS	*Proceedings of the Scottish Antiquarian Society*
RB	*Revue Bénédictine*
RBPH	*Revue Belge de Philologie et d'Histoire*
RC	*Rotuli Clausarum Litterarum*
RChart	*Rotuli Chartarum*
RH	*Revue Historique*
Rigord	*Oeuvres de Rigord et Guillaume le Breton*, ed. H.F. Delaborde (SHF, 1882–85)
RLib	*Rotuli de Liberate*
RParl	*Rotuli Parliamentorum*, I, ed. J. Strachey (London, 1767)
RPat	*Rotuli Patentium Litterarum*
RRS	*Regesta Regum Scotorum*
RS	Rolls Series
Rymer	T. Rymer, *Foedera* (Record Commission, 1816)
Salisbury	John of Salisbury, *Letters*, ed. W.J. Millor and C.N.L. Brooke (Oxford, I, 1955; II, 1979)
SATF	Société des Anciens Textes Français
SHF	Société de l'Histoire de France
Shirley	*Royal and other historical Letters illustrative of the reign of Henry III*, ed. W.W. Shirley (RS 27, 1862–66)
SHR	*Scottish Historical Review*
Smith	*Britain and Ireland 900–1300*, ed. B. Smith (Cambridge, 1999)
SRS	Scottish Record Society
SS	Surtees Society
TJHE	*Transactions of the Jewish Historical Society of England*
VCH	Victoria County History
Wendover	Roger de Wendover, *The Flowers of History*, ed. H.G. Hewlett (RS 84, 1886–89)
WHR	*Welsh History Review*

Notes

Chapter 1

1. R.S. Rait, *The Parliaments of Scotland* (Glasgow, 1924); A.A.M. Duncan, 'The early parliaments of Scotland', *SHR* 55 (1966), 38–58.
2. HH, i, 2; *Gesta Stephani*, ed. K.R. Potter and R.H.C. Davis (2nd edn, Oxford, 1976), i, 21; Gerald, VI: Itinerary, ii, 7; *CPR 1266–72*, 142.
3. A. Grant, *Independence and Nationhood, Scotland 1306–1469* (London, 1984), pp. 72–75; T.M. Cooper, 'The numbers and the distribution of the population of medieval Scotland', *SHR* 26 (1947), 2–9.
4. A.A.M. Duncan, *Scotland: The making of the Kingdom* (Edinburgh, 1975), pp. 94–100.
5. Gerald, VI: Description, i, 6.
6. J. Stevenson, 'The beginnings of literacy in Ireland', *PRIA* 89 C (1989), 127–55; *Literacy in Medieval Celtic Societies*, ed. H. Pryce (Cambridge, 1998).
7. H.G. Richardson and G.O. Sayles, *Law and Legislation* (Edinburgh, 1966), pp. 1–13.
8. CM, V, 603; likewise, Peter Philomenus, *In Algorismum vulgarem Johannis de Sacrobosco commentarius*, ed. M. Curtze (Hanniae, 1897), p. 31.
9. Bede, *Ecclesiastical History*, ii, 2.
10. Gervase, II, p. lxxxi.
11. *Magna Vita Sancti Hugonis*, ed. D.L. Douie and D.H. Farmer (repr. Oxford, 1985) i, 13.
12. *Brut*: 1045.
13. A. López Ferreiro, *Historia de la Sancta A.M. Iglesia de Santiago de Compostela* (Santiago, 1901), IV, p. 307; D. Lomax, 'The first English pilgrims to Santiago', in *Studies in Medieval History Presented to R.H.C. Davis*, ed. H.M. Mayr-Harting *et al.* (London, 1985), pp. 165–75.
14. *Visio Thurkilli*, ed. P.G. Schmidt (Leipzig, 1978); P.G. Schmidt, 'The vision of Thurkill', *JWCI* 41 (1978), 50–64.
15. *Memorials of St Edmund's Abbey*, ed. T. Arnold (RS 96, 1890), I, Hermann, s. 40; Samson, ii, 2.
16. Reginald of Durham, *Libellus de vita S. Godrici*, ed. J. Stevenson (SS 20, 1847).
17. *Cartulaire du Chapitre de la cathédrale d'Amiens* (Amiens, 1912), pp. 125–6.
18. C.H. Lawrence, *St Edmund of Abingdon* (London, 1960).
19. C. Plummer, 'Vie et Miracles de S. Laurent archevêque de Dublin', *AB* 33 (1914), 121–86.
20. *Flores*, II, 257.
21. *English Historical Documents c.500–1042*, ed. D. Whitelock (2nd edn, London, 1979), no. 51, cl. 6; G.C. Dunning, 'Trade relations between England and the continent in the late Anglo-Saxon period', in *Dark Age Britain*, ed. D.B. Harden (London, 1956), pp. 218–33.
22. Aelfric, *Colloquy*, ed. G.N. Garmonsway (2nd edn, London, 1947).

23. R.S. Lopez and I.W. Raymond, *Medieval Trade in the Mediterranean World* (New York, 1955), pp. 57–8, no. 20, cl. 3.
24. *ASC*, E: 1031 (for 1027); Whitelock (see note 21 above), no. 53. When Edward I promised to send Charles of Salerno 'harriers' in 1279, it is not clear whether he meant hounds or hawks. Rymer I, ii, 568.
25. A.J. Robertson, *The Laws of the Kings of England from Edmund to Henry I* (Cambridge, 1925): Aethelred IV, pp. 1–9.
26. C.W. Jones, *Saint Nicholas of Myra, Bari and Manhattan, biography of a legend* (Chicago, 1978); A.I.E. Langfors, *Histoire de l'abbaye de Fécamp en vers français du xiiie siècle* (Helsinki, 1928); Reginald of Durham, *Libellus de admirandis beati Cuthberti virtutibus*, ed. J. Raine (SS 1, 1835): nos 23, 28, 30–33, 52, 75, 83; *MTB*, I (William) Miracles: i, 30, 41; iii, 42, 45; iv, 6, 11, 13, 14; vi, 75, 77, 145, 146; *MTB*, II (Benedict): i, 68; iv, 41–46; *Memorials* (see note 15 above) I, Hermann, ss. 33, 53; Samson i, 11; ii, 3, 7, 15, 16.
27. Gerald, I, 117; Adam, ii, 17, 22, 52; iv, 1, 10, 35.
28. *The Map of Great Britain circa 1360 known as the Gough Map*, ed. E.J.S. Parsons (Oxford, 1958).
29. Bracton, *De Legibus Angliae*, trans. S.E. Thorne (Cambridge, Mass., 1968), III, pp. 198–9.
30. J. MacInnes, 'West Highland sea-power in the middle ages', *Transactions of the Gaelic Society of Inverness* 48 (1972–74), 518–56.
31. Gerald, V: Topographia, pt. 3, s. 90; *The Book of the Taking of Ireland*, ed. R.A.S. Macalister (Dublin, 1938–56); J. Carey, *The Irish National Origin-legend: synthetic pseudo-history* (Cambridge, 1994).
32. Dicuil, *Liber de Mensura orbis terrae*, ed. J.J. Tierney (Dublin, 1967), vii, 6, 7, 11–15; G.J. Marcus, *The Conquest of the North Atlantic* (Woodbridge, 1980).
33. Bernard of Clairvaux, *Life of Malachy*, trans. H.J. Lawlor (London, 1920).
34. T.W. Fulton, *The Sovereignty of the Sea* (Edinburgh, 1911).
35. *ASC*, E: 1008–9; C: 1049; D, E: 1050.
36. *Stubbs' Select Charters*, 9th edn, ed. H.W.C. Davis (Oxford, 1913, repr. 1951), pp. 181–4, cl. 12.
37. *CS*, 1085, 1111, 1119, 1127; *AFM*, I–II, 947.
38. M.V. Taylor, *Liber Luciani de laude Cestrie* (Record Society of Lancashire and Cheshire, 64, 1912).
39. *GR*, ss. 347–50, 355–89; sugar, 374.
40. Hoveden, III, 43–55, 155–61.
41. Bartholomew Anglicus, *On the Properties of Things, John Trevisa's translation* (Oxford, 1975), book 15.
42. P.D.A. Harvey, 'The Sawley map and other world maps in twelfth-century England', *Imago Mundi* 49 (1997), 33–42.
43. P. Meyer, 'Notice sur les Corrogationes Promothei d'Alexandre Neckam', *NEMBN* 35 (1896), 641–82.
44. B. Hauréau, 'Un poème inédit de Pierre Rigor, chanoine de Reims', *BEC* 44 (1883), 5–11.
45. *The Political Songs of England*, ed. T. Wright (Camden Society, 1839), pp. 63–8.
46. *HF*, 24 (1904), 760.
47. B. Dickins, 'The cult of St Olave in the British Isles', *Saga Book of the Viking Society* 12 (1937–45), 53–80.
48. Dialogue, 53.
49. *Rotuli Hundredorum* (1818) II, 171b; *RPat*, 146; *CPR 1232–47*, 73; *CPR 1247–58*, 239; *CPR 1258–66*, 352, 547, 551, 653; *CPR 1272–81*, 203–4; *RParl*, I, 32, n. 21.
50. A. Grant, 'Scotland's "Celtic Fringe" in the late middle ages: the McDonald Lords of the Isles and the Kingdom of Scotland', in Davies, pp. 118–41; 119: 'institutionalised racism'.
51. J.B. Gillingham, 'The beginnings of English imperialism', *Journal of Historical Sociology* 5 (1992), 392–409; id., 'Killing and Mutilating political enemies in the British Isles', Smith, pp. 114–34; id., 'Civilizing the English? The English histories of William of Malmesbury and David Hume', *HR* 74 (2001), 17–43.
52. R. Bartlett, 'Cults of Irish, Scottish and Welsh saints in twelfth century England', in Smith, pp. 67–86; M. Philpott, 'Some Interaction between the English and Irish churches', *ANS* 20 (1997), 157–204.

Chapter 2

1. Wipo, The deeds of Conrad II, *Imperial Lives and Letters of the eleventh century*, ed. T.F. Mommsen and K.F. Morrison (New York, 1962), pp. 52–100: ch. 35.
2. OV, II, 256–7.
3. William of Poitiers, *Gesta Guillelmi*, ed. R.H.C. Davis and M. Chibnall (Oxford, 1998), ii, 29.
4. Lambert, 113.
5. M. Mathews, 'Forms of Social Mobility: the example of Zensualita', in *England and Germany in the High Middle Ages*, ed. A. Haverkamp and H. Vollrath (Oxford, 1996), pp. 357–69.
6. DB, f. 118; f. 52; H. Ellis, *A general introduction to Domesday Book* (London, 1833), II, pp. 428, 430, 444, 449, 454, 457, 463, 465, 468, 469, 474, 480, 486, 499, 502, 505, 512; A. Ballard, 'The Law of Breteuil', *EHR* 30 (1915), 646–58.
7. *Frutolfs und Ekkehards Chroniken*, ed. F.J. Schmale and I. Schmale-Ott (Darmstadt, 1972), 78; E. van Houts, 'The Norman Conquest through European Eyes', *EHR* 110 (1995), 832–53; D. Berg, *England und der Kontinent* (Bochum, 1987); K.E. Gade, 'Northern light on the battle of Hastings', *Viator* 28 (1997), 65–82.
8. Adam, iii, 52.
9. *ASC*, D: 1051 (for 1050); GP, s. 164; *A brief history of the bishoprick of Somerset, Ecclesiastical Documents*, ed. J. Hunter (Camden Society, 1840), 19.
10. *Monumenta Arroasiensia*, ed. B.M. Tock (Corpus Christianum, contin. med., Brépols, 2000), 175.
11. H.E.J. Cowdrey, 'Gregorian reform in Anglo-Norman lands and Scandinavia', *Studi Gregoriani* 13 (1985), 321–52.
12. HN, 55–69.
13. Herbert Losinga, *Letters*, ed. R. Anstruther (London, 1846), nos 5, 3.
14. L.F. Salzman, *Building in England down to 1540* (Oxford, 1952), pp. 135–6.
15. E. Fernie, *The Architecture of Norman England* (Oxford, 2000).
16. C.M. Kauffmann, *Romanesque Manuscripts 1066–1190* (London, 1975); F. Wormald, 'The survival of Anglo-Saxon illumination after the Norman Conquest', *PBA* 30 (1944), 1–19.
17. O. Pächt, *The Rise of Pictorial Narrative in Twelfth-Century England* (Oxford, 1962).
18. D. Matthew, *The Norman Monasteries and their English Possessions* (Oxford, 1962).
19. E.A. Freeman, *The History of the Norman Conquest of England: its causes and its results* (2nd edn, Oxford, 1876), IV, App. K; *Chronica abbatiae de Evesham*, ed. W.D. Macray, xliv; P. King, 'English influence on the church of Odense in the early middle ages', *JEH* 13 (1962), 144–53.
20. Adam, iii, 54.
21. Anselm, nos 447, 449; *The Orkneyinga Saga*, trans. A.B. Taylor (Edinburgh, 1938), 52.
22. GC, IX (1874), instrumenta cols 217–24; J. Le Patourel, 'Geoffrey of Montbray, bishop of Coutances, 1049–1093', *EHR* 59 (1944), 129–61.
23. HN, 111–12, 114.
24. J. Shepard, 'The English and Byzantium', *Traditio* 29 (1973), 53–92; K.N. Ciggaar, 'L'émigration anglaise à Byzance après 1066', *Revue des Etudes Byzantines* 32 (1974), 301–42; R.J. Godfrey, 'Defeated Anglo-Saxons at Constantinople', *ANS* 1 (1978), 63–74.
25. OV, II, 202–3; IV, 16–17; Geoffrey of Malaterra, *De rebus gestis Rogerii Calabriae et Siciliae comitis*, ed. E. Pontieri (Bologna, 1927, 1974).
26. V. Laurent, 'Byzance et l'Angleterre au lendemain de la conquête normande', *Numismatic Circular* 71, 5 (May 1963), 93–6.
27. GR, s. 225.
28. K.A.H. Kellner, *Heortologie* (2nd edn, Freiburg im Breisgau, 1906), pp. 174–92.
29. C.H. Haskins, 'A Canterbury monk at Constantinople', *EHR* 25 (1910), 293–5.
30. HH, i, 38.
31. V. Laurent, 'Un sceau inédit du patriarche de Jérusalem, Sophrone II trouvé à Winchester', *Numismatic Circular* 72, 1 (January 1964), 49–50.
32. GP, s. 425.
33. Vita de B. Mariano Scoto, *AASS*, Feb. II, 361–72, cap. 4.

34. H. Loyn, *The Vikings in Wales* (Viking Society, 1976); C. Etchingham, 'North Wales and the Isles: the insular Viking zone', *Peritia* 15 (2001), 145–87.
35. *A Medieval Prince of Wales: The life of Gruffydd ap Cynan*, ed. D.S. Evans (Llanarch, 1990).
36. B. O'Cuiv, The impact of the Scandinavian invasions on the Celtic-speaking peoples *c*.800–1100, *International Congress of Celtic Studies, Dublin 1959*, (1975); S. Duffy, 'Ostmen, Irish and Welsh in the eleventh century', *Peritia* 9 (1995), 378–96.
37. L. Abrams, 'The conversion of the Scandinavians of Dublin', *ANS* 20 (1997), 1–29; *CS*, 1026.
38. G. Goudie *The Celtic and Scandinavian Antiquities of Shetland* (Edinburgh, 1904); Adam, iv, 35.
39. D. Broun, 'The origins of Scottish identity in its European context', in *Scotland in the Dark Ages*, ed. B. Crawford (St Andrews, 1994), pp. 21–31.
40. *Orkneyinga* (see note 21 above), 41.
41. R. Power, 'Magnus Barelegs' expeditions to the West 1093–1103', *SHR* 65 (1986), 107–32: *id.*, 'The death of Magnus Barelegs', *SHR* 73 (1994), 216–22; *Orkneyinga* (see note 21 above), 78, 82–3, 93, 100, 106.
42. Adam, iii, 24, 72–3, 77; iv, 10.
43. DB, f. 262v.
44. DB, f. 163; GP, s. 154; *Gesta Stephani* (see Chapter 1, note 2), 27, 29–30; *AM*, I, 11: 1124.
45. *Vita Wulfstani*, ed. R. Darlington (Camden Society, 1928), 43, 91.
46. Gerald of Wales, *Expugnatio Hibernica*, ed. A.B. Scott and F.X. Martin (Dublin, 1978), 18.
47. S. Duffy, 'Irishmen and Islesmen in the kingdoms of Dublin and Man 1052–1171', *Eriu* 43 (1992), 93–133; I. Beuermann, 'Metropolitan ambitions and politics: Kells-Mellifont and Man and the Isles', *Peritia* 16 (2002), 419–34.
48. *ASC*: 1030, 1054.
49. *ASC*, D, E: 1072.
50. *ASC*, E: 1093.
51. HH, vii, 2; *ASC*, E: 1092.
52. Marianus Scottus, *Chronicon*, ed. G. Waitz (*MGH, SS*, 13), 74–9.
53. *Orkneyinga* (see note 21 above), 31: *c*.1048.
54. Lanfranc, *Letters*, ed. H. Clover and M.T. Gibson (Oxford, 1979), no. 50.
55. Turgot, *Vita S. Margaretae Scotorum reginae*, ed. H. Hinde (SS 51, 1867).
56. Hugh the Chanter, *The history of the church of York 1066–1127*, ed. C. Johnson, rev. M. Brett *et al.* (Oxford, 1990), xlv–liv, 67.
57. *ASC*, E: 1063.
58. A.G. Williams, 'Norman lordship in southeast Wales during the reign of William I', *WHR* 16 (1993), 445–66.
59. Gerald, VI: Itinerary, ii, 12.
60. Anselm, no. 270; *The Text of the Book of Llan Dav*, ed. J. Gwenogvryn Evans and J. Rhys (Oxford, 1893).
61. *AI*: 1068; B. Hudson, 'The family of Harold Godwinsson and the Irish sea province', *JRSAI* 109 (1979), 92–100.
62. GR, s. 409; OV, VI, 30, 48, 50.
63. *AI*: 1079.
64. *AI*: 1028, 1042, 1064; *ALC*: 1051, 1064.
65. A. Wilmart, 'La Trinité des Scots à Rome', *RB* 41 (1929), 218–30.
66. *AI*: 1080.
67. A. Gwynn, 'Ireland and the Continent in the eleventh century', *IHS* 8 (1953), 193–216.
68. *AU*: 1023, 1027, 1038, 1042, 1052.
69. A. Gwynn, 'Gregory VII and the Irish Church', *Studi Gregoriani* 3 (1948), 105–28.
70. J.E.C. Williams, 'The court poets of medieval Ireland', *PBA* 57 (1971), 85–135.
71. M.T. Gibson, *Lanfranc of Bec* (Oxford, 1978), pp. 122–4.
72. Lanfranc (see note 54 above), nos 9, 10.
73. Gregory VII, *Epistolae Vagantes*, ed. H.E.J. Cowdrey (Oxford, 1972), no. 57.
74. D. Bethell, 'English monks and Irish reforms in the eleventh and twelfth centuries', *Historical Studies* VIII (1971), 111–35; D.N. Dumville, *Councils and Synods of the Gaelic Early and Central Middle Ages*, Quiggin Pamphlets (Cambridge, 1997).

75. Lanfranc (see note 54 above), no. 49.
76. Anselm, nos 198, 201.

Chapter 3

1. GR, s. 251.
2. See now, C. Tyerman, *England and the Crusades* (Chicago, 1988).
3. Raimond d'Aguilers, *Liber*, ed. J.H. and L.L. Hill (Paris, 1969).
4. Anselm, no. 195.
5. *De expugnatione Lyxbonensi*, ed. C.W. David (New York, 1936, repr. 1976).
6. GR, s. 410; G. Barnes, 'The medieval Anglophile: England and its rulers in Old Norse history and saga', *Parergon*, n.s. 10, 2 (1992), 11–26.
7. GR, ss. 347–50, 355–89; R.M. Thomson, 'William of Malmesbury, historian of crusade', *Reading Medieval Studies* 23 (1997), 121–34.
8. *Peregrinationes tres*, ed. R.B.C. Huygens and J.H. Pryor (Corpus Christianum, contin. med. 84, 1994), 35–57.
9. Lambert, 113.
10. W. Holtzmann, 'Zur Geschichte des Investiturstreits', *Neues Archiv* 50 (1935), 270–82: letter 280–2.
11. *Gesta Francorum*, ed. R.M.T. Hill (Oxford, 1962).
12. *Brut*: 1125, 1143.
13. Guibert of Nogent, *Gesta Dei per Francos*, ed. R.B.C. Huygens (Corpus Christianum, contin. med. 127, 1996), 89; A.D. Macquarrie, *Scotland and the Crusade 1095–1560* (Edinburgh, 1985).
14. *AI*: 1105.
15. *CS*: 1147.
16. B. Lees, *Records of the Templars in England in the Twelfth Century* (London, 1935).
17. J. Bédier, *Les chansons de croisade* (Paris, 1909), pp. 3–16.
18. R.L. Poole, 'The appointment and deprivation of St William of York', *EHR* 45 (1930), 273–8.
19. Dialogue, pp. 18, 35–6.
20. John of Salisbury, *Policraticus*, ed. C.C.J. Webb (Oxford, 1909), vii, 19.
21. *Orkneyinga* (see Chapter 2, note 21), 52, 66, p. 379, n. 1, pp. 384–5, nn. 6–7; R.G. Cant, 'Settlement, society and church organization in the northern isles', *The Northern and Western Isles in the Viking World*, ed. A. Fenton and H. Palson (Edinburgh, 1984), pp. 169–79.
22. F. Brittain, *Saint Giles* (Cambridge, 1928); E.J. Kealey, *Medieval Medicine, a social history of Anglo-Norman medicine* (Baltimore, 1981).
23. J. Stow, *The Survey of London* (Everyman edn, 1912), pp. 438–41.
24. P.K. Hitti, *Memoirs of an Arab-Syrian Gentleman* (Beirut, 1964), pp. 165–6; *Gesta Stephani* (see Chapter 1, note 2), i, 28; *MTB*, I, vi, 6; Melrose: 1265.
25. L.M. de Rijk, *Garlandus Compotista Dialectica* (Assen, 1959); GP, s. 164.
26. C.H. Haskins, *Studies in the History of Medieval Science* (Cambridge, Mass., 1924); *Adelard of Bath*, ed. C. Burnett (Warburg Institute Surveys and Texts 14, London, 1987); D. Metlitzki, *The Matter of Araby in Medieval England* (Princeton, 1977).
27. C. Henry, 'Prologus N. Ocreati in Helceph', *Abhandlungen zur Geschichte der Mathematik* III (1880), 129–39.
28. Petrus Alfonsi, *The Disciplina Clericalis*, trans. P.R. Quarrie, ed. E. Hermes (London, 1977).
29. J. Kritzek, *Peter the Venerable and Islam* (Princeton, 1964); G. Sarton, *Introduction to the History of Science* II Part 1: From Rabbi ben Ezra to Roger Bacon (Washington, 1931), pp. 175–7.
30. I. Lancaster, *Deconstructing the Past, Abraham ibn Ezra's introduction to the Torah* (London, 2003).
31. *PL*, 163: 759–70; R. Foreville and J. Leclercq, Un débat sur le sacerdoce des moines au xiie siècle, *Analecta Monastica* 4e série, fasc. 41 (Rome, 1957), 9–14.
32. *PL*, 156: 962–1018, Liber II.

33. MS Darmstadt Cod. 2202: E. Zimmermann and K.H. Staub, *Buchkunst des Mittelalters* (Wiesbaden, 1980), pp. 31–2.
34. B. Hauréau, *Notices et Extraits* (Paris, 1891) III, pp. 212–13; L. Minio-Paluello, 'The "Ars Disserendi" of Adam of Balsham "Parvipontanus"', *MARS* 3 (1954), 116–69; J. Pitra, *Spicilegium Solesmense*, III (Paris, 1855), Anonymus Anglus Cisterciensis monachus, Distinctionum Monasticum et Moralium, V, 476, note 8; E. Faral, *Les arts poétiques du xiie et xiiie siècles* (Paris, 1924), under Geoffrey of Vinsauf.
35. *Brut*: 1115.
36. *HMC Reports on Manuscripts in Various Collections* (1901), I 217.
37. L.V. Delisle, *Rouleaux des Morts* (SHF, Paris, 1866), p. 110.
38. Stephen de Fougères, Vita S. Vitalis, ed. E.P. Sauvage, *AB* I (1882), 355–90, ii, 11, pp. 378–9.
39. Meyer (see Chapter 1, note 43).
40. *Rouleaux* (see note 37 above), 168–71; OV, IV, 326.
41. E.A. Escallier, *L'abbaye d'Anchin* (Lille, 1852); K.F. Werner, 'Andreas von Marchiennes und die Geschichtsschreibung', *Deutches Archiv* 9 (1952), 402–63.
42. A. Boutemy, 'Enluminures d'Anchin au temps de l'abbé Gossuin (1131/33 à 1165)', *Scriptorium* 11 (1957), 234–48; *id.* 'Un monument capital de l'enluminure anglo-saxonne', *CCM* 1 (1958), 179–82; E. Salter, *English and International: Studies in the Literature, Art and Patronage of medieval England*, ed. D. Pearsall and N. Zeman (Cambridge, 1988).
43. H. Dauphin, L'érémitisme en Angleterre au xie et xiie siècles, *Eremitismo in Occidente nei secoli xi e xii* (Milan 1965), pp. 271–310.
44. M.D. Knowles and R.N. Hadcock, *Medieval Religious Houses: England and Wales* (London, rev. 1971).
45. Walter Map, *De Nugiis Curialium: Courtiers' Trifles*, ed. M.R. James *et al.* (Oxford, 1983), v, 5.
46. HP, 40.
47. *Memorials of the Abbey of St Mary of Fountains*, ed. J.R. Walbran (SS 42, 1863), 89–90.
48. *PL.*, 172: 1363–1446: Vita beati Bernardi: 1426–27; J.G. Dunbar, *The Historic Architecture of Scotland* (London, 1966).
49. *Chronica regum Manniae et Insularum*, trans. G. Broderick (Belfast, 1979); B.R.S. and E.M. Megaw, 'The Norse heritage in the Isle of Man', in *The Early Cultures of North West Europe*, ed. C. Fox and B. Dickins (Cambridge, 1950), pp. 143–70.
50. Vita S. Mochullei Hibernensi episcopi, ed. K. Pertz (*MGH, SS* 20), 512–14.
51. D. Binchy, 'The Irish Benedictine congregation in medieval Germany', *Studies* 18 (1929), 194–210.
52. M. Dolley, *Anglo-Norman Ireland* (Dublin, 1972), p. 35.
53. *Miscellaneous Irish Annals 1114–1457*, ed. S. Ohlnnse (Dublin, 1947): 1134; Liam de Por, 'Cormac's chapel: the beginnings of Irish Romanesque', in *North Munster Studies*, ed. E. Rynne (Limerick, 1967), pp. 133–45.
54. P.J. Dunning, 'The Arrouaise Order in Medieval Ireland', *IHS* 4 (1946), 297–316.
55. R. Stalley, *The Cistercian Monasteries in Ireland* (London, 1987).
56. W. Dugdale, *Monasticon Anglicanum* (1820 edn) III, 635–40; Jaffe 10863; G. Desjardins, *Cartulaire de l'abbaye de Conques en Rouergue* (Paris, 1879), nos 497, 516, 519–22.
57. D.M. Dunlop, 'The British Isles according to medieval Arabic authors', *Islamic Quarterly* 4 (1957), 11–28.
58. *The Anglo-Norman Chronicle of Wigmore Abbey*, ed. J.C. Dickinson and P.T. Ricketts, *Transactions of the Woolhope Naturalists' Field Club* 39 (1967), 413–46.
59. A. Gransden, *Historical Writing in England c.500–c.1307* (London, 1974).
60. G. Gaimar, *L'estoire des Engleis*, ed. A. Bell (Oxford, 1960).
61. P. Verbrist, 'Reconstructing the past: the Chronicle of Marianus Scotus', *Peritia* 16 (2002), 284–334.
62. E. Könsgen, 'Zwei unbekannte Briefe zu der Gesta Regum Anglorum des Wilhelms von Malmesbury', *Deutsches Archiv* 31 (1975), 204–14.
63. R.W. Southern, 'The English origins of the "Miracles of the Virgin"', *MARS* 4 (1958), 176–216.
64. C. Bullock-Davies, *Professional Interpreters and the Matter of Britain* (Cardiff, 1966).

65. Geoffrey of Monmouth, *Historia Regum Britanniae*, ed. A. Griscom (London, 1929, repr. 1977); M. Schlauth, 'Geoffrey of Monmouth and early Polish historiography', *Speculum* 44 (1969), 258–63.

66. T.M. Charles-Edwards, 'The date of the four branches of the Mabinogi', *Transactions of the Honourable Society of Cymmrodorion* (1970), 263–78.

67. *Book of Leinster*, ed. R. Atkinson (1880), ed. R.I. Best, 6 volumes, (Dublin, 1954–83); U. Mac Gearailt, 'The language of some late Middle Irish texts in the Book of Leinster', *Studia Hibernica* 26 (1991–92), 167–216.

68. Hugh the Chanter (see Chapter 2, note 56), xxx–xlv.

69. *Llan Dav* (see Chapter 2, note 60); F.G. Cowley, 'The church in Glamorgan', *Glamorgan County History* III (1971); Gerald, IV, 268.

70. *Cartae et alia munimenta quae ad dominium de Glamorgan pertinent*, ed. G.T. Clark, rev. G.L. Clark (Cardiff, 1910).

71. *Rhigyfarch's Life of Saint David*, ed. J.W. James (Cardiff, 1967); *Vitae Sanctorum Britanniae et Genealogiae*, ed. A.W. Wade-Evans (Cardiff, 1944).

72. G. Donaldson, 'Scottish bishops's sees before the reign of David I', *PSAS* (1952–53), 106–17; D.E.R. Watt, *Fasti Ecclesiae Scoticane Medii Aevi ad annum 1638* (SRS, n.s. 1, 1969).

73. J. Fleming, *Gille of Limerick (c.1070–1145): Architect of a medieval church* (Dublin, 2001).

74. *CS*: 1107, for 1111; J. MacErlean, 'Synod of Ráith Breansail', *Archivium Hibernicum* 3 (1914), 1–33.

75. M. Holland, 'Dublin and the reform of the Irish church in the eleventh and twelfth centuries', *Peritia* 14 (2000), 111–60; K. Hughes, *Early Christian Ireland* (London, 1972), ch. 9.

76. J. Ryan, *Toirdelbach O Conchubair (1088–1156), King of Connaught, king of Ireland* (Dublin, 1966).

77. *ALC, AU*: 1129.

78. H. Immenkötter, 'Ecclesia hiberniana: Die Synode von Inis Padraig im Jahre 1148', *Annuarium Historiae Conciliorum* 17, I (1985), 19–69.

79. J.F. O'Doherty, 'Rome and the Anglo-Norman invasion of Ireland', *Irish Ecclesiastical Record* 42 (1933), 131–45; John of Salisbury, *The Metalogicon*, trans. D.D. McGarry (Berkeley, 1955), iv, 42.

80. *Purgatorium S. Patricii, Das Buch von Espurgatoire*, ed. K. Warnke (Halle, 1938).

81. *Visio Tundali*, ed. A. Wagner (Erlangen, 1882); N.F. Palmer, *Visio Tungdali, The German and Dutch translations* (Munich, 1982).

82. *Die texte des Normannischen Anonymus, Anonymus Eboracensis*, ed. K. Pellens (Wiesbaden, 1966).

83. *GR*, s. 420; Holtzmann (see note 10 above), 282–301.

84. E. Narducci, 'Intorno a due trattati inediti d'Abaco', *Bullettino di Bibliografia e di Storia delle scienze matematiche e fisiche* 15 (1882), 135–54; Philippe of Thaon, *Cumpoz c.1113*, ed. I. Short (Anglo-Norman Text Plain Text series 2, 1984); Haskins *Studies* (see note 26 above), pp. 327–35: 'The abacus and the exchequer'; B. Lyon and A. Verhulst, *Medieval Finance: a comparison of financial institutions in northwestern Europe* (Bruges, 1967).

85. Suger, *Vie de Louis VI le Gros*, ed. H. Waquet (2nd edn, Paris, 1964), pp. 98–103, trans. as *The deeds of Louis the Fat* by R. Cusiman and J. Moorhead (Washington, 1992).

86. F.L. Ganshof, 'Note sur le premier traité anglo-flamand de Douvres', *Revue du Nord* 40 (1959), 245–57; *Dip. Docs*, no. 1, renewed, nos 2, 3, 4.

87. J.H. Round, 'The counts of Boulogne as English lords', *Studies in Peerage and Family History* (London, 1901), 147–80.

88. Galbert of Bruges, *The Murder of Charles the Good*, trans. J.B. Ross (New York, 1967), 113.

89. *Historia Ecclesie Abbendonensis*, vol. II, ed. J. Hudson (Oxford, 2002), pp. 68–9.

90. *AASS*, July, III, 113–41.

91. *AASS*, July, VII, 98–131.

92. Snorre Sturluson, *Heimskringla, or the Lives of the Norse Kings*, ed. E. Monsen (Cambridge, 1932), XIV, 8; C. Hohler, 'The cathedral of St Swithun at Stavanger in the twelfth century', *Journal of the British Archaeological Association* 27 (1964), 92–118;

H.G. Leach, 'The relations of the Norwegian with the English church 1066–1399 and their importance to comparative literature', *Proceedings of the American Academy of Arts and Sciences*, 44 (1909), 531–60.

93. H.K. Mann, *Nicholas Breakspear, the only English Pope* (London, 1914); R.W. Southern, 'Pope Adrian IV', in *Medieval Humanism* (Oxford, 1970), 234–52.

94. Vita et miracula B. Henrici episcopi, *Monumentorum veterum ecclesiae Suegothicae, pars prima*, ed. E. Benzelius (Uppsala, 1709); J. Messenius, *Chronicon episcoporum per Sueciam* (Stockholm, 1611), 105.

95. T. Schmid, *Liber ecclesiae Vallentunensis* (Stockholm, 1945), 29–31.

96. OV, VI, 394–7; Anselm, no. 263; M. Defourneaux, *Les français en Espagne au xie et xiie siècles* (Paris, 1949), p. 132.

97. C. Verlinden, *L'esclavage dans l'Europe Médiévale, t. 1. Péninsule Ibérique, France* (Bruges, 1955), p. 147.

98. G. Loisel, *Histoire des Ménageries de l'Antiquité à nos jours* (Paris, 1902); Lambert, 128.

99. F. Bar, *Les Epitres latines de Raoul le Tortuaire* (1937), ep. 9.

100. *Brut*: 1115.

101. R.A. McDonald, *The Kingdom of the Isles, Scotland's western seaboard 1100–1336* (East Linton, 1997).

102. *ALC, AU*: 1118.

103. *Brut*: 1114.

104. GR, s. 400; G.W.S. Barrow, *David I of Scotland (1124–1153): the balance of the old and the new* (Reading, 1984); *The Acts of Malcolm IV, king of Scots 1153–65*, ed. G.W.S. Barrow (*RRS*, I, Edinburgh, 1960).

105. B.H.I.H. Stewart, *The Scottish Coinage* (rev. edn, London, 1967).

106. Richard of Hexham, *Historia de gestis regis Stephani et de bello de Standardo, Chronicles of the reigns of Stephen, Henry II and Richard I*, ed. R. Howlett (RS 82, 1886), III, 139–78; R.D. Oram, *The Lordship of Galloway* (Edinburgh, 2000).

107. *Brut*: 1108; L. Toomians, 'Wizo Flandrensis and the Flemish settlement in Pembrokeshire', *Cambridge Medieval Celtic Studies* 20 (1990), 99–118.

108. *Gruffydd ap Cynan: a collaborative biography*, ed. K.L. Maunde (Woodbridge, 1996).

109. O. Davies, *Celtic Christianity in Early Medieval Wales* (Cardiff, 1996), ch. 5: 'The poets of the princes'; C.W. Lewis, 'Court poets', in *Guide to Welsh Literature*, ed. A.O.H. Jarman and G.R. Hughes (Cardiff, 1992); J. Lloyd Jones, 'The court poets of the Welsh princes', *PBA* 34 (1948), 167–97.

110. *Gruffydd* (see Chapter 2, note 35).

111. T.E. McNeill, *Castles in Ireland. Feudal Power in a Gaelic World* (London, 1997); M.T. Flanagan, 'Irish and Anglo-Norman warfare in twelfth-century Ireland', in *A Military History of Ireland*, ed. T. Bartlett and K. Jeffery (Cambridge, 1996), pp. 52–75.

112. *Heimskringla* (see note 92 above), XIII, 33; XIV.

113. GR, s. 409.

114. *Memorials* (see Chapter 1, note 15), II (1892), 290.

115. Anselm, no. 428.

116. C.R. Sneddon, 'Brendan the navigator: a twelfth-century view', in *The North Sea World in the Middle Ages*, ed. T.R. Liszka and L.E.M. Walker (Dublin, 2001), pp. 211–29.

Chapter 4

1. J.B. Gillingham, *The Angevin Empire* (2nd edn, London, 2001); W.L. Warren, *Henry II* (London, 1973).

2. J. Alers, *Die Welfen und die Englische Könige* (Hildesheim, 1987).

3. *Gesta* I, 310; Hoveden, II, 283.

4. *Chronicon Universale anonymi Laudunensis 1154–1219*, ed. A. Cartellieri (Leipzig, 1909).

5. J.H. Round, 'Hornchurch Priory', *Transactions of the Essex Archaeological Society* n.s. vi, 1 (1896), 1–12; VCH Essex, II, 195; J. Gremaud, *Documents relatifs à l'histoire du Valdais* (Lausanne, 1875), I, 102–7, n. 156; II, 122–3, n. 736; A. Simonetta, 'Hoard of

coins found along the Great St Bernard Pass', *The Numismatic Circular* 57 (1949), cols 356–7.
6. *Chronicon . . . Laudunensis* (see note 4 above); *HF*, 13, 683.
7. Diceto, II, 7–8.
8. *MTB*, III, 526: GC, IX (1751), 172; L. Falkenstein, 'Zu Entstehungsort und Redaktor des Collectio Brugensis', *Proceedings of the Eighth International Congress of Medieval Canon Law*, ed. S. Chodorow (Vatican City, 1992), 117–51; *Epistolae Cantuarienses 1187–1199*, ed. W. Stubbs (RS 38, 1865), nos 14, 109, 142, 239, 456; p. 559.
9. Gervase, I, 203.
10. *The Acts of William I 1165–1214*, ed. G.W.S. Barrow (*RRS*, II, Edinburgh, 1971), 10.
11. Melrose: 1166.
12. J.A. Kossmann-Putto, 'Florent V count of Holland, claimant to the Scottish throne in 1291–92, his personal and political background', *Scotland and the Low Countries 1124–1994*, ed. G.G. Simpson (East Linton, 1996), pp. 15–27.
13. *Gesta*, I, 313–14, 322; Hoveden, III, 298–9, 308; IV, 138, 174.
14. *Jordan Fantosme's Chronicle*, ed. R.C. Johnston (Oxford, 1981), 69, ll. 637–44.
15. Walter of Coventry, *Memoriale*, ed. W. Stubbs (RS 58, 1872–73), 206.
16. R.A. McDonald and S.A. McLean, 'Somerled of Argyll: a new look at an old problem', *SHR* 71 (1992), 3–22.
17. Faral (see Chapter 3, note 34); B. Hauréau, Notice sur un manuscrit de la Reine Christine à la bibliothèque du Vatican (344), section xxvi, pp. 314–18, section xlv, pp. 348–9, *NEMBN* 29/2 (1880).
18. P. Latimer, 'Henry II's campaign against the Welsh in 1165', *WHR* 14 (1989), 523–52.
19. Gerald, III, 166.
20. Gerald, VI: Itinerary, i, 5; ii, 7; VII, 68; VIII, 33; Salisbury, II, nos 173, 228, 231; *MTB*, III, 56, 528.
21. H. Pryce, 'Owain Gwynedd and Louis VII: the Franco-Welsh diplomacy of the first prince of Wales', *WHR* 19 (1998–99), 1–28.
22. *Brut*: 1173.
23. *Histoire de Guillaume le Maréchal*, ed. P. Meyer (SHF, 1901), 87.
24. Gerald, VI: Description, i, 8.
25. Devizes, 33; Gerald, VI: Description, i, 6.
26. *PR 3 J*, 1201, 128, 137, 264.
27. S. Duffy, 'The 1169 invasion as a turning point in Irish-Welsh relations', Smith, pp. 98–113; *Brut*: 1168.
28. *The Song of Dermot and the Earl*, ed. G.H. Orpen (Oxford, 1892), ll. 1849–58.
29. Gervase, I, 234–5; *Gesta*, I, 102–3.
30. M.T. Flanagan, 'Henry II, the Council of Cashel and the Irish bishops', *Peritia* 10 (1996), 184–211.
31. Gerald, VIII, 156.
32. *MTB*, III, 525.
33. *Thomas Becket: Actes du Colloque international de Sédières*, ed. R. Foreville (Paris, 1975); C. Renardy, 'Notes concernant le culte de saint Thomas Becket dans le diocèse de Liège', *RBPH* 55 (1977), 381–9.
34. *MTB*, I, iv, 52; v, 10; vi, 25, 37, 39, 44, 51, 65; II, vi, 5, 6.
35. *Thomas Saga Erkibyskups*, ed. E. Magnusson (RS 65, 1875–83).
36. T. Borenius, *St Thomas Becket in Art* (London, 1932).
37. *Epistolae* (see note 8 above), nos 104, 177, 382; *Layettes du Trésor des Chartes*, ed. J.B.A.T. Teulet (Paris, 1863–1909), II, no. 2221.
38. Guernes de Pont de Ste Maxence, *La vie de Saint Thomas*, ed. E. Walberg (repr. Paris, 1936); I. Short, 'An early draft of Guerne's Vie de Saint Thomas Becket', *Medium Aevum* 46 (1977), 20–34.
39. Gervase, I, 3–29, esp. 6–7, 20–1; C. Wilson, *The Gothic Cathedral* (London, 1990).
40. *Epistolae* (see note 8 above), nos 288, 197.
41. C. Duggan, *Twelfth-century Decretal Collections* (London, 1963).
42. L. Wahrmund, *Quellen zur Geschichte des Römish-Kanonischen Processes im Mittelalter*, Bd II, Heft III: *Die Summa de ordine judiciario des Ricardus Anglicus* (Innsbruck, 1915).
43. *MTB*, III, 525; *Gesta*, I, 199–206.
44. *Magna Vita* (see Chapter 1, note 11).

45. Hoveden, IV, 30; E.A. Winkelmann, *Philipp von Schwaben und Otto von Braunschweig: Jahrbücher der deutschen Geschichte* (Leipzig, 1873–78), 488–90, App. 1, s. 2.
46. Salisbury, I, xxvii–viii; J. González, *El reino de Castilla en la época de Alfonso VIII, I, Estudio* (Madrid, 1960), p. 190.
47. *MTB*, VI, 396; VII, 26, 143; D. Matthew, *The Norman Kingdom of Sicily* (Cambridge, 1992), pp. 216–18.
48. H.G. Leach, *Angevin Britain and Scandinavia* (Cambridge, Mass., 1921), pp. 28–9.
49. G.M. Gathorne-Hardy, *A Royal Imposter, King Sverre of Norway* (Oxford, 1956).
50. GC, X, 1548–49; Salisbury, II, nos 142, 214.
51. GC, II, 1352; *PL*, 190: 1027; G. Raciti, 'Isaac de l'Etoile et son siècle', *Citeaux Commentarii Cistercienses* 13 (1962), 135–41.
52. Gervase of Tilbury, *Otia Imperialia, recreation for an emperor*, ed. S.E. Banks and J.W. Baines (Oxford, 2002).
53. G.B. Flahiff, 'Ralph Niger', *Medieval Studies* 2 (1940), 104–26; Ralph Niger, *De re militari*, ed. L. Schmugge (Berlin, 1917); Ralph Niger, *Chronica*, ed. R. Anstruther (London, 1851).
54. M. Gullick, 'Professional scribes in eleventh and twelfth-century England', in *English Manuscript Studies 1100–1500*, 7 (1998), ed. P. Beal and J. Griffiths, pp. 1–24; L.V. Delisle, *Notice de douze livres royaux* (Paris, 1902), app. ix; F. Avril and P.D. Stirnemann, *Manuscrits enluminés d'origine insulaire vii–xx siècles* (Paris, 1987); F. Deuchler, *Der Ingeborgpsalter* (Berlin, 1967).
55. *PL*, 215: 298–9; *HMC Various* (see Chapter 3, note 36), 235–6, no. 227.
56. Rigord, 120, 86: 1192.
57. *Chronicon . . . Laudensis* (see note 4 above): 1212.
58. *PL*, 207: 452–3, n. 158.
59. Jaffe, 12787.
60. Jaffe, 14963.
61. Gerald, III, 240, 287, 290–1, 293, 297.
62. Gerald, III, 248; IV, 268–305.
63. *Brut, AC*: 1153.
64. HP, 40.
65. Winkelmann (see note 45 above).
66. Magister Gregorius, *Narracio de mirabilibus urbis Romae*, ed. R.B.C. Huygens (Leiden, 1970); *Llan Dav* (see Chapter 2, note 60); GR, ss. 351–2; Gerald, IV, dist. iv, 2.
67. Tilbury (see note 52 above), pp. 576–87, 802–5.
68. Hoveden, II, 67, 98; Niger, *Chronica* (see note 53 above).
69. E. Jamison, 'The Sicilian Norman kingdom in the mind of Anglo-Norman contemporaries', *PBA* 24, 1938.
70. A.M. Tommasini, *Irish Saints in Italy* (London, 1937); L. Gougaud, *Les saints irlandais hors d'Irlande* (Louvain, 1936); M. Halsall, 'Vercelli and the Vercelli Book', *PMLA* 84/6 (1969), 1545–51; J.F. Foster, 'The connection of the church of Chesterton with the abbey of Vercelli', *Proceedings of the Cambridge Antiquarian Society* 13 (1909), 185–212; *CPL*, 97; V. Mandelli, *Il comune di Vercelli nel medio evo* (Vercelli, 1857), II, p. 323.
71. Gerald, III, Invectiones, i, 2.
72. Jocelin of Brakelond, *Chronicle*, ed. H.E. Butler (Edinburgh, 1949), pp. 48–9.
73. A.L. Gabriel, 'English masters and students in Paris in the twelfth century', *Garlandia* (Frankfurt, 1969), 1–37; Jocelin (see note 72 above), p. 44.
74. Salisbury, II, nos 167, 275.
75. Map (see Chapter 3, note 45); Potthast, 584; and see Chapter 7, note 28.
76. *PL*, 207, 428–32, n. 143.
77. Jocelin (see note 72 above), p. 55.
78. Nigel de Longchamp, *Speculum Stultorum*, ed. J.H. Mozley and R.R. Raymo (Berkeley, 1960).
79. Pseudo Boethius, *De disciplina scholarium*, ed. O. Weijers (Leiden, 1976).
80. Johannes de Hauvilla, *Architrenius*, ed. W. Wetherbee (Cambridge, 1994).
81. *Dictionnaire de Spiritualité* (Paris, 1988), XIII, 593–654.
82. D. Lohrmann, 'Ernis abbé de S. Victor, rapports avec Rome, affaires financières', in *L'abbaye parisien de St Victor an moyen âge*, ed. J. Longère (Paris, 1991), pp. 181–93.
83. A.O. Johnsen, *Om Theodoricus og hans Historia de antiquitate regum Norwagiensium* (Oslo, 1939), Appendix, Letters I–III.

84. B. Smalley, 'Andrew of St Victor', *Recherches de théologie ancienne et médiévale* 10 (1938), 358–73.
85. *Magna Vita* (see Chapter 1, note 11), v, 10.
86. Gerald, III, 66, 239–40; I, 117, 248.
87. Potthast, 1357, *PL*, 216: 1249.
88. D.E.R. Watt, *A Biographical Dictionary of Scottish Graduates to A.D. 1410* (Oxford, 1977).
89. J. Bulloch, *Adam of Dryburgh* (London 1958); *PL*, 198: 723.
90. K. Hughes, *Early Christian Ireland* (London, 1972), ch. 9; Gwynn (see Chapter 2, note 67).
91. D.O. Corrain, 'Foreign connections and domestic politics', in *Ireland in Early Medieval Europe*, ed. D. Whitelock *et al.* (Cambridge, 1982), pp. 213–31; W.W. Heist, *Vitae Sanctorum Hiberniae* (1965), 285–301, Vita S. Flannani episcopi, 286; *ALC*: 1174.
92. H. Mackinnon, 'William de Montibus: a medieval teacher', in *Essays in Medieval History Presented to Bertie Wilkinson*, ed. T.A. Sandquist and F.M. Powicke (Toronto, 1969), pp. 32–45.
93. R.W. Hunt, *The Schools and the Cloister*, ed. M.T. Gibson (Oxford, 1984); Alexander Neckam, *Speculum speculationum*, ed. R.M. Thomson (Oxford, 1988).
94. Sarton (see Chapter 3, note 29), II, pp. 437–8.
95. R.M. Thomson, 'Liber Marii de Elementis, The work of a hitherto unknown Salernitan master', *Viator* 3 (1972), 78–89.
96. *Gesta abbatum monasterii S. Albani*, ed. H.T. Riley (RS 28, 1867), I, 194–6, 217–53.
97. *Evesham* (see Chapter 2, note 19), xx–xxiii.
98. T. Silverstein, 'Daniel Morley, English cosmogonist and student of Arabic science', *Medieval Studies* 10 (1948), 179–96; G. Maurach, 'Daniel v. Morley "Philosophia"', *Mittellateinisches Jahrbuch* 14 (1979), 204–55.
99. J.K. Otte, The life and writings of Alfredus Anglicus, *Viator* 3 (1972), 275–91.
100. Sarton (see Chapter 3, note 29), II, p. 404.
101. Gerald, III, 228; VIII, 65.
102. *PR 5 R I*, 122; *6 R I*, 88, 89; *7 R I*, 142; *8 R I*, 70; *9 R I*, 215.
103. *Chronicon Werumanensium*, ed. L. Weiland (*MGH, SS*, 23), 467.
104. Peter of Celle, *Letters*, ed. J. Haseldine (Oxford, 2001).
105. A.W. Burridge, 'L'immaculée conception dans la théologie de l'Angleterre médiévale', *Revue d'histoire ecclésiastique* 32 (1936), 570–97.
106. W. Wattenbach, 'Verse aus England', *Neues Archiv* 1 (1876), 600–4; R.W. Southern, *Medieval Humanism* (Oxford, 1970), 143, n. 1; P. Lehmann, 'Mittellateinische Verse', *Sitzungsberichte der bayerischen Akademie der Wissenschaften, Philos. Philolog. and hist. Klasse* 22, Abteilung 2 (Munich, 1922), 45.
107. Eystein Erlendsson, *Passio et miracula beati Olavi*, ed. F. Metcalfe (Oxford, 1881); K. Larsen, *A History of Norway* (Princeton, 1948); A. Albertsen, *A Guide to the Cathedral of Nidaros* (Trondheim, 1946).
108. G. Turville-Petre and E.S. Olszewska, *The Life of Gudmund the Good, bishop of Holar* (Viking Society, 1942), xiv–xvi, cc. 48–50, 55–59.
109. R.H. Pinder-Wilson and C.N.L. Brooke, 'The Reliquary of St Petroc and the ivories of Norman Sicily, *Archaeologia* 104 (1973), 261–305; K. Jankulak, *The Medieval Cult of St Petroc* (Woodbridge, 2000).
110. H. Price, 'Church and Society in Wales, 1150–1250', in Davies, pp. 27–47.
111. *AM*, I, 15: 1163.
112. *Statuta capitulorum generalium ordinis Cisterciensis 1116–1786*, ed. J. Canivez, VIII (Louvain, 1941).
113. L. Musset, 'Quelques problèmes posés par l'annexion de la Normandie au domain royal français', in *La France de Philippe Auguste*, ed. R.H. Bautier *et al.* (Paris, 1982), pp. 291–309.
114. P.M. Barnes, 'The Anstey case', in *A Medieval Miscellany for Doris Mary Stenton*, ed. P.M. Barnes and C.F. Slade (PRS, n.s. 36, 1960), pp. 1–24.
115. *Recueil des actes de Henri II*, ed. L.V. Delisle, rev. E. Berger (Paris, 1916–27).
116. P. Hyams, 'The common law and the French connection', *ANS* 4 (1981), 77–92.
117. *Gesta*, I, 139–54.

118. J.L. Barton, 'Bracton as a civilian', *Tulane Law Review* 42 (1968), 555–83; F. de Zulueta and P. Stein, *The teaching of Roman law in England around 1200* (Selden Society, supplementary series, 1990).

119. Glanvill, *Tractatus de legibus et consuetudinibus regni Anglie*, ed. G.D.G. Hall (Edinburgh, 1965).

120. Gerald, VIII, De principis instructione, dist. i, 20; Niger, *Chronica* (see note 53 above); W.P. Muller, 'The recovery of Justinian's Digest in the middle ages', *Bulletin of Medieval Canon Law*, n.s. 20 (1990), 1–29; L. Boyle, 'The beginnings of legal studies at Oxford', *Viator* 14 (1983), 107–31; R.W. Southern, 'Master Vacarius and the beginning of an English Academic Tradition', in *Medieval Learning and Literature*, ed. J.J.G. Alexander and M.T. Gibson (Oxford, 1976), pp. 257–86.

121. Dialogue, 18, 35–6.

122. K.L. Maund, *Handlist of the Acts of Native Welsh Rulers 1132–1283* (Cardiff, 1996).

123. H.D. Emanuel, *The Latin Texts of the Welsh Laws* (Cardiff, 1967); H. Pryce, 'The Prologues to the Welsh Law Books', *Bulletin of the Board of Celtic Studies* 33 (1986), 151–87; *id.*, 'The context and purpose of the earliest Welsh lawbooks', *Cambridge Medieval Celtic Studies* 39 (2000), 39–63.

124. A.A.M. Duncan, 'Regiam maiestatem: a reconsideration', *Juridical Review* (1961), 199–217; *RRS*, I, 62–7; II, 71–4.

125. R. Somerville, *Scotia Pontificia* (Oxford, 1982); *id.*, 'Pope Alexander III and King William', *Innes Review* 24 (1973), 121–4.

126. *Scotia Pontificia*, no. 110; *The Acts of the Parliament of Scotland*, ed. T. Thomson and C. Innes (*RC*, 1844), I, 107.

127. A.D.M. Barrett, 'The background to *Cum Universi*: Scoto-papal relations 1159–92', *Innes Review* (1995), 116–38.

128. R.D. Oram, 'In obedience and reverence: Whithorn and York c.1128–c.1250', *Innes Review* 42 (1991), 83–100.

129. M.T. Flanagan, 'The context and uses of the Latin Charter in twelfth-century Ireland', in *Literacy* (see Chapter 1, note 6), pp. 113–32.

130. D.O. Riain-Raedel, 'Diarmaid MacCarthaigh King of Cork', *Journal of the Cork Historical and Archaeological Society* 90, no. 249 (1985), 26–30.

131. L. Felkenstein, 'Ein vergessener Brief Alexanders III an einem Rex Hibernorum', *Archivum Historiae Pontificiae* 10 (1972), 107–60.

132. A. Gwynn and R.N. Hadcock, *Medieval Religious Houses of Ireland* (London, 1970).

133. *The Manuscript Irish Missal*, ed. F.E. Warren (London, 1979).

134. M.P. Sheehy, *Pontificia Hibernica* (Dublin, 1962–65).

135. *Chartularies of St Mary's Dublin*, ed. J.T. Gilbert (RS 80, 1884), I, 354–8, n. 289.

136. A. Gwynn, 'Tomaltach Ua Conchobair, Coarb of St Patrick 1181–1201', *Seancha Ardmaca* 8 (1977), 231–74.

137. S. Duffy, 'The first Ulster plantation: John de Courcy and the men of Cumbria', in *Colony and Frontier in Medieval Ireland*, ed. T. Barry *et al.* (London, 1995), pp. 1–27; M.T. Flanagan, 'John de Courcy, the first Ulster plantation and Irish churchmen', in Smith, 154–78.

138. *Dermot* (see note 28 above), ll. 1089–1137, 2061–2154.

139. Gerald, V: Expugnatio (see Chapter 2, note 46); Topographia Hibernica.

140. W.L. Warren, 'John in Ireland', in *Essays presented to Michael Roberts*, ed. J. Bossy and P. Jupp (Belfast, 1976), pp. 11–23; *id.*, 'King John and Ireland', in *Ireland and England in the Late Middle Ages*, ed. J.F. Lydon (Dublin, 1981), pp. 26–42; S. Duffy, 'John in Ireland: the origins of England's Irish problem', in Church, pp. 221–45.

141. M. Lenihan, *Limerick, its history and antiquities* (Dublin, 1866), pp. 546–7.

142. *MTB*, I, ii, 25, 27, 29; iii, 45, 54; iv, 52; v, 7; vi, 19, 55, 80, 118, 144, 168.

143. R. Barber and J. Barker, *Tournaments, Jousts, Chivalry and Pageants in the Middle Ages* (Woodbridge, 1989).

144. M. Aurell, *L'Empire des Plantagenets 1154–1224* (Paris, 2003); W.F. Schirmer and U. Broich, *Studien zum literarischen Patronat im England des 12. Jahrhunderts* (Cologne, 1962): *Heinrich II als Patron der Literatur seiner Zeit*; L.M. Ayres, 'English painting and the continent', in *Eleanor of Aquitaine*, ed. W.W. Kibler (Austin, 1976), pp. 138–42.

145. Brut: 1176; M. Surridge, 'Romance linguistic influences on Middle Welsh', *Studia Celtica* 1 (1966), 63–92.

146. *Tales of the Elders of Ireland*, trans. A. Dooley and H. Roe (Oxford, 1999); J.E.C. Williams, 'The court poets of medieval Ireland', *PBA* 57 (1971), 85–135; D.O. Corrain, 'Nationality and Kingship in pre-Norman Ireland', *Historical Studies* 11 (1975), 1–35; B. O'Cuiv, 'Literary creation and Irish historical tradition', *PBA* 49 (1963), 233–62.
147. R.L.G. Ritchie, *Chrétien de Troyes and Scotland* (Oxford, 1952).
148. *The Romance of Fergus*, ed. W. Frescolin (Philadelphia, 1983).
149. M.D. Legge, 'La précocité de la littérature anglo-normande', *CCM* 8 (1965), 327–49; I. Short, 'Patrons and polyglots, French literature in twelfth-century England', *ANS* 14 (1991), 229–49.
150. *La Chanson de Roland*, ed. F. Whitehead (Oxford, 1970); GR, s. 242.
151. R.T. Pickens, 'The literary activity of Philippe de Thaün', *Romance Notes* 12 (1970), 1–5.
152. *La vie d'Edouard le confesseur*, ed. O. Sodergard (Uppsala, 1948).
153. Thomas of Britain, *Tristram*, ed. S. Gregory (New York, 1991); M. Benskin, T. Hunt and I. Short, 'Un nouveau fragment du Tristan de Thomas', *Romania* 113 (1992–95), 289–319.
154. Faral (see Chapter 3, note 34), pp. 34–7.
155. R.W. Hunt, 'The "lost" preface to the *Liber Derivationum* of Osbern of Gloucester', *MARS* 4 (1958), 267–82.
156. D. James, 'Two medieval Arabic accounts of Ireland', *JRSAI* 108, 5–9.
157. Maréchal (see note 23 above), 20, 52, 66.
158. W. Rothwell, 'The teaching of French in medieval England', *Modern Language Review* (1968), 37–46; E. Faral, *Mimes français du XIIIe siècle* (Paris, 1910).
159. *MTB*, I, iv, 36; Devizes, 66.
160. J. Flinn, *Le Roman de Renard* (Paris, 1963); K. Varty, *Reynard the Fox* (Leicester, 1967); H. Schwarzbaum, *The Mishle Shu' alim of Rabbi Berechiah Ha Nakdan* (Kiran, 1979).
161. Lambert: 96.
162. *HF*: Limoges chronicle; Gerald, VII, 304: dist. iii, 28.
163. A.M. Duncan, 'The Dress of the Scots', *SHR* 29 (1950), 210–12; *PL*, 203: 729–30.
164. *Orkneyinga* (see Chapter 2, note 21), *passim*; R.A. McDonald, 'Images of Hebridean lordship in the late twelfth and early thirteenth centuries: the seal of Raonall MacSorley', *SHR* 74 (1995), 129–43.
165. Hoveden, II, 102–4; *PR 23 H II*, 166, 187, 192, 207, 208; *PR 24 H II*, 19; *PR 25 H II*, 125; *PR 31 H II*, 216; R.M. Dawkins, 'The Later history of the Varangian Guard', *Journal of Roman Studies* 37 (1947), 39–46.
166. Gerald, I, 60; VIII, 159, 202, 204, 207–12.
167. *Les oeuvres de Simund de Freine*, ed. J.E. Matzke (SATF, 1909), 61–117; J. Barrow, 'A twelfth-century bishop and literary patron: William de Vere (1186–98)', *Viator* 18 (1986), 175–89.
168. G.W.S. Barrow, 'The reign of William the Lion, king of Scotland', *Historical Studies* 7 (1969), 21–44; Macquarrie (see Chapter 3, note 13).
169. *AC, Brut*: 1190; Gerald, VI, Itinerary.
170. Ambroise, *The crusade of Richard Lion-heart*, trans. M.J. Hubert, notes J.L. La Monte (New York, 1941, repr. 1976), ll. 3731–70.
171. Hoveden, III, 35.
172. Devizes, 23; A. Ailes, *The origins of the royal arms of England* (Reading Medieval Studies Monograph no. 2, 1982).
173. *PL*, 215: 298–9, no. 15; H. Géraud, Le comte-evêque, *BEC* 5 (1843–44), pièces justificatives, 4, 35–6.
174. Diceto, I, 429.
175. Newburgh, Hoveden, Diceto, *passim*.
176. J. Baldwin, 'La décennie décisive: les années 1190–1203 dans le règne de Philippe Auguste', *RH* 266 (1981), 311–37.
177. U. Hucker, *Otto IV* (MGH Schriften 34, 1990).

Chapter 5

1. *Dip. Docs*, nos 5, 9.
2. F.M. Powicke, *The Loss of Normandy* (Manchester, 1907); Rigord, II.
3. Ralph of Coggeshall, *Chronicon Anglicanum 1066–1223*, ed. J. Stevenson (RS 66, 1875), 146.
4. Baldwin (see Chapter 4, note 176).
5. C. Petit-Dutaillis, *Etude sur la vie et le règne de Louis VIII 1187–1224* (Paris, 1894), 72–96.
6. Musset (see Chapter 4, note 113).
7. *Maréchal* (see Chapter 4, note 23), 38, 49.
8. *Rotuli Normanniae*, ed. T.D. Hardy (London, 1835): Rotulus de valore terrarum Normannorum, 122–43.
9. CM, IV, 288; *CPR 1232–47*, 420.
10. *AM*, I, 57; II, 256; IV, 392.
11. *Loss of Normandy* (see note 2 above), 327–8.
12. *RChart* I, 133b–134a; *RPat*, 45b; Gervase, 95–6.
13. M.D. Legge, *Anglo-Norman Literature and its Background* (Oxford, 1963).
14. Guillaume le Clerc, *The Bestiary*, trans. G.C. Druce (Ashford, 1936).
15. N. Vincent, 'Isabella of Angoulême', John's Jezebel, in Church, pp. 165–219.
16. N. Vincent, *Peter des Roches: an alien in English Politics 1205–38* (Cambridge, 1996); *CPR 1258–66*, 269–70.
17. J.C. Holt, *Magna Carta* (Cambridge, 1965), App. II, The unknown charter, 296–303, cl. 7.
18. R.F. Treharne, 'The Franco-Welsh Treaty of Alliance in 1212', *Bulletin of the Board of Celtic Studies* 18 (1960), 60–75.
19. MGH, SS 29: Danish Annals 1216; Rigord, I, 245–6, 303–4; *HF*, XVIII, 227–31, 240, 350, 354, 357.
20. A. Wilmart, 'Les mélanges de Mathieu, préchantre de Rievaulx', *RB* 52 (1940), 15–84; Faral (see Chapter 3, note 34), 35.
21. HA, II, 146–8, 507; Petit-Dutaillis (see note 5 above).
22. Rymer, I, 65; Hoveden, III, 268; Newburgh, 422–3: v, 4.
23. *Histoire des ducs de Normandie et des rois d'Angleterre*, ed. F. Michel (SHF, 1840); L.V. Delisle, 'Notice sur la Chronique d'un anonyme de Béthune', *NEMBN* 34 (1891), 365–97; C. Petit-Dutaillis, 'L'anonyme de Béthune', *RH* 50 (1892), 63–71; *HF*, 24 (1904), 754–75.
24. V.H. Galbraith, *Roger of Wendover and Matthew Paris* (Glasgow, 1944).
25. R. Vaughan, *Matthew Paris* (Cambridge, 1958).
26. M.T. Clanchy, *From Memory to Written Record, England 1066–1307* (2nd edn, Oxford, 1993).
27. *RPat*, 42–3: 1204; *RC*, 70b: 1206.
28. M. Bateson, *Records of the Borough of Leicester* (London, 1899).
29. B.K.V. Weiler and I.W. Rowlands, *England and Europe in the Reign of Henry III 1216–72* (Aldershot, 2002).
30. Dip. Docs, no. 28; *CR 1227–31*, 233–4, 545.
31. Shirley, nos 208, 216, 217.
32. Rymer, I, 219–20.
33. F. Mugnier, 'Les Savoyards en Angleterre au xiiie siècle', *Mémoires et Documents publiés par la Société Savoisienne d'histoire et d'archéologie* 29 (1890), 155–476.
34. CM, III, 319–24; Rymer, I, 223.
35. H. Kantorowicz, 'Petrus de Vinea in England', *Mitteilungen des Osterreichischen Instituts für Geschichtsforschung* 51 (1937), 43–88.
36. CM, III, 485, 491; *CR 1237–42*, 165.
37. Shirley, no. 434.
38. *CR 1247–51*, 88; CM, V, 71, 99.
39. Shirley, no. 302.
40. L.V. Delisle, 'Mémoire sur une lettre inédite adressée à la reine Blanche par un habitant de La Rochelle, *BEC* 17 (1856), 513–55; A. Jeanroy, 'Le soulèvement de 1242 dans la poésie des troubadours', *Annales du Midi* 16 (1904), 311–29; C. Bémont, 'La campagne de Poitou 1242–43: Taillebourg à Saintes', *Annales du Midi* 5 (1893), 289–314.

41. *RC* , 156b; *PatR 1216–25*, 5; Dip. Docs, 29: no. 18.
42. *RC*, 180; *CR 1225–32*, 39.
43. D.M. Williamson, 'The legation of Cardinal Otto in England', *EHR* (1949), 145–73.
44. *CPL*, 43, 59, 75.
45. *CPL*, 55.
46. G.R. Stephens, 'Joan of Scotland', *Speculum* (1945), 300–9.
47. D. Williamson, 'The legate Otto in Scotland and Ireland', *SHR* 28 (1949), 12–30.
48. *CPL*, 85, 93, 109, 153, 164, 183; *Littere*, nos 303, 304; *Brut*: 1236.
49. J.E. Lloyd, 'The Welsh Chronicles', *PBA* (1928); T. Jones Pierce, 'Strata Florida abbey', *Ceredigion* 1 (1950), 18–33.
50. *Brut*: 1214, 1230, 1242.
51. *Brut*: 1212.
52. M.H. d'Artois de Jubainville, *Histoire des ducs et des comtes de Champagne*, V (Paris, 1863), no. 1221; E. Martène and U. Durand, *Thesaurus Novus Anecdotarum* I (Paris, 1717), 872–3.
53. P. Topping, 'Harald Maddadson, earl of Orkney and Caithness 1139–1206', *SHR* 62 (1983), 105–20.
54. Melrose: 1216.
55. K.J. Stringer, 'Periphery and Core in thirteenth century Scotland, Alan son of Roland, lord of Galloway and Constable of Scotland', *Medieval Scotland, Crown, Lordship and Community*, ed. A. Grant and K.J. Stringer (Edinburgh, 1993), pp. 82–113.
56. *CPL*, 69, 91, 92; Rymer, I, 190, 217, 227, 231, 272, 289; *CR 1254–56*, 292.
57. K. Helle, 'Anglo-Norwegian relations in the reign of Hakon Hakonsson 1217–63', *Medieval Scandinavia* I, 1968; id., 'Norwegian consolidation and expansion during the reign of king Hakon Hakonsson', *Orkney Miscellany* 5 (1973); *Diplomatarium Norwegicum*, 19, nn. 272–5, 277–80; CM, IV, 612–13, 626–7; V, 195, 201, 222, 230.
58. *The Norwegian Account of Haco's Expedition against Scotland AD MCCLXIII*, ed. J. Johnstone (Edinburgh, 1782), x, 15.
59. *The Life of Gudmund the Good, bishop of Holar*, trans. G. Turbeville-Petre and E.S. Olszewska (Viking Society, London, 1942), 48–9.
60. *RRS*, II, n. 462: 1205; *Exchequer Rolls*, 6, 34; *CDI*, I, n. 2407.
61. *CPL*, 245.
62. G.G. Simpson, 'The familia of Roger de Quinci, earl of Winchester and constable of Scotland', in *Essays on the Nobility of Medieval Scotland*, ed. K.J. Stringer (Edinburgh, 1985), pp. 102–30; G.A. Moriarty, 'The Balliols in Picardy, England and Scotland', *New England Historical and Genealogical Register* 106 (1952), 273–90.
63. *Histoire des ducs* (see note 23 above) pp. 112–14.
64. P. Brand, 'Ireland and the literature of the early common law', *Irish Jurist* 16 (1981), 95–113.
65. J.R.S. Phillips, 'The Anglo-Norman nobility', in *The English in Medieval Ireland*, ed. J. Lydon (Dublin, 1984) pp. 87–104; Shirley, n. 509.
66. *CDI, passim*.
67. *ALC*, I, 375–81.
68. *Chronicles of Stephen* (see Chapter 3, note 106), II, 517; *AM*, IV, 254.
69. Magna Carta, cl. 50.
70. *Chronicles of Stephen* (see Chapter 3, note 106), II, 517, 519–20; *AM*, III, 43–7, 50–1.
71. *Memoriale* (see Chapter 4, note 15), 247.
72. CM, II, 635; Shirley, no. 199.
73. CM, III, 217–19, 609–11; IV, 47; VI, 477; H. MacKenzie, 'The Anti-Foreign Movement in England 1231–32', in *Haskins Anniversary Essays in Medieval History*, ed. C.H. Taylor and J.L. La Monte (Boston, 1929), pp. 183–203.
74. CM, IV, 628; V, 514.
75. CM, IV, 650; V, 204–5, 263, 344, 650, 696; D.A. Carpenter, 'English peasants in Politics 1258–67', *Past and Present* 136 (1992), 3–42.
76. W. Cunningham, *Alien Immigrants to England* (London, 1897); H. Ridgeway, 'King Henry III and the "aliens" 1236–72', *Thirteenth-century England* II (1987), 81–92; D.A. Carpenter, *The Minority of Henry III* (London, 1990), pp. 4, 394–5; id. 'King Henry III's "statute" against aliens, July 1263', *EHR* 107 (1992), 925–44.
77. *Documents of the Baronial Movement of Reform and Rebellion 1258–67*, ed. I.J. Sanders (Oxford, 1973) doc. 38, cl. 15, 16.

78. J. Maddicott, *Simon de Montfort* (Cambridge, 1994).
79. *ALC*; *AConnacht*, 1243.
80. CM, III, 189.
81. G.L. Harriss, *King, Parliament and Public Finance in Medieval England to 1369* (Oxford, 1975).
82. H.G. Richardson, *The English Jewry under Angevin Kings* (London, 1960).
83. *Ibid.*, 120, 132.
84. D. Berger, 'Mission to the Jews and Jewish-Christian contacts in the polemical literature of the high middle ages', *AHR* 91 (1986) 576–91.
85. Jocelin (see Chapter 4, note 72), 45–6.
86. *CR 1231–34*, 515; *1242–47*, 149; *CPR 1258–66*, 153, 613; *CCR 1272–79*, 50, 130.
87. Newburgh, iv, 7–10.
88. *PR 2 R I*, 68–70; *PR 3 R I*, 147, 203; *PR 4 R I*, 145.
89. Gerald, VI: Itinerary, ii, 13; Devizes, 69; *MTB*, II, ii, 20.
90. I. Epstein, 'Pre-expulsion England in the Responsa', *TJHE* 14 (1935–39), 187–205.
91. S. Krauss, 'L'émigration de 300 rabbis au Palestine en l'an 1211', *Revue des Etudes Juives* 82 (1926), 333–52.
92. J. Jacobs, 'Une lettre française d'un juif anglais au xiiie siècle', *Revue des Etudes Juives* 18 (1889), 256–61; P. Hyams, 'The Jewish Minority in Medieval England 1066–1290', *Journal of Jewish Studies* 25, 1974, 270–93; C. Roth, *History of Jews in England* (3rd edn, Oxford, 1964).

Chapter 6

1. Gerald, VIII: De principis instructione, dist. iii, 30.
2. Bartholomew (see Chapter 1, note 41), book 15.
3. Map (see Chapter 3, note 45), v, 6.
4. *PR 4 J*, 104, 131; *RC*, 607, 622b; *RChart*, 60; *CR 1227–31*, 80.
5. *RC*, 108; *RC*, II, 61; *RPat*, 61b.
6. *RPat*, 43.
7. T.H. Lloyd, *The English Wool Trade in the Middle Ages* (Cambridge, 1977).
8. *RPat*, 65b, 76, 191; *PatR 1216–25*, 102; *RC*, 625.
9. J. Hatcher, *English Tin Production and Trade before 1550* (Oxford, 1973); *PR 10 R I*, 182; *CPR 1258–66*, 454; W. Heyd, *Histoire du Commerce du Levant*, rev. F. Raynaud (Leipzig, 1923), p. 422; CM, IV, 151; Shirley, no. 168; *CChtR*, II, 304.
10. J. Blair and N. Ramsey, *English Medieval Industries* (London, 1991); *CPR 1281–92*, 227; PL, 171: 1737.
11. H. Heaton, *The Yorkshire Woollen and Worsted Industries* (Oxford, 1920).
12. *Orkneyinga* (see Chapter 2, note 21), 280–1.
13. A.G.I. Christie, *English Medieval Embroidery* (Oxford, 1938); A.F. Kendrick, *English Needlework*, rev. P. Wardle (London, 1967); CM, IV, 546–7; *Gesta Abbatum*, I, 127.
14. W.N. Yates, 'Bishop Peter de Aquablanca (1240–68): a reconsideration', *JEH* 22 (1971), 303–17; Mugnier (see Chapter 5, note 33); *Chartes du diocèse de Maurienne*, ed. A. Billiet (Chambéry, 1861), 95–103: no. 62.
15. *RPat*, 73b, 77, 173; *RC*, 82; *Heinrich der Löwe und seine Zeit, Katalog der Ausstellung* (Brunswick, 1995), Bd. I, 331–71: E. 9.
16. *Diplomatarium Norwegicum*, ed. A. Bugge (Kristiana, 1910), nos 214, 252; *CPR 1247–58*, 400; A.J. Taylor, 'Count Amadeus of Savoy's visit to England in 1292', *Archaeologia* 106 (1979), 123–32.
17. Blair and Ramsey (see note 10 above), 180.
18. *Liber Sancte Marie de Melros Munimenta Vetustiora*, ed. C. Innes (Edinburgh, 1837), nos 14, 15; *PatR 1216–25*, 519; L.A. Warnkoenig and A.E. Gheldolf, *Histoire de la Flandre et de ses institutions civiles et politiques jusqu'à l'année 1305* II (Brussels, 1836), no. 35.
19. *Gesta*, I, 101–3; Gerald, VI: Topography, I, 8; *Irish Pipe Roll of 14 John 1211–12*, ed. O. Davies and D.B. Quinn (Belfast, 1941).

20. T. O'Neill, *Merchants and Mariners in Medieval Ireland* (Dublin, 1987), p. 130; *Municipal*, nos 34, 36; A.F. O'Brien, 'The royal boroughs, the sea-port towns and royal revenue in medieval Ireland', *JRSAI* 118 (1988), 13–26; *CDI*, II, nos 188, 191; IV, nos 197, 204, 256, 307–10, 318, 321, 399, 455, 570; *RC*, 335b.

21. *Registrum Episcopatus Glasguensis*, ed. C. Innes (Maitland Club, 1842), lxxxiii–iv; A.A.M. Duncan, 'Documents relating to the Priory of the Isle of May c.1140–1313', *PSAS* 90 (1956–57), 56; *RRS*, I, nos 162, 169; II, nos 93, 303; W. Herbert, *The history of the twelve great Livery Companies of London* II (London, 1837); *Rotuli de Oblatis et Finibus tempore regis Johannis*, ed. T.D. Hardy (London, 1835), p. 191; *RC*, II, 91; *ALC*, I, 257.

22. J. MacInnes, 'The Gaelic perception of the Lowlands', in *Gaelic and Scotland*, ed. W. Gillies (Edinburgh, 1989), pp. 89–100.

23. T. Madox, *The history and antiquities of the Exchequer of England 1066–1327* (London, 1711), 526; *RC*, 44, 45, 120,124, 163, 190b, 631b; *PR 14 J*, 45.

24. M. Bateson, 'A London municipal collection of the reign of John', *EHR* 17 (1902), 496–502.

25. J.C. Parsons, *The Court and Household of Eleanor of Castile in 1290* (Toronto, 1977).

26. Simon de Quentin, *Histoire des Tartares*, ed. J. Richard (Paris, 1965), xxxi, 43, *c*.1248.

27. *PR 4 H II*, 113; *PR 8 J*, 47–8; *PR 9 J*, 31; *RC*, 96, 352; *CLibR 1245–51*, 179, 288.

28. *Exchequer Rolls*, 5, 6, 28, 34.

29. *PatR 1216–25*, 450, 457, 528; *PatR 1225–31*, 47.

30. E.M. Carus-Wilson, 'La guède française en Angleterre', *Revue du Nord* 35 (1953), 89–105; *PR 10 R I*, 12; *PR 9 J*, 71; *RC*, 217b.

31. R. Doehaerd, 'Les galères génoises dans la Manche et la Mer du Nord à la fin du xiiie siècle', *Bulletin de l'Institut historique belge de Rome* 19 (1938) 5–76, nos 13, 14; R.S. Lopez, 'Majorcans and Genoese on the North Sea route in the thirteenth century', *RBPH* 29 (1951), 1163–79.

32. *CPR 1281–92*, 11; *CCR 1288–96*, 363, 365.

33. Arnold of Lübeck, *Chronica Slavorum*, ed. J.M. Lappenberg (*MGH, SS* 21, 1868), iii, 5; *RC*, 100, 117b, 163, 176b, 180, 190b; *RC, II*, 133; W.R. Childs, *Anglo-Castilian Trade in the Later Middle Ages* (Manchester, 1978); *Dip. Pract*, no. 248; *Liber Quotidianus Contrarotulatoris Garderobae 28 Edward I*, ed. J. Topham (London, 1787); *CPR 1272–81*, 171, 184, 191, 193–4, 212; *CPR 1281–92*, 11.

34. *RC*, 132, 156b, 182b, *CR 1227–31*, 353, 517, 523.

35. *RC*, 509; Shirley, no. 302; *CLibR 1251–60*, 73, 84; Rymer I, ii, 533, 569, 575, 645, 654, 662, 667.

36. *HA*, II, 380.

37. *CM*, V, 275, 489; *CR 1254–56*, 46; *CLibR 1251–60*, 197; *The Chronicle of Lanercost 1272–1346*, trans. H. Maxwell (Glasgow, 1913), p. 37; Rymer, I, 533.

38. Rigord, I, 34–5, s. 21; *PR 17 H II*, 147–8; *PR 21 H II*, 15.

39. *RC*, 126b; Rymer I, 169–70; *Dip. Docs*, no. 11.

40. *HMC Various* (see Chapter 3, note 36), I, 219.

41. *The Local Custom Accounts of the Port of Exter 1266–1321*, ed. M. Kowaleski (Devon and Cornwall Record Society, n.s. 36, 1993); *RC*, 651; *RC, II*, 91; *CR 1234–37*, 38.

42. *Municipal*, nos 27, 39, 42, 53; *CDI*, II, nos 314, 1038; III, no. 864.

43. *PR 19 H II*, 13, 29, 50, 130, 196; *PR 20 H II*, 14, 54, 103, 131; *PR 21 H II*, 175.

44. Barnes (see Chapter 3, note 6); *RPat*, 52b.

45. *Recueil* (see Chapter 4, note 115), n. xiv, 1150–51.

46. A. Giry, *Histoire de la Ville de St Omer* (Paris, 1877).

47. *Hansisches Urkunden Buch*, ed. K. Höhlbaum (Halle, 1876), I, no. 40; T.H. Lloyd, *Alien Merchants in England in the High Middle Ages* (Harvester Press, 1982); *id.*, *England and the German Hanse 1157–1611* (Cambridge, 1991); J.F. Huffmann, *Family, Commerce and Religion in London and Cologne* (Cambridge, 1998), 184; A.L. Poole, 'Richard the First's Alliances with the German Princes in 1194', *Studies in Medieval History presented to Frederick Maurice Powicke*, ed. R.W. Hunt, W.A. Pantin and R.W. Southern (Oxford, 1948), pp. 90–9; *CChR*, I, 214.

48. T.F. Ruiz, 'Castillian Merchants in England 1248–1350', *Order and Innovation in the Middle Ages*, ed. W.C. Jordan, B. McNab and T.F. Ruiz (Princeton, 1976), pp. 173–85; Childs (see note 33 above); *RC, II*, 116; *RChart*, 96b.

49. J. Balasque, *Etudes historiques sur la ville de Bayonne* (Bayonne, 1862); *CCR 1272–79*, 420–1; *CCR 1288–96*, 324.

50. HMC, 9th report, Appendix, 61–68; Lambert, 100; Géraud (see Chapter 4, note 173).
51. *RPat*, 5, 9, 10, 39b, 65b; *RChart*, 99; A. Schaube, *Handelsgeschichte der romanischen Völker des Mittelmeergebiet bis zum Ende des Kreuzzüge* (Munich, 1906), 392–417.
52. PL, 215: 298–9; *RC*, 146b.
53. *PatR 1216–25*, 248; *PatR 1225–32*, 85, 133; *RC*, 611; *RC*, II, 137.
54. *Les relations commerciales entre Gênes, la Belgique et l'Outremont*, ed. R. Doehaerd (Brussels, 1941), III–IV, no. 326.
55. *PatR 1216–25*, 472; *RLib*, 8, 46, 143, 148; *RChart*, 96b.
56. *RC*, II, 9, 13b; *CR 1227–31*, 94; *PatR 1225–32*, 180; *CPR 1232–47*, 282, 480.
57. Lopez (see note 31 above).
58. *RC*, 146b; *PatR 1216–25*, 448, 472, 478; *RC*, II, 137; *PatR 1225–32*, 574–5; *CR 1234–37*, 254–5; *CPR 1232–47*, 480.
59. E.A. Bond, 'Extracts from the Liberate Rolls', *Archaeologia* 28 (1840), 207–326; *CR 1237–42*, 160, 509; *CR 1242–47*, 143, 314–15; *CPR 1247–58*, 548; R.C. Stacey, *Politics, Policy and Finance under Henry III, 1216–45* (Oxford, 1987).
60. *CR 1242–47*, 314–15; *CPR 1232–47*, 239; *CPR 1247–58*, 184.
61. R.W. Kaeuper, *Bankers to the Crown, The Riccardi of Lucca and Edward I* (Princeton, 1973).
62. *RC*, II, 91; *CR 1237–42*, 509; *PatR 1225–32*, 258, 265, 336; *Rôles Gascons*, ed. F. Michel I (Paris, 1885), p. x, n. 4.
63. *PatR 1216–25*, 39, 384, 457, 491–2; *PatR 1225–32*, 35, 144; *CR 1227–31*, 458, 576; *CR 1237–42*, 509; *CR 1242–47*, 143; *CPR 1266–72*, 599, 695; *CPR 1281–92* 341, 352, 383, 481; *CPR 1292–1301* 73, 76, 557, 558; F. Avens, 'Wilhelm Servat von Cahors als Kauffmann zu London 1273–1320', *Vierteljahrschrift für Sozial und Wirtschaftsgeschichte* 11 (1913), 477–514; *De Antiquis legibus Liber*, ed. T. Stapleton (Camden Society, 1846), 62, 118; N. Denholm-Young, 'The merchants of Cahors', *Collected Papers* (Oxford, 1969), 290–7; HA, II, 382.
64. H. van Werveke, 'Les statuts latins et les statuts français de la Hanse Flamande de Londres', *Bulletin de la Commission Royale d'Histoire* 118 (1958), 289–320; *RPat*, 85, 98, 146; *RC* 120a, b, 124, 132, 145; *RC*, II, 97, 207b.
65. Rymer, II, ii, 747–8.
66. *RC*, 81; *RPat*, 85; *RC*, 613.
67. *RC*, 419, 464b; *RParl*, 200/56.
68. *PatR 1216–25*, 384; *RC*, 419.
69. *CR 1227–34*, 367.
70. *Curia Regis Rolls* (HMSO, 1922–), XII, no. 2108; *CChR 1226–57*, 227; *CLibR 1226–40*, 264–5; *CLibR 1245–57*, 315.
71. Madox (see note 23 above), 529; *PR 5 J*, xii–xiii, 11, 12; *PR 6 J*, xliii, 218–20; *PR 7 J*, 116; *PR 8 J*, 50, 58; *PR 9 J*, 33, 51; *RPat*, 42–3; *RLib*, 35.
72. *CChR 1226–57*, 214; *CR 1234–37*, 216, 399; *CPR 1232–47*, 130.
73. S.E. Rigold, 'The trail of the Easterlings', *BNJ* 26 (1949–51), 31–55.
74. J.M. Lappenberg, *Urkundliche Geschichte des Hansischen Stahlhofes zu London* (Hamburg, 1851); *RPat*, 102; *PatR 1216–25*, 40, 474, 476, 500, 509; *PatR 1225–32*, 40, 415; *Codex Diplomaticus Lubecensis*, II (Lübeck, 1858), no. 35; *CPR 1247–58*, 553; *CR 1242–47*, 543.
75. *Munimenta*, I, 418–24.
76. *PatR 1216–25*, 476, 506; *PatR 1225–32*, 502.
77. Shirley, nos 186, 187; *RC*, 238, 625b, 645; *RC*, II, 13b, 91, 119b, 120a, b, 124.
78. *CPR 1247–58*, 114–15, 141; *Calendar of Fine Rolls*, 106; *Liber Quotidianus* (see note 33 above), 161.
79. E.W. Moore, *The Fairs of Medieval England* (Toronto, 1985).
80. *RRS*, II, 308; *Exchequer Rolls*, 8, 37; *Municipal*, nos 10, 11, 37, 41, 44; Michel (see note 62 above), no. 117.
81. C. Gross, *Select Cases Concerning the Law Merchant* (Selden Society 23, 1908); *PatR 1225–32*, 23.
82. E.C. Varenbergh, *Histoire des relations diplomatiques entre le comté de Flandre et l'Angleterre au moyen âge* (Brussels, 1874), pièces justificatives nos 4, 5, 7; G. Espinas, *La vie urbaine de Douai au moyen âge* (Paris, 1913), no. 633; Hoveden, IV, 172; *CPR 1232–47*, 480; *CPR 1247–58*, 430; *CPR 1266–72*, 456–7, 524, 526; *CPR 1272–81*, 307; *CCR 1272–79*, 333.

83. *RPat*, 173b; *RC*, 209; *PatR 1216–25*, 84; *CR 1247–51*, 135.

84. Bateson (see Chapter 5, note 28).

85. *CR 1261–64*, 351, 388, 392–4; *CR 1264–68*, 75; *CPR 1258–66*, 320, 398.

86. *RPat*, 76.

87. J.J. McCusker, 'The wine prise and medieval merchant shipping', *Speculum* 41 (1966), 279–96.

88. M. Allen, 'The volume of the English currency 1158–1470', *EcHR* 54 (2001), 595–611.

89. D.F. Allen, *A Catalogue of English Coins in the British Musum, The Cross and Crosslets ('Tealby') Type of Henry II* (London, 1951).

90. *PatR 1216–25*, 366; *Liber Rubeus*, ed. H. Hall, III (London, 1896), 979–80; *CPR 1247–58*, 114–15, 141.

91. *CPR 1232–47*, 21, 508; *CPR 1247–58*, 10, 21, 657; *CR 1247–51*, 107.

92. J. Craig, *The Mint, A History of the London Mint from AD 287 to 1948* (Cambridge, 1953); *CPR 1272–81*, 322, 449; *CCR 1279–88*, 32–3.

93. D.A. Carpenter, 'Gold and gold coins in England in the mid-thirteenth century', *Numismatic Chronicle* 147 (1987), 106–13; *CPR 1247–58*, 558, 576; G.C. Brooke, *English Coins from the Seventh Century to the Present Day* (3rd edn, London, 1950).

94. D.M. Metcalf, *Coinage in South-east Europe, 820–1396* (London, 1978), p. 180; P. Spufford, *Money and its Rise in Medieval Europe* (Cambridge, 1988).

95. N. Mayhew, 'Numismatic evidence and falling prices in the fourteenth century', *EcHR* (1974), 1–15.

96. P. Grierson, *The Coins of Medieval Europe* (London, 1991); *CR 1247–51*, 549; *CR 1253–54*, 2.

97. *AM*, IV, 222–3.

98. *RPat*, 173; *PatR 1216–25*, 100; *CR 1234–37*, 205; J.H. Round, *The Commune of London* (Westminster, 1899); *Municipal*, nos 24, 25; *Liber Primus Kilkenniensis*, ed. C. McNeill (Dublin, 1931).

99. *PR 4 J*, 40; *PR 7 J*, 34.

100. *MTB*, III, 2–13; Wattenbach (see Chapter 4, note 106); Devizes, 65; H. Hall, *Select Cases Concerning the Law Merchant 1251–1779* (Selden Society 49, 1932), 137–40; P. Nightingale, *A Medieval Mercantile Community: The Grocers' Company and the politics and trade of London 1000–1485* (New Haven, 1995).

101. *CChR 1226–57*, 407; *CPR 1258–66*, 519; *CCR 1272–79*, 408; *CPR 1272–81*, 431; *CPR 1281–92*, 9; S. Reynolds, *An Introduction to the History of English Medieval Towns* (Oxford, 1977), 125.

102. *Calendar of Pleas and Memoranda Rolls*, ed. A.H. Thomas (Cambridge, 1929), 281; *Munimenta*, 418–24, 485–8; *CPR 1272–81*.

103. *GP*, s. 208.

104. G.S. Pryde, *Burghs of Scotland* (Oxford, 1965); M.R. Spearman, 'Early Scottish Towns', in *Power and Politics in Early Medieval Britain and Ireland*, ed. S.T. Driscoll and M.R. Nieke (Edinburgh, 1988), pp. 96–110.

105. *Selected Texts on British Urban History before the Mid-Thirteenth Century*, ed. S. Reynolds *et al.* (Elenchus Fontium Historiae Urbanae, vol. 2, pars 2, Brill, 1988), no. 2.

106. *Fantosme* (see Chapter 4, note 14), 38, 85, 86, 120; Watt (see Chapter 4, note 88); *CDS*, nos 2237, 2646.

107. *Parliament of Scotland* (see Chapter 4, note 126), 671–2; *Exchequer Rolls*, p. lxxxiii.

108. Walter Bower, *Scotichronicon*, ed. D.E.R. Watt (Aberdeen, 1987–99), IV, viii, 55; *PatR 1216–25*, 132.

109. W.W. Scott, 'The use of money in Scotland 1124–1230', *SHR* 58 (1979), 105–31; Stewart (see Chapter 3, note 105); *CPR 1272–81*, 456.

110. Gerald, VI: Description, i, 8; ii, 8.

111. Reynolds (see note 105 above), no. 3; *PatR 1216–25*, 87; *Brut*: 1275.

112. I. Soulsby, *The Towns of Medieval Wales* (Phillimore, 1983); L. Butler, 'Planned Anglo-Norman towns in Wales 950–1250', in *The Comparative History of Urban Origins in Non-Roman Europe*, ed. H.B. Clarke and M. Simms (BAR international series 255, 1985), II, pp. 469–504.

113. *CPR 1281–92*, 2–3.

114. E. Besley, 'Short Cross and other medieval coins from Llanfaes, Anglesey', *BNJ* 65 (1996), 46–82.

115. *Littere*, 328.
116. *Municipal*, nos 1, 2.
117. *Municipal*, nos 38, 46.
118. *The Dublin Guild Merchant Roll c.1190–1265*, ed. P. Connolly and G. Martin (Dublin, 1992).
119. W. Sayers, 'Anglo-Norman verse on New Ross and its founders', *IHS* 28 (1992–93), 113–23.
120. *PatR 1216–25*, 114, 115, 136, 168; *CDI*, II, 413–18.
121. *RC*, 118b; *CPR 1272–81*, 198, 250, 397.
122. *Memorials* (see Chapter 1, note 15), I, s. 33.
123. *PR 7 H II*, 56, 59; *PR 18 H II*, 86; *PR 19 H II*, 13, 29, 43; *PR 22 H II*, 199; *PR 23 H II*, 177, 188, 207–8; *PR 29 H II*, 104, 148, 160; *PR 31 H II*, 216; *PR 33 H II*, 23, 203, 210.
124. F.W. Brooks, *The English Naval Forces 1199–1272* (London 1932); *British Naval Documents 1204–1960*, ed. J.B. Hattendorf *et al.* (Navy Records Society, 131, 1993); *PatR 1225–32*, 34, 36, 276; *CPR 1232–47*, 27; *CLibR 1267–72*, nos 2191, 2297 E; *CR 1242–47*, 245; *CR 1251–53*, 245, 508; *CR 1261–64*, 356, 384.
125. K.M.E. Murray, *The Constitutional History of the Cinque Ports* (Manchester, 1935); N.A.M. Rodger, 'The naval service of the Cinque Ports', *EHR* 111 (1996), 636–51.
126. *CPR 1247–58*, 90.
127. A. Ballard, 'The early municipal charters of the Sussex Boroughs', *Sussex Archaeological Collections* 55 (1912), 35–40; *CR 1261–64*, 391.
128. *RParl*, I, 32, 98; *CPR 1232–47*, 73; *CPR 1247–58*, 239; *CPR 1258–66*, 352.
129. *CPL*, 43; *AM*, I, 283.
130. *CPR 1232–47*, 99, 188; *RPat*, 52; *PatR 1216–25*, 119; *PatR 1225–32*, 53; *CPR 1232–47*, 99, 188; *CPR 1258–66*, 655; *CLibR 1226–40*, 503; *CR 1234–37*, 194.
131. *RC*, 118b, 209b, 631b; *RC*, II, 91; *CR 1227–31*, 212; *CR 1234–37*, 194; *CR 1237–42*, 401, 429, 431–2; *CR 1253–54*, 124; *CPR 1247–58*, 230.
132. *RPat*, 52; *CM*, IV, 208; Rymer, I, 246; *PatR 1216–25*, 119; *PatR 1225–32*, 56; *CLibR 1245–51*, 503; *CPR 1232–47*, 99; *CR 1234–37*, 194.
133. *RC*, 69, 70b, 91, 352; *RC*, II, 48, 96, 129; *RPat*, 84; *CR 1234–37*, 194, 513; *PatR 1225–32*, 56; Shirley, no. 238.
134. *PR 19 H II*, 2, 13, 31, 117, 132–4; *CPR 1258–66*, 368, 421.
135. Gerald, III, 238.
136. Gerald, VI: Itinerary, i, 5; *CM*, V, 633; *CR 1253–54*, 124.
137. *Exchequer Rolls*, 5, 14, lxiii; *CM*, V, 93; *RC*, 211.
138. Shirley, no. 1; *CDI*, II, no. 310; IV, nos 307, 308, 368; P.F. Wallace, 'Anglo-Norman Dublin, continuity and change', *Irish Antiquity*, ed. D.O. Corrain (Dublin, 1981), pp. 247–67.
139. *Municipal*, 100–1, no. xxxi; *CDI*, I, no. 2532; *PatR 1216–25*, 337; *CPR 1232–47*, 27, 35, 428.
140. C. Bémont, 'Un rôle gascon', *Bulletin philologique et historique du comité des travaux historiques et scientifiques* (1915), 92–139.
141. *RC*, 110b, 117, 118b, 120, 127b, 203b; *RC*, II, 116, 129; *RPat*, 65, 70b, 80, 81b, 83b; *PatR 1225–32*, 44–6, 370–7; *Municipal*, no. 53.
142. *RC*, 620b–623b, 631b; *CR 1254–56*, 443.
143. *RC*, 65, 70b, 110b, 127b; *PatR 1225–32*, 44–6, 370–7.
144. *CR 1261–64*, 388.
145. N.S.B. Gras, *The Early English Customs System* (Cambridge, Mass., 1918), pp. 225–44.
146. *The Laws of Oléron*, ed. P. Studer (Southampton Record Society 1910–11); 'Les bons usages et les bonnes coutumes et les bons jugemenz de la commune d'Oléron', ed. C. Bémont, *Bulletin philologique et historique du comité des travaux historiques et scientifiques* (1917), 246–340; *RC*, 44, 47, 166b, 509b; *PatR 1216–25*, 422; *CR 1237–42*, 509; *CPR 1232–47*, 59, 499; *RChart*, 197b.
147. *CPR 1266–72*, 593–5; H. Berken, 'Het verdraag van Montreuil, 1274', *RBPH* (1944), 89–126.
148. Saxo Grammaticus, *Danorum Regum heroumque historia*, trans. E. Christiansen (BAR international series 84, 118, 1980–81), 514: xiv, 11.
149. Benjamin of Tudela, *The Itinerary*, ed. M.N. Adler (London, 1907).
150. *Elenchus Fontium Historiae Urbanae*, I, ed. C. van de Kieft and J.E. Niermeijer (Leiden, 1967).

151. *RC*, 419; *RC*, II, 116, 129; *CR 1242–47*, 543; *CR 1247–51*, 551; *CPR 1272–81*, 325; *RParl*, 200/56.
152. *RPat*, 133b.
153. D. Matthew, *The English and the Community of Europe in the Thirteenth Century* (Reading, 1997).
154. A. Schulte, *Geschichte des mittelalterlichen Handels und Verkehr* (Leipzig, 1900), 162; A. Longnon, *Documents relatifs au comté de Champagne et de Brie 1172–1361*, III (Paris, 1914), 13.
155. *Dip. Docs*, no. 370.
156. *CPR 1247–58*, 385.
157. S. Lyons, 'Copy of a Roll of Purchases made for the tournament of Windsor Park', *Archaeologia* 17 (1814), 297–310; *Records of Wardrobe and Household*, ed. B.F. and C.R. Bayley (London, 1977); B. Botfield, *Manners and Household Expenses of England* (Roxburghe Club 57, 1841).
158. J. Higgitt, *The Murthly Hours* (London, 2000).
159. R.L. Reynolds, 'Some English settlers in Genoa in the late twelfth century', *EconHR* 4 (1932–34), 317–23.
160. *Calendar of State papers and Manuscripts Relating to English Affairs in the Archives of Venice*, ed. R. Brown (1864), no. 2, 1224.
161. *CM*, V, 662; H. Géraud, *Paris sous Philippe le Bel, Le Rôle de la Taille de Paris, 1292* (Paris, 1837).
162. B. Hauréau, *Notices et Extraits*, IV (Paris, 1892), 143, 173.
163. *Histoire Littéraire de la France*, 23 (1856), 752.
164. *CLibR 1251–60*, 388; Rymer, 523, 529; *CPR 1247–58*, 264, 275.
165. *RPat*, 26; *PatR 1225–32*, 36; *CR 1251–53*, 508; *CR 1259–61*, 487, 495–7; *CPR 1272–81*, 128, 137, 184; *RParl*, 154; *Dip. Docs*, no. 280; Michel (see note 62 above), p. xv; R.J. Bartlett, 'Techniques militaires et pouvoir politique', *Annales* 41 (1986), 1135–59; *CPL*, 397, 428; *Flores*, ii, 478; iii, 256; Rymer, I, 797, 815, 820.
166. A.J. Taylor, 'The castle of St Georges d'Espérance', *Antiquaries Journal* 33 (1952), 33–47.
167. Wilson (see Chapter 4, note 39); T.A. Heslop, 'Art, Nature and St Hugh's Choir at Lincoln', in *England and the Continent in the Middle Ages: studies in memory of Andrew Martindale*, ed. J. Mitchell and M. Moran (Stamford, 2000), pp. 60–74.
168. P. Binski, *Westminster Abbey and the Plantagenets* (New Haven, 1995); R. Branner, 'The Montjoies of Saint Louis', in *Essays in the History of Architecture*, ed. D. Fraser, H. Hibbard and M.J. Lewine (London, 1967), pp. 13–16.
169. N. Pevsner and J. Harris, *Lincolnshire, Buildings of England*, rev. N. Antram (London, 1989), p. 452; A.A.F. Lindblom, *La peinture gothique en Suède et en Norvège* (Stockholm, 1916); A. Anderson, *English Influence in Norwegian and Swedish Figure Sculpture in Wood 1220–70* (Stockholm, 1949); J. Bony, *The English Decorated Style* (Oxford, 1978).
170. J. Harvey, *English Medieval Architects* (London, 1954); A.J. Taylor, 'Master James of St George', *EHR* 65 (1950), 433–57.
171. P. Binski, 'The Cosmati at Westminster', *Art Bulletin* 77 (1990), 6–34.
172. *RPat*, 9.
173. *RLib*, 78; *RC*, 535.
174. *RC*, 82b, 108.
175. *RC*, 145.
176. N. Didier, 'Henri de Suse en Angleterre 1236–44', *Studi in onore di Vicenzo Arangiò-Ruiz* (Naples, 1952), ii, pp. 333–51; G.L. Haskins and E.H. Kantorowicz, 'A diplomatic mission of Francis Accursius and his oration before Pope Nicholas III', *EHR* 58 (1943), 424–47; *CPR 1272–81*, 127; E.H. Kantorowicz, 'A Norman Finale of the Exultet and the Rite of Sarum', *Harvard Theological Review* 34 (1941), 129–43; *id.*, 'The Prologue to Fleta and the school of Petrus de Vinea', *Speculum* 32 (1957), 231–49.
177. *CPR 1272–81*, 61, 76, 143, 209.
178. N. Denholm-Young, 'The cursus in England', in *Oxford Essays in Medieval History presented to H.E. Salter* (Oxford, 1934), pp. 68–103; L.B. Dibben, 'Secretaries in the thirteenth and fourteenth centuries', *EHR* 25 (1910), 430–44.
179. *CLibR 1245–51*, 57.
180. *RC*, 606; *CPR 1258–66*, 249, 255, 256, 304; *CR 1261–64*, 187, 349, 406.

181. J.C. Russell, 'Master Henry of Avranches as an international poet', *Speculum* 3 (1928), 24–63.
182. *CLibR 1251–60*, 388.
183. Parsons (see note 25 above); CM, V, 513.
184. *Liber Quotidianus* (see note 33 above), 166.
185. *CPR 1247–58*, 591.
186. *CPL*, 232.
187. CPL, 137; *CPR 1272–81*, 142, 144, 185, 216, 300; *CPR 1292–1301*, 433.
188. *RPat*, 10, 108; *PatR 1216–25*, 201; *CR 1216–25*, 201; *CPR 1232–47*, 179, 180; *CPR 1272–81*, 459; *CPR 1292–1301*, 138.
189. *RChart*, 123; *RPat*, 106; *CPR 1225–32*, 87; *CPL*, 50; *CLibR 1226–40*, 273; *CPR 1272–81*, 546; *CPR 1292–1301*, 187; A. Francesco La Cava, *Liber Regulae S. Spiritus* (Milan, 1947); Rymer, 648.
190. *Survey of London*, XVIII, ed. G.H. Gater and E.P. Wheeler (London, 1937), pp. 1–5; *CPR 1272–81*, 283, 382, 447.
191. *CLibR 1226–40*, 273; *CPR 1272–81*, 546.
192. *PatR 1225–32*, 87.
193. Philippe de Beaumanoir, *Jehan et Blonde*, ed. S. Lecuyer (Paris, 1984); R.H. Bautier, Philippe de Beaumanoir, *Colloque scientifique international organisé pour la commémoration du VIIe centenaire des coutumes et usages du Beauvaisis de Philippe de Beaumanoir* (1983), 5–15.
194. *Liber Quotidianus* (see note 33 above), 155.

Chapter 7

1. N. Mengozzi, 'Il Pontefice Onorio III e la sua relazione col regno di Inghilterra', *Bullettino Senese di Storia patria* 18 (1911), 235–324.
2. Melrose: 1213; CM, III, 266–74; *AM* I Margam: 1163; *RPat*, 124; Neckam (see Chapter 4, note 93).
3. *Interdict Documents*, ed. P.M. Barnes and W.R. Powell (PRS, 1960); C.R. Cheney, 'King John and the Papal Interdict', *Bulletin of the John Rylands Library* 31 (1948), 295–317.
4. *ALC*: 1215.
5. P. Csendes, *Philip von Schwaben* (Darmstadt, 2003).
6. *RPat*, 186b.
7. S. Lloyd, 'King Henry III, the Crusade and the Mediterranean', in *England and her neighbours 1066–1453*, ed. M.C.E. Jones and M.G.A. Vale (London, 1989) ch. 6.
8. C.R. Cheney and M.G. Cheney, *The Letters of Pope Innocent III* (Oxford, 1967), no. 261; *PL*, 216: 1261; *HMC Various* (see Chapter 3, note 36), pp. 235–6; *RPat*, 5.
9. Macquarrie (see Chapter 3, note 13).
10. *Brut*: 1201.
11. *Histoire des ducs* (see Chapter 5, note 23); *HF*, 24, 760.
12. F. Wormald, 'The rood of Bromholm', *JWCI* 1 (1937–38), 31–45; F.M. Powicke, 'The oath of Bromholm', *EHR* 56 (1941), 529–48.
13. *Memoriale* (see Chapter 4, note 15), II, 241–3; *RPat*, 157.
14. *CDS*, I, no. 703.
15. Macquarrie (see Chapter 3, note 13); Melrose: 1219.
16. *Brut*: 1219, 1221.
17. CM, III, 126; *AM*, I, Margam: 1228.
18. CM, IV, 146, 166.
19. G. Murphy, 'Two Irish poems written from the Mediterranean in the thirteenth century', *Eigse* 7 (1953–55), 71–9.
20. Melrose: 1238; *CPL*, 169, 175.
21. CM, V, 93; Melrose: 1248, 1250.
22. *Brut*: 1249.
23. B.Z. Kedar, 'The passenger list of a crusader ship 1250', *Studi Medievali* 13 (1972), 267–79.

24. CM, IV, 274–5: J.J. Saunders, 'Matthew Paris and the Mongols', in *Essays in Medieval History presented to Bertie Wilkinson*, ed. T.A. Sandquist and F.M. Powicke (Toronto, 1969), pp. 116–32.
25. *Monumenta Franciscana*, ed. J.S. Brewer (RS 4, 1858), 213.
26. Potthast, 7349; CM, III, 102; C.R. Cheney, *Innocent III and England* (Stuttgart, 1976), pp. 94–6.
27. CM, III, 217; H. Cole, *Documents Illustrative of English History* (London, 1844), pp. 351–3; Potthast, 14983; D. Wilkins, *Concilia Magnae Britanniae et Hiberniae* (London, 1737), I, 700; C. Harper-Bill, 'The diocese of Norwich and the Italian connection 1198–1261', in *England and the Continent* (see Chapter 6, note 167), pp. 75–89.
28. J. Le Neve, *Lincoln: Fasti Ecclesiae Anglicanae 1066–1300*, III, ed. D.E. Greenway (London, 1977).
29. Harriss (see Chapter 5, note 81).
30. Shirley, 532, App. V, no. 4.
31. *CPL*, 122; CM, III, 184, 186–9.
32. W.E. Lunt, *Financial Relations of the Papacy with England to 1327* (Cambridge, Mass., 1939); C. Johnson, 'The Keeper of Papal Bulls', in *Essays in Medieval History presented to Thomas Frederick Tout*, ed. A.G. Little and F.M. Powicke (Manchester, 1925), pp. 135–8.
33. T. Mathews, *Welsh Records in Paris* (Carmarthen, 1910).
34. *AC*, 90, 91, 103, 105; *CR 1266–72*, 115; *CPR 1266–72*, 7; *CPR 1272–81*, 199, 368.
35. D. Waley, 'A register of Boniface VIII's chamberlain, Theodoric of Orvieto', *JEH* 8 (1957), 141–52, no. 27.
36. *Le Liber Censuum de l'Eglise Romane*, ed. P. Fabre and L. Duchesne (Paris, 1910); B.E. Crawford, 'Peter's Pence in Scotland', in *The Scottish Tradition*, ed. G.W.S. Barrow (Edinburgh, 1974), pp. 14–22.
37. *CPL*, 89; Melrose: 1222.
38. *CPL*, 166, 219, 264, 257: Glasgow; 106, 188, 192, 228, 271: St Andrews; 225: Kelso.
39. *CPL*, 225, 258.
40. Melrose: 1201, 1216, 1217, 1221, 1239.
41. *CPL*, 74, 83, 87.
42. J. Bannerman, 'The king's Poet and the inauguration of Alexander III', *SHR* 68 (1989), 120–49.
43. *CPL*, 270.
44. *CPL*, 243.
45. *CPL*, 261.
46. *Registrum de Dunfermelyn*, ed. C.N. Innes (Edinburgh, 1842), nos 281, 285, 290–1; R. Folz, *Les saintes reines du moyen âge en Occident* (Brussels, 1992), pp. 93–104.
47. Watt (see Chapter 4, note 88).
48. D.L. Galbreath, 'Scottish seals from the continent', *SHR* 27 (1948), 127–41.
49. Potthast, 16725, 16880, 22837, 22906; *CPL*, 346, 497.
50. P.J. Dunning, 'Pope Innocent III and the Irish kings', *JEH* 8 (1958), 17–32.
51. W.L. Warren, 'Church and State in Angevin Ireland', *Peritia* 13 (1999), 276–91.
52. *CPL*, 9, 75, 77; *AConnacht*: 1224.
53. Shirley, nos 141, 198.
54. *CDI*, I, no. 736; *PatR 1216–25*, 22, 23.
55. Potthast, 6323, 6325, 7227; *CDI*, I, no. 736; Sheehy (see Chapter 4, note 134), 158.
56. *ALC*; *AConnacht*: 1249.
57. J.A. Watt, *The Church and the Two Nations in Medieval Ireland* (Cambridge, 1970); A.F. O'Brien, 'Episcopal elections in Ireland c.1254–72', *PRIA* 73 (1973), 129–76; A. Cosgrove, 'Irish Episcopal Temporalities in the thirteenth century', *Archivium Hibernicum* 32 (1974), 63–71; K.W. Nicholls, 'Medieval Irish Cathedral Chapters', *Archivium Hibernicum* 31 (1973), 102–11.
58. *CPL*, 283, 304 (Potthast, 15488); *CPR 1247–58*, 398; E. Curtis, 'Sheriff's accounts of county Tipperary', *PRIA* 42 C 5 (1934), 65–95; J.R.S. Phillips, 'David MacCarwell and the proposal to purchase English Law', *Peritia* 10 (1996), 253–73.
59. Potthast, 14670; *CPR 1247–58*, 511, 512; G.O. Sayles, *Documents of the Affairs of Ireland* (Dublin, 1979), no. 4.
60. *CPL*, 98, 184.

61. *Les registres d'Urbain IV 1261–64*, ed. J. Guiraud (Paris, 1901), I, *Registre dit Caméral*, nos 209–11; II, *Registre Ordinaire*, no. 518.

62. A. Paravicini Bagliani, *Cardinali di Curia e 'Familiae' cardinalizie dal 1227 al 1254* (Padua, 1972); *ALC*: 1242; *AConnacht*: 1241; *CPR 1242–47*, 64, 255, 398; E. St J. Brooks, *The Irish Cartularies of Llanthony Prima et Secunda* (I.M.S., Dublin, 1953), 23–6, nos 16, 17; *ALC*, 361: 1243; Potthast, 15636.

63. *CPL*: Cloyne, 145; Ardfert, 146; Meath, 148; Ardagh, 279, 286; Raphoe, 275; Ossory, 260; Ross, 425.

64. *CR 1234–37*, 368; *CPR 1232–47*, 145, 146.

65. *AConnacht*: 1245; *CPL*, 218.

66. *CPL*, 134; Sheehy (see Chapter 4, note 134), pp. 307, 308; Potthast, 16658.

67. *ALC*: 1206.

68. *CPL*, 117, 168.

69. *CPL*, 190.

70. *Dip. Docs*, nos 344, 352, 353.

71. F. Ughelli, *Italia Sacra* (2nd edn, Venice, 1717), I, 1295–9.

72. *CPL*, 131, 242, 272, 308; Sheehy (see Chapter 4, note 134), pp. 253, 298, 322.

73. *CPL*, 253, 277, 295, 301, 321, 380, 392–3, 423.

74. *CPR 1272–81*, 146.

75. K.W. Nicholls, 'The Register of Clogher', *Clogher Record* VII, 3 (1971–72), 361–431, esp. 412–17.

76. M.E. Gibbs and J. Lang, *The Bishops and Reform 1215–72* (London, 1934).

77. R. Foreville, *Le jubilé de saint Thomas Becket* (Paris, 1958); F.M. Powicke, *Stephen Langton* (Oxford, 1928).

78. *CPL*, 13, 91, 96, 103, 209, 332.

79. *Rotuli Hugonis de Welles, episcopi Lincolniensis*, ed. W.P.W. Phillimore and F.N. Davis (Canterbury and York Society 1907–9, Lincoln Record Society 1912–14); *Rotuli Roberti Grosseteste episcopi Lincolniensis*, ed. F.N. Davis (LRS, 11, 1914); *The Register or Rolls of Walter Gray, archbishop of York*, ed. J. Raine (SS 56, 1870).

80. D.E.R. Watt, *Medieval Church Councils in Scotland* (Edinburgh, 2000).

81. *CPL*, 146, 163, 237.

82. M.H. Vicaire, *Saint Dominic and His Times* (London, 1964).

83. *CM*, III, 119, 131–5.

84. Thomas of Eccleston, *De adventu fratrum minorum in Anglia*, ed. A.G. Little (Manchester, 1951), 331.

85. R. Brooke, *Early Franciscan Government* (Cambridge, 1959), 195–209.

86. *Monumenta Franciscana* (see note 25 above), 146–7, ep. 43; M. Reeves, *The Influence of Prophecy in the Later Middle Ages* (Oxford, 1969).

87. Gwynn and Hadcock (see Chapter 4, note 132).

88. Knowles and Hadcock (see Chapter 3, note 44).

89. I.B. Cowan and D.E. Easson, *Medieval Religious Houses Scotland* (2nd edn, London, 1976).

90. Melrose: 1230.

91. R.H. Britnell, 'The proliferation of markets in England, 1200–1349', *EcHR* 34 (1981), 209–21; J.L. Cate, 'The English mission of Eustace of Flay (1200–01)', *Etudes dédiées à la mémoire de Henri Pirenne* (Brussels, 1937), pp. 67–89; D. Lohrmann, St 'German de Flay und der Anglo-Norman Reich', *Francia* I (1993), 193–256.

92. R. Bartlett, *Trial by Fire and Water: the medieval judicial ordeal* (Oxford, 1986).

93. Legge (see Chapter 5, note 13); Rauf de Lenham, *Art de Kalender*, ed. O. Södergård (Stockholm, 1989).

94. Bartholomew (see Chapter 1, note 41).

95. C. Duggan, *Twelfth-century Decretal Collections* (London, 1963), 23; J.E. Sayers, 'William of Drogheda and the English canonists', *Proceedings of the Seventh International Congress of Medieval Canon Law*, ed. P. Linehan (Vatican City, 1988), 205–22.

96. *CPL*, 49.

97. Paravicini (see note 62 above).

98. L. Boyle, 'Canon Law before 1380', in *The Early Oxford Schools, History of the University of Oxford*, I, ed. J.I. Catto (Oxford, 1984), pp. 531–64.

99. Bracton, *On the Laws and Customs of England*, trans. S.E. Thorne (Cambridge, Mass., 1968–77).

100. *Chartularium Studii Bononiensis*, I (1909); V (1921), 1265–66; VII, (1923); VIII (1929); IX (1931); X (1936); XI (1937).
101. *Select Scottish cases of the Thirteenth Century*, ed. T. Cooper (Edinburgh, 1944).
102. *Chartularium Studii Bononiensis*, I (1909), 108.
103. Lawrence (see Chapter 1, note 18); R.W. Southern, 'From Schools to University', in Catto (see note 98 above), pp. 1–36.
104. *RC*, II, 98b, 112; *CPR 1225–32*, 257; CM, III, 166–9.
105. *CPL*, 225.
106. B. Lawn, *The Salernitan Questions* (Oxford, 1963); *id.*, *I quesiti salernitani* (La Cava dei Tirreni, 1969); Kealey (see Chapter 3, note 22).
107. Gilbert Anglicus, *Compendium medicinae* (Lyon, 1510); H.E. Handerson, *Gilbert Anglicus, Medicine of the Thirteenth Century* (Cleveland, 1918); C.H. Talbot and E.A. Hammond, *The Medical Practitioners in Medieval England* (London, 1965), pp. 58–60.
108. Talbot and Hammond (see note 107 above), p. 25; L. Thorndike, *A History of Magic and Experimental Science*, I (New York, 1929), pp. 688, 740.
109. CM, V, 299.
110. *CDS*, II, no. 222; Rymer, II, 206–7; Watt (see Chapter 4, note 88), pp. 306–8.
111. A. Paravacini Bagliani, *Medicina e scienze della natura alla corte dei Papi nel duecento* (Spoleto, 1991).
112. *CPL*, 481, 495.
113. Talbot and Hammond (see note 107 above).
114. Bodley MS e Mus 219; Balliol College MS 285; Sloane MSS 348, 420; Additional MS 25031; Harley MS 5228; N. Morgan, *Early Gothic Manuscripts 1190–1250* (London, 1982), no. 78.
115. Sarton (see Chapter 3, note 29), III, I, pp. 880–2.
116. L. Thorndike, *Michael Scot* (London, 1965); *CPL*, 94, 96, 98, 102, 117.
117. D.A. Callus, 'Introduction of Aristotelian Learning to Oxford', *PBA* 29 (1943), 229–81; B.G. Dod, 'Aristoteles Latinus', in *Cambridge History of Later Medieval Philosophy*, ed. N. Kretzmann, A. Kenny and J. Pinborg (Cambridge, 1982), pp. 45–79; G. Lacôme, *Aristoteles Latinus* (Rome, 1939), 341–425; C.H. Lohr, 'Medieval Latin Aristotle Commentaries', *Traditio* 23, 24, 26–30 (1967, 1968, 1970–74).
118. M.T. d'Alverny, 'Avicenna Latinus', *Archives d'histoire doctrinale et littéraire du moyen âge* 32 (1965), 264–302; *id.*, 37 (1970), 335–48; *id.*, 39 (1972), 329–37.
119. M. and C. Dickson, 'Le cardinal Robert de Courson, sa vie', *Archives d'histoire doctrinale et littéraire du moyen âge* 9 (1934), 53–142.
120. L.J. Paetow, 'The life and works of John Garland, Morale Scolarium', in *Memoirs of University of California*, 4, 2 (Berkeley, 1927), pp. 69–273; A.C. Friend, 'Master Odo of Cheriton', *Speculum* 23 (1948), 641–58; Faral (see Chapter 3, note 34).
121. R.M. Huber, 'Alexander of Hales, his life and influence on medieval scholasticism', *Franciscan Studies*, V (1945), 353–65.
122. L. Thorndike, *The Sphere of Sacrobosco and its commentators* (Chicago, 1949); G.F. Hill, *The development of Arabic numerals in Europe* (Oxford, 1915).
123. H. Denifle and E. Chatelain, *Chartularium Universitatis Parisiensis* (Paris, 1889–97) I, 227–32; 201, 202; G.C. Boyce, *The English-German Nation in the University of Paris* (Bruges, 1927).
124. Denifle and Chatelain, 153.
125. John Le Romeyn, archbishop of York, *Register*, ed. W. Brown (SS 123, 128, 1913, 1917).
126. John Peckham, *Registrum Epistolarum*, ed. C.T. Martin (RS 77, 1882), no. 462; M.D. Knowles, 'Some aspects of the career of archbishop Peckham', *EHR* 7 (1942), 1–18, 178–201; *CPL*, 501–3.
127. N. Ker and W.A. Pantin, 'Letters of a Scottish student at Paris and Oxford *c*.1250', *Formularies which bear on the history of Oxford, c.1240–1420* (Oxford Historical Society n.s. 5, 1947), 472–91.
128. P. Glorieux, *Répertoire des maîtres en Théologie de Paris au xiiie siècle* (Paris, 1933); G.W.S. Barrow, 'A Scottish Master at Paris', *Recherches de Théologie Ancienne et Médiévale* 17 (1950), 126–7.
129. Galbreath (see note 48 above).
130. *CPL*, 287; Denifle and Chatelain (see note 123 above), 530, 589, 602.
131. *Histoire Littéraire de la France* 21 (Paris, 1847), by V.L.C.

132. *CPL*, 345.
133. M.B. Crowe, 'Peter of Ireland, teacher of saint Thomas Aquinas', *Studies* 45 (1956), 443–54.
134. M. Esposito, 'Friar Malachy of Ireland', *EHR* 33 (1918), 359–66; *id.*, 'Notes on Latin learning in Medieval Ireland', *Hermathena* 48 (1933), 221–49; *ALC*, 315; K. Simms, 'Guesting and Feasting in Gaelic Ireland', *JRSAI*, 108 (1978), 67–100.
135. J. Swanson, *John of Wales* (Cambridge, 1989).
136. R.W. Southern, *Robert Grosseteste, the Growth of an English Mind in Medieval Europe* (Oxford, 1986); Grosseteste, *Epistolae*, ed. H.R. Luard (RS 25, 1861); G. Stephens, *Knowledge of Greek in England in the Middle Ages* (Philadelphia, 1933).
137. CM, V, 284–7; T.H. Aston, 'Oxford's medieval alumni', *Past and Present* 74 (1971), 3–40.
138. CM, III, 324, 627; IV, 196; V, 400–1, 705; Talbot and Hammond (see note 107 above), pp. 179–81.
139. R. Bacon, *Opera Quaedam hactenus inedita*, ed. J.S. Brewer (RS 15, 1859).
140. *Munimenta Academica*, ed. H. Anstey (RS 50, 1868), 78–81; *Historical Papers and Letters from the Northern Registers*, ed. J. Raine (RS 61, 1873), 122–3, no. 76.
141. M. Cauville, 'Illustration in Harley MS 3487', in *England in the thirteenth century* (1985), 31–44.
142. C.R. Cheney, *Gervase Abbot of Prémontré* (Manchester, 1950); *id.*, 'Gervase abbot of Prémontré: a medieval letter writer', *Bulletin of the John Rylands Library* 33 (1951–52), 25–56.
143. GC, IX, 648; *CR 1227–31*, 358; *MGH, SS*, XXIII, 573: 6.
144. Stephen of Lexington, *Letters from Ireland 1228–1229*, trans. B.W. O'Dwyer (Kalamazoo, 1982); B.W. O'Dwyer, 'The problem of reform in the Irish Cistercian monasteries and the attempted solution of Stephen of Lexington', *JEH* 15 (1964), 186–91; *id.*, 'The impact of the native Irish on the Cistercians in the thirteenth century', *Journal of Religious History* 4 (1967), 287–301; *id.*, 'The Annals of Connacht and Loch Cé and the monasteries of Boyle and Holy Trinity', *PRIA* 72 C (1972), 83–101; see Chapter 4, note 8.
145. J.E. Lloyd, 'The Welsh Chronicles', *PBA* 14 (1928), 369–91.
146. J. Goering and H. Pryce, 'The de modo confitendi of Cadwgan, bishop of Bangor 1215–1235/6', *Medieval Studies* 62 (2000), 1–27.
147. F.M. Powicke, *The Loss of Normandy* (2nd edn, Manchester, 1961).
148. Melrose: *passim*.
149. *Charters of the Abbey of Coupar Angus*, ed. D.E. Easson (Edinburgh, 1947), I, no. 49; J. Wilson and A.C. Laurie, 'Charter of the abbot and convent of Cupar 1220', *SHR* 8 (1911), 172–7.
150. *PL*, 185, ii: 1759–60.
151. S.R. Macphail, *History of the Religious House of Pluscardyn* (Edinburgh, 1881); *The Douce Legacy, Bodleian Library Exhibition Catalogue* (Oxford, 1984), 44, no. 70: Douce MS 50.
152. G. Charvin, *Statuts, Chapitres Généraux et visites de l'ordre de Cluny* (Paris, 1965).
153. CM, IV, 612, 626, 650; V, 195, 201, 222, 230.
154. CM, IV, 626–7, 650–1; V, 230.
155. CM, V, 397.
156. *CPL*, 106; P. Henderson, *Prereformation Pilgrims from Scotland to Santiago de Compostela* (Confraternity of St James, occasional papers, 4, 1997).
157. *Registrum Prioratus Omnium Sanctorum iuxta Dublin*, ed. R. Butler (Dublin, 1845).

Chapter 8

1. CM, V, 191–7.
2. *The Book of Ser Marco Polo*, ed. H. Yule (3rd edn, London, 1903), I, 36, n. 2.
3. Rusticiano de Pisa, *Meliadus de Leonnys*, intro. C.E. Pickford (London, 1980); R.S. Loomis, 'Edward I, Arthurian enthusiast', *Speculum* 28 (1953), 114–27.

4. *CPR 1272–81*, 116, 265; *CPR 1281–92*, 496; Rymer, I, ii, 520, 564, 586, 641, 666, 674, 705, 712–13, 741–3; C. Desimoni, 'I conti dell'ambasciata al Chan di Persia', *Atti della Società Ligure di Storia Patria*, III (1877–84), 339–698.

5. *CPR 1272–81*, 247, 296, 457, 546; *CPR 1292–1301*, 465; *CCR 1272–79*, 104; *CChR 1257–1300*, 214, 240; C.L. Kingsford, 'Sir Otho de Grandison 1238?–1328', *Transactions of the Royal Historical Society* 3rd s III (1909), 125–95.

6. *AASS*, May III, 654; *CCR 1279–88*, 73, 145; Rymer, I, 618.

7. *CPL*, 237, 261.

8. *Chronicle of Holyrood*, ed. M.O. Anderson (SHS, 1938), 176: 1266.

9. K. Hampe, 'Aus einem register des Cardinal Ottobonus von S. Adriano', *Neues Archiv* 22 (1896–97), 337–72.

10. Melrose: 1270.

11. A. Dunlop, *Bagimond's Roll*, SHS Misc. V (1933), 79–106; VI (1939), 1–77; X (1965), 1–9; D.E.R. Watt, 'Bagimond de Vezza and his roll', *SHR* 80 (2001), 1–23; *CPL*, 449.

12. *CPL*, 480.

13. Lunt (see Chapter 7, note 32).

14. N. Denholm-Young, *Richard of Cornwall* (Oxford, 1947); H.E. Hilpert, 'The Election of Richard of Cornwall as king of Germany', *JMH* (1980), 185–98; B. Weiler, 'Image and reality in Richard of Cornwall's German career', *EHR* 113 (1998), 111–42; id., 'Matthew Paris, Richard of Cornwall's candidacy for the German throne and the Sicilian business', *JMH* 26 (2000), 71–93.

15. CM, V, 366, 371.

16. *CR 1256–59*, 135; *CR 1259–61*, 207.

17. CM, V, 388, 606, 636.

18. CM, V, 690.

19. *Littere*, no. 317.

20. B. Weiler, 'The Sicilian Business', *HR* 74 (2001), 127–50.

21. M. Gavrilovitch, *Etude sur le traité de Paris* (Paris, 1899).

22. Joinville, *Histoire de Saint Louis*, ed. N. de Wailly (Paris, 1906), 137, s. 679; comp are CM, V, 713.

23. F.R. Lewis, 'The election of Richard of Cornwall as senator of Rome', *EHR* 52 (1937), 657–62.

24. *Dip. Docs*, nos 312, 321, 341, 415.

25. P. Chaplais, 'English arguments concerning the feudal status of Aquitaine in the fourteenth century', *BIHR* 21 (1948), 203–13.

26. H. Johnstone, 'The county of Ponthieu, 1279–1307', *EHR* (1914), 435–52.

27. *Dip. Pract*, nos 245, 248, 401; Rymer, I, ii 677, 679, 681, 683–4, 687, 712, 713.

28. *Dip. Pract*, nos 40, 120, 347; Rymer, I, ii 545, 548, 554–7, 563, 568, 615.

29. *Account of the expenses of John of Brabant and Thomas and Henry of Lancaster 1292–93*, ed. J. Burtt (Camden Miscellany II, 1853); J. De Sturler, *Les relations politiques et les échanges commerciaux entre le duché de Brabant et l'Angleterre au moyen âge* (Paris, 1936); Rymer, 550–1, 553, 566, 672, 731, 734, 739.

30. P. Chaplais, *English Diplomatic Practice in the Middle Ages* (London, 2002), 86, no. 50.

31. M.C. Hill, *The King's Messengers 1199–1377* (London, 1961).

32. *Dip. Pract*, no. 4, 1282; Bugge (see Chapter 6, note 16), 267: 1256; Rymer, I, ii, 588.

33. *Dip. Pract*, no. 116; *CR 1256–59*, 149–50, 154; J.O. Baylen, 'John Mansell and the Castilian treaty of 1254: a study of the clerical diplomat', *Traditio* 17 (1961), 482–91.

34. *NEMBN* 35/2; *Dip. Pract*, no. 182; *CLibR 1259–60*, 249; Rymer, I, ii, 567, 569, 570.

35. Chaplais (see note 30 above), *passim*.

36. *Dip. Docs*, no. 182.

37. Rymer, I, ii, 813–14; *CPR 1292–1301*, 103; Chaplais (see note 30 above), 168, no. 63.

38. M.H. d'Artois de Jubainville, *Historie des ducs et des comtes de Champagne*, IV (Paris, 1865).

39. *Scotland under Alexander III*, ed. N.H. Reid (Edinburgh, 1990).

40. R.I. Lustig, 'The treaty of Perth: a re-examination', *SHR* 58 (1979), 35–37; F.J. Cowan, 'Norwegian Sunset – Scottish Dawn: Hakon IV and Alexander III', in Reid (see note 39 above), pp. 103–31; A.O. Johnsen, 'The payments from the Hebrides and Isle of Man to the crown of Norway 1153–1263', *SHR* 48 (1969), 18–32; B. Megaw, 'Norsemen and natives in the kingdom of the Isles', *Scottish Studies* 20 (1976), 1–44.

41. *SHR* 69 (1990): G.W.S. Barrow, 'A kingdom in crisis: Scotland and the Maid of Norway', 120–141; K. Helle, 'Norwegian Policy and the Maid of Norway', 142–56; M. Prestwich, 'Edward I and the Maid of Norway', 157–74.
42. Varenbergh (see Chapter 6, note 82); Rymer, 613.
43. B.E. Crawford, 'North Sea kingdoms and North Sea bureaucrats', *SHR* 69 (1990), 175–84.
44. *CCR 1272–79*, 505.
45. W.D.H. Sellar, 'The common law of Scotland and the common law of England', in Davies.
46. G.H. Hand, 'The opinions of the Paris lawyers upon the Scottish succession *c*.1292', *Irish Jurist*, n.s. (1970), 141–55.
47. *AC*: 1260, 1286; compare *Flores*, II, 456, 466.
48. *Brut*: 1252, 1265, 1267, 1270, 1272.
49. Surridge (see Chapter 4, note 145).
50. See Chapter 3, note 109.
51. *Brut*: 257–9.
52. *Littere*, n. 206; Rymer I, ii, 515, 528.
53. *ALC*, 409, 427–9, 431–2.
54. K. Simms, 'The O'Hanlons, the O'Neills and the Anglo-Normans in thirteenth century Armagh', *Seanchas Ardmaca* 9 (1978), 70–94; R.F. Frame, 'Ireland and the Barons' Wars', in *Ireland and Britain 1170–1450* (London, 1998), pp. 56–69.
55. *ALC*, 487.
56. Paravicini (see Chapter 7, note 62), *passim*.
57. *Richard de Swinfield, bishop of Hereford, A roll of the household expenses*, ed. J. Webb (Camden Society, 62, 1855), clxxvii.
58. Peckham (see Chapter 7, note 126).
59. Romeyn (see Chapter 7, note 125), nos 238, 950, 962, 1114, 1487, 1503.
60. See Chapter 6, note 7.
61. *Dip. Docs*, nos 363, 426, 428; Rymer I, i, 418; I, ii, 564.
62. *CR 1261–64*, 391–4; *CR 1264–68*, 34, 84, 98; *CPR 1258–66*, 388, 393, 482, 650; *CPR 1266–72*, 320, 462, 646–7, 706; *CLibR 1260–67*, 141–2; *Dip. Docs*, nos 392, 398, 402.
63. *CPR 1258–66*, 388, 551, 575–6, 580; *CPR 1266–72*, 1, 24, 129, 558–61.
64. *CPR 1258–66*, 505; *CPR 1266–72*, 141, 469, 558–66.
65. *CR 1264–68*, 46–7, 137, 155; *CPR 1258–66*, 398, 509; *CPR 1266–72*, 462, 486, 646–7, 706; *CPR 1272–81*, 95; Rymer I, ii, 555, 659.
66. Melrose: 1264, 1265.
67. P.H. Briegger, 'A statue of Henry of Almain', in *Wilkinson Essays* (see Chapter 4, note 92), pp. 133–8; Flores II, 501; Rymer I, ii, 566, 568, 577, 584, 586–7.
68. G.E. Cokayne, *Complete Peerage* (new edn, London, 1910–59), *passim*.
69. F.R. Lewis, 'Beatrice of Falkenberg', *EHR* 52 (1937), 279–82.
70. *Complete Peerage*, V, 628–31; *CR 1251–53*, 142, 268, 303.
71. Rymer, I, ii, 826.
72. P. Grosjean, 'Thomas de la Hale, moine et martyr à Douvres en 1295', *AB* 72 (1954), 167–91.
73. *RParl*, petition no. 135.
74. W. Ullmann, 'The development of the medieval idea of sovereignty', *EHR* 64 (1949), 1–33.
75. *Chronica monasterii S. Albani, Willelmi Rishanger Annales Regis Edwardi Primi*, ed. H.T. Riley (RS, 1865), 448–9; E. Amort, *De origine, progressu valore et fructu indulgentiarum* (Venice, 1738), 67; H.F. Kessler, *Rome 1300: on the path of the pilgrim* (New Haven, 2000).

Further reading

The notes have been deliberately kept as simple as possible, providing only references and not guidance to the copious literature devoted to almost every aspect of the subject. It does not seem appropriate to provide a long bibliography for a book designed to give a general overview. The following suggestions comprise, as far as possible, only recent or standard books not always cited in the notes but which offer fuller discussion of some of the principal themes of this book.

Standard histories, the two volumes of the Oxford History of England, R. Bartlett, *England under the Norman and Angevin kings* (Oxford, 2000), and F.M. Powicke, *The Thirteenth Century* (Oxford, 1953), deal with the main issues of continental relations only indirectly. More focused studies are J. Le Patourel, *The Norman Empire* (Oxford, 1976), M. Chibnall, *Anglo-Norman England 1066–1166* (Oxford, 1986) and J.C. Holt, *Colonial England 1066–1215* (London, 1997). Comparable works for other parts of the British Isles are R.R. Davies, *Conquest, Coexistence and Change: Wales 1063–1485* (Oxford, 1987), A.A.M. Duncan, *Scotland: the Making of the Kingdom* (Edinburgh, 1975), G.W.S. Barrow, *The Anglo-Norman Era in Scottish History* (Oxford, 1980) and A. Cosgrove, ed., *A New History of Ireland II: Medieval Ireland 1169–1534* (Oxford, 1987). For the British Isles as a whole, there is nothing to match R.F. Frame, *The Political Development of the British Isles 1100–1400* (Oxford, 1990), though recent collections of essays offer some interesting ideas: *Britain and Ireland 900–1300: insular responses to medieval European change*, ed. B. Smith (Cambridge, 1999), *The British Isles 1100–1500: comparisons, contrasts and connections*, ed. R.R. Davies (Edinburgh, 1988).

For international relations the only comprehensive view is provided by F.L. Ganshof, *The Middle Ages: a history of international relations*, trans. R.I. Hall (New York, 1970). D. Berg, *England und der Kontinent* (Bochum, 1987) has more recently focused on English foreign policy in this period. For formal diplomacy there is now P. Chaplais, *English Diplomatic Practice in the Middle Ages* (London, 2003). Several recent volumes of studies by various authors discuss relations with particular countries: *England and her Neighbours 1066–1453: essays in honour of Pierre Chaplais*, ed. M.C.E. Jones and M.G.A. Vale (London, 1989), *England and Germany in the High Middle Ages*, ed. A. Haverkamp (London, 1996), *England and Europe in the Reign of Henry III 1216–72*, ed. B.K.V. Weiler and I.W. Rowlands (Aldershot, 2002), *Medieval Europeans: studies in ethnic identity and national perspectives in Medieval Europe*, ed. A. Smyth (Basingstoke, 2002). *England and the Continent in the Middle Ages: studies in memory of Andrew Martindale, Harlaxton Symposium 1996*, ed. J. Mitchell and M. Moran (Stamford, 2000), concentrates on cultural connections, as does E. Salter, *English and International: studies in the literature, art and patronage of medieval England*, ed. D.A. Pearsall and N. Zeeman (Cambridge, 1988).

Influential works on specific topics are F.M. Powicke, *The Loss of Normandy 1189–1204: studies in the history of the Angevin empire* (2nd edn, Manchester, 1961) and J.B. Gillingham, *The Angevin Empire* (London, 2001).

On the church, see V. Ortenberg, *The English Church and the Continent in the Tenth and Eleventh Centuries* (Oxford, 1992) and C. Morris, *The Papal Monarchy* (Oxford, 1989). J.W. Baldwin, *Masters, Princes and Merchants* (Princeton, 1970), J. Sumption, *Pilgrimage: an image of medieval religion* (London, 2002) and C. Tyerman, *England and the Crusades* (Chicago, 1988) show how religious teaching affected the laity.

For secular culture: R. Barber and J. Barker, *Tournaments, Jousts, Chivalry and Pageants in the Middle Ages* (Woodbridge, 1989), D. Crouch, *The Image of Aristocracy in Britain 1000–1300* (London, 1992), M.D. Legge, *Anglo-Norman Literature and its Background* (Oxford, 1963), M.T. Clanchy, *From Memory to Written Record: England 1066–1307* (2nd edn, Oxford, 1993) and E.C. Fernie, *The Architecture of Norman England* (Oxford, 2000).

The activities of seamen and merchants provide the subject matter for G.J. Marcus, *The Conquest of the North Atlantic* (Oxford, 1981), N.A.M. Rodger, *The Safe-guard of the Sea: a naval history of Britain vol I 660–1649* (London, 1997), T.H. Lloyd, *Alien Merchants in England in the High Middle Ages* (Sussex, 1982) and C. Dyer, *Making a Living in the Middle Ages* (New Haven, 2002).

Index